New Songs of Celebration Render

Congregational Song in the Twenty-First Century

Compiled and edited by
C. Michael Hawn

New Songs of Celebration Render

Congregational Song in the Twenty-First Century

Compiled and edited by
C. Michael Hawn

Foreword by John L. Bell

Preface by Pablo Sosa

Contributors

James Abbington

Emily R. Brink

Kathleen Harmon, SNDdeN

C. Michael Hawn

Lim Swee Hong

Deborah Carlton Loftis

David W. Music

Greg Scheer

GIA Publications, Inc.
Chicago

Library of Congress Cataloging-in-Publication Data

New songs of celebration render : congregational song in the twenty-first century /
    compiled and edited by C. Michael Hawn ; foreword by John L. Bell ; preface by
    Pablo Sosa ; contributors: James Abbington [and seven others].
  pages cm
Includes bibliographical references and index.
ISBN 978-1-57999-985-8 (alk. paper)
1. Church music. 2. Hymns--History and criticism. I. Hawn, C. Michael. II.
    Abbington, James.
ML3000.N49 2013
782.27--dc23
                            2013019958

© 2013 GIA Publications, Inc.
All rights reserved.

7404 S. Mason Ave.
Chicago, Illinois 60638
www.giamusic.com
 G-7658
ISBN: 978-157999-985-8

In honor of Carl P. Daw, Jr., FHS,

priest, poet,

and Executive Director of the Hymn Society

in the United States and Canada (1996 - 2009),

who has encouraged the fullness of

congregational singing in its many forms.

Table of Contents

Acknowledgments XI

Foreword by John L. Bell XV

Preface by Pablo Sosa XVII

Introduction: Streams of Song by C. Michael Hawn XXV

STREAM ONE
Roman Catholic Liturgical Renewal Song 1
CHAPTER 1   Singing the Paschal Mystery 3
    Roman Catholic Liturgical Music after Vatican II
    Kathleen Harmon, SNDdeN

STREAM TWO
Classic Contemporary Protestant Hymnody 37
CHAPTER 2   When in Our Music God Is Glorified 39
    Classic Contemporary Protestant Hymnody
    Emily R. Brink

STREAM THREE
African-American Congregational Song 69
CHAPTER 3   If It Had Not Been for the Lord on My Side . . 71
    African-American Congregational Song
    James Abbington

STREAM FOUR
Gospel and Revival Songs 103
CHAPTER 4   I Sing for I Cannot Be Silent 105
    Gospel and Revival Hymnody in the Twentieth Century
    David W. Music

STREAM FIVE

FOLK HYMNODY 129
CHAPTER 5   DANCE THEN WHEREVER YOU MAY BE 131
   Folk Influences in Hymnody
   Deborah Carlton Loftis

STREAM SIX

PRAISE & WORSHIP MUSIC 173
CHAPTER 6   SHOUT TO THE LORD 175
   Praise & Worship, From Jesus People to Gen X
   Greg Scheer

STREAM SEVEN

GLOBAL AND ECUMENICAL CONGREGATIONAL SONG 207
CHAPTER 7   THROUGH EVERY LAND, BY EVERY TONGUE 209
   The Rise of Global and Ecumenical Song
   C. Michael Hawn and Lim Swee Hong
   PART I HISTORICAL PERSPECTIVES IN AND
   DISSEMINATION OF ECUMENICAL GLOBAL SONG 209
   PART II REGIONAL PERSPECTIVES:
   AN INTRODUCTION TO AFRICAN HYMNODY 228
   PART III REGIONAL PERSPECTIVES:
   AN INTRODUCTION TO CARIBBEAN, CENTRAL
   AND SOUTH AMERICAN HYMNODY 262
   PART IV REGIONAL PERSPECTIVES:
   AN INTRODUCTION TO ASIAN HYMNODY
   BY LIM SWEE HONG 281
   PART V A EUROPEAN ADDENDUM
   MUSIC FROM ECUMENICAL CHRISTIAN COMMUNITIES 302

THE FINAL STANZA

   STREAMS AND TRIBUTARIES 347
   C. Michael Hawn

APPENDIXES
    Appendix A: Seven Streams of Song:
        An Overview of Congregational Song since Vatican II . 355
    Appendix B: Stream Seven — Sources for Hymns Cited 359

BIBLIOGRAPHY 367
CONTRIBUTORS 385
Tables and Examples Index 391
List of Recorded Musical Examples 393
Index of Hymns and Songs 395
Index of Hymnals and Hymnal Supplements, Hymnaries, Psalters
    and Hymn Collections Cited 411
Index of Hymn Tunes 419
Name Index 421
Subject Index 447

ACKNOWLEDGMENTS

C. Michael Hawn

This book has been in some stage of formation for over fifteen years. It appears appropriately within a year of the fiftieth anniversary of the Second Vatican Council in October 2012. Regretfully, my memory does not serve to provide a comprehensive list of all who have influenced this project. I am grateful to Dean William B. Lawrence and the Perkins School of Theology, Southern Methodist University, who have assisted in several substantial ways, including a Scholarly Outreach Award in 2006 that provided resources for completing the initial manuscript, and sabbatical study leaves for the 1998–1999 academic year and the spring semesters of 2004, 2008, and 2012, which were of immense help in pursuing the innumerable details of this project. In addition, Perkins School of Theology provided funding for a research assistant during the 2012–2013 academic year. Lisa Hancock, a Master of Sacred Music student, has been most helpful in preparing the many indexes for the book.

The Hymn Society in the United States and Canada provided an impetus for this study in the early 1990s when they requested that I attempt to discern the emerging patterns in congregational song evident in North American hymnals. The data base that I was using at the time was filled to capacity and would not accept any further information.

The over arching outline of this book — Seven Streams of Congregational

States, Canada, and Australia. Thanks to the feedback from many in attendance at these presentations who sharpened the ideas in this book.

I am grateful to my students in the Master of Sacred Music program who read and commented on the manuscript in the fall of 2009 as well as the comments by Eric Mathis, now an instructor in Church Music and Worship at Samford University, who, along with his students, used this manuscript as an outline for a course.

Carlton R. Young, FHS, has been a partner in the study of global song for many years and offered many probing and insightful comments, especially on Stream Seven. John Thornburg, a hymn writer and an international enlivener of congregational song, has also been a significant dialogue partner on the practice and pedagogy of congregational song.

Anyone who studies congregational song is deeply indebted not only to those who have conceived hymns throughout the ages, but also those who planted the seeds of congregational singing in their hearts and minds. I am grateful for three mentors who bequeathed to me a love for the people's song: Donald Hustad and Hugh McElrath opened me to the joy and understanding of hymnology. Jay Wilkey first taught me that music making is a worldwide phenomenon. I have been claiming their inheritance for forty years.

My fellow writers represent some of the most knowledgeable persons in their respective areas. Thanks for providing carefully prepared manuscripts and for your willingness to dialogue about your sections of the book.

I am especially in debt to friends at GIA including Robert Batastini, FHS, retired vice president and senior editor, who initially invited me to submit a proposal and helped me envision this project, and Kelly Dobbs Mickus, then senior editor, who patiently pursued this project during its initial phases. The final stages of the book have benefited immensely from current GIA staff who worked with the project and improved it in many ways: David Anderson, Vice-President for Church Music; Michael Silhavy, Assistant Senior Editor; Alec Harris, who worked with the preparation of the compact disc; Martha Chlipala who prepared the layout of the manuscript; and Michael Boschert who searched for dates for composers and secured copyrights. In addition, Carroll Gonzo, editor for the *Choral Journal*, worked with me to edit the final manuscript in a thorough and timely manner. Through their efforts,

GIA has become the leading North American publisher of not only hymnals, song supplements, single-author collections, hymn-based anthems and musical arrangements of congregational song in many styles, but also current scholarship in the study of hymnology.

Finally, I am grateful for the congregations in forty countries in North America, the Caribbean, Central and South America, Europe, sub-Saharan Africa, Australia, and various parts of Asia that have been gracious enough to sing with me over the last thirty years in festivals, liturgies, and informal gatherings. They remind us of the truth in the final phrase of "Holy God, We Praise Thy Name," Clarence Walworth's nineteenth–century translation of the eighteenth–century text by Ignaz Franz, paraphrasing the fourth–century hymn, *Te Deum*: "through the church the song goes on." This project has convinced me that the reverse is also true: through the song the church goes on.

FOREWORD

John L. Bell

In past centuries, the Christian Church showed its schismatic potential in disruptions over ecclesiastical governance and theology. In recent years, aesthetic taste has become a similar source of division. Where in the early church some said, "I am for Apollos," and others, "I am for Paul," their twenty-first century counterparts create ructions when some exalt Taizé over Wesley, or Praise & Worship songs over Catholic devotional favorites.

In the middle of this unconscious exaltation of personal taste over spiritual and liturgical integrity, the song offered to God becomes a self-referential exercise rather than a duty and a joy. This circumstance is undoubtedly aided and abetted by a performance culture whereby worshippers consume and rate what the choir or praise band do, oblivious to how that same culture causes a creeping paralysis to affect congregational singing.

What we always need is an understanding of the bigger contexts—liturgically, historically, globally and stylistically—in which hymnody finds its place. The aficionados of high-octane choruses need to learn that there is biblical justification for lament; the devotees of six-versed strophic songs have to appreciate the power in the repeated singing of simple truths. The defenders of the denominational canon have to recognize that hymnody has always been an ecumenical activity. And, those who believe that the Western traditions in Christian worship are the only ones that carry a divine imprimatur have to wake up to the fruits of creativity, which the Holy Spirit has richly engendered in churches below the equator.

There could not be a better time for this book to appear because, in a highly imaginative way, it enables readers to have both an overview and an informed, scholarly appraisal of the genres or streams of hymnody that flow and intermingle in contemporary worship. This book makes no claim to be exhaustive; there can be few if any publications that offer such a panorama of practice and potential, drawing on the insight and experience of academics who are also practitioners.

Nor can there be a better person to edit such a volume. Michael Hawn combines within himself a rare passion for facilitating congregational song, an extensive intellectual grasp of the history and purposes of hymnody, and an enviable global view of current practice gleaned from observation and engagement in Christian music making in all continents.

I unreservedly commend this book to all who love the song of God's people.

PREFACE

Pablo Sosa

"Many are the voices, one is the song…"
(Imaginary verse for an ancient hymn)[1]

Church worship services, pop music recitals, civil rights rallies, and soccer field games, are nowadays some of the scarce remaining occasions, at least in our Western society, that still can provide people a meaningful chance to sing together.[2] In fact, to a larger or lesser extent, they actually rely on people singing as an essential element for the fulfillment of their objectives

Liturgies for these events have many elements in common—many more than we church people are sometimes ready to admit. The systematic, continuous practice of trying to identify these elements eventually becomes a very healthy exercise for the worship life of the church. It helps it expand its boundaries over the framework of the Christian community to encompass society at large, and even beyond that, the entire spectrum of humanity, which should actually be the scope of all worship addressed to the God of the universe.

Group singing is undoubtedly one of the strongest and most important of these elements, cutting across all lay liturgies. That is, granted that we can assume that human beings are the same when singing a hymn in church, or voicing a refrain in some public event.

What is Group Singing?

It was the insightful Charlene Spretnak who twenty years ago beautifully articulated the concept of "states of grace" and counted group singing as one of them:

> When we experience consciousness of the unity in which we are embedded, the sacred whole that is in and around us, we exist in a state of grace. At such moments our consciousness perceives not only our individual self, but also our larger self, the self of the cosmos.... Sometimes the consciousness of grace comes on quite suddenly and so intensely that the moment is never forgotten. More frequently, we experience slight versions of it, as in the act of group singing when the alignment of vibrations evokes in us awareness of the vibratory ocean of flux and form in and around us. Touching the ultimate truth in that way, and many others, brings us joy, release, connection, and peace.[3]

The first time I read this paragraph, I could not help thinking of our own congregational singing and feeling both a profound joy for the privilege of leading people through such an experience, and at the same time the uncomfortable suspicion that our singing might not always be worthy of such a lofty description. But then, the reassuring thought came to my mind that, whatever our definitions of "grace," it is essentially a gift. Grace is given, not acquired. Consequently, after we have made our best efforts to help the people of God sing their praises, by providing what we consider suitable music and proper advice to perform it, the only thing left for us is to pray that in their voices this music may become a channel through which God's grace can be received.

As we sail through the various "streams" of congregational music introduced in this volume, we experience a similar feeling: they all come from the same fountain of grace and run through the fields of this world, under different circumstances, watering the plants in the vast garden of the Creator, hoping to keep them growing strong. In more specific words, they show us how poets, composers, musicians, pastors, creators of all kinds in different parts of the world during the last fifty years have striven to bring about music to keep the faithful singing and maintain congregational song alive and growing as an instrument of God's grace.

This perspective is certainly something we have to thank the editor of this book: the possibility of listening to the navigators of these streams tells us about their voyages. As it happens, it is a rather unusual experience, especially for us church folks, to be able to consider these various currents each one alongside the others, and on an equal level. For various reasons, we have been more often bent on holding the value of our own musical tradition and resistant to others, thus missing the chance to watch the complete fascinating picture of Christian song today. Hopefully, the exposure to this book will motivate all of us to throw some of these reasons over board! There are two aspects of congregational singing in the last fifty years, made evident to me in this work, which I would like to point out: the role of music and the relation between song and society.

Let Music be Music!

I remember Dieter Trautwein (1928–2002), German pastor, poet, and composer, a leading person in the renewal of hymnody in the Lutheran church, facetiously lamenting the fact that many of his parishioners were "Philharmonic Christians." By this he meant they attended church only out of love for the music performed—much of which he composed. I believe this is actually true, not only in Germany, but also not necessarily to be lamented. If music is ministering to people in ways sermons or even liturgy evidently are not, instead of blaming music for it, we should thank God for music, and then question ourselves about the relationship of church worship to ordinary people, because it seems to be leading so many of them to consider music as their only remaining tie with some form of faith.

I was recently told by the director of a fashionable all-day classical music radio station here in Buenos Aires that "liturgical music is the reservoir of something singular and valuable, which should be extended to other musical expressions and communicated to the rest of society." There is a *quality* in the act of performing liturgical music, he continued to say, however modest and imperfect it may be, that calls to the fact that something *is happening* that relates us to the transcendent.[4]

Elaborating on that, we should add that when music, any music, but especially group singing comes so close to the mystery of our own existence, it has a chance to become a revealing instrument, a healing balm, and a strengthening power, as I am certain all of us have some time or other experienced, which is what my eventual colloquial partner considered should be shared with other fellow human beings. This surprisingly positive statement coming from a secular source could nevertheless be readily validated on the other end of the line by "praise music" theorists, quoting Psalm 22:3, for instance, as their basic thesis: "God inhabits the praises of Israel." That something singular and valuable would then be nothing less than God's very presence.

The Role of Music in Worship

All this postulating points to the growth of the role of music in church worship, which I believe can be traced to a gradual two-fold process. First, the recognition of music as the possible *locus* of worship, however unorthodox this may sound to our Christian ears, and second, a change in the status of music from "servant" to "partner" of the Word is needed.

There is an undeniable possibility of music provoking within us an awareness of God's presence and our own human condition. "We are such stuff as dreams are made of," Shakespeare wrote.[5] The nature of music (the stuff it is made of) is paralleled by the nature of worship. The evanescent, vanishing nature of both music and worship is very often the source of true worship. Worship begins with the first sound of a musical composition and music may provide an authentic response to the worshipful intention of an assembly. The Spanish philosopher, writer, and poet Miguel de Unamuno would go farther, much farther, to imagine that human lives are but dreams God is dreaming, and all our liturgical lullabies we sing to keep God dreaming us, in order to preserve our existence, less he (or she) should wake up and let us vanish away.[6] Secondly, the growing role of music in worship has to do with a change in its status, from "servant" to "partner" of the Word.

Throughout history, the church's many important leaders have insisted on considering music as the servant of the Word, mostly I believe due to their notion of a singular word of God confined to the pages of the Bible, and submitting all human expressions to it. I evaluate this attitude as opposite to what any song calls for from an artistic point of view, and furthermore alien to the spirit of freedom that the gospel proclaims. Paraphrasing the words of Jesus: the Word comes to us not to be served, but to serve.

At any rate, at all times many believe—some still do—they are entitled to exert control on music whenever it supposedly attracted undue attention to the detriment to the Word. This, of course, always resulted in the production of correct church music and very poor artistic expressions. In fact, whenever the church has been keen on "using" music, or any other artistic form, no matter for how lofty a purpose, it has impoverished its significance and diminished its power.

In the last half of the twentieth century, we have been experiencing a change from this dogmatic attitude to the recognition of music as a true partner of the Word. Of course, we still speak of *hymns* when referring to their *texts,* separately from their *tunes,* and hymnological studies are much more concentrated on poetry than the music. It continues to be common place for many parishioners to attach more importance to the words of a song as "bearing the message" rather than to the music. But, we are gradually learning to take much more seriously into consideration the language of music and to acknowledge to what extent it also bears and modifies "the message." Human beings are made so that they can listen or sing *synergetically*. We can perceive words and music as two currents of energy uniting in our mind to produce a *greater* impact, and especially a *different* impact, from that produced by each one of them separately. And, although in churches of the northern hemisphere, it is still customary to sing alternatively different sets of words to a single tune, a remnant from musically precarious times, the recognition of the unity of words and music giving birth to a new form of expression, has given a strong impulse to church music writing, evident in what is heard in worship services all around. In some cases, the idea seems to be less words, more music. It is not always a *good* idea, but it evidently reflects a need and a trend.

Song and Society

The relationship of Christian song to society is marked, first of all, by a change in the notion of what is sacred. The precise traditional lines determining the limits of the holy spaces have become more diffuse, often times bringing about as much fear and uncertainty as freedom and relief. The long-winded arguments about what music and instruments should and should not be allowed in worship have by now become obsolete. And, even more important, the meticulous evaluation of what is and what is not sacred has been replaced by a search for the sacred in all human expressions.

The sacralization of a style of worship music is also no longer admissible, for all styles are the product of definite cultural frameworks, and there is not one that will guarantee the validity of worship (as far as human worship of God can be deemed valid). We must recognize God's presence in all styles, searching to establish an authentic bond with God.

This situation is reinforced by the fact of God's incarnation. God became a human being within a particular culture, not because of its perfection, but in spite of its faults. And, this process of incarnation is an open one. God continues to be revealed in different cultures and forms as they are touched by the gospel, giving us a chance to enjoy new visions of the divine.

God's incarnation in Christ is one of the reasons for the unparalleled richness in church music, and particularly in congregational singing developed in the last fifty years, made evident also in this book—so much so that we should not speak of church music, but church musics. Are they all sacred? Insofar as they relate us to the Holy One, and they all can, through God's grace they are most sacred.

The second factor influencing the relation of congregational song to society is the awareness of God's action in the world. "The arm of God is much longer than the arm of the church," it has been said. God's action in the world is a permanent call to us to stand alongside human beings affirming the dignity of their lives. And, the last century has encompassed a period of human history in which the need for this kind of solidarity has certainly been felt in ways not known before. It has been a time when congregational song had to learn new concrete words, hard and edged, to cry out to God:

> O God of earth and altar,
> bow down and hear our cry,
> our earthly rulers falter,
> our people drift and die;
> the walls of gold entomb us,
> the swords of scorn divide,
> take not thy thunder from us,
> but take away our pride.
> —*Gilbert K. Chesterton, 1906*

The twentieth century had just begun when Chesterton wrote these words, and it must have been hard then to even imagine that the worst was yet to come: two world wars, at least two genocides (the Armenians by the Turks, the Jews by the Germans) countless minor wars, social and political crises, economic imperialism, and devastation of the planet. Christian song would no longer abandon the suffering of the world.

The last fifty years have seen, especially in Africa and Latin America, as well as in Asia, Europe, and North America, the rising of movements giving voice and strength to peoples struggling for their legitimate rights. Many of their songs are sung in church. Are they sacred? Insofar as they relate us to each other as children of God, in human solidarity, they are most sacred.

Who Dares?

This book is a provoking work. Michael Hawn is known for his ability to challenge people to get into other people's shoes, and learn to enjoy it! He has traveled around the world, meeting all kinds of church musicians and congregations, interpreting faithfully for each other what the rest are doing in a sort of middle way ministry for which we are all grateful. This book will undoubtedly widen this service to a much larger audience within and outside the limits of our Christian communities. Let us rejoice and be glad for it!

Notes—

1. Cyprian of Carthage wrote in 252, "De unitate ecclesiae" (Of church unity). Paraphrased in 1972 by Swedish hymn writer Anders Frostenson (1906-2006) as "Lågorna är många", and set to music by his fellow countryman Olle Widestrand (b. 1932), it became widely known through the Vancouver Assembly of the World Council of Churches in 1983, when it was translated into several languages, including English, as "Many are the light beams, one is the light."
2. I recently heard a North American musician regret that the only spontaneous group singing left to their society is the annual "Happy Birthday to You."
3. Charlene Spretnak, *States of Grace: The Recovery of Meaning in the Postmodern Age* (San Francisco: Harper Collins, 1991).
4. Santiago Chotsourian, Argentine composer and conductor. Director of Amadeus FM Radio Station, Buenos Aires.
5. These are the words of Prospero in *The Tempest* Act 4, scene 1, but are actually "We are such stuff as dreams are made on." Humphrey Bogart misquoted Shakespeare ("made OF") at the end of the film *The Maltese Falcon*, 1941.
6. Miguel de Unamuno (1864-1936). This image is taken from his tragicomic novel *Niebla* (Mist) published in 1914, available in an edition by M. J. Valdés (Madrid: Cátedra, 1982).

Introduction

Streams of Song

C. Michael Hawn

Come, thou fount of every blessing;
Tune my heart to sing thy grace;
Streams of mercy never ceasing
Call for songs of loudest praise.
—Robert Robinson, 1758

Are hymns relevant to Christians today? Albert van den Heuvel of the World Council of Churches reflected on the problem of finding relevant hymns in a preface written for a collection of new material in 1966:

> There was a minister in a European country not very long ago, who told his congregation on a Sunday morning that they would only sing one hymn: "What we should like to sing about," he said, "is not in the hymnal; what is in the hymnal about our subject is obsolete or heretical. So let us be silent and listen to the organ."
>
> This little story is, of course, irritating. I can already hear lots of people say: 'but there are beautiful hymns in our hymnal! Our fathers have sung them for many centuries! We have learned them from our mothers! What is wrong with

> Ambrosius's hymns, Luther's hymns, the Psalms, the Wesleyan treasury, and all the others?' The man in our story would have shrugged his shoulders, I am afraid. His point is not that there are not good hymns, but that there are very few [that] support his preaching and that of his generation. I am with him on this. There are many things in the life of the denominations [that] are frustrating, but few are so difficult to live with as this one. Choosing the hymns for Sunday morning worship is an ever-recurring low ebb in my ministry.[1]

This book attempts to respond to the concerns raised by the European minister and echoed by van den Heuval by reviewing what has happened in the people's song since the Second Vatican Council. In the forty years that have followed this quotation, their concerns have been answered many times over by an abundant outpouring of congregational songs. Indeed, the mid 1960s signaled the beginning of an explosion of congregational song around the world. It is only now, at the beginning of the twenty-first century, that scholars are in a position to begin to understand the diversity and wealth of congregational music available to the church since these years of liturgical reform—diversity and wealth of hymnody unprecedented in Christian history.

Why must Christians sing? Albert van den Heuvel proposed the following reason:

> It is the hymns, repeated over and over again, which form the container of much of our faith. They are probably in our age the only confessional documents, which we learn by heart. As such, they have taken the place of our catechisms . . . . There is ample literature about the great formative influence of the hymns of a tradition on its members. Tell me what you sing, and I'll tell you who you are![2]

This book contains a close examination of the smorgasbord of congregational song that has emerged, since the time of van den Heuvel's observation with the hope that congregations will be more intentional about their diet of singing and broaden their tastes.

In the historic dialogue between *lex credendi* [law of believing] and *lex orandi* [law of praying], there is ample precedent for saying not only that belief and prayer are related, but also that sung prayer shapes belief.[3] The words we sing and the rituals we practice in Christian worship provide pedagogical foundations for belief. Erik Routley noted that "when a congregation sings [a hymn], they are not far from saying, 'We think this. This is our own idea.'"[4] Argentinean church musician Pablo Sosa affirmed this premise in perhaps even stronger terms: "The doctrines of the church do not become faith until they are sung."[5]

Van den Heuvel, Routley, and Sosa, all involved in the ecumenical movement in the 1960s and 1970s, could not have predicted the explosion of congregational song in the world-wide Christian church that has followed in the years since they articulated the significance of hymn singing in the formation of faith—an explosion characterized by such quantity and diversity that it challenges earlier parochial conceptions of quality. This book attempts to reflect the breadth of congregational singing in the church during the final decades of the twentieth century, beginning with the reforms of the Second Vatican Council (1962–1965).

Methodology

In the early 1990s, this author embarked on a project for the Hymn Society in the United States and Canada that examined hymnody from an ecumenical perspective. In the 1970s, soon after Vatican II, the Consultation on Ecumenical Hymnody (CEH) prepared a list of 227 hymns for ecumenical use. The first stage of my work was to survey the impact of the CEH in thirty-eight North American English-language hymnals published between 1976 and 1995.[6] The results of this study revealed some of the same concerns that were raised following the early attempts at common lectionaries. For example, some liturgical theologians examining lectionaries of their day lamented the lack of scripture readings that bore the witness of women. Later lectionary attempts have attempted to respond to these and other imbalances and omissions.

Likewise, I observed that the excellent work of the CEH was limited in its recommendations, failing to include congregational songs from many voices in the North American Christian community, especially minority groups and songs widely known in free-church traditions. The participants in the CEH were aware of these shortcomings, but could not muster a fuller participation from these groups in their process. The primary purpose of the CEH was formative—that is, to provide a body of hymns that would influence the shape of the church's sung faith, balancing theological and liturgical concerns. The participants hoped that future hymnal committees, creating a common body of sung faith at least in the church in the United States, would choose the hymns on this list. I attempted to discern the impact of this noble effort in the article.

Following this article, I realized that the data I had collected revealed a much more complex picture of congregational song than the CEH process was able to demonstrate. What about newer hymns written since the CEH report in 1977?[7] What about rich congregational resources that seemed to fall outside of earlier definitions of "hymn"?

It was at this point that I continued my research, but with a different goal from that of the CEH. Rather than developing a prescriptive list for guidance, I chose to develop a descriptive list that might inform future hymnal committees concerning the items that appear most often in North American hymnals, making no value judgments on the quality or ecumenical possibilities of a given item. The goal of this list was modest—simply to indicate what was being included in hymnals. Items written before 1960 comprised one list and items composed after 1960 a second list, the latter group needing to be separated out, since they had not had the benefit of time and may not have been recognized by hymnal committees to the same degree. The results of this list produced from forty English-language hymnals published in Canada and the United States between 1976 and 1996 were then published.[8]

It was from this raw data that this current project evolved. After living with these results for some years in my teaching, patterns emerged. I realized that students, pastors, and church musicians were not equipped to appreciate the variety and quantity of the flood of new materials available to the church since the mid-1960s. In many hymnals, hymns tend to look more or less the same on the page, regardless of their cultural, ecclesiological, and historical origins. Hymnology texts offered glimpses of more recent literature, but had neither the space nor the perspective to organize current congregational song into a more comprehensible shape. This book is an attempt to discern meaningful patterns in the wealth of recent congregational song that reflects an outpouring of the Holy Spirit in myriad confessional and ethnic traditions for our time.

Streams of Song

In a conference celebrating the publication of the Spanish-language United Methodist hymnal *Mil Voces Para Celebrar* in 1996 in Dallas, Texas, Bishop Joel Martínez proposed in his sermon "each generation must add its stanza to the great hymn of the church." He went on to observe, "the stanza of our generation is the most diverse of any era in the history of the church." We have been nourished by the witness of past generations through the singing of their stanzas, but there must be new songs that reflect the experience of God's work in our lives and in the world today.

This metaphor, describing our generation's "stanza" in the great, ongoing hymn of the church universal, is rich with possibilities. It implies that we should sing earlier stanzas from previous generations. Can you really understand a hymn if you start on the last stanza? The metaphor not only suggests that we should not just sing the songs from previous generations, but also adds new songs from our age. After all, who stops on the penultimate stanza without finishing the hymn?

The quantity and diversity of our generation's stanza does not lend itself easily to organization—the work of the Holy Spirit rarely manifests itself in ways that are easily discernable to human patterns of understanding. Yet, there are reasons why it may be valuable to attempt to recognize the gifts of the Spirit that have been given to the church in our age.

I have chosen "streams of song" as the overarching organizational metaphor. Streams have a source, and each of the proposed seven streams of song came from particular sources of faith—a particular expression of piety. Streams come in various widths and depths. Not all streams are the same. Some of the song streams are rushing and seem to be overflowing their banks because of the musical outpouring generated from their particular piety source. Others are steady in their flow, and yet still others may be either drying up or merging with other streams. Streams meander; they do not flow in straight lines such as canals. They occasionally crisscross each other. Such is the case with many songs in this overview. Some songs fit comfortably in two or more streams.

This fluid model stands in contrast to a pigeonhole approach in which everything is neatly organized. The fluidity of this model reflects how these songs usually appear in hymnals: songs from one tradition organized around a particular season of the Christian year or theological theme are placed in juxtaposition to songs in other streams. Hymns demonstrate flexibility in their liturgical possibilities. Many hymns embody a range of themes, and one often notices that the same hymn appears in varying sections of different hymnals.

Finally, streams are vibrant parts of creation, carrying us along with them, offering constant changes in depth, rate of flow and character. Some parts of a stream are smooth with almost no sense of movement while others rush to a waterfall. Some songs still our souls while others raise us to an emotional apex. Streams are always changing. Every time we sing a song, it is a new experience. More familiar hymns still may surprise us with a new insight or provide security in a constantly changing world. Similar to an unforeseen turn in the bend of a river or an unanticipated crosscurrent, new songs often challenge us in unexpected ways, catching us off guard, delighting us as they provide words for feelings never before articulated, or confronting our previously held notions.

Few, if any, reading this book will navigate all these streams with equal confidence. We all have our primary source of piety and preferences for expressing this piety in song. Yet, the people of God who gather in the common assembly we call Christian worship may enrich their prayer by expanding the number of streams from which they draw.

The Organization of This Book⁹

My research and experience of singing in a wide variety of Christian traditions indicates seven streams of song, drawing on seven sources of piety, each with its own identity while overlapping in some cases with others in varying degrees.

Stream One

Roman Catholic Liturgical Renewal Song reflects directly the reforms of Vatican II and the outpouring of song for the assembly that came and continues to come from this historic council. Virtually no hymnal is untouched by at least some congregational songs from this stream. At the center of this stream are songs for the sacraments, music for the lectionary, compositions for the Christian year, responsorial psalms, and ritual music. Because of the breadth of the Catholic Church, these songs come to us from various parts of the world, but especially from Spanish-speaking locations as well as Euro-North American English speakers. Sr. Kathleen Harmon, SNDdeN, Music Director for programs of the Institute for Liturgical Ministry in Dayton, Ohio, guides us through this stream.

Stream Two

Classic Contemporary Protestant Hymnody is a swelling stream originating in the "hymnic explosion" of Great Britain in the 1960s and 1970s, and joined by rivers in other English-speaking countries, especially Australia, Canada, New Zealand, and the United States. Although quite varied, the center of this stream includes paraphrases of scripture, including fresh metrical paraphrases of the Psalms, hymns for the Christian year and sacraments, prophetic hymns on justice themes such as inclusion, peace and ecology, hymns on ministry, and, in some sections of the stream, a strong interest in inclusive language. Emily Brink, experienced hymnal editor in the Reformed tradition, author, and past president of The Hymn Society in the United States and Canada, knows the range of this literature well.

Stream Three

The **African-American Congregational Song** finds a voice in virtually all confessional traditions. Here, one will find a variety of musical expressions from spirituals and hymns to various styles of gospel music. This stream offers us songs born in the crucible of struggle, reflecting scripture and, often, expressing faith in the first-person. Since the middle of the twentieth century, virtually all hymnals include songs from this stream, even in predominately Anglo confessional traditions. Many see songs from this stream as a major, even singular, contribution from the United States to the larger church. James Abbington, organist, professor, hymnal editor, author, co-director of the annual Hampton University Ministers' and Musicians' Conference, and one of today's leading scholars in African-American congregational song, introduces us to the richness of this stream.

Stream Four

Gospel and Revival Songs are perhaps on the wane as a separate stream. It appears to be merging with others, especially with streams three and six. These songs of praise, personal salvation and experience continue, however, to find their way into a remarkable number of hymnals, even in some traditions where they have not been a dominant voice. David Music, Baptist professor, author, composer, and past editor of *The Hymn*, speaks with experience and appreciation about this literature.

Stream Five

Folk Hymnody draws from several sources of piety and has always been a part of the church's song. This stream experienced a revival in the Civil Rights Movement and the anti-Viet Nam era of the 1960s, spreading into folk masses and continuing as an idiom in its own right today. The use of the acoustic guitar lends informality to songs of praise and protest as well as narrative ballads that are immediately accessible to groups. Deborah Carlton Loftis, Baptist church music professor, church musician, and scholar, explores the depths of folk music in the church and the panoply of composers in this idiom today.

Stream Six

Praise & Worship Music finds its piety source in early twentieth-century American Pentecostal traditions, but has expanded into a worldwide expression of Christianity in many languages. Its electric sounds have influenced other streams, especially stream three, and those devoted to this stream have their spiritual roots in a wide variety of confessional traditions. These songs, often rooted in scriptural fragments, range from ecstatic praise to intense prayer, and often address God directly in the second person and petition Christ in the first person. Greg Scheer, college music teacher, Reformed church musician, author, and versatile leader of songs in this stream as well as many others, guides us through the artists, publishers, and changing styles of this popular genre of song.

Stream Seven

The Ecumenical and Global Stream attempts to bring into focus the contributions of two-thirds of the world's Christians, especially those that come from Africa, Asia, Latin America, and the Caribbean. A European addendum focuses on the contributions of two well-known ecumenical communities, Taizé and Iona, to global song. A direct result of the reforms of Vatican II and the pronouncement to "respect ... and foster ... the genius and talents of the various races and peoples,"[10] this stream offers a bird's-eye view of songs around the world from many confessional traditions that have been included in North American hymnals. C. Michael Hawn, professor of church music, author, and leader of congregational song in many ecumenical settings around the world, joins Lim Swee Hong, professor of church music from Singapore, Methodist church musician, and composer, in the exploration of this rich and diverse stream of congregational song.

Limitations of This Study

This study focuses, for the most part, on the breadth rather than the depth of current congregational song practice. Although this study demonstrates the considerable breadth of the church's song in the last half of the twentieth and early years of the twenty-first centuries, taking a broad perspective sacrifices a deeper focus on any one particular aspect of the church's song. Where individuals or movements in a given stream have played a significant role, they have been given more space. Additional space is also given to those about whom less is known in North America and information is not as available. A deeper understanding may be found in sources cited in the footnotes and in the hymnals listed at the end of chapters.

A helpful source for most streams is Erik Routley's *A Panorama of Christian Hymnody*, revised and expanded by Paul A. Richardson (Chicago: GIA Publications, Inc., 2005). This handy compendium provides hymn texts for many of the precursors of each stream before Vatican II, complete stanzas that are not possible to cite in their entirety in this book, and texts by additional authors not included in this study.

Each stream's song and its unfolding story have determined how each chapter has been organized. In some cases more background understanding is required and provided. In others, more biographical information and musical examples have been included because this material is generally less available. All chapters, however, focus on the story, the major representatives, and the distinctive theological contributions of each stream.

This study is limited by its social location. The writers, though representing a broad range of confessional traditions, come, save one, from the United States. The songs from North American hymnals have determined, for the most part, the contents of this study. These contents reveal substantial breadth, and considerable effort has been made to incorporate materials from other parts of the world. However, a similar study conducted in England, Argentina, Australia, or Korea, for example, would reveal a significantly different reality. Some of the streams in this book might be reduced to a rivulet in other cultural settings (if they exist at all), and others might be added.

This study is based upon what is published rather than on congregational song practice. Our focus is on what appears in hymnals and hymnal supplements since the Second Vatican Council, not on what congregations are actually singing. Some congregations, especially those who draw heavily on streams three, six and seven, have often moved on to more recent material not available in the hymnals reviewed. By the time a hymnal comes out, some of its contents are, for many churches, out of date. Other congregations do not use hymnals at all, relying on the projection of texts on screens or transmitting of songs through oral/aural means. Most recently, leaders of Emerging Church worship make extensive use of "home grown" compositions. Though locally composed music is not sung exclusively in emerging worship, many Web sites from these congregations contain mp3 files of their original compositions. Although the pastors and church musicians of every church are, in effect, the hymnal editors for their congregation, those who do not use hymnals bear a greater responsibility for selecting a breadth of sources that they use to shape the congregation's sung faith.

I do not want to suggest that there is no correlation between congregational song collections and congregational practice, but many congregations sing only a small percentage of their hymnal's contents, shaping, in essence, their own, sung canon; others supplement their hymnals with additional resources by using one of several copyright licenses available to churches. Basing a study of the breadth on congregational song practice, while desirable, would be a very difficult, perhaps overwhelming project to organize and report. Although such a study based upon actual practice would be valuable, I hope that the approach taken in this book lends insight into the breadth and depth of our generation's stanza.

Some groups are not included. The ritual music and chants of various Orthodox Christian traditions are not included though a few examples appear in hymnals. Many hymnals include hymns originally in Greek and translated into English, usually in the nineteenth century. Since Orthodox congregations do not use hymnals and draw heavily on long-established traditional repertoire, however, it was difficult to include them in this study. Christian songs from the Middle East are rarely sung in North America. Translations of hymns emerging from Eastern Europe following the fall of the Soviet Union have not found their way into many hymnals yet.[11] Relatively little Native-American hymnody is available to the larger church. Though there are many singing traditions in Oceana in the South Pacific, they seldom find their way into North American hymnals. These are but a few of the many song traditions that are currently practiced, but not included in this study. These gifts of the Spirit may yet come to us in the future, however.

General Trends Observed

Various patterns emerge in this study. The following overview highlights some of these patterns with the hope that awareness of them may enhance the reader's appreciation of the various streams.

Solo/Congregational Balance

Although congregational song is the focus of this study, several streams employ soloists or cantors in a variety of ways. Cantors, in stream one, are essential to the performance of responsorial psalmody. Stream three often draws upon soloists as catalysts for call-and-response singing—a standard feature of many African-American styles. The gospel songs of stream four were often solos initially and later claimed by the congregation. The irregular meter of many folk songs in stream five is more conducive to solo singing than congregational participation in many instances. Contemporary Christian artists have extensive solo careers. Those who participate in the songs in stream six often learn them from CDs and DVDs as solo or ensemble selections, and then sing them as congregational selections. Many songs of the world church, the focus of stream seven, draw upon solo singers in a variety of ways, especially call-and-response songs in Africa. Cantors enhance the sung prayer of the Taizé Community. Only stream two, classic contemporary Protestant hymns, does not regularly make use of solo singing to enhance the performance of congregational song. Yet, when one examines the average hymnal, the importance of cantors or soloists is not apparent. This calls upon church musicians to understand the wide variety of performance practices needed to bring alive various musical styles.

Written and Oral Traditions

A popular notion of the compositional process often imagines a creative and thoughtful hymn writer sitting at the computer composing a hymn text or a musician seated at the piano notating the melody of a hymn tune on staff paper as it emerges from her or his artistic imagination. This may be true for many composers, but songs throughout the spectrum of streams are often composed and sung without the benefit of, or even the need for, a written score. Notation on a physical piece of paper may be an afterthought in many African-American styles. Musicians who perform from a written score in stream three often see musical notation as a general guide to be melodically and harmonically modified on the spot or as a basis for extensive improvisation. Choirs in streams three, six, and seven often learn music through a process of oral transmission—totally without any written music. Written music is notoriously unrevealing in African music, providing only the barest outline that is enhanced through improvised solos, percussion parts, dance, and improvised harmonies. What looks so simple on the page becomes complex in performance for those who know the style. Many songs from the Asian subcontinent depend upon heterophonic improvisation around a melody and minute melodic variations, all of which resist notation.

Regardless of the musical style, a written score should never be confused with the sound and experience of singing a congregational song. Much, perhaps most, of the world's Christian song is sung by people who do not read music and, as a result, is primarily an oral experience. Those congregations who participate primarily in stream two, the most consistently literate of the seven streams, may feel disoriented as they attempt to participate in oral or semi-oral musical styles. Church musicians trained only in classical Western music may have difficulty in bringing orally conceived music to life.

Text/ Music Independence

As will become clearer in the discussion of stream two, the English hymn tradition has a heritage of tunes and texts composed by different people. Furthermore, the metrical nature of the texts allows numerous melodies to be paired with the same text. Depending upon which side of the Atlantic you reside, a different melody may be sung to the same text in England and the United States. Various faith traditions also sing different tunes to the same words. The majority of popular meters with the most options for tunes are common in English hymnody, e.g., SM, SMD, CM, CMD, LM, and LMD. These and other commonly used meters are still used by current text writers in stream two, but many poets explore new meters that demand new tunes. Only a few composers in stream two have the skill to successfully compose both texts and tunes, e.g., Dan Damon, Marty Haugen, Michael Joncas, Jane Marshall, Thomas Pavlechko in the United States, Pablo Sosa from Argentina, Per Harling in Sweden, and the late Spanish priest Cesáreo Gabaráin. Erik Routley, the eminent hymnologist, could also write both texts and tunes of lasting value.

By contrast, hymnals contain an increasing number of congregational songs with universally fixed text and tune pairings or where the tune and text are integrally linked and composed together because of the nature of the text or original language. Most selections listed as "irregular" in the metrical indexes at the back of hymnals have fixed text/tune pairings. Irregular meters include African-American spirituals and gospel songs from stream three, gospel and revival songs from stream four, folk songs from stream five, contemporary choruses from stream six, global songs from stream seven, as well as hymns from stream two with stanzas of varying metrical length. In general, stream two demonstrates the most independence between texts and tunes while other streams require a more integral, fixed relationship between words and music.

Variety of Accompanying Instruments

The pipe organ once was the dominant instrument for leading congregational song. In our age, the organ has become one of many instrumental possibilities for supporting the people's song. Although the range of possible instruments varies widely within a stream, each stream has its normative instrumental sounds. Stream one may use organ extensively, but also piano and acoustic guitar are common in various Catholic masses. The pipe organ has traditionally been the domain of stream two, though piano is commonly used along with other instruments such as handbells. African-American styles call upon a variety of instrumental sounds; thus, one will find everything from pipe and electronic organs and electronic keyboards to electronic guitars and percussion in stream three. The gospel and revival songs of stream four have usually been notated for piano and organ (pipe or electronic) in combination. The acoustic guitar is the normative sound of the folk idiom of stream five, though piano is common along with light percussion of tambourines and congas. Stream six is associated primarily with electronic guitars and keyboards and heavy use of percussion—both trap sets and congas. It is not uncommon in congregations with more resources, however, to have the bands of praise teams augmented with brass sections, including saxophones, electrified strings, and other wind instruments. With streams six and seven the center of instrumental gravity switches from a keyboard sound to a percussion-dominant sound, especially in various styles of world Christian music. Stream seven may include a wide array of instruments associated with specific ethnic groups or regions of the world, ranging from particular kinds of drums and specialized percussion to string and wind instruments not common in Western music. For example, the sruti box, producing open fifth drones, is a staple of music from India and other countries in the Asian subcontinent. The guitar either supplants or enhances various keyboards (electronic, organ, or piano) in steams five, six and seven. The increasing role of church orchestras has made the sounds of woodwind, brass, and string instruments more common, especially in streams two, four, and six.

A cappella singing also takes place in a number of the streams to varying degrees; indeed, singing without instruments is an option throughout the spectrum of musical styles. Unaccompanied plainsong is characteristic of stream one. Several musical styles used to support the strophic hymns of stream two were essentially *a cappella* in their origins, e.g., the music of the Sacred Harp or oblong tune-book tradition. The music of the African-American Spirituals may be best experienced when unaccompanied and harmonized by ear. Streams four, five and six employ unaccompanied singing more sparsely, but effectively, as points of variety. The unaccompanied voice is characteristic of various African and Asian musics. Within broader parameters of artistic creativity, one can identify each stream by its instrumental soundscape alone without texts.

Many Songs Demonstrate Characteristics of Several Streams

The artistic imagination of poets and composers often bridges streams. For example, Fred Kaan's celebrative communion text, "Let Us Talents and Tongues Employ," essentially from stream two, a strophic hymn with a refrain, is paired effectively with Doreen Potter's Caribbean-based tune LINSTEAD, performed effectively with guitar, claves, shakers and tambourines—sounds associated with the world church in stream seven. Many examples of text and musical exchanges take place between streams three and four. For example, Andraé Crouch's *My Tribute* is one of the signature songs of African-American gospel music, but alludes directly to Fanny Crosby's "To God be the Glory" and draws upon the metaphors of the redemptive power of the blood of Christ common in the gospel and revival music of stream four. Increasingly, a classic strophic hymn associated with stream two receives a musical treatment common to the charismatic music of stream six. The folk styles of stream five still influence music written out of the piety of stream one. Some of the music composed by David Haas, Marty Haugen, and others still easily fits an acoustic guitar and has echoes of earlier folk masses.

Bridging streams may be a sign of vitality in the life of the church and is increasingly a sign of our stanza in the great hymn of the church. When a text from one stream is placed in counterpoint with a musical style from another stream, the result may be enlivening to both. A number of text and tune writers appear in more than one stream. These are signs of the Holy Spirit at work and fly in the face of those who take refuge in divisive camps that segregate musical styles from each other.[12]

Variety of Song Structures

I have written extensively about the significance of various structures employed in congregational song, especially strophic, a form that I call sequential, cyclic, and refrain forms and the relationship of these structures to worship.[13] Each structure has many variations that serve the text in a different way. Strophic hymns consist of several stanzas with many words that form a progression (sequence) of thought. Cyclic songs use fewer words that are repeated with musical variations, i.e., a theme and variation approach to structure. Refrain forms have attributes of both: sequential stanzas with cyclic refrains. Stream two, the classic Protestant hymn, has characteristically though not exclusively used the strophic structures, a form that defines what a hymn "looks like" for many singers. This study indicates that other structures have gained in their prominence during the last half of the twentieth century. The refrain form has long been associated primarily with both streams three and four as a characteristic of gospel songs. Refrain structures are also a primary feature of much Roman Catholic Renewal music (stream one) since Vatican II. Cyclic structures appear in several streams, but especially in stream six, the music of the charismatic movement, and seven, principally music from Africa and the Taizé Community. Stream five, the folk stream, uses primarily refrain and cyclic structures, but may employ variations of all.

The importance of this observation is ontological in nature: What is a hymn? Some definitions recall the Greek *hymnos*, a term indicating a song praising "a god or gods, a hero, a nation, or some other entity or reality."[14] Augustine's classic definition of a hymn places God as the object of worship. Thus, a hymn is "a song in praise of God." From a literary perspective, "a hymn is usually a lyric poem with a metrical and strophic text. Literally, a lyric poem suited for singing to the accompaniment of a lyre or a harp, but more broadly, it is simply a poem appropriate for singing."[15] S. Paul Schilling continues this train of thought, indicating that a lyric poem "gives voice to the poet's feelings rather than to external events. Hymns are ... lyrics [that] express the feelings, attitudes, needs, and commitments of their authors and those who use them."[16] It is this definition that may broaden our ontological response to the questions, what is a hymn and what does singing do in worship?

The structures of hymns have always demonstrated variety; historically strophic poetry (in stanzas) has shaped Western consciousness about the nature of hymns and how they communicate. Other structures were thought of as alternative or supplementary at best and, perhaps, inferior at worst. Although strophic hymnody remains vital, even a cursory look at the most recent hymnals reveals that refrain and cyclic structures are on the rise. Depending upon the liturgical tradition represented in a hymnal, cyclic structures appear, in part, in a section of the hymnal labeled, "Service Music."[17] Others include cyclic structures throughout on a thematic basis. Often both approaches are followed in the same book. Diversity of structure characterizes twenty-first-century congregational song to such an extent that our notion of what constitutes a valid hymn has been challenged. Those who plan worship may benefit from an understanding of the liturgical possibilities inherent in the various structures so that they might integrate the congregation's song more purposefully and effectively into worship.

Physical Responses to Congregational Song

Since the middle of the twentieth century, streams three, six, and seven insert another element into congregational singing: movement or dance. To those who sing in these streams extensively, part of the piety is expressed through kinesthetic involvement while singing. Movement is not optional, but is integral to the experience of singing. Specific musical styles and song structures, especially cyclic forms, lend themselves to a physical response. As these songs have become a part of our hymnals, they bring into our worship the possibility of congregational singing that is more fully embodied. Dance is a part of the diverse landscape of congregational singing in the twenty-first century.

The discussion in this section indicates the diversity of this generation's stanza and some of the challenges in leading the breadth of congregational song available to the church.

Purposes of This Study

Assuming that what we sing plays a significant role in shaping our faith, this study attempts to examine the breadth of our sung prayer. Prayers of praise, thanksgiving, adoration, invocation, confession, intercession, and blessing all come in sung forms. Although not all congregational singing is prayer, even in this expanded sense, learning to pray well is part of our liturgical responsibility. In an essay entitled "The Integrity of Sung Prayer," Don Saliers notes:

> At the heart of our vocation as church musicians and liturgical leaders is the question of how we enable the Church to 'pray well'—to sing and dance faithfully and with integrity.... When we are engaged in sung prayer, we are not simply dressing out words in sound; rather, we are engaged in forming and expressing those emotions, which constitute the very Christian life itself.[18]

The Holy Spirit has provided today's church with a diverse spectrum of possibilities for praying well. This book explores ways in which our sung prayer is changing.

The diversity of congregational song discussed in this book may be overwhelming to many. I encourage the reader to delight in the gifts of the Spirit. Mark Bangert uses the metaphor of varied cuisine to express the richness of sampling diverse, authentic musical styles in worship. He cautions us, however, that, "Great cuisine is not an end in itself. Feasts and everyday meals are occasions for conversation and the building of community. It is across food that we get to know each other."[19] It is through the sharing of our songs that we gain a broader understanding of the universal Christian church.

This book is for the church musician, pastor, musical layperson, or hymn lover who wants to better understand the nature of congregational singing in what many feel is the most diverse, rich and complex age in the life and worship of the church.

A Hypothesis and a Challenge

When I examined the forty hymnals as well as additional hymnal supplements that have shaped this study, a noteworthy pattern seemed to emerge. *I sensed, in broad terms, a correlation between musical style and theological emphasis.* This hypothesis challenges some widely held assumptions that musical style, as an artifact of culture, is neutral and conveys nothing in and of itself, i.e., a given content may fit into any style and communicate the same content. Although it is true that some theological themes emerge across streams, specific differences appear from stream to stream; some theological themes are more prominent in some streams than in others.

Don Saliers acknowledges the link between musical style and theology:

> The musical idiom conveys a great deal about how the community conceives of God. Acoustic images reflect theological imagination at work. When the quality of the music is grandiose or pompous, the projected image of God may

> contain more of the self-image of the worshiping community than the community realizes. When the quality of music is pleasant and folksy, the projected image of God may be strong on intimacy and ease, but lacking in awe or mystery.... [M]uch depends upon the language used to address God or to describe God's relation to the world and to human beings. Gregorian chant is simple in one sense, but not without mystery. This may be said for melodies from folk traditions ... such as are found in Appalachian traditions or in the Spirituals. So we must attend to the wedding of text and tune, and to the way in which the assembly actually sings—what musicians refer to as the 'performance practice' of the words set to music.[20]

For Saliers and for us, music matters in worship not just as a conveyor of emotion, though music certainly has affective import, but as a window into the piety of a worshiping body and a partner the process of articulating the sung theology of a tradition.

The unprecedented musical eclecticism of congregational song styles since the Second Vatican Council replaces hundreds of years when a given tradition could be recognized more or less monolithically by a single musical style, for example, plainsong or Renaissance polyphony for the Roman Catholic Church, gospel songs for nineteenth- and early twenty-century Revival traditions in the United States, or Victorian hymnody for nineteenth-century Anglicanism. To some, the eclecticism of our era connotes a fragmented church. From these who are perplexed by the sheer variety of musical options, we hear the questions, "Where is all of this leading? What style will finally win out?" To others, the diversity of musical styles found in church music indicates a hopeful trend. Rather than asking where we are headed, these people relish a time when the musical fullness of the church, manifested through stylistic diversity and theological perspectives, seems to be at hand. Rather than a fragmented church, myriad styles of music may be a theological indication that this is a time of unprecedented creativity in the Spirit, a time of unparalleled cross-cultural and ecumenical exchange, and a time to conceive God and God's actions among humanity in the broadest, least-restricted terms.

Congregational song styles are more restrictive than many other forms of music because they must be effective with large groups of people that rehearse very little (if at all) and who are, as a whole, untrained in music or singing. Effective congregational singing requires accessibility and, to varying degrees, immediacy. Because all congregational song has its fulfillment in worship, some music—albeit within a wide variety of musical styles and forms—is better than others for this purpose.

The assumption that music carries no inherent meaning and is, therefore, a neutral conveyer of content is largely an assumption of Western, classical aesthetics that values "absolute" music. Move into popular culture or traditional societies and this assumption breaks down very quickly. Based upon this study, the poets in each stream tend to prefer a general musical style or a group of closely related styles to convey their theology. This book does not explain this assumption completely, but hopefully brings it to a greater awareness as an important factor.

If this is indeed true, one can assume a general relationship between musical style and theology. Congregations in North America have the possibility of singing many more musical styles than their forbearers in any other time in history. We may also deduce that singing out of only one stream, as varied as it might be and as comfortable as it may seem to the congregation, could limit the breadth of sung theology a congregation encounters.

This book challenges all that lead worship not to limit their songs to a single stream, but to dip into several streams for an abundant, sung faith with the hope of broadening the theological perspectives of their congregation and enjoying the variety of ways of praying that congregational singing offers.

Each congregation will have its own starting place or preference within this spectrum of current congregational song practice. Regardless of where a given faith community centers its sung faith, a vital singing congregation should broaden the range of its sung (and prayed) faith by incorporating songs from the depth of its particular confessional historical tradition and from the breadth of the current streams suggested in this book.

I quoted Albert van den Heuval at the beginning of this introduction who boldly claims: "Tell me what you sing, and I'll tell you who you are!" I hope that you discover through this book who you are—and who you may become as a singing people.

—Epiphany, 2013

Notes—

1 From Albert van den Heuvel, *Risk: New Hymns for a New Day* (Geneva: World Council of Churches, 1966), Preface.
2 Albert van den Heuvel.
3 Geoffrey Wainwright discusses the history and significance of *lex orandi* and *lex credendi* in depth in *Doxology: The Praise of God in Worship, Doctrine, and Life* (New York: Oxford University Press, 1980), Chapters VII and VIII.
4 Erik Routley, *Hymns Today and Tomorrow* (Nashville: Abingdon Press, 1964), 21.
5 An unattributed quotation in Pablo Sosa, "Spanish American Hymnody: A Global Perspective," *The Hymnology Annual: An International Forum on the Hymn and Worship*, Vol 3, ed., Vernon Wicker (Berrien Springs, MI: Vande Vere Publishing Ltd, 1993), 60-61.
6 C. Michael Hawn, "The Consultation on Ecumenical Hymnody: An Evaluation of its influence in Selected English Language Hymnals Published in the United States and Canada since 1976." *The Hymn* 47:2 (April, 1996), 26-37.
7 This report was published as "Hymns and Tunes Recommended for Ecumenical Use," *The Hymn*, 28:4 (October 1977), 192-209.
8 C. Michael Hawn, "'The Tie That Binds': A List of Ecumenical Hymns in English Language Hymnals Published in Canada and the United States Since 1976," *The Hymn* 48:3 (July 1997), 25-37.
9 One of the contributors to this volume has authored a helpful study that has also attempted to organize twentieth-century hymnody: David W. Music, *Christian Hymnody in Twentieth-Century Britain and America: An Annotated Bibliography* (Westport, Connecticut: Greenwood Press, 2001). Though the vast majority of the book contains extremely helpful bibliographic information, there is a brief introductory chapter that suggests a structure for approaching twentieth-century hymnody. Music's categories include (1) Mainstream Hymnody (streams one and two of the current study); (2) Popular Congregational Song (primarily stream six of the current study); (3) Ethnic, Global and Insular Hymnody (primarily streams three and seven of the current study); and (4) Congregational Psalmody (partially covered in streams one and two of this study). In addition, streams four and five focusing on gospel and folk hymnody respectively receive specific treatment in the current study. Finally, Music's summary includes the entire twentieth century, where the current volume focuses on hymnody since the Second Vatican Council.

10 *Sacrosanctum Concilium*, paragraph 37, 1963.
11 This is changing gradually. *Evangelical Lutheran Worship* (2006), the most recent hymnal of the Evangelical Lutheran Church in America, has included hymns in translation from Eastern Europe. Some of these will undoubtedly be included in future hymnals.
12 Variety of musical styles with the same text can make a significant difference. *Evangelical Lutheran Worship* (2006) has, for example, ten Eucharistic settings with different musical styles. The different musical settings open up new realms of meaning in the established structure and traditional Eucharistic texts.
13 See C. Michael Hawn, *One Bread, One Body: Exploring Cultural Diversity in Worship* (Bethesda, MD: The Alban Institute, 2003), 126-139, and *Gather into One: Praying and Singing Globally* (Grand Rapids, MI: Wm. B. Eerdmans, 2003), chapter seven.
14 See S. Paul Schilling, *The Faith We Sing* (Philadelphia: The Westminster Press, 1983), 5.
15 Schilling.
16 Schilling.
17 *The New Century Hymnal* (1995) takes this approach by listing a number of cyclic songs from the global Christian community in the index of service music rather than in the alphabetical index of first lines and titles. *Evangelical Lutheran Worship* (2006) includes many cyclic global songs in the index of "First Lines and Titles of Liturgical Music."
18 Don Saliers, "The Integrity of Sung Prayer," *Worship* 55:4 (July 1981), 291-292, 293.
19 Mark Bangert, "Welcoming the Ethnic into our Church Musical Diet," *Cross Accent: Journal of the Association of Lutheran Church Musicians*, 5 (January 1995), 7.
20 Don E. Saliers, *Music and Theology* (Nashville: Abingdon Press, 2007), 28.

— STREAM ONE —
ROMAN CATHOLIC
LITURGICAL RENEWAL SONG

Chapter 1
Singing the Paschal Mystery:
Roman Catholic Liturgical Music after Vatican II

Kathleen Harmon, SNDdeN

We hold the death of the Lord deep in our hearts.
Living, now we remain with Jesus, the Christ.

We are the presence of God, this is our call:
Now to become bread and wine—
Food for the hungry;
Life for the weary.
For to live with the Lord, we must die with the Lord.

We hold the death of the Lord deep in our hearts.
Living, now we remain with Jesus, the Christ.[1]

The vision of Vatican II that liturgy required the full, conscious, active participation of the people and that communal singing was a necessary means to that participation did not occur in a vacuum. Effective groundwork had been laid by papal documents[2] and by the liturgical movement[3] that burgeoned for more than fifty years prior to the Council. This groundwork culminated in 1963 with the nearly unanimous passage[4] at

Vatican II of *Sacrosanctum Concilium* (SC), the Constitution on the Sacred Liturgy.[5]

SC espoused liturgy as the means whereby the paschal mystery of Christ is made present and the people's participation in that mystery is actualized. Through the paschal mystery of "his blessed passion, resurrection from the dead, and glorious ascension" (SC 5) Christ redeemed humanity. Through baptism the faithful are "plunged into the paschal mystery of Christ" (SC 6). Made sons and daughters of God and members of the Body of Christ, they die and rise with Christ in sacramental celebration and in daily Christian living. In the liturgy, they "come together to celebrate the paschal mystery" (SC 6), reaffirming and deepening their identity as the Body of Christ called to give their bodies and pour out their blood for the sake of the world's redemption.

SC based its liturgical and ecclesiological approach upon the understanding of the early Church that there exists an essential, ontological relationship between the mystery of Christ, the meaning of baptism, and the celebration of liturgy. The very nature of the liturgy calls for the full, conscious, and active participation of the faithful because this is "their right and duty by reason of their baptism" (SC 14). This active participation of the people, then, was to be the primary consideration in all the liturgical reforms flowing from Vatican II (SC 14).

To this end, SC mandated revisions in the Order of Mass (SC 50). Subsequent directives preserved the substance of the rite but simplified it, eliminating unnecessary accretions and restoring important lost elements. The revisions led to a fuller Liturgy of the Word with more readings, a sung responsorial psalm, a homily related to the scriptural texts and the liturgical year, and a restored Prayer of the Faithful (Universal Prayer). The revisions also resulted in a Liturgy of the Eucharist incorporating acclamations sung by the people and communal singing during the Communion procession.

SC acknowledged and endorsed music as one of the essential means of promoting the fuller participation of the assembly. The people were to enter actively into the celebration through "acclamations, responses, psalmody, antiphons, and songs" (SC 30). SC balanced competing factors as it strove to meet the musical challenges generated by its liturgical reforms.

The document called for preserving and fostering musical treasures from the Church's tradition (SC 114) while also permitting other kinds of music that accorded with "the spirit of the liturgy" (SC 116). It granted Gregorian chant "pride of place" (SC 116) while also making room for the "people's own religious songs" (SC 118). It preserved the Latin tongue while extending use of the vernacular for the sake of the people (SC 36). It directed that the people be enabled to say or sing in Latin those parts of the Ordinary of the Mass[6] belonging to them, but also permitted people to sing their own songs in their own language (SC 54). It esteemed the pipe organ as the traditional instrument of the Church's liturgy, but also allowed use of other instruments considered suitable for liturgy and given local ecclesiastical approval (SC 120). The document instructed composers to create works to meet the needs not only of choirs, but also of the entire assembly (SC 121).

SC opened the floodgates for an outpouring of diverse streams of music in Roman Catholic liturgy. As a result, music used in the liturgy today includes folk, pop, rock, and traditional hymn styles and Gregorian chant. Fed by global awareness, the migrations of peoples, and the growing number of parishes with multicultural and multilingual assemblies, the music also includes songs with bilingual and multilingual texts; repertoire from African-American, Hispanic, Filipino, Vietnamese, Pacific Rim sources; and world music idioms from Asia, Africa, and Latin America.

But, SC also channeled the flow of these diverse streams of music by naming the liturgy as the primary underlying current. The principal role of music is to support the action of the liturgy (SC 112). It is this ministerial function that makes music essential and necessary to the liturgy. For Roman Catholics, then, a liturgical purpose always guides the music. The streams of music are tributaries feeding into the central current of the liturgy. Whatever its form or style, the music must always facilitate the people's immersion in this deeper, more essential current.

It is impossible in this short chapter to explore all the streams of music used today in Roman Catholic liturgy in North America. Hence this author takes an eclectic, and selective, approach to the flow of three broadly defined streams of music—contemporary, traditional, and culturally diverse—in a representative selection of hymnbooks and song resources produced by the three major publishers of Roman Catholic liturgical music.[7] This examination is organized by mingling two separate but interrelated schemas. A typological schema classifies the music sung by the people at Mass according to the three broadly conceived categories previously identified. This schema traces *what* music was being introduced into Roman Catholic worship. A chronological schema describes the content of the selected musical resources in the order of their dates of publication. This schema reveals *when and from where* the different streams were introduced.

The examination begins chronologically with the first resource relevant to this study, the *Hymnal for Young Christians: Volume I* (1967), then traces the growth of contemporary styles of music in Roman Catholic usage from this root. The narrative then moves chronologically through developments in the traditional stream, beginning with the first edition of the *People's Mass Book* in 1961. Along the way, the narrative introduces how the culturally diverse music stream grew concomitantly with the first two streams, appearing in resources intended for specific linguistic or cultural groups, in resources created for congregations with multicultural and multilingual memberships, and becoming integrated into traditional and contemporary stream resources.

The examination verifies the incremental use of these multiple streams of music in post-Vatican II Roman Catholic worship in the United States. The second half of the chapter presents, some critical assessment of these musical developments, identifying patterns appearing in the stream of hymn and song resources, and challenges generated by the streams of music.

Streams of Music in Post-Vatican II Hymnbooks and Song Resources

Hymnal for Young Christians.

The introduction of folk music into liturgical celebrations began with the Folk Mass movement of the 1960s.[8] The ecclesial context for the Folk Mass movement was the call of SC for full, active, conscious liturgical participation in the language of the people. The socio-political context was the civil rights movement; the Vietnam War protests; the assassinations of

John Kennedy, Martin Luther King, Jr, and Robert Kennedy; and the overall reaction throughout the 1960s against what were perceived to be outdated social structures. The folk music associated with the socio-political scene exploded onto the liturgical scene. Catholics sang "We Shall Overcome," "If I Had a Hammer," and "Where Have All the Flowers Gone" at Mass. Guitar was the primary instrument, jeans and T-shirts were the typical garb of this new kind of ensemble leading the music at Mass.

The leading publisher of the Folk Mass repertoire was F.E.L. Publications, founded by Dennis Fitzpatrick (b. 1937). A classically trained musician, Fitzpatrick collaborated with Roger Nachtwey (1930–2007) in 1961 to produce the *Demonstration English Mass*, the first complete setting of the Mass sung from beginning to end in English. The notable achievement of *The Demonstration Mass* was its successful adaptation of Gregorian chant to the English language. In 1963, in an effort to show that the vernacular could be wed to the Gregorian tradition, Fitzpatrick mailed recordings of his Mass setting to every Roman Catholic bishop in the United States. He was financially supported in this project by a group he called the "Friends of the English Liturgy." Thus, the groundwork was laid for what would later be named F.E.L. Publications.

In 1965, F.E.L. published the *English Liturgy Hymnal* with numerous English refrains for the appointed Mass Propers,[9] and only a few hymns. When this hymnal failed to succeed in the way he had anticipated, Fitzpatrick initiated collaboration with Ray Repp (b. 1942), whose Folk Mass music was becoming widely sung in the U.S. Together, they recorded and published Repp's popular *Mass for Young Americans*. The album included what are today considered to be "classics" of this period, among these being the Mass setting, "Sons of God," "Here We Are," "Clap Your Hands," and "Shout from the Highest Mountain."

F.E.L. went on to produce the premiere folk-music collection *Hymnal for Young Christians* (HYC): volume one in 1967, volume two in 1970, and the third and final volume in 1973. HYC made available the most popular folk-style composers of the day, among them Ray Repp, Robert Blue, Paul Quinlan (b. 1939), James Thiem (b. 1942), Ian Mitchell (1927–1969), Germaine Habjan (b. 1944), Roger Nachtwey, and the Dameans.[10] Using HYC, people sang and clapped folk settings of the Mass and songs for use at Mass, songs for catechetical situations, songs for children, and songs for raising social awareness. In an ironic twist, then, the success of HYC contributed to the demise of Fitzpatrick's initial dream of creating a vernacular liturgy in which the people would be singing the Mass Propers.

There was a point in the 1960s when folk-style music became mainstream in the average American parish and in many mainline Protestant congregations. Despite its musical and liturgical shortcomings, this music provided an avenue for the people to respond to the new mandate calling for liturgical participation through song. The music filled a vacuum. It was engaging and accessible. Its progenitors connected liturgy to the people and to the needs of the times. As Ken Canedo points out:

> The Folk Mass brought social justice themes into the liturgy and encouraged American Catholics to embrace congregational singing. The Folk Mass introduced the use of modern instrumentation and song styles in liturgy, planted the seeds for multicultural participation, and raised awareness in copyright justice. Lastly, the Catholic Folk Mass helped spark a similar movement in Protestant circles that eventually exploded as the multimillion dollar Contemporary Christian Music industry.[11]

GLORY AND PRAISE REPERTOIRE

The banner of the folk music movement was picked up in the 1970s by a new breed of composers whose work generally exhibited more sophisticated compositional technique. Notable among these were the St. Louis Jesuits—John Foley (b. 1939), Roc O'Connor (b. 1949), Dan Schutte (b. 1947), Bob Dufford (b. 1943) and Tim Manion, (b. 1951)—whose "Be Not Afraid," "One Bread, One Body," and "Here I Am, Lord" remain significant Catholic favorites. The St. Louis Jesuits earned wide, popular appeal because of their accessible melodies, memorable refrains, and varied rhythms. They earned liturgical stature because they drew their lyrics primarily from scriptural sources.

Carey Landry (b. 1944), whose work began during the Folk Mass movement, gained widespread popularity with songs such as "The Spirit Is A-Movin'," "Hail Mary, Gentle Woman," "Abba, Father," and "Peace Is Flowing Like a River." Landry's compositions were noted for their accessibility and easily sung by children and adults on first hearing. Along with the music of the St. Louis Jesuits, Landry's songs were the principal reason for the success of what became the most popular Roman Catholic hymnal ever marketed. *Glory and Praise* (G&P) was published by the North American Liturgy Resources (NALR) of Phoenix in 1977. Volume 2 followed in 1980, and Volume 3 in 1982. This third volume contained the addition to the G&P repertoire of several pieces in classical style by the French liturgist/composer Lucien Deiss (1921–2007), early evidence of the merging of musical streams that would eventually occur in most mainline hymnbooks.

The first three volumes of G&P were released in a single hardbound edition in 1983. In 1994, OCP purchased the rights to the products and materials of NALR, subsequently producing a new edition of the hardbound version, *G&P—Second Edition*, to which they added a number of the most popular songs from their own repertoire as well as a considerable number of traditional hymns.

Gather Hymnbooks

Hailing from the Minneapolis area, David Haas (b. 1957), Marty Haugen (b. 1950) and Michael Joncas (b. 1951) were the central figures in a third wave of new liturgical music in contemporary, popular idioms. All three were prolific composers, versatile in their use of woodwinds, brass, percussion, guitar, and keyboard. They were also skillful in creating melodic lines and harmonic progressions that effectively set the texts being sung. David Haas continues to produce work in a wide range of primarily pop and folk idioms, as does Haugen. Joncas's work appeared in the second volume of G&P; his *On Eagle's Wings* from that collection remains one of the most frequently requested songs for Catholic funeral liturgies. Joncas continues to compose songs across a wide range of styles: contemporary idioms; classically composed hymns; polyphonic settings of Latin texts; psalmody in various styles; and vernacular settings of the Mass.

Much of the work of these three musicians was disseminated through the *Gather* hymnal they helped edit, under the leadership of Robert Batastini (b. 1942). Published jointly in 1988 by GIA and NALR, *Gather* was a collection of music in popular idioms drawn from numerous publishers and intended to be used concomitantly with GIA's classical hymnody collection, the third edition of *Worship* (1986). The music in *Gather* exhibited greater complexity in vocal scoring and instrumental arranging than previous publications of guitar-based, folk-style music for liturgical use. Moreover, in order to draw the assembly into the unfolding pattern of the liturgical year, the editors used the Lectionary as their guide in making song selections. In addition to songs by Haas, Haugen, and Joncas, *Gather* also contained works by other significant composers such as Tom Conry (b. 1951), the St. Louis Jesuits, the Dameans, and the Dutch team of Huub Oosterhuis (b. 1933) and Bernard Huijbers (1922–2003). *Gather* introduced Roman Catholics to Haugen's *Mass of Creation,* the most widely sung vernacular setting of the Mass until the implementation of the third edition of the Roman Missal (RM3) in 2011.[12]

In 1994, GIA published *Gather—Second Edition*, greatly expanding its repertoire. The second edition included new songs by composers published in the first edition; works by other leading musicians such as Rory Cooney (b. 1952), Bernadette Farrell (b. 1957), Rob Glover (b. 1950), Bob Moore (b. 1962), and Francis Patrick O'Brien (b. 1958); songs from Hispanic and African-American sources; music from Taizé; and world music from John Bell (b. 1949) and the Iona Community as well as Nigeria, Paraguay, Zimbabwe, and South Africa. *Gather Comprehensive* was published the same year, combining the contents of *Gather—Second Edition* with a collection of standard classical hymns. In this edition of the *Gather* series, there is a confluence of the three streams of contemporary, traditional, and culturally diverse music in one volume. *Gather Comprehensive—Second Edition* appeared in 2004, offering an updated mix of contemporary, classical, multicultural, and global music and adding notable composers such as Tony Alonso (b. 1980), Kate Cuddy (b. 1953), Jaime Cortez (b. 1963), Lori True (b. 1961), and Steve Warner (b. 1954). The current *Gather—Third Edition* (2011) maintains the *Gather* pattern of integrating traditional hymnody, contemporary musical forms, and multicultural and multilingual pieces into one volume.

The first edition of *Gather* included Joncas's *Psallite Mass* with a Gloria set for cantor/choir stanzas in English and assembly refrains in Latin. *Gather—Second Edition* offered *Mass for the Life of the World*, a bilingual setting by Joe Camacho (b. 1951) and David Haas. *Gather Comprehensive* added two Mass settings in classical style, Richard Proulx's (1937–2010) *A Community Mass* and his adaptation of Franz Schubert's *Deutsche Messe*. To its contemporary, classical mix, *Gather Comprehensive—Second Edition* added two chant-based Mass settings, Proulx's *Missa Emmanuel* based upon "O Come, O Come, Emmanuel" and his *Corpus Christi Mass* based upon "Adoro te devote." *Gather—Third Edition* includes twelve settings of the Mass in various styles, among them Ronald Krisman's (b. 1946) Spanish/English *Misa Una Santa Fe/One Holy Faith Mass*, Norah Duncan's (b. 1952) African American *Unity Mass*, the *Cantus Missae* chanted in Latin, and the English chanted Mass from RM3.

Spirit and Song Collections

In 1999, OCP issued a new type of contemporary songbook for worship titled *Spirit and Song* (S&S). Subtitled *A Seeker's Guide to Liturgy and Prayer*, S&S was aimed intentionally at youth and young adults and provided music for youth ministry activities, retreat experiences, college campuses, as well as for liturgical celebrations. Songs for liturgical use were arranged in sections according to ritual function; songs for non-liturgical settings were gathered separately in a section titled "Prayer and Praise Songs." The resource offered a wide variety of contemporary pieces by such composers as Tom Booth (b. 1961), Ken Canedo (b. 1953), Janet Vogt (b. 1953), Steve Angrisano (b. 1965), Tom Tomaszek (b. 1950), and Ricky Manalo (b. 1965); a limited number of bilingual songs, such as "Pescador de Hombres" ["Lord, You Have Come"] by Cesáreo Gabaráin (1936–1991) and "Somos el Cuerpo de Cristo" ["We Are the Body of Christ"] by Jaime Cortez (b. 1963). The collection also included such crossover pieces from the Christian contemporary genre as Rich Mullins's (1955–1997) "Awesome God" and Twila Paris's (b. 1958) "He Is Exalted." Many of the songs exhibited the highly syncopated rhythms characteristic of the popular music of the time. In 2005, OCP published the second volume of S&S, adding repertoire from composers such as Sarah Hart, Matt Maher (b. 1974), and more Contemporary Christian Music artists such as Chris Tomlin (b. 1972), Matt Redmon (b. 1974), and Kathy Troccoli (b. 1958).[13]

Volume 1 of S&S contained the highly syncopated contemporary Mass settings *Mass of a Joyful Heart* by Steve Angrisano and Tom Tomaszek and *Mass of Life* by Tom Booth, and the Gloria from Fr. Richard Ho Lung's (b. 1939) *Caribbean Mass*. Volume 1 also provided the most multilingual Mass setting ever to appear in any resource, Jesse Manibusan's (b. 1958) energetic *Misa del Mundo* incorporating texts in Tongan, Tagalog, Spanish, Polish, German, English, Indonesian, Vietnamese, Korean, Creole, Mandarin, Japanese, and Italian. Volume 2 included the *Mass of St. Timothy* by Matt Maher, Tom Booth, and Tim E. Smith and Bobby Fisher's *Misa Santa Barbara* with interwoven Spanish/English texts.

Voices as One Collections

In the same years that OCP published S&S, WLP produced its comparable *Voices as One* (VO) songbooks. These contemporary collections were also intended for use within liturgy and for prayer gatherings, retreats, praise and worship events, teen ministry, concerts, and as the preface to the second volume states, "any other time when you rely on music to open a path to an encounter with our God." The wide range of contemporary styles included settings for traditional choirs, praise band arrangements, rock, rap, and quiet meditative pieces. Leading composers within these genres included Ed Bolduc (b. 1969), Paul Tate (b. 1968), Joe Mattingly (b. 1957), John Angotti (b. 1961), David Yackley (b. 1954), and Steve Warner. Although Volume 1 contained no settings of the Mass, Volume 2 included Ed Bolduc's *Mass of Celebration* that mixed pop and rock styles, and John Angotti's rock setting, *Mass of Rejoicing*.

People's Mass Book

The period after Vatican II also ushered a new stream of vernacular hymnody into Roman Catholic liturgy. One of the most influential initiators of this stream was Omer Westendorf (1916–1997). In 1950, Westendorf, a classical musician with advanced training in Gregorian chant, founded the World Library of Sacred Music (WLSM) in Cincinnati. Influenced by contemporary European liturgical music, Westendorf brokered deals with several European publishers to distribute their music in the United States. In 1955, WLSM issued the *People's Hymnal*, containing sixty-eight hymns. In 1961, WLSM released the first edition of the *People's Mass Book* (PMB), followed by the second edition in 1964. When American bishops mandated the changeover to vernacular language in 1964, PMB became a market success because it was the only available hardcover vernacular hymnal.

PMB merited its warm reception not only by the default of being the sole hard-bound option available, however, but also because of its broadened inclusivity and attentiveness to theological and liturgical principles underlying the use of music in the liturgy. PMB contained traditional Protestant hymns such as "A Mighty Fortress Is Our God" as well as a number of Flemish, Dutch, and Welsh tunes given newly composed texts by American writers such as Melvin Farrell (1930–1986), Michael Gannon (b. 1927), and Westendorf, under the pen name J. Clifford Evers. It introduced the well known and still widely published hymn "Where Charity and Love Prevail," a Westendorf (J. Clifford Evers) paraphrase of the Latin text "Ubi Caritas" set to a chant-style melody by Dom Paul Benoit, OSB (1893–1979). The notable exception to the classical hymn collection in PMB was "God Is Love" from Clarence J. Rivers's (1931–2004) acclaimed *An American Mass Program* set for cantors and *a cappella* choir in the style and rhythms of the African-American spiritual. The resource included two Gregorian chant Masses, one in English, the other in Latin; and a number of classically composed Mass settings, the most time-tested one to be Jan Vermulst's (1925–1994) *Mass for Christian Unity*.

The third edition of PMB appeared in 1970 and included music by Lucien Deiss who wrote in a classical style, employing a verse-refrain format to facilitate the singing of the people. Among his compositions still in use today are "All the Earth," "Priestly People, "Keep in Mind," and "Grant to Us, O Lord." This edition added Jan Vermulst's *People's Mass,* which, as with his earlier *Mass for Christian Unity*, was to become widely used. The hymnal also added considerable folk repertoire from composers such as Joe Wise (b. 1939), Jack Miffleton (b. 1942), and Sebastian Temple (1928–1997).

J. S. Paluch acquired WLSM in 1971, moved its operations to the Chicago area, and renamed it World Library Publications (WLP). WLP produced the fourth edition of PMB in 1984, including contemporary hymn texts from such writers as Fred Pratt Green (1903–2000) and Frederick Kaan (1929–2009), and earlier texts amended for inclusive language. The current edition of PMB, dating to 2003, includes many more musical styles and traditions than previous editions. Alongside Western-European style hymns are songs with African origins (such as the Ghana folk song "Jesu, Jesu, Fill Us With Your Love" with text by Tom Colvin (1925–2000) and the South African freedom song "We Are Marching in the Light of God" ["Siyahamba"], bilingual English/Spanish songs such as, "When We Are Living" ["Pues Si Vivimos"], songs from the African-American tradition such as Doris Akers' (1922–1995) "Lead Me, Guide Me," songs drawn from popular musical repertoire such as Kathleen Thomerson's (b. 1934) "I Want to Walk as a Child of the Light," pieces from the contemporary folk-style genre such as Dan Schutte's "Here I Am, Lord," and Peter Scholtes' (b. 1938) "They'll Know We Are Christians By Our Love," the Folk Mass song that remains popular in the repertoire of almost every Christian denomination.

We Celebrate Worship Resource

In 1994, WLP began publishing *We Celebrate Worship Resource* (WC) as a revision of *We Celebrate with Song*, its companion resource for its annual missalette, *We Celebrate*. Issued every three years, WC includes a mix of traditional and contemporary songs with a limited number of bilingual pieces. Noted composers include James Marchionda (b. 1947), Deanna Light (b. 1967), Paul Tate, Paul Page (b. 1947), Steve Warner, and Steven Janco (b. 1961). The 2011–2014 edition contains Mass settings in chanted, traditional, contemporary, and bilingual (English/Spanish) styles.

Worship Hymnbooks

GIA produced the first edition of *Worship* in 1971, following it with a major revision, *Worship II*, in 1975. The contents of this hymnbook deliberately offered the more traditional repertoire of classical hymnody, selections from Gregorian chant, and works from composers such as Richard Proulx, C. Alexander Peloquin (1918–1996), Calvin Hampton (1938–1984), and Howard Hughes (b. 1930). The resource included the psalmody of the French Jesuit and liturgist Joseph Gelineau (1920–2008) who, in the mid 1950s, translated the Hebrew Psalter into French then set it to original psalm tones created to match the "sprung meter"[14] of the Hebrew poetry. Translated from French into English under the auspices of the Ladies of the Grail, and disseminated in the United States by GIA, these psalm settings became widely used.[15] *Worship* also introduced into the liturgical repertoire the beloved Communion hymn, "I Am the Bread of Life" by Suzanne Toolan (b. 1927). Eventually translated into twenty-five languages, this hymn continues to be sung around the world.

Worship—Third Edition (W3) appeared in 1986. As with its companion volume *Gather*, the hymns in W3 were selected with the Lectionary in mind. Where possible, texts were altered for inclusive language. New hymn writers such as Frederick Kaan, Fred Pratt Green, and Thomas Troeger (b. 1945) were included. A number of contemporary-style pieces from composers such as David Haas, Marty Haugen, Michael Joncas, and music from Taizé and John Bell were added to the traditional repertoire. Mass settings included the classically based *Mass of the Bells* by C. Alexander Peloquin and *Community Mass* by Richard Proulx, the Latin chant setting *Cantus Missae*, and David Hurd's (b. 1950) *New Plainsong* Mass.

Worship—Fourth Edition (2011) contains greater musical diversity than its predecessors with more contemporary and multicultural repertoire interspersed among its traditional hymnody. The volume includes Mass settings in all styles, plus an English/Spanish setting.

RitualSong

In 1996, GIA combined content from *Worship* and *Gather* into the single hymnal, *RitualSong* (RS). Aiming for a clearer expression of the ritual purpose of music used in liturgy, RS included much more service music and many more psalm settings than previous GIA resources. In addition, RS mixed the contemporary and classical content taken from its parent resources more evenly than had *Gather—Comprehensive* and added a number of hymns and songs appearing for the first time in the GIA repertoire.

Journeysongs Hymnbooks

In 1994, OCP published its first hardbound hymnal, *Journeysongs* (JS). The resource contained a mix of traditional hymns, chant pieces (some with Latin text and some with English texts), and contemporary music by a number of composers, most notably Bob Hurd (b. 1950), Bernadette Farrell, Christopher Walker (b. 1947), Paul Inwood (b. 1947), Owen Alstott (b. 1947), Randall DeBruyn (b. 1947), Scott Soper (b. 1961), M. D. Ridge (b. 1938), and others whose work had appeared in the G&P resources. In terms of culturally diverse repertoire, there were a half-dozen bilingual songs, a half-dozen songs by Cesáreo Gabaráin, and a number of compositions by Grayson Warren Brown (b. 1948). Settings of the Mass included two in Spanish, one by Mary Frances Reza, the other by Alejandro Mejia; parts of the bilingual Spanish/English *Misa de las Americas* by Bob Hurd and Barbara Bridge (b. 1950); Grayson Warren Brown's gospel-styled *Cast Your Bread Upon the Water*; and the standard Latin chant Mass.

In 2003, the second edition of *Journeysongs* (JS2) appeared, offering an increased repertoire of traditional and contemporary hymns, Latin/English chant, spirituals and gospel-style music, and bilingual songs in Spanish/English. In addition, JS2 introduced new hymn texts by writers such as Genevieve Glen (b. 1945) and Harry Hagan (b. 1947). Mass settings included Bob Hurd's *Missa Ubi Caritas*, based on motifs from the Latin chant, and Hurd and Ken Canedo's *Mass of Glory*, incorporating jazz and blues elements. *Journeysongs—Third Edition* (2012) followed the implementation of RM3 and contained a wide selection of Mass settings in multiple styles, and a broader selection of repertoire from the G&P and the S&S collections than previous editions.

Breaking Bread Resource

In 1996, OCP began publishing the annual paperback missal *Breaking Bread* (BB). Published annually, BB contained some variation in content from year-to-year as music deemed no longer useful was removed and new music added. The 2013 edition includes an extensive collection of hymnody from various historical periods: contemporary repertoire from Carey Landry, the St. Louis Jesuits, David Haas, Marty Haugen, Michael Joncas; culturally diverse pieces from Jesse Manibusan, Grayson Warren Brown, Pedro Rubalcava (b. 1958) and Ricky Manalo; a considerable number of bilingual songs such as Jaime Cortez's "Somos el Cuerpo de Cristo" ["We Are the Body of Christ"], Bob Hurd's "Ubi Caritas" and "Pan de Vida"; popular pieces re-set in bilingual format such as "One Bread, One Body" ["Un Pan, Une Cuerpo"], "Here I Am, Lord" ["Aquí Estoy, Señor"] and "Be Not Afraid" ["No Temas Más"); and music from other contemporary composers such as Christopher Walker, Paul Inwood, Ernest Sands (b. 1949), Bernadette Farrell, M.D. Ridge. As with other song resources published after the implementation of RM3, BB provides updated Mass texts in a variety of musical styles.

Lead Me, Guide Me Hymnbooks

GIA published *Lead Me, Guide Me: The African-American Catholic Hymnal* (LMGM) in 1987. The National Black Catholic Clergy Caucus authorized the development of LMGM, and the coordinating team of Marjorie-Gabriel Burrow, Rawn Harbor (b. 1947), and Leon Roberts (1950–1999) oversaw the collection and arrangement of its musical materials. The hymnal was oriented toward celebrating Roman Catholic liturgy in African-American style and included an introduction to African-American religious song by Thea Bowman (1937–1990) and an introduction to the role of music in African-American inculturated liturgy by J. Glenn Murray (b. 1950). The resource represented the variety characteristic of the Black Catholic musical heritage, including Gospel music, spirituals, hymns, contemporary compositions; motets, hymns, and Latin chants drawn from Euro-American roots; and pieces from Bantu, Swahili, and West Indian roots. In keeping with its liturgical intent, the resource organized songs according to the liturgical year, and included ritual music for the Mass and other rites of the Church.

Lead Me, Guide Me—Second Edition (2012) continued in the direction set by LMGM, adding more complete liturgical offerings and employing musical editing more in keeping with African-American performance practices. The edition contains gospel-style Mass settings by Kenneth W. Louis (b. 1956), M. Roger Holland II, Norah Duncan IV, Leon C. Roberts; a spirituals-based setting by Kim R. Harris and M. Roger Holland II; Marty Haugen's contemporary-style *Mass of Creation*; Richard Proulx's traditional *A Community Mass*; and English and Latin chant settings.

Flor y Canto Hymnbooks

OCP published the first edition of the Spanish hymnal *Flor y Canto* in 1989, drawing music from the United States, Mexico, Cuba, Puerto Rico, and Spain. Most of the music was newly composed in folk-style idioms by composers such as Mary Frances Reza, Carmelo Erdozain (b. 1939), Carlos Rosas (b. 1939), J. A. Espinosa (b. 1940), José Luis Castillo (b. 1958), Juan J. Sosa (b. 1947), and, most notably, the Spaniard Cesáreo Gabaráin. Gabaráin, one of the most beloved priests in Spain following the Second Vatican Council and the best known internationally from this country, was known for his singable folk-song style hymns, especially on Marian themes and for the Eucharist, and his athletic achievements, including ministry to cyclists on long journeys.

In response to changing needs within the Hispanic community, OCP issued *Flor y Canto, segunda edición* in 2001. In addition to new songs from the United States, Mexico, and Spain, the second edition contained songs in Caribbean styles, songs from Central and South America, and nearly one hundred bilingual songs. More Mass settings were added, with Mary Frances Reza's popular *Misa San José* given special prominence. *Flor y Canto, tercera edición* (2011) continues the intent of its predecessors, adding several new songs to the existing collection and the new Spanish Mass settings, *Misa Dominicana* and *Misa Puertoriqueña*.

One Faith/Una Voz

Published in 2005 by OCP, *One Faith/Una Voz* offered music for English-speaking assemblies, Spanish-speaking assemblies, and bilingual titles for multicultural celebrations. The resource contained a wide variety of Mass settings, some in English, some in Spanish, some bilingual, and one in Latin. The hymnal also contained a mixture of traditional and contemporary hymns and songs. The intent of this resource was to enable bilingual communities to celebrate liturgy together as one Body of Christ, appreciating the different musical traditions of each group and entering into the celebration with "one voice."

Oramos Cantando/We Pray in Song

This GIA (2013) resource is the first fully bilingual hymnal in the United States, with every piece of music appearing in both English and Spanish. The resource includes hymns and songs for the rites of the Church and for the liturgical year, and many of the Spanish songs originally published by OCP.

Thánh Ca Dân Chúa

Desiring to meet the needs of Vietnamese-American assemblies, OCP published *Thánh Ca Dân Chúa* in 2009. Intended for both Vietnamese and bilingual liturgical celebrations, the resource contains over three hundred traditional and newly composed Vietnamese hymns from more than one hundred Vietnamese composers and as well as popular English songs from composers such as Bernadette Farrell, Bob Hurd, and Dan Schutte. The hymnbook contains the text of the newly approved Vietnamese Order of Mass and two Vietnamese Mass settings with revised translations.

Assessing the Streams of Music
Emerging Patterns

We can discern some broad patterns in the development of hymnals originally oriented toward the contemporary stream of music (that is, from HYC to VO). First, there is a gradual progression in musical sophistication from rather simply written guitar-only folk styles to complex rock styles and full praise band repertoire. Second, there are differences in the groups to which the various hymnbooks are targeted. The *Gather* books are intended for inter-generational assemblies; HYC, S&S, and VO for youth and young adults. Although the *Gather* hymnals offer music intended only for liturgical use, the youth-oriented resources contain songs for non-liturgical purposes and for liturgy. Moreover, with each edition the *Gather* series includes more culturally diverse and bilingual and multilingual repertoire, and with *Gather Comprehensive* moves beyond solely folk-pop repertoire to include a large number of traditional hymn forms. The S&S and VO youth-oriented resources, on the other hand, include only minimal repertoire of either traditional or culturally diverse types, and move the contemporary stream into its current expressions in rock and Contemporary Christian Music.

We can also see a pattern of development in the hymnals focused on traditional repertoire. The PMB and *Worship* resources eventually expand to include the contemporary and culturally diverse streams, although with varying degrees of balance. There is a chronological thrust to this development; hymnals appearing before 1990 tend to start with a single orientation that eventually expands, while hymnals appearing after 1990 tend to merge the streams at their inception. Moreover, in their chronological progressions, these resources add an increasing number of contemporary hymn writers such as Fred Pratt Green, Frederick Kaan, Brian Wren (b. 1936), Sylvia Dunstan (1955-1993), Carl P. Daw (b. 1944), Delores Dufner (b. 1939), Ruth Duck (b. 1947), Herman G. Stuempfle (1923-2007), Alan J. Hommerding (b. 1956), Harry Hagan, Mary Louise Bringle (b. 1953), and Genevieve Glen. Such writers provide fresh texts, using imagery drawn from the modern world and from new developments in scriptural exegesis and theological studies. It is clear that publishers of these hymnbooks are committed to preserving the best from the past and to making available the best from the present.

Overall, traditional hymnody drawn from many periods and places has high representation. By comparison, culturally diverse music, although included in many resources, is less well represented. The same can be said for the tradition of chant; although examples of Gregorian chant increase in the chronological progression of the hymnals, chant continues to stand in the shadows of the non-chant hymn repertoire and contemporary music.

The publication of hymnals intended for diverse and multicultural communities has grown considerably. Since the late 1980s, composers and publishers have increasingly collaborated to produce hymnals in response to a new cultural complexity in the American Church. Typically, these culturally diverse resources are liturgically oriented and organized, indicating that those involved in their production possess pastoral sensitivity to diverse groups in the Church and a clear understanding that music, whatever its cultural or linguistic roots, must always serve a liturgical purpose.

Emerging Challenges

The flood of multiple musical streams since Vatican II has stretched the cultural and ethnic boundaries of the People of God, facilitated the vernacular vision of SC, and brought new life to liturgical celebration. But, this flood of music has also raised a number of challenges concerning the use of music in the liturgy. In order to respond fully and faithfully to all the possibilities the flood of music opens up for the liturgy, we must also address these challenges. The following section identifies some of these challenges and their implications.

How best to honor the hierarchy of musical elements.[16] STL 115 outlines a hierarchy of musical elements to be sung in the liturgy. Those responsible for musical decision-making need to see this hierarchy as an avenue for selecting music with a clear understanding of the liturgical rite and the role of music in the rite. At the same time, they need to avoid a rigidity that allows no room for different interpretations, different congregational abilities and needs, and different modes of implementation.

In the hierarchy, first preference is given to the dialogues[17] "sung by the priest or the deacon or the lector, with the people responding, or by the priest and people together."[18] These ritual texts express the dialogical relationship between specific ministers (i.e., presider, deacon) lector, and the assembly in the enactment of the rite. The dialogue responses endorse the participative role of the entire assembly in the rite. In the decades since Vatican II, much attention has been given to how the people participate through the singing of hymns; considerably less attention has been given to their participation through the singing of the dialogues. The singing of the dialogues, however, is ritually more important and needs to become normative practice.

Likewise, the acclamations are also texts through which the people enact the rite. Through their singing of the acclamations, the people assent to the action of God (STL 115a). Singing the acclamations,[19] then, has priority over singing hymns and is to be normative in every liturgical celebration.

Second in importance is the singing of antiphons and psalms. Antiphons with accompanying psalm verses comprise the proper chants for the entrance and Communion processions. These proper antiphons have not been fully available, however, as no vernacular collection has ever been produced, and the chants offered in the revised Latin *Graduale Romanum* of 1974 follow a one-year cycle not always in accord with the three-year cycle of the revised Lectionary. Moreover, singing these chants requires trained choirs capable of dealing with the intricacies of the Latin language and Gregorian chant. Even the chants contained in the *Graduale Simplex* of 1975, although simplified, remain beyond the reach of the average congregation. It is not surprising, then, that these proper chants have been widely supplanted by more accessible hymns and songs.

STL 144 and 190 address this situation by reiterating the range of options outlined in the General Instruction of the Roman Missal GIRM 48 and 87. For the entrance and Communion chants, an antiphon and psalm drawn from the *Graduale Romanum* or the *Graduale Simplex* may be used. An antiphon and psalm from another episcopally approved collection may be chosen. A hymn or song that is in keeping with the purpose of the entrance or Communion chant and that carries the stamp of episcopal approval may be sung. This openness to options balances Church tradition with contemporary needs while upholding the normative priority of psalmody in the liturgy.

The psalm with which people are most familiar in the liturgy is the responsorial psalm sung as part of the Liturgy of the Word. The three-year Lectionary for Sunday Mass introduced in 1969 included a three-year cycle of responsorial psalms. Sung between the first and second readings, the responsorial psalm replaced the gradual sung after the epistle in the former rite (the Tridentine Mass of Pius V).

The singing of the responsorial psalm has become commonplace; understanding its function has not, however. How the function of the responsorial psalm is perceived is crucial because this perception shapes musical decisions, liturgical praxis, and liturgical catechesis of the people. GIRM 61 indicates the purpose of the psalm is to enable meditation on the word of God, and STL 155 adds that the psalm "is in effect a reading from Scripture." A more accurate definition, however, would be that the psalm is a ritual response to other readings. The Introduction to the Lectionary for Mass does not call the psalm a ritual response, and GIRM is nebulous on this point. The most explicit statement about the psalm as ritual response is found in The Introduction to the Order of Mass that states:

> The Responsorial Psalm follows the first reading and is an integral part of the Liturgy of the Word. After hearing and taking to heart God's word, all respond with words that are themselves God-given. Words that have expressed the faith of God's people over the centuries are selected by the Church to express the appropriate response, whether of wonder and praise, repentance and sorrow, hope and trust, or joy and exultation.[20]

The responsorial psalm is not the presentation of a psalm *per se,* but a pericope of a psalm incorporating specific lines of the text that accord with and shed light upon the Liturgy of the Word, particularly the first reading and gospel of the day.[21] The revised Lectionary restructured psalm texts to fit this liturgical hermeneutic, truncating and regrouping verses in ways that transformed a psalm's original sense and form. In order to meet a specific liturgical purpose, the Lectionary essentially created a new psalm form.

Early Church history gives evidence of the practice of singing the responsorial psalm as a reading.[22] The shift during the Middle Ages from a psalm sung responsorially with the people to an elaborate gradual sung only by a *schola* provides speculation as to how the psalm came to be seen as a meditation.[23] There is no clear historical evidence of the responsorial psalm being understood as a ritual response. Rather, this viewpoint is a post-Vatican II development hinted at in GIRM, articulated in select scholarly and pastoral writings,[24] but only now beginning to be grasped as liturgical practice aligns more fully with the intent of the post-Vatican II Lectionary.

According to Harry P. Nasuti the psalms possess the sacramental power to effect what they represent.[25] The psalms transform the internal landscape of the person praying them, and do so through the very act of being prayed.[26] As a prescribed text, the responsorial psalm does not necessarily express what those gathered for liturgy feel like praying at that moment.[27] Rather, the psalm offers the assembly what they are called upon to pray at that moment as response to a particular word God has spoken. Through the agency of the psalm, assembly members become persons "conform[ed] to the words of the psalm."[28] Liturgically, the responsorial psalm actualizes the word of God in the gathered believers, transforming them into "the type of persons that God wants them to be."[29] The psalms are "the means by which the rest of Scripture is actualized in the believer. Indeed, they are not so much the human response to what is found in the rest of Scripture as they are the means by which such a response is made possible."[30]

Thus, the responsorial psalm is the ritual response through which the assembly members assent to how God's word heard in this liturgy is reshaping their identity. The psalm leads the assembly members into the Liturgy of the Word as a transformative experience through which they become more fully who God calls them to be: baptized members of the Body of Christ. This response begun in the liturgy is then completed in the conscious choices believers make concerning the kinds of persons they opt to be in daily Christian living. The psalm is not a reading. But, it is the proclamation of the assembly choosing to be transformed by a new self-understanding and a new commitment to discipleship.

Such understanding has a bearing on the musical settings composed for the responsorial psalms and how psalmists render the singing of these psalms. Preferably, the text is the psalm of the day assigned in the Lectionary (GIRM 61). Discernment is then needed about what musical setting of the psalm will best enable a particular assembly to surrender to what God is saying in these particular readings and what God is doing through this particular psalm. There is no single or simple answer. Discernment must consider the make-up and culture of a particular assembly, and the liturgical season or solemnity being celebrated. Whatever choice is made, the text of the psalm needs to be given priority so that both psalmist and assembly members can grapple with its challenges, surrender to its meaning, and enter more deeply into the action of the Liturgy of the Word.

Third in STL's hierarchy of elements to be sung are refrains and repeated responses, such as those comprising part of the Kyrie and the Lamb of God. Fourth—and last—in the hierarchy are hymns. STL directs us first to sing the dialogues, acclamations, antiphons, psalms, and responses because these texts constitute the rite; in other words, in singing these texts the people are enacting the rite. At its deepest level, liturgy makes present Christ's paschal mystery. In every liturgical celebration God calls the assembly into divine presence, Christ leads the assembly in prayer as his Body, and the Spirit transforms the assembly into being more perfectly that Body in the world. The singing of these liturgical texts is a living, breathing actualization of the rite, or more accurately, is the Holy Spirit's actualization of the rite in the assembly, an actualization to be internalized and lived.

By contrast, hymns that are not prescribed texts of the liturgy merely embellish or accompany the rite. Nonetheless, "the people's own religious songs" have a place and their use in the liturgy is to be encouraged (SC 118). Careful discernment must be followed, however, to ensure that the hymns are appropriate to the spirit of the liturgy, support the liturgical action, and express content that conforms to Catholic teaching (STL 115d).

Resolving the conflict over Propers vs. hymns. Although last in priority, in common practice hymns are most often the first consideration when planning music for the liturgy. Our survey of hymnbook and song resources reveals that aside from the call for the active participation of the people, the Folk Mass Movement largely ignored other directives of SC concerning music. The movement paid little heed to retaining the treasury of Gregorian chant and polyphony (SC 114, 116) or to setting texts drawn primarily from scriptural and liturgical sources (SC 121). MS, issued in 1967 to clarify the musical intent of SC, was also largely ignored and in some quarters even considered irrelevant.[31] At the time, the euphoria of singing musical idioms the people recognized in a language the people knew simply overshadowed all other considerations. Consequently, the folk-music movement exacerbated

25

the practice begun even before Vatican II of the "four-hymn Mass" in which the people sang vernacular hymns in place of the Propers. Inadvertently, the folk-music movement contributed to the nearly total disappearance of the Propers from current liturgical practice. Traditionally-oriented resources such as PMB contributed to this loss by providing hymns to be used at the ritual points where Propers would have been sung.

Debate about whether singing a hymn is even appropriate in Roman Catholic liturgy remains intense. Frank C. Quinn, O.P. (1932–2008), for example, considered the introduction of hymns into the liturgy to be the natural outgrowth of SC's endorsement of active participation of the people, and proposed liturgically appropriate ways to use them.[32] Edward Schaefer, on the other hand, decries the use of hymns as detrimental to the integrity of the liturgy, arguing that the singing of hymns instead of Propers has destroyed the unity of the Church's prayer from parish to parish (and even from Mass to Mass in a single parish), and that hymns "are, in fact, little more than reflections of the personal piety and taste of the individual who happens to select them."[33] Schaefer acknowledges that the use of hymns is now a decades-old practice deserving fuller consideration, but argues that critique must be brought to bear on the liturgical appropriateness of this practice and study must be made of the theological contents and formative consequences of the texts used in these hymns.[34]

The fact remains, however, that the custom in the United States of singing hymns and songs during the liturgy has become cemented in place by more than two generations of use. Moreover, Anthony Ruff presents exhaustive evidence[35] that the singing of hymns during the Mass is not a new phenomenon. He also demonstrates that historically the singing of the Propers has never been the sole, universal practice of the Church.[36] He makes a balanced argument for use of both Propers and hymns, both Latin and the vernacular, both Gregorian chant and contemporary musical forms. At a 2013 gathering of musicians to discuss the debate about singing Propers or hymns in the liturgy, he offered the following questions to guide the discussion:

> What personal experiences do I bring to the table? What are my positive (or not so positive) liturgical experiences with

hymns, songs, English antiphons, Latin chant antiphons? What is my method for thinking about antiphons and hymns? What do I value most—history/tradition, official documents, spirituality/prayer, liturgical theology, evangelization, artistic beauty, or something else? What would be the gains (spiritual, liturgical, musical) in using antiphons rather than hymns and songs, and what would be the losses? What would be the losses (spiritual, liturgical, musical) in replacing hymns and songs with antiphons? How do we respond to the seeming popularity of hymns and songs? What are the criteria for selecting hymns and songs? Should hymns attempt to take up the function of antiphons and be more like them? What are hymns there for?[37]

Questions such as these move musical decision-making beyond polemics to the reflective discernment that serves the liturgy and, ultimately, the people who gather to celebrate the liturgy. In the end, those responsible for making musical choices need to be attentive to whether their selections enable the assembly to participate more fully in the liturgy. Whether Propers or hymns, it is clear the music must support the liturgical action and accord with the spirit of the liturgy. Whether Propers or hymns, the music must help the assembly members surrender more fully to the action of God unfolding through the rite. Whether Propers or hymns, the music must enable assembly members to encounter the prayer of Christ in the songs they sing and to recognize this prayer as their own.

Addressing issues of musical quality. The flood of musical styles and genres after Vatican II has raised intense debate about the quality of music used in the liturgy. The signatories of *The Snowbird Statement on Catholic Liturgical Music* (SS),[38] for example, argue that much of the music introduced after Vatican II lacks the necessary quality of beauty. Although admitting the term "beauty" remains elusive, this group nonetheless maintains that beauty can be adjudicated using objective criteria of musical standards (SS 6). They argue against a purely functionalist approach to liturgical music in favor of "a liturgical music practice that is beautiful and artistically well-formed" (SS 5).

In addition to the loss of beauty, SS also decries "the indiscriminate incorporation of an entertainment or therapeutic ethos into liturgical music" (SS 7). Much music currently in use in the liturgy draws the assembly into "sentimentality, consumerism, individualism, introversion, and passivity" (SS 7), frames of mind diametrically opposed to the spirit and purpose of the liturgy. SS endorses the reforms of Vatican II and the call of SC for full, conscious, active participation of the faithful in the liturgy, but asks for more thorough and discriminating dialogue about the nature and role of liturgical music, especially in the English-speaking world.

The Milwaukee Symposia for Church Composers: A Ten-Year Report[39] (MilS), issued in 1992, considers the claim that there exist objective criteria whereby we can evaluate the quality of a given style or piece of music to be an example of Western European ethnocentricity (MilS) 60). MilS argues for a cross-cultural frame of reference that challenges Western musical biases, and a functional understanding of the role of music that judges a given piece of music for its ability to serve the rite and to enable the participation of the people (MilS 60).

This report presents a theology of liturgical music based upon its sacramentality and its ministerial role. Sacramentally, music is a "vehicle of God's self-revelation," enabling union with God and the other worshipers "in a particular and unparalleled way" (MilS 13). Ministerially, music serves the word that is central to liturgical celebration (MilS 15). Holiness does not inhere in the music but in "the joining of music and texts in the enactment of rite" (MilS 6). Hence, a functional approach to evaluating the appropriateness of a given piece of music for the liturgy is fundamental and must be primary.

SS and MilS express significant aspects of the ongoing debate about musical quality and function within the liturgy. Both were issued with the intent of stimulating deeper discussion and discernment about liturgical music in current Roman Catholic practice. Although the two documents disagree on their starting points and come to differing conclusions, they need to be read together with thoughtful consideration given to their points of agreement and their points of contention.

Preserving Tradition in the Midst of Innovation. Another of today's challenges is to treasure more fully the place of Gregorian chant and Latin language in the heritage[40] of the Church. Church documents guiding music in the liturgy all indicate the value and importance of maintaining this heritage and the implementation of RM3 provides added impetus to do so. The survey of hymnbooks traversing the period from immediately after Vatican II to the present revealed an overall increase in the inclusion of chant and of Latin texts. More must be done, however, to ensure the inclusion of these elements from the Church's tradition in today's multicultural, multilingual, multi-musical liturgical celebrations. Although Gregorian chant and Latin language are not essential elements of the liturgy (though some today would argue they are) but are merely, like all forms of music and language, vehicles for revealing the deeper nature and purpose of the liturgy and drawing the assembly into its dynamic, chant and Latin are nonetheless part of the culture of the Roman rite. The overarching challenge here is a balanced use of music generated by the Church's past with use of music being generated by the Church's present and its future.

Grappling with the Meaning of Inculturation. The current liturgical/musical situation raises the need to grapple more deeply with the nature of liturgical inculturation vis-à-vis the nature of the liturgy. Discrimination is needed about what cultural patterns and practices of prayer and song belong in the liturgy because these patterns and practices support the liturgy in its work of drawing the people more deeply into their identity and mission as Body of Christ and what cultural patterns and practices do not belong because they deflect the people from this purpose. More reflection is needed about the nature and purpose of the liturgy. Pastoral musicians and liturgists across all cultural, ethnic, and linguistic groups need to identify the essential elements of the liturgy: that is, what makes the liturgy what it is such that without those elements liturgy loses its identity and, therefore, its power to transform the Church more fully into being the Body of Christ. Deeper discernment is needed about how to inculturate the liturgy in ways that are true to the essential elements of the rite, that honor diverse cultures, and that embrace the Church's tradition.

Also needed is a more nuanced understanding of what is meant by "culture." Culture encompasses far more than language, far more than musical idioms. Anthropologists and social scientists in the field of cultural studies today define the term "culture" in several ways, evidencing the complexity of the topic.[41] When those making musical and liturgical decisions speak of cultural diversity, they need to be knowledgeable about these multiple approaches and the merits and limitations of each. Leaders need clarity in the application of the appropriate approach because it will determine the outcome of critical analysis, the shaping of recommendations concerning music and liturgy, and the parameters of evaluation.

Clarifying What Music is Appropriate for liturgy. Early on, the folk hymnbooks introduced the practice of printing songs about social protest and awareness, catechetical songs meant for the classroom, and devotional songs intended for non-liturgical prayer experiences side-by-side with music intended for the liturgy. Needing to fill the vacuum created by the shift to the vernacular, many liturgically uneducated parish musicians made use of the available repertoire without discernment as to liturgical appropriateness. This situation is compounded when current resources juxtapose liturgical and non-liturgical music without distinguishing which music is intended and appropriate for liturgical celebration and which is not. The result is confusion not only for music ministers, but also for people in the pews who do not understand why the music and texts they are singing in devotional prayer services or hearing in concert performances may not be suitable for use in the liturgy.

There is a need to differentiate when, where, and how to respond to the unbaptized in need of evangelization, to the baptized in need of catechesis, and to those seeking encounters with the sacred outside the parameters of the liturgy, and to delineate what forms of music best support each of these aspects of the mission of the Church. The underlying challenge is to distinguish between liturgical and devotional prayer, between subjective piety and piety rooted in the liturgy.

Liturgy is not a catechetical event, even though it contains elements that teach the faith; liturgy is not evangelization, even though it proclaims, in both word and action, the Good News of salvation; liturgy is not private prayer, even though it includes silent moments in which the people encounter God/Christ in the personal depths of their hearts. Rather, liturgy is the communal, public prayer of the Church engaged in ritual surrender to the paschal mystery. There are many kinds of sacred music that nourish people's faith and lift their hearts in prayer. Each genre has its own purpose and its own place, however, and not all sacred music is suitable for liturgical use. Music better suited for private devotional prayer, or for retreat or renewal experiences, youth rallies, or the concert hall is misplaced when used in the liturgy because it is at cross purposes with the liturgy.

The music used in the liturgy must share the same purpose as the liturgy. This means it must be music that draws the people into ecclesial identity, into the corporate prayer of the Body of Christ, and into sacramental, ritual celebration. Whatever its style or form, origins or instrumentation, the music must enable the assembly to surrender itself fully, consciously, actively to the paschal mystery being made present. This is music's primary liturgical function, and the principle that must guide all musical decision-making.

Understanding the Ministerial Relationship of Music to Liturgy. Today, more than ever, greater clarity is needed concerning the relationship of music to the liturgy. Although no style of music is inherently more sacred than another, some styles are, by nature, more appropriate for the liturgy than others. The key evaluative discernment here is whether the music is directing the liturgy or the liturgy is directing the music. Whenever music replaces the action of the liturgy as the basis of decision-making, music becomes peripheral rather than integral to the liturgy. And, even when peripheral, the music will dominate by drawing the people away from the liturgy into itself.

Grasping the Purpose of the Liturgy. To celebrate liturgy well requires understanding the purpose of the liturgy and the role liturgical music plays in supporting this purpose. According to SC, liturgy is the making present of the paschal mystery (SC 6). The paschal mystery refers to the whole of the Christ event: his life, passion, death, resurrection, ascension, sending of the Spirit, and promised second coming. But, it also refers to the participation of the Christian community in the Christ event: the paschal mystery is *their* mystery; it is they who live, die, and rise today as the Body of Christ in the world (Rom 6:3–11). In daily living, the paschal mystery is made present in myriad ways the faithful choose fidelity to their baptismal identity by dying to self so that they, and others, may have a fuller life. In the liturgy the paschal mystery is made present in the unfolding dynamics of the rite. Every time the baptized gather for liturgy, they are the Church, visibly united in communal surrender to the dying and rising mystery that defines their lives.

Conclusion
Now We Remain: Singing the Paschal Mystery

The context of this study of streams of music entering Roman Catholic liturgy after Vatican II has been the liturgical vision that guides the celebration of Roman Catholic liturgy. Within this context, we have traced the emergence of multiple streams of music in a loosely chronological survey of significant hymnbooks from Vatican II to the present. We have reflected on some patterns evident in the emergence of these streams. We have identified some of the challenges these musical developments place before us. We must continue to ask how well the music we sing meets the challenge of a changing liturgy in a changing world vis-à-vis the liturgical vision that frames this challenge. In other words, we must keep asking ourselves how far we have come and how far we yet need to go to reach a fully renewed, fully inculturated, fully intercultural liturgy. We must also keep asking ourselves how far we have come and how far we yet need to go to completely surrender ourselves to a liturgy that requires our death that others may be given life.

From SC onward, the liturgy of the Roman Catholic Church has allowed for many streams of music, but under these varying currents has always flowed a single, deep and steady current of liturgical understanding and practice that channels all the streams toward an eschatological destination in which all humankind is drawn into the communitarian life of the Trinity. Each stream of music, then, must be critiqued not in terms of its ability to give immediate satisfaction but in terms of its teleological capability. And, this teleological capability is evaluated existentially in the manner in which and to the extent that the music—whatever its form, style, genre, or roots—draws the baptized community into its paschal mystery identity and mission as Body of Christ given over for the life of the world.

Liturgical prayer arises not from a single language or a single style of music but from people's hearts united through diverse languages and musics in offering themselves with Christ in the power of the Holy Spirit to the Father, to one another, and to the world as the one Body of Christ. This is the liturgical/musical vision of SC. As we continue to rejoice in the multiplicity of musical streams in today's liturgy and to struggle with the challenges this multiplicity brings, may this remain the vision that inspires and guides us.

Notes —

1. Excerpt from "Now We Remain" by David Haas, © 1983, GIA Publications, Inc.
2. Pope Pius X's *Tra le sollecitudini* of 1903 urged the participation of the people in the liturgy through the singing of the chants proper to the Mass; Pope Pius XII's *Mediator Dei* of 1947 promoted congregational singing in the liturgy; and his *Musica sacra disciplina* of 1955 endorsed the singing of popular hymns during the liturgy.
3. The Liturgical Movement flowered in the first half of the twentieth century in Europe, the United Kingdom, and the United States. Convinced that the Church would be revitalized through a reinvigorated liturgy, participants in the Movement pursued liturgical research, established centers for liturgical education and formation, sponsored liturgical conferences, published liturgical journals, and experimented with new forms of pastoral-liturgical practice. This renewal movement influenced nearly every mainstream Western Christian church tradition.
   For more on the Liturgical Movement see Keith F. Pecklers and Bryan D. Spinks, "The Liturgical Movement," in *The New Westminster Dictionary of Liturgy and Worship*, ed., Paul Bradshaw (Louisville/London: Westminster John Knox Press, 2002), 283-289. For an in-depth look at the Liturgical Movement in the United States, see Keith F. Pecklers, *The Unread Vision: The Liturgical Movement in the United States of America: 1926-1955* (Collegeville: Liturgical Press, 1998). For discussion of the Liturgical Movement and music, see Anthony Ruff, OSB, *Sacred Music and Liturgical Reform: Treasures and Transformations* (Chicago/Mundelein: Liturgy Training Publications, 2007), chapters 11 and 12; hereafter, *Sacred Music and Liturgical Reform.*
4. The Council vote was 2147 in favor; four against.
5. Vatican Council II, *Sacrosanctum Concilium*, 1963 (*Acta Apostolicae Sedis* 56 [1964]), 97-138. English trans. in *Documents on the Liturgy, 1963-1979: Conciliar, Papal, and Curial Texts* © 1982 International Committee on English in the Liturgy (Collegeville: Liturgical Press), 1-131.
6. The Ordinary of the Mass consists of the Kyrie, the Glory to God, the Eucharistic Prayer acclamations (Holy, Holy; Mystery of Faith; and Great Amen), and the Lamb of God.
7. GIA Publications, Inc., in Chicago (GIA); Oregon Catholic Press in Portland, Oregon (OCP); World Library Publications in Franklin Park, IL (WLP). Since the purpose is not to present a comprehensive survey of music but rather to demonstrate the appearance of specific streams of music in Roman Catholic repertoire over the period of time from Vatican II to the present, a representative sampling is sufficient. Inevitably, I fail to acknowledge some composers and pieces other writers would have cited as significant; such is not a judgment on their work, but a consequence of needing to place limits on an extremely vast topic.
8. For more detailed exploration of the Folk Mass movement see Ken Canedo, *Keep the Fire Burning: The Folk Mass Revolution* (Portland, OR: Pastoral Press, 2009), hereafter, *Keep*

33

the Fire Burning; Tim Schoenbachler, *Folk Music in Transition: The Pastoral Challenge* (Phoenix: Pastoral Arts Associates, 1979); and Donald Boccardi, SM, *The History of American Catholic Hymnals Since Vatican II* (Chicago: GIA Publications, Inc., 2001).

9. The Mass Propers consist of the introit, offertory, and Communion chants appointed for—that is, proper to—the day. Each is comprised of an antiphon and a verse taken from a psalm or other scriptural source.

10. In 1968, Darryl Ducote, Mike Balhoff, Dave Baker, Buddy Ceasar, and Gary Ault, seminarians at Notre Dame Seminary in New Orleans, formed a musical group and called themselves the Dameans. The group became a leading contributor to contemporary, Catholic liturgical music in the 1980s.

11. Canedo, *Keep the Fire Burning*, 10.

12. The Roman Missal is the official book containing all the texts of the Mass. In November 2011 the third edition, an English retranslation more in accord with original Latin sources and containing Vatican chant settings of the sung parts of the Mass was mandated for use in the United States. The mandate created a need for new musical settings of the Mass in accord with the new textual requirements. Composers subsequently generated new or revised settings of the Mass, and publishers produced new hymnbook and music resources.

13. For more on Contemporary Christian Music, see chapter six.

14. "Sprung meter" is a rhythmic pattern in which a varying number of syllables is distributed over a fixed number of stresses. This pattern is typical of many English-language nursery rhymes ("Three Blind Mice," for example), and is the underlying pattern in Hebrew psalmody.

15. In 2010, a new and revised translation of the Grail psalms undertaken by Abbot Gregory Polan and the monks of Conception Abbey, Missouri, was granted *recognitio* by the Vatican as the official translation to be included in future revisions of all liturgical rites in the United States.

16. From this point forward the terms "hymn" and "song" will be used interchangeably to refer to all sorts of musical forms sung by the congregation.

17. For example, the priest's address, "The Lord be with you" with the people's response, "And with your spirit" or the lector's "Word of the Lord" at the conclusion of a reading with the people's response, "Thanks be to God."

18. STL 115a, citing the General Instruction of the Roman Missal (Washington, D.C.: United States Conference of Catholic Bishops, 2003) 40; hereafter GIRM; and *Musicam sacram* (*Acta Apostolicae Sedis* 56 [1967]) 7,16; English trans. in *Documents on the Liturgy, 1963-1979:Conciliar, Papal, and Curial Texts* © 1982 International Committee on English in the Liturgy (Collegeville: Liturgical Press), 1293-1306; hereafter MS.

19. The acclamations include the Gospel Acclamation, and the people's parts of the Eucharistic Prayer (the Sanctus, the Mystery of Faith, and the Great Amen).

20. Introduction to the Order of Mass: A Pastoral Resource of the Bishops' Committee on the Liturgy (Washington, DC: USCCB, 2003), 86.

21. The responsorial psalm aligns with the first reading and the gospel primarily during Ordinary Time. During Advent, Christmas, Lent, and Easter the readings and psalm are not directly related but have been juxtaposed because of their relationship to the focus of the liturgical season. Even during Ordinary Time, the psalm is not related to the second reading that is running along its own semi-continuous track. Nonetheless, the responsorial

psalm does play an interpretive role vis-à-vis the Liturgy of the Word. For fuller discussion of this point, see Ralph Kiefer, *To Hear and To Proclaim, Introduction, Lectionary for Mass with Commentary for Musicians and Priests* (Washington, D.C.: The Pastoral Press, 1983), 81: "the Responsorial Psalm constitutes a summation of the word for that day"; J. Michael McMahon, *Singing our Worship: A Pastoral Musician's Guide to the General Instruction of the Roman Missal* (Silver Spring, MD: NPM Publications, 2003, 2007) 12: the psalm and its refrain often provide "an interpretive key to the readings of the day;" Irene Nowell, *Sing a New Song: The Psalms in the Sunday Lectionary*, (Collegeville, MN: Liturgical Press, 1993); Peter Purdue, "The New Lectionary," in *Doctrine and Life* 19 (1969), 666-679; and Kathleen Harmon, *The Ministry of Cantors* (Collegeville, MN: Liturgical Press, 2004).

22   For example, see Augustine, Sermon 165, PL, 38, 902: "We have heard the Epistle, the psalm and the Gospel; all these three readings are in agreement." Cited in Joseph Gelineau, *Voices and Instruments in Christian Worship*, trans. Clifford Howell, S. J. (Collegeville: Liturgical Press, 1964), n. 139, p. 79.

23   Robert Cabié, *The Church at Prayer—Vol. II: The Eucharist*, new ed., trans. Matthew J. O'Connell (Collegeville: Liturgical Press, 1986), 63.

24   See, for example, Lucien Deiss, *Celebration of the Word* (Collegeville, MN: Liturgical Press, 1993), 43: "The Responsorial Psalm may be considered as the *response* of the community to the Word that is given to it. Certainly, it is clear that the essential response is obedience to God and adoration of God's holy will. The Responsorial Psalm ritualizes this response;" italics in original; Deiss, *Visions of Liturgy and Music for a New Century* (Collegeville, MN: Liturgical Press, 1996), 102–103; Kathleen Harmon, SNDdeN, *The Ministry of Cantors* (Collegeville, MN: Liturgical Press, 2004); Harry P. Nasuti, "The Sacramental Function of the Psalms in Contemporary Scholarship and Liturgical Practice" in *Psalms and Practice: Worship, Virtue, and Authority*, ed. Stephen Breck Reid (Collegeville, MN: Liturgical Press, 2001), 78-89.

25   Harry P. Nasuti, "The Sacramental Function of the Psalms in Contemporary Scholarship and Liturgical Practice" in *Psalms and Practice: Worship, Virtue, and Authority*, ed. Stephen Breck Reid (Collegeville, MN: Liturgical Press, 2001), 78-89.

26   Nasuti, 81.

27   Nasuti, 82.

28   Nasuti, 82.

29   Nasuti, 86.

30   Nasuti, 81.

31   Gordon E. Truitt, "Musicam sacram," in *The Song of the Assembly: Pastoral Music in Practice*, eds. Bari Colombari and Michael Prendergast (Portland, OR: Pastoral Press, 2007), 21.

32   Frank C. Quinn, "Liturgical Music as Corporate Song 2: Problems of Hymnody in Catholic Worship," in *Liturgy and Music: Lifetime Learning*, ed. by Robin A Leaver and Joyce Ann Zimmerman (Collegeville, MN: Liturgical Press, 1998), 308-323.

33   Edward Schaefer, *Catholic Music through the Ages* (Chicago/Mundelein, IL: Liturgy Training Publications, 2008), 173-174.

34   Schaefer, 196.

35   Anthony Ruff, OSB, *Sacred Music and Liturgical Reform: Treasures and Transformations* (Chicago/Mundelein: Liturgy Training Publications, 2007), 564–592.

36 Ruff, 470.

37 Anthony Ruff, OSB, "Antiphons and their Use in the Liturgy," Colloquium of the National Association of Pastoral Musicians, Jan. 27-29, 2013, Washington D.C.

38 *The Snowbird Statement on Catholic Liturgical Music* (Salt Lake City: The Madeleine Institute, 1995). At the invitation of Msgr. M. Francis Mannion, seventeen liturgists and musicians from the US, Canada, England, and Ireland engaged in a series of discussions concerning Roman Catholic liturgical music in English-speaking countries, producing this statement that they named after the town in Utah where their dialogue began.

39 *The Milwaukee Symposia for Church Composers: A Ten-Year Report* (Washington, DC: The Pastoral Press and Chicago: Liturgy Training Publications, 1992). This document resulted from a ten-year series of symposia on the quality of liturgical music in the United States sponsored by Theophane Hytrek, SSSF, and Archbishop Rembert Weakland, OSB.

40 See SC 68; MS 50; STL 72-80.

41 Ricky Manalo, "Sing to the Lord: Cultural Perspectives" in *Perspectives on Sing to the Lord: Essays in Honor of Robert W. Hovda, Series V*, 39-54. Silver Spring, MD: NPM Publications, 2010.

—Stream Two—
Classic Contemporary Protestant Hymnody

Chapter 2

When in Our Music God Is Glorified:
Classic Contemporary Protestant Hymnody

Emily R. Brink

Many living rooms in North American homes a couple of generations ago displayed a painting of a pastoral scene with a stream coursing through the middle of wooded landscape. Imagine for a moment that the stream represented congregational song in North American Protestant worship about fifty years ago. That stream would represent the long history of hymns that nourished the faith and worship of Protestant Christians since the days of the sixteenth-century Reformation. About the middle of the twentieth century, hymns represented the main stream of congregational song in Protestant churches.

That stream was nourished not only in Sunday morning worship, but also many Protestant churches held Sunday evening and Wednesday night prayer services in which more hymns were sung than on Sunday mornings. In addition, many people sang hymns at home; living rooms often included a piano or small organ. The singing of hymns was an important part of the spiritual nurture of adults and children at home as well as in church.

When speaking of the congregational song of the church, many of these Protestants might have argued that the tradition of hymnody was more than a stream; it was more like a river, and the only river on the map. That river still runs deep, but now with many other streams joining it; other chapters in this book trace those other streams. The intention of this chapter is to trace the movements in classic contemporary Protestant hymnody composed by Anglo writers since the middle of the twentieth century. The chapter is in three parts: a brief description of classic Protestant hymnody is followed by a broad overview of changes in recent hymns and hymnals, and then a more specific view by region and country.

Classic Protestant Hymnody

Classic Protestant hymnody covers a very wide range. The words "classic" and "hymnody" in this chapter refer primarily to recent English texts in metrical and strophic structures intended for congregational singing, rooted in the English hymn tradition that began in the eighteenth century. That tradition was rooted in an even older one—metrical psalmody that dates back to the earliest days of Protestantism in the sixteenth century. In this chapter, some recently composed tunes for these texts will be mentioned, though many newer texts have been set to older tunes both composed and folk. So, it will be necessary to treat texts and tunes somewhat separately. In fact, the tradition of treating texts and tunes as separable components of congregational song is one that is deeply rooted in the classic English hymn tradition, more so than in the continental European tradition or in much contemporary worship song, where texts and tunes are more likely to be considered as integral phenomenon.

The word "Protestant" covers a lot of territory, both geographically and ecclesiastically. To narrow the range somewhat, this chapter will focus especially on hymn texts that come from the pens of Anglo Protestant writers from the English-speaking world, including England, Scotland, Australia and New Zealand, the United States and Canada. Ecclesiastically, the territory is very broad. Speaking only of North American Protestantism, James F. White delineates nine traditions: Lutheran, Reformed, Anabaptist, Anglican (Episcopalian), Separatist, Quaker, Methodist, Frontier, and Pentecostal.[1] Those traditions have been losing some of their distinctive edges in the last half century. More recently, John D. Witvliet listed "five very distinct movements—the Charismatic Movement, the Liturgical

Movement, the Ecumenical Movement, the Church Growth Movement, and a neo-Confessional movement—each with its own magnetic pull."[2] Changes in classic Protestant hymnody come especially from the Liturgical and Ecumenical Movements.

An Overview of Changes

During the 1950s, denominational hymnals were filled especially with eighteenth- and nineteenth-century hymns that did not address the kinds of political, social, and economic conditions affected by two world wars and a great depression. A whole new youth culture began, and the United States was in its "second childhood, with nostalgic theme parks (Disneyland) and ... Barbie [Doll], ... a Hollywood sexpot in plastic."[3]

Beginning in the 1950s, four levels of change in Protestant hymnody began somewhat simultaneously around the English-speaking world, indicating a widespread and ecumenical readiness for new beginnings for the song of the church. Continuing the earlier imagery of the river of hymnody, recent changes can be described in terms of becoming deeper, broader, more active, and more diverse.

Deeper

First, the river became deeper. In the second half of the twentieth century, most Protestant traditions reached back to their roots to regain a sense of identity after denominational mergers and realignments in the preceding half-century.[4] Many new denominational hymnals worked at recovering older texts and tunes that reflected their particular tradition. The *Lutheran Book of Worship* (LBW, 1978) is generally considered the first of a new generation of North American hymnals, so much so that the *Dictionary of American Hymnology* chose 1978 as the cutoff date for a comprehensive listing of all hymns and hymnals produced in North America since 1640.[5] The LBW became the hymnal of the Evangelical Lutheran Church in America (ELCA), but it was actually released ten years before the formal beginning of the ELCA. That hymnal was crucial in bringing together three different Lutheran de-nominations into institutional unity. One critical strategy in that union was to reach back to common, early Christian and historic Lutheran roots of liturgy, psalmody, and hymnody.[6]

At the same time, other Protestant denominations were reshaping their worship books, liturgical forms, and approach to preaching, stimulated both by the ecumenical movement and the reforms of Vatican II. Those changes in turn stimulated many hymn writers also to reach back deeply, especially to the Scriptures themselves as a primary source for hymnody.

Much Protestant worship had included only three or four congregational hymns on a Sunday morning: an opening hymn of praise, perhaps a sung prayer of confession, a sermon hymn of dedication, and a parting hymn of praise or commitment. Each was usually formed as a prayer, addressed to God. But, hymns can also be formed as proclamation, addressed to others. With a new emphasis on scripture as a source for hymnody, especially the psalms, and with increased interest in exegetical preaching, more congregational song restored the tradition of hymns as proclamation, either in metrical settings of scripture or in hymnody. The Lutheran tradition, in particular, is filled with hymns that proclaim in song the scripture preached in sermon. A renewed interest among Protestants in singing the psalms—filled with both proclamation and prayer—resulted in many new settings of psalms and canticles.[7] Since metrical psalmody matches the form and structure of classic hymnody, they can also be included as part of this stream of hymnody, though other forms of psalmody—especially the remarkable introduction of responsorial psalmody in Protestant worship—are beyond the scope of this book.[8]

The very title of this book reflects the bond between old and new, between the ancient texts and newer forms for contemporary singing. "New Songs of Celebration Render" [*Panorama*: 628] is a metrical psalm setting of Psalm 98 by Erik Routley (1917–1982), one of the most significant leaders of a new generation of hymn writers. This text, from 1972 and first published in 1974, is set to the tune assigned to that same psalm in the Genevan Psalter of 1562. The text, one of proclamation, calls on all creation to praise the God who has "made known his great salvation," and will one day return with justice and truth victorious to establish the world in peace.

Example 2:1
"New Songs of Celebration Render" by Erik Routley, stanza 1, compared with
Psalm 98:1-2 (NRSV)

New songs of celebration render	O sing to the LORD a new song,
to him who has great wonders done:	for he has done marvelous things!
Love sits enthroned in ageless splendour-	His right hand and his holy arm
come and adore the Mighty one!	have gotten him the victory.
He has made known his great salvation,	The LORD has made known his victory, he has revealed his vindication
which all his friends with joy confess;	in the sight of the nations.
he has revealed to every nation	
his everlasting righteousness.	

©1974, Hope Publishing Company, Carol Stream, IL 60188. All rights reserved. Used by permission.

Another facet of reaching back deeply into the history and practice of the Christian church was to recover the Christian year. Most Protestant churches have joined the more liturgical traditions of Episcopalians and Lutherans in welcoming visual arts and symbols along with expanded sections in hymnals for the liturgical year. Now almost every Protestant church celebrates Advent, Epiphany, Lent, and Holy Week. Hymn writers have responded with many more hymns for those seasons and for hymns celebrating the arts in worship.

Yet, another recovery has been the growing recognition, though not widespread recovery, of the ancient pattern of Word and Table as normative for Sunday worship—a pattern disrupted during the sixteenth-century Reformation. A century ago, many Protestant churches celebrated the sacrament of Holy Communion infrequently, often four or five times a year. The predominant practice was somber, even funereal. But, when Protestant churches started recovering the idea of Eucharist (meaning Thanksgiving) and celebrating the sacrament of Holy Communion on Christmas, Easter, and more often throughout the year, more hymns were needed. The Lord's Supper section became one of the most expanded sections of hymnals in the second half of the twentieth century. The greatest number is found in the *Chalice Hymnal* of the Christian Church (Disciples of Christ), with its heritage of weekly communion; one fourth of the hymns are related to the Lord's Supper.[9] "All Who Hunger, Gather Gladly" [*Panorama:* 872] by Canadian hymn writer Sylvia Dunstan (1955–1992) is a good example of a communion text that is both joyful and deeply biblical; already in the first stanza there are references to Isaiah 55:1, Exodus 16, and Psalm 34:8.

Broader

On a second level of change, the river of classic Protestant hymnody also became broader, more ecumenical. Many beloved hymns in Protestant hymnals already reached back beyond the English hymn tradition. The nineteenth century witnessed important translations of early Greek and Latin hymns and of Lutheran chorales. But, a whole new level of ecumenicity started during the twentieth century. Many new denominational hymnals, especially in North America, Australia, and New Zealand, reached beyond their immigrant roots.

In the middle of the twentieth century, with denominational mergers and realignments, ecumenical efforts moved first within denominations with a similar confessional heritage, and then expanded. In North America, the Inter-Lutheran Commission on Worship that prepared the *Lutheran Book of Worship* (LBW) first formed a list of 227 such hymns, and LBW included 175 of them. That ecumenical list of 227 hymns proved to be influential on subsequent hymnal committees as well. Another more ecumenical consultation became "the primary force in the formation of a core of ecumenical congregational song in the United States during the last half of [the twentieth] century."[10] There is now a large body of shared hymns in mainstream Protestant hymnody, as shown not only in denominational hymnals but also in several non-denominational hymnals.

The development of a common lectionary was another ecumenical effort affecting hymnody that was directly influenced by the reforms of Vatican II. *The Revised Common Lectionary* (1992) was prepared by the Consultation on Common Texts (CCT: www.commontexts.org), an ecumenical consultation of liturgical scholars and denominational representatives, both Catholic and

Protestant, from the United States and Canada. The remarkable spread of *The Revised Common Lectionary* (RCL), even among communions that had not ever followed a lectionary, is a direct consequence of the ecumenical movement. The twentieth anniversary annotated edition of the RCL (Minneapolis: Fortress Press, 2012) provides helpful ancillary materials after twenty years of use. The use of a lectionary—a schedule of assigned scripture readings from both Old and New Testaments, including a psalm for each week, repeated in two-or three-year cycles—has resulted in an increase in the amount of scripture read in worship, more exegetical preaching, and a great number of new hymns based upon or responding to those passages.

The swift spread of the RCL across the entire English-speaking world was unexpected: "After all the centuries since the sixteenth-century reformation, many of the churches that divided at that time are now committed to reading the scriptures together Sunday by Sunday. This is a kind of ecumenism nobody anticipated, least of all the Roman See. And, it makes possible wonderful weekly clergy gatherings all over the world for the purpose of mutual work on sermons and homilies."[11] It also makes possible ways for hymn writers to work ecumenically, offering new psalm settings and hymns on those scripture texts. The result has been a change from the predominantly experiential hymns of late nineteenth-century Protestant hymnody to more objective exposition of the truths of scripture. One happy result of this closer tie of new hymns to scripture has been to include scripture indexes in most hymnal collections—a wonderful tool for worship planning. Two early examples of separately published collections of new lectionary-based hymns are *New Hymns for the Lectionary* (1986) with fifty-two texts by Tom Troeger (b. 1945) [See *Panorama*: 751–759 for representative hymns] and tunes by Carol Doran (b. 1936), and two collections by Carl Daw, Jr. (b. 1944), one of hymns, *A Year of Grace* (1990), and one of metrical psalms, *To Sing God's Praise* (1992). Another collection of texts by multiple hymn writers on passages from the New Testament was *Hymns for the Gospels* (2001).[12]

Example 2:2
"These Things Did Thomas Count as Real" by Thomas Troeger, stanza 1, based on John 20:19-31, a reading for the Second Sunday of Easter [See *Panorama*: 751 for complete text]

These things did Thomas count as real:
the warmth of blood, the chill of steel,
the grain of wood, the heft of stone,
the last full twitch of flesh and bone.

©1994, Oxford University Press. Used by Permission.

More Active

A third level of change in recent hymnody came from the many new springs that started bubbling up in response to changes in the culture. In the second half of the twentieth century, the river of hymnody began rushing with a tremendous increase in the number of hymns written, resulting in the often-used phrase "hymn explosion," soon to be followed by a hymnal explosion. New hymnals and, increasingly, separate supplements were published, including many collections of texts and tunes by individual authors and composers.

Many new hymns included issues and topics never before addressed in hymnody, reflecting profound changes in the world and in society. In the 1950s, the Hymn Society in the United States and Canada started publishing little collections of hymns to fill gaps such as "Five New Hymns on the City" (1954), "Fourteen New Rural Hymns" (1955), and "Seven New Social Welfare Hymns" (1961).[13] Fred Kaan (1929–2009) [See *Panorama*: 603–610 for representative hymn texts], beginning as pastor of the Pilgrim Church in Plymouth, England, in 1963, started writing hymns regularly then; he said "becoming a hymn writer had its origins in the frustration created by what I could not find in the hard-cover hymnbook."[14]

One of the most challenging issues has been the matter of language change. On one level, language changes were simple. Following new translations of the Bible, many hymn writers also began using pronouns and verb forms that reflected contemporary English usage, and writers of new hymn texts increasingly followed contemporary usage. Hymnals are always collections of old and new, but the contrast had never been greater between the older language and contemporary usage, so hymnal committees struggled with whether to update older texts. Again, LBW broke new ground, reviewing and changing many older, classical texts, so much so that the index includes indented entries of changed first lines. For example, "Break Thou the Bread of Life" became "Break Now the Bread of Life." *Hymns for Today's Church*[15] in England also opened controversial doors of language change, discussed later in this chapter. However, more recently, many hymnals have returned to original language, and many are not bothered by "thee" and "thou" language.

On a deeper level, language changes opened up both issues of theology and justice that challenged new hymn writers as they struggled with language for God and issues of gender, class, origin, and all those who are least among us. The most radical and controversial approach to inclusive language was taken by the *New Century Hymnal,*[16] which, similar to LBW, included an index with old and adapted titles. Anyone interested can read several lively responses to their approach.[17] Inclusive language with respect to human beings is the pattern for new hymns in North America, but is still not considered an issue among many British hymn writers, for whom the term "man" is often still used generically.

The inclusive language issue is related to broader concerns for justice that have always characterized the church, from the psalms to our own day, but these concerns have become more urgent after two world wars and increasing global conflicts and terrorism that cause great suffering. Through the efforts of some individual congregations, and especially the hymn searches of the Hymn Society in the United States and Canada, many new hymns have been written that include concern for children, the elderly, urban poverty, and environmental issues. Paul Westermeyer addresses themes of justice in *Let Justice Sing: Hymnody and Justice,* providing many examples.[18] Some of those hymns include praise, the posture of most hymns, while others offer repentance, lament, and intercession. The balance of lament and praise is better in the current generation of hymnals than in previous ones, and some churches are once more finding a place for singing laments in worship. See, for examples, "Our Cities Cry to You, O Lord" [*Panorama*: 849] by Canadian hymn writer Margaret Clarkson (1915–2008), and the following text by English writer Martin Leckebusch (b. 1962).

Example 2:3
"In an Age of Twisted Values," stanza 1, by Martin E. Leckebusch.[19]

In an age of twisted values we have lost the truth we need.
In sophisticated language we have justified our greed.
By our struggle for possessions we have robbed the poor and weak.
Hear our cry and heal our nation; your forgiveness, Lord, we seek.

© 1995, Kevin Mayhew Ltd. Used by permission.

Diverse

Finally, a fourth level of change in the river of congregational song in Protestant worship is the sheer diversity of sources, both in style and origin. Hymnody is now clearly one stream among many explored in this volume. Those different streams now sometimes converge in cross-over ways that make definitions and distinctions difficult. The word "hymn" used to stand for most of congregational song, and most denominational song collections were called hymnals. No more; increasingly, new publications look for other titles, because the contents are so much more stylistically inclusive than previous collections. Another reason for the name change stems from the greater attention paid to the liturgical context of hymnody, for example, the *Lutheran Book of Worship*, *The Worshiping Church, and* two hymnals scheduled for publication in 2013: *Lift Up Your Hearts* (Faith Alive) and *Glory to God* (Presbyterian Publishing Corporation).

Traditional classic hymnody may still be the dominant stream in most mainline Protestant congregations, but more often, especially in congregations influenced by the charismatic movement, other streams of congregational song are represented as well. The power in some of those more recent streams has resulted in the virtual disappearance of traditional classic hymnody in many Protestant congregations that two generations ago sang only hymns.

At the same time, some contemporary musical groups rooted in rock and jazz traditions are rediscovering hymns. To further reveal this story—of the deeper, wider, and more rushing river of Protestant hymnody in North American in the last fifty years, now clearly one stream of congregational song among others—we now turn to an overview of hymn writers and movements in different English-speaking countries.

England and Scotland

The classic tradition of English hymnody began in England and Scotland, which also provides a good place to begin tracing recent movements. During the 1960s, two groups of people in the United Kingdom started work simultaneously and separately on creating new hymns for worship. At first, neither group knew about the other. One ecumenical group began rather quietly in the small village of Dunblane, Scotland, and another group of Anglican clergy and musicians began much more publicly in London.[20]

The Dunblane Gatherings

In 1962, a new ecumenical center in the small village of Dunblane, Scotland, hosted a meeting with representatives of several denominations to discuss the role of the music in the church. Ian Fraser, (b. 1917) the leader of the center and minister in the Church of Scotland, chose the topic and invited some twenty-four clergy and musicians from the seven major denominations in Scotland. Fraser hoped to contribute some fresh ideas to hymnody since the Church of Scotland was currently at work on a revision of their hymnal, *The Church Hymnary*. The group met with anticipation, since there was a need to address the relationship of classic hymnody to contemporary society and to the growing popularity of folk music in the church, especially after the publication of Geoffrey Beaumont's *Folk Mass* in 1957.

That meeting, and a few subsequent ones, marked a significant new beginning. The remarkable thing in retrospect is how influential that group of writers was, not only for British hymnody, but also for the entire English-speaking world. The first little collection of sixteen new hymns was informally published in 1964, called *Dunblane Praises;* a second collection, *Dunblane*

Praises 2 came out two years later. The meetings at Dunblane, Scotland, proved to be a catalyst for a number of new writers who stood clearly in the tradition of classical Protestant hymnody.

Erik Routley (1917–1982), pastor in the United Reformed Church, contributed both texts and tunes at these meetings, and with his outstanding knowledge of hymnody, became an important mentor to the other members. His very first hymn dealt with urban issues; "All Who Love and Serve Your City" (1966, *Dunblane Praises 2*) [*Panorama*: 504] soon found its way into many hymnals.[21] Other members of the group, some joining later, are now represented in most English language hymnals, including especially Brian Wren (b. 1936). As with Routley, Wren was a pastor in the United Reformed Church; his first hymns include "I Come with Joy to Meet My Lord" (1966) [Now revised as "I Come with Joy, a Child of God"; see *Panorama*: 498 A. and B.] and "Thank You, Lord, for Water, Soil, and Air" (1973) [*Panorama*: 500], introducing ecological issues into hymnody.

There were other writers at work as well in different hymnal projects, sometimes without awareness of each other, as they prepared other hymnals or supplements. Already in the 1970s, Routley started to speak of an "English hymn renaissance" with respect to especially three writers, Brian Wren, Fred Pratt Green (1903–2000), and Fred H. Kaan (1929–2009).[22]

Methodist pastor Fred Pratt Green started serious work as a hymn writer only after retirement, when he joined a hymnal committee in 1966 to prepare the Methodist supplement *Hymns and Songs* (1969). Erik Routley came to consider him the finest writer since Charles Wesley.[23] The Dutch ecumenist Fred Kaan, another pastor in the United Reformed Church, spent several years as executive secretary of the World Alliance of Reformed Churches, and with his extensive international experience became interested in filling gaps not covered in older hymnals, particularly in the area of social responsibility. His text "Father, Help Your People" (1966) is a prayer that worship on Sunday be connected with all of life, at home or in the marketplace, "that in work and worship love may set the tone."[24]

One pivotal figure is Timothy Dudley-Smith (b. 1926), ordained in the Church of England in 1950. His early role as a hymn writer began with another group, this time of Anglicans—the Jubilate Group.

The Jubilate Group

Also in the 1960s, a group of Anglican clergy and musicians involved in youth work began to address the increasing dissonance between the older song tradition of the church and the newer songs of popular culture that appealed to teenagers. Not much had changed in the song of the church between the two great world wars, but after World War II, popular culture changed greatly, and many church youth groups started exploring folk music and guitar accompaniments. Michael Baughen (b. 1930), an ordained Anglican priest, was among others who worked with youth, also seeking to provide new songs for them. Several Anglican clergy began working together, eventually forming Jubilate Group Limited, a team that worked on increasingly ambitious projects to help reform the song of the church.[25]

When joining the staff of the Church Pastoral Aid Society (CPAS), Baughen approached Timothy Dudley-Smith, then general secretary of CPAS, who agreed to publish a collection of new songs. Dudley-Smith also contributed texts, though he was not involved in the editing of the collection. *Youth Praise 1* was released in 1966 in the heart of London at an event that drew more than two thousand youth. Three years later, *Youth Praise 2* was introduced at Royal Albert Hall; this time more than 10,000 people attended two events the same day, with choirs, more than a hundred guitarists, and a wide range of new songs. Those two collections, totaling 299 hymns and songs, sold over a million copies. Of the songs in classic hymn style, the song most often found in hymnals today is Timothy Dudley-Smith's setting of the Song of Mary, "Tell Out My Soul" (1961) [*Panorama*: 501], eventually paired with the tune WOODLANDS. Few today would guess that this text was prepared for youth.

The same group of Anglican clergy focused next on psalms and canticles, which were increasingly neglected in Anglican parishes. *Psalm Praise* (1973) was the first collection of psalm settings that revealed the diversity that has marked congregational song ever since: contemporary texts, revisions of older texts, and many different styles, from chant to folk to metrical. GIA Publications, Inc. made *Psalm Praise* immediately available in North America.

In 1980, the *Psalm Praise* team members incorporated as Jubilate Group Limited and moved forward to a larger hymnal project, releasing *Hymns for*

Today's Church (HTC) in 1982 with John W. Wilson (1905–1992) as music editor and Michael Saward (b. 1932) as text editor, a collection of more than 500 hymns and songs both old and new. Their approach in revising classical texts proved to be polarizing both on account of texts and tunes. Many writers standing in the classical tradition were indignant regarding changes to beautiful, older poetry, others were delighted that some previously awkward texts were rescued and now intelligible to contemporary worshipers. At the same time, those who honored the classical hymn-tune tradition associated with the organ did not appreciate the move to a much more popular style of tune, often led by guitars and keyboard. HTC included 277 texts and tunes by the now eight members of the group, plus forty-six texts by Dudley-Smith. One of the best known hymns from HTC is "Baptized in Water" [*Panorama*: 671] by Michael Saward. In 1999 the Jubilate Group released their next major hymnal, *Sing Glory: Hymns, Psalms, and Songs for a New Century.* This collection of 698 songs has not created the stir that HTC did, partly because it represents a maturing of their approach, now including a much wider range of authors and composers, and partly because stylistic diversity had become so widespread.

The Iona Community

The ecumenical and international Iona Community <www.iona.org.uk>, based on the island of Iona in Scotland, has made many liturgical and musical contributions to worship around the world. Ian Fraser, who convened the first 1962 meetings in Dunblane, Scotland, was also a friend of the Iona Community that began in 1938 during the Depression. The rebuilding of an ancient abbey on the island of Iona became a symbol of the need to rebuild a community based upon a belief that work and worship were one. The themes of a common life rooted in justice pervade the many hymn texts that have come from that community, especially under the musical leadership of John Bell (b. 1949) [*Panorama*: 702–716]. Their music ranges from collections of global songs, to hymns, to metrical psalm settings—some lively and joyful psalms of praise, others haunting psalms of lament, to choruses ("wee" songs), and choral anthems. They have also published collections of prayers and liturgies that integrate song into a larger liturgical context. *Common*

Ground (1998) is the largest collection of their congregational song. One small but telling example of how concerns for justice are imbedded in their work is found in the word "protest" in Bell's hymn "For All the Saints Who've Shown Your Love" (GIA–4540). He includes thanks for those who saw God's kingdom come "through selfless protest, prayer, and praise." See stream seven, "Through every land, by every tongue; The Rise of Global and Ecumencial Song," for a fuller account of the history of the Iona Community and the John Bell's contributions.

Example 2:4
"Sing to God with Joy and Gladness"; refrain and stanzas 1 and 2 (Psalm 147:1–6)
For the full text and tune GLENDON, also by John L. Bell, see *Psalms of Patience, Protest, and Praise,* by John L. Bell

Refrain:
Sing to God, with joy and gladness, hymns and psalms of gratitude;
with the voice of praise discover that to worship God is good.

1. God unites his scattered people, gathers those who wandered far,
heals the hurt and broken spirits, tending every wound and scar.

2. Such is God's great power and wisdom none can calculate or tell;
keen is God to ground the wicked and with humble folk to dwell.

(The Iona Community, © 1993, available through GIA Publications, Inc.).

In addition to those directly involved with the Dunblane meetings, Jubilate Group, and the Iona Community, many other writers had been active in England in the last part of the twentieth century.[26] Earlier, the mention of "cross-over" songs indicated that some songs were hard to categorize, since they are influenced both by folk music and the charismatic movement.

One such song from 1987 that became immediately popular is *Shine, Jesus, Shine*, by Graham Kendrick; it is unrhymed, yet metrical and strophic in structure. A more recent example even more clearly stands in the classic metrical tradition: "In Christ Alone" (2002) by Stuart Townend (b. 1963) and Keith Getty (b. 1974) is in a very familiar meter (88 88 D), rhymed, and in every way matches the definition of classical Protestant hymnody, though many of those who sing it would be surprised by that analysis, since it became popular first among youth. Both of these songs exemplify the increasing trend in contemporary popular worship music to treat text and tune as integral.

Example 2:5
"In Christ Alone," stanza 1
[See full text and hear song on www.gettymusic.com/hymns-inchristalone.aspx.]

In Christ alone my hope is found;
He is my light, my strength, my song.
This cornerstone, this solid ground;
firm through the fiercest drought and storm.
What heights of love! What depths of peace,
When fears are stilled, when strivings cease.
My comforter, my all in all;
here in the love of Christ I stand!

© 2002, Thankyou Music (admin. By EMI Christian Music Publ.). Used by permission.

Australia and New Zealand

Australia was settled mostly by British Protestant and Irish Catholic immigrants—in the early days many were convicts expelled from Great Britain. As in North America, Australian Protestants sang from hymnals they had taken with them. Immigration from several other countries, both from Europe and especially Asia and the South Pacific, grew rapidly after the two world wars, bringing much more diversity. The church has always been small in Australia, and several different denominations began working on a joint hymnal; the participants were Anglicans, Methodists, Congregationalists, and Presbyterians. The publication of *The Australian Hymn Book* in 1977 marks the first ecumenical and distinctly Australian hymnal, even though the contents came mainly from outside of Australia. That same year, Methodists, Congregationalists, and some Presbyterians merged to form the Uniting Church in Australia. *The Australian Hymn Book* was published under the title *With One Voice* in both England (1979) and New Zealand (1982), which included a *New Zealand Supplement.* Some Presbyterians continued to publish their own separate hymnal.[27]

Whereas the 1977 hymnal included primarily hymns in the classical Protestant tradition, a variety of supplements introduced more stylistic diversity and more recent hymns from across the English-speaking world.[28] In 1999, a major revision of the 1977 hymnal was published: *Together in Song: The Australian Hymn Book II.* This collection was even more ecumenical, involving Roman Catholics and Lutherans on the editorial committee; the bodies represent fully eighty percent of the Christians in Australia.[29] *Together in Song* includes still more stylistic diversity and more distinctly Australian voices, including songs from the Pentecostal tradition and a small sampling of songs from indigenous aboriginal groups. Reasons for the revision centered on the desire for broader content and about language issues, both with respect to contemporary usage and to gender-inclusive language. Certainly, another reason for the revision: by then, many Australians were writing hymns; Erik Routley said that Australia "has been rather slower in getting off the ground,"[30] but in *Together in Song,* seventy-six different Australians are represented and half the book consists of material written since 1950; yet the songs come from forty-eight countries. Two significant Australian text writers are Elizabeth Smith (b. 1956) [See *Panorama*: 877–882 for representative hymns] and Robin Mann (b. 1949), who also composes music.[31] In New Zealand, Shirley Erena Murray (b. 1931) [*Panorama*: 883-890] is the outstanding hymn text writer, with three collections of her hymns published in North America; her work is the most widely known.[32] Murray's hymns reflect a wide variety of theological themes, including prophetic issues about topics of justice and ecology.[33]

Example 2:6
"God Weeps" by Shirley Erena Murray, stanza 1 (1994)
[See *Panorama*: 886 for full text]

God weeps
>   at love withheld,
>   at strength misused,
>   at children's innocence abused,
> and till we change the way we love,
>   God weeps.

©1996, Hope Publishing Company, Carol Stream, IL 60188. All rights reserved. Used by permission.

THE UNITED STATES AND CANADA

Similar to Australia and New Zealand, the United States and Canada were formed as nations by different groups of immigrants in addition to the slaves who came to the United States from Africa. Classic Protestant hymnody was the mainstay of the older North American churches rooted in England and Scotland, and hymnals such as the Episcopal *Hymnal 1940* reflected strong continuity with hymnody in Great Britain. Though Canada is more closely related to the British tradition and has often been treated together with Great Britain in hymn studies originating in Great Britain, it makes sense to consider Canada together with the United States.

It should come as no surprise that recent hymns from Great Britain have found their way into North American hymnals. After all, the language is the same, and the classical Protestant hymn tradition was well represented by the older Anglican, Episcopal, Baptist, Methodist, and Reformed and Presbyterian immigrants who came from Great Britain to North America. The traffic across the ocean increased when in the 1970s, George Shorney (1931–2012), then president of Hope Publishing Company, began a publishing relationship with many significant British hymn writers. He met them in England, procured the publishing rights to their hymns for North American audiences, and introduced them to North Americans at several conferences of the Hymn Society in the United States and Canada. His work of "publisher as patron" mutually introduced North Americans and several British hymn writers mentioned earlier such as Timothy Dudley-Smith, Erik Routley, Brian Wren, and Fred Kaan.[34] Both Routley and Wren eventually moved to North America, each becoming completely devoted to hymnody, Wren as hymn writer, lecturer, and professor, and Routley as teacher of hymnology, hymn writer, and editor of *Rejoice in the Lord* (1985), the hymnal of the Reformed Church in America.

GIA Publications, Inc. also contributed to the traffic from Great Britain; they hold North American rights to all music from the Iona Community and have helped sponsor travel by John Bell. The fact that GIA began as a Roman Catholic publisher, yet is the North American publisher of two ecumenical communities—the Iona Community as well as the Community of Taizé—is a clear indication of the ecumenical spirit at the end of the twentieth century.

With fresh examples of creative hymn writing from Great Britain and Scotland, the creative spark spread to North America. Pastor and hymn writer Richard Leach (b. 1953) recounts his introduction to some of the new hymn writers when taking a worship course at Yale Divinity School taught by theologian and hymn writer Jeffrey Rowthorn:

> The words of Thomas Troeger and Brian Wren were so vivid and so energized, compared to what I was leading the congregation in every Sunday morning, that my first reaction was 'Wow!' And then I thought, 'I wonder if I could do that?' And then, 'I want to do that.' So I began to try. [See *Panorama*: 779–783 for representative hymns][35]

The Hymn Society in the United States and Canada (www.thehymnsociety.org) serves as an important catalyst in North America and beyond for the writing of new hymns in the classical Protestant tradition. Their annual conferences bring together writers, composers, editors, and publishers, and their quarterly publication *The Hymn* not only includes articles about hymnody old and new, but also provides a book service offering a wide range of hymnals, supplements, and single author and composer collections published in North America. Carl P. Daw, Jr. (b. 1944), former executive director of the Hymn Society, is one of the most significant hymn writers in North America, with several published collections; his texts are found not only in North American hymnals, but also across the world, many translated into other languages. [See *Panorama*: 760–768 for representative hymns.]

But, not all recent North American hymn writers stand in the tradition of English hymnody. Immigration patterns to North America, especially after World War II, continued from Western Europe, and many cities consisted largely of ethnic neighborhoods with different denominational traditions, each with their own hymn traditions as well. In the last quarter of the twentieth century, immigration has become much more global and diverse, with many refugees coming from around the world.

The strong heritage of Lutheran hymnody from Germany, Scandinavia, and more recently, from Eastern Europe found new expressions in North America. When several Lutheran bodies from different European roots combined forces in hopes of preparing a new Lutheran hymnal that would serve most of them, they reached back to their roots, moving beyond the German pietism that still characterized so much of immigrant Lutheran culture to deeper Lutheran roots. Significant Lutheran hymn text writers include Jaroslav Vajda (1914–2008) [See *Panorama*: 724–729 for representative hymns], who not only contributed original hymn texts, but also translated many from Slovak, and especially the pastor theologian Herman Stuempfle (1923–2007) [See *Panorama*: 769–778 for representative hymns], whose hymns are found in many hymnals.

Other significant hymn text and tune writers stand in a variety of traditions, but their ecclesiastical roots are not always clear. Many hymn writers today have moved from the tradition in which they were reared, so it is less helpful than before to identify hymn writers in terms of their theological traditions. Rae Whitney (b. 1927), for example, moved from England to the United States, and had been affiliated with Baptist, Methodist, and Congregational churches before becoming an Anglican [see *Panorama* 742–747]. Marty Haugen (b. 1958) grew up as a Lutheran, has been composer-in-residence in the United Church of Christ, and has worked most of his career as a pastoral musician in Roman Catholic parishes. (See stream five for further analysis of hymns by Marty Haugen.)

Yet, denominational roots still offer a starting point for a theological and liturgical orientation to hymn writers, including the following names listed with examples found in *Panorama:* Bryan Jeffrey Leech (b. 1931, Evangelical Covenant) [*Panorama*: 740–741], Jeffrey Rowthorn (b. 1934, Episcopal)

[*Panorama:* 748–750], John Thornburg (b. 1954, United Methodist) [*Panorama:* 784–785], Ruth Duck (b. 1947, United Church of Christ) [*Panorama:* 788–793], Joy Patterson (b. 1931, Presbyterian) [*Panorama* 823–824], John Core (b. 1951, Disciples of Christ) [*Panorama:* 838], and Mary Louise Bringle (b. 1953, Presbyterian) [*Panorama:* 846].

In Canada, the three most significant hymn writers in the last half of the twentieth century are Margaret Clarkson (1915–2008) [*Panorama*: 848–849], whose texts are collected in *A Singing Heart,* Sylvia Dunstan (1955–1993) [*Panorama*: 869–874], whose work as a prison chaplain strongly affected her writing; some of her texts are found in *In Search of Hope and Grace,* and in *Where the Promise Shines,* and Walter H. Farquharson (b. 1936) [*Panorama*: 850], a minister in the United Church of Canada with thirteen hymns in the United Church hymnal, *Voices United* (1996) and two additional hymns in the supplement *More Voices* (2007).

Hymn Tune Composers

So far, the narrative of this chapter has concentrated on hymn texts with very little mention of tunes, which of course, can more easily cross language barriers. But, since this chapter is focused on recent English texts in the classical hymn tradition, a few words would be appropriate about some tunes also in the classical tradition by English-speaking composers.

The challenge of composing tunes that are fresh and yet accessible for congregational singing is considerable, so there is no hymn tune "explosion" during the last half of the twentieth century. Often, new texts are sung to familiar, older classical hymn tunes or to folk tunes from a variety of cultures. In discussing hymn tunes in the first half of the twentieth century in *Let the People Sing: Hymn Tunes in Perspective* (LTPS), Paul Westermeyer includes examples of tunes by only eight composers, all from England. For the second half of the twentieth century, he includes tunes from eighteen representative composers; of those, fifteen are North American by birth or by immigration. Four tunes included there that have had wide acceptance and rather consistent pairing with particular texts are listed below.

- KINGDOM, by V. Earle Copes (b. 1921), set to "For the Bread Which You Have Broken" by Louis F. Benson (LTPS 369)
- BRIDEGROOM, by Peter Cutts (b. 1927) set to "Like the Murmur of the Dove's Song" [*Panorama*: 763] by Carl Daw (LTPS 370)
- MERLE'S TUNE, by Hal Hopson (b. 1933), set both to the *Benedictus* ("Blest Be the God of Israel") by Michael Perry (1942–1996) (LTPS 376), and to Arlo Duba's (b. 1929) setting of Psalm 84, "How Lovely, Lord, How Lovely."
- ANNIVERSARY SONG, by Jane Marshall (b. 1924) (LTPS 377), set to her own text "What Gift Shall We Bring" [*Panorama*: 928]

Other representative tunes are a bit more musically challenging, for example:

- VINEYARD HAVEN, by Richard Dirksen (1921–2003) (LTPS 372)
- EARTH AND ALL STARS, by Herbert Brokering (1926–2009) (LTPS 376)
- AUGUSTINE, by Erik Routley (LTPS 38)
- NOW, by Carl Schalk (b. 1929) (LTPS 381), who is one of the foremost composers of hymn tunes and other music for the church, and has written many tunes to texts by Jaroslav Vajda.

Twentieth-century hymn tunes paired with recent Protestant contemporary classical hymnody reflect at least three approaches. (1) *Melody-dominant settings* are a continuation of the unison, melody-dominant tune tradition with independent organ accompaniment found in the early twentieth century by Ralph Vaughan Williams (1872–1958), composer of KING'S WESTON, SALVE FESTE DIES, and SINE NOMINE, and Charles Villiers Stanford (1852–1924), composer of ENGLEBERG. Carl Schalk and Carol Doran (b. 1936) often compose hymn tunes in this manner. ANNIVERSARY SONG by Jane Marshall (b. 1924) is an example of this style:

Example 2:7

© 1982 Hope Publishing Co., Carol Stream, IL, 60188. www.hopepublishing.com
All rights reserved. Used by permission

(2) *Harmonic settings* are a continuation of four-part settings as found in the nineteenth-century Victorian period; some congregations still sing well in harmony. Whereas tunes set in four-part harmony was once the dominant style, contemporary composers choose it much less frequently. (3) *Anthem style settings,* also for singing in harmony, but with more anthem-like harmonic writing and increased contrapuntal movement. Erik Routley's AUGUSTINE, set to George Herbert's "Let All the World in Every Corner Sing," mixes melody-dominant and anthem-style approaches. UNION SEMINARY by Harold Friedell (1905–1958) began as an anthem setting of Percy Dearmer's (1867–1926) text, "Draw Us in the Spirit's Tether." In several recent hymnals, Friedell's anthem setting has been adapted for a four-part hymn. EAST ACKLAM by Francis Jackson (b. 1917), written for Fred Pratt Green's "For the Fruits of this Creation" [*Panorama:* 593] is an example of an anthem-style setting:

Example 2:8

1. For the fruits of this cre-a-tion, Thanks be to God;
For his gifts to ev-'ry na-tion, Thanks be to God; For the plow-ing, sow-ing, reap-ing, Si-lent growth while we are sleep-ing, Fu-ture needs in earth's safe-keep-ing, Thanks be to God.

Words: Fred Pratt Green © 1970 Hope Publishing Co.; Carol Stream, IL, 60188, www.hopepublishing.com
All rights reserved. Used with permission Music © 1960 Francis Jackson

Although these categories do not account for all of the tunes paired with hymn texts in this chapter, they represent the vast majority.[36]

Conclusion

This chapter began with a living room scene, with a pastoral painting and church-going families who often gathered around the piano to sing the old hymns they also sang in church. That scene was perhaps idyllic, but certainly not uncommon for many Protestants. However, that scene would certainly not be representative of home life at the beginning of the twenty-first century in which pianos in homes are rare, iPods make it possible for individuals to carry their own musical library with them, and a wide range of popular music has often replaced classical hymnody, indeed, classical music. The river of hymnody has been replaced by multiple streams. In a 2000 survey, college students at a Christian college were asked what worship songs they knew. Hymns did not fare that well. For example, only nineteen percent of the students recognized the classic Wesley hymn "Love Divine, All Loves Excelling."

Older Protestant hymnody excelled in praise of God and thanksgiving for salvation in Christ. It also often emphasized the pilgrim nature of the Christian's life and the hope of eternal life, whether in the stately phrases of Wesley's hymn "Love Divine" or in the more humble and escapist "This world is not my home, I'm just a passin' through." But, there is not as much "other worldly" emphasis in Protestant hymnody as in the first half of the twentieth century. There is much more cultural engagement.

Ironically, during the hymn explosion in the last part of the twentieth century, with excellent new denominationally produced hymnals that introduced many new hymns and metrical psalms for congregational singing, church attendance plummeted in main-line churches that had best upheld the tradition of classical Protestant hymnody. Meanwhile, many new churches have emerged, often independent and not tied to a denominational heritage of hymnody. The cultural emphasis has shifted away from longer texts found in classical hymnody toward much shorter texts and choruses. Many Protestant churches no longer have hymnals in the pews and sing few hymns from the classical tradition, usually a few older hymns often led by bands rather than by the organ. Instead, many churches have turned to more popular worship songs from CDs and the Internet that have found their way from Western culture to the entire world. It is the sound, the music, which has captured the interest of many worshipers, more than the texts. In many shorter texts, praise of God is not directly connected to the work of God in the world and the need for cultural engagement.

Yet, there is an interesting return to substantive older hymn texts in popular culture. In Great Britain, Kingsway has released three recordings of live festivals and events featuring classic hymns (and a few modern ones), describing these collections as "Traditional church choirs this ain't!" Tracks feature worship bands from these events interpreting traditional hymns for today's generation, seeking to preserve the dignity and power of such classics as "Be Thou My Vision," "Guide Me, O Thou Great Jehovah," "Crown Him With Many Crowns," and "When I Survey The Wondrous Cross." The Christian band Jars of Clay from the United States released *Redemption Songs* (2005) that includes new musical settings of several hymns, including "God Be Merciful to Me" and "I Need Thee Every Hour." None of these musical treatments fit into the classic Protestant hymn tradition of congregational song, because these recordings are sung by members of the bands, not by congregations, but they are singing hymns. An article by Kevin Twit summarized a new interest in the substantive texts of older hymn texts in the article "My Grandmother Saved It, My Mother Threw It Away; and Now I'm Buying It Back: Why Young People Are Returning to Old Hymn Texts."[37] And, so the stream of classic Protestant hymnody continues to flow in new directions and more diverse ways than ever before.

Summary

In the second half of the twentieth century, Protestant churches reached deeply back to scripture and their own histories to regain a new sense of identity after two world wars and a great depression. The churches also reached out broadly and ecumenically, in response to many immigrant experiences and the migration of millions of people away from their ancestral homes. Hymn writers responded to changes in church life that placed renewed emphasis on scripture, especially the psalms, as a primary source for hymnody; on congregational song as proclamation as well as prayer; on a recovery of the Christian year; and on more frequent celebrations of Holy Communion. With the wide-spread adoption of the *Revised Common Lectionary* among main-line Protestant churches, hymn writers found inspiration again in the psalms, many Old Testament prophets, and the teaching and ministry of Christ, with new psalm settings, hymns and Scripture paraphrases on lectionary texts. The use of the lectionary also stimulated the arts in visually honoring the Christian year, and new hymns have also celebrated the use of the arts in worship.

With many changes in the English language during this period, reflected in many new Bible translations, hymn writers also began using fresh language and took on topics seldom addressed in traditional hymnody. They turned once again to lament, confession, prophetic proclamation, and intercession—needed counterparts to the predominant themes of praise and thanksgiving in classic Protestant hymnody and worship.

Perhaps two words best exemplify the approach of hymn writers in the last half of the twentieth century: inclusivity and justice. The word "inclusive" as a basic issue of justice came to expression in the use of language with respect to gender, disabilities, and race, and extends to many translated hymns into English from around the world. Hymn writers also encouraged cultural engagement by dealing with major issues facing people everywhere: the need for justice with respect to creation and the environment, children, the elderly, the urban and rural poor, those affected by war and terror—not only locally, but also globally. The hymns of classic English Protestant hymnody from the last half of the twentieth century and into the twenty-first century provide a rich repertoire for worship among Christians who pray in song for shalom.[38]

Notes —

1 James F. White, *Protestant Worship: Traditions in Transition* (Louisville: Westminster/John Knox, 1989).
2 John D. Witvliet, "Expanding the Conversation: Knitting Together Worship and Congregational Life," in *Reformed Worship* 79 (March, 2006), 2.
3 "The Boomer Files," by Jerry Adler, *Newsweek*, November 14, 2005, 52.
4 Denominational mergers included, for example, in Great Britain, the United Reformed Church (1972); in Australia, the Uniting Church (1977); in Canada, the United Church of Canada (1925); and in the United States, the United Church of Christ (1957), the United Methodist Church (1969), the Presbyterian Church USA (1983), and the Evangelical Lutheran Church in America (1988).

5 *Dictionary of North American Hymnology: A Comprehensive Bibliography & Master Index of Hymns and Hymnals Published in the United States and Canada 1640–1978.* CD-ROM published by the Hymn Society in the United States and Canada, 2003.

6 *The Lutheran Book of Worship* (1978) was replaced by *Evangelical Lutheran Worship* in 2006. Similarly, the Lutheran Church-Missouri Synod replaced *Lutheran Worship* (1982) in 2006 with the *Lutheran Service Book;* these two collections represent the beginning of the next generation of denominational hymnals and worship books in North America.

7 For an excellent overview, see *The Biblical Psalms in Christian Worship: A Brief Ecumenical Introduction and Guide to Resources,* by John D. Witvliet (Grand Rapids: Wm. B. Eerdmans, 2007).

8 Examples of recent complete metrical Psalters include the *Psalter Hymnal* (Grand Rapids: CRC Publications, 1987) and *The Psalms:150 Metrical Psalms for Singing to Well-Known Hymn Tunes,* by Martin E. Leckebusch (Kevin Mayhew, 2006.). See also the large collection *Psalms for All Seasons* (Grand Rapids: Faith Alive Publications, 2012) for multiple settings of all the psalms in multiple styles. Many other hymnals and separate collections include metrical settings of especially those psalms found in the *Revised Common Lectionary;* examples include *The Presbyterian Hymnal* (Louisville: Westminster/John Knox Press, 1990) and *A New Metrical Psalter* by Christopher L. Webber (New York: The Church Hymnal Corporation, 1986).

9 For a review of this 1995 hymnal see Nancy M. Turner, "The *Chalice Hymnal:* Broken Bread—One Body," *The Hymn,* 48.1 (January, 1997), 33–38.

10 C. Michael Hawn, "The Consultation on Ecumenical Hymnody: An Evaluation of its Influence in Selected English Language Hymnals Published in the United States and Canada since 1976," *The Hymn* (April, 1996), 26. A broader list of common hymns followed in C. Michael Hawn, "'The Tie That Binds': A List of Ecumenical Hymns in English Language Hymnals Published in Canada and the United States Since 1976," *The Hymn* 48:3 (July 1997), 25–37.

11 Horace B. Allen, from an interview prepared for the August 1997 meeting of *Societas Liturgica* held in Turku, Finland.

12 Thomas Troeger and Carol Doran, *New Hymns for the Lectionary* (New York: Oxford University Press, 1990); Carl P. Daw, Jr., *A Year of Grace: 66 hymns for the church year* (Carol Stream, IL: Hope Publishing Co., 1990) and *To Sing God's Praise: 18 Metrical Canticles Set to Both Traditional and Contemporary Tunes* (Carol Stream, IL: Hope Publishing Co., 1992); W. Thomas Smith and Robert Batastini, comps., *Hymns for the Gospels* (Chicago: GIA Publishing, Inc., 2001).

13 A list of all thirty-three collections (1952–1982) published by the Hymn Society is included in *Holding in Trust: Hymns of the Hymn Society in the United States and Canada,* ed. George Black, Emily Brink, and Nancy Faus (Carol Stream: Hope Publishing Co., 1992), 176.

14 Quoted in *Duty and Delight: Erik Routley Remembered* (Carol Stream, IL: Hope Publishing Company, 1985), 218.

15 *Hymns for Today's Church*, eds. Michael Saward and John F. Wilson (London: Jubilate Group, 1982).

16 *The New Century Hymnal*, ed. Arthur G. Clyde (Cleveland: (Pilgrim Press, 1995).

17 Arthur G. Clyde, *The Language of the New Century Hymnal* (Cleveland: The Pilgrim Press, 1996), fifty-six pages, provides a defense of the committee's approach written by the hymnal editor. Richard L. Christensen edited a counterpoint critique in *How Shall We Sing the Lord's Song: An Assessment of The New Century Hymnal,* 160 pages, published in 1997 by Confessing Christ, a movement of laity and clergy in the United Church of Christ.

18 Paul Westermeyer, *Let Justice Sing: Hymnody and Justice* (Collegeville: The Order of St. Benedict, Inc., 1998), 118 pages.

19 The full text, set to CHURCH UNITED by American composer Alfred V. Fedak (b. 1953), is found in *Sing! A New Creation* (Grand Rapids: CRC Publications, 2001), 61.

20 For an insider's account of these developments, see the article by the Welsh hymn scholar Alan Luff, "The Twentieth-Century Hymn Explosion: Where the Fuse Was Lit," *The Hymn* 58:4 (Autumn 2007), 11–21.

21 For an overview of Routley's texts and tunes found in North American hymnals, see "Erik Routley as Hymn Writer and Composer," by Emily R. Brink, part of a larger tribute to his work in *The Hymn.* Vol. 53 (October 2002), 4–7.

22 Chapter 23 of *Panorama,* "British Hymnody, 1952-1975," includes thirty-four texts from these and other writers of that period (*Panorama:* 487–520).

23 "It is fair to say that [Fred Pratt Green] has become the finest hymn writer in Methodism since Charles Wesley (if it be not an anachronism to call either of the Wesleys a Methodist). For a long time, the magnificence and sheer volume of Charles Wesley's output stifled the hymn-writing genius in English Methodism, but in Pratt Green the lost time is amply made up." Erik Routley's commentary on Pratt Green's "Christ is the world's light," #7 in *Companion to Westminster Praise* (Chapel Hill, NC: Hinshaw Music, 1977).

24 Three published collections of Kaan's hymn texts are available from the Hymn Society Book Service (1-800-THE HYMN).

25 Much of the material that follows was gathered from *Jubilate Everybody: The Story of Jubilate Hymns,* by Michael Saward, published in Great Britain by Jubilate Hymns in 2003. Their Web site, www.jubilate.co.uk includes more than 1500 texts and 526 tunes by members of the group. For more information, contact <info@jubilate.co.uk>.

26 For a more extensive overview of hymns in Great Britain from 1976–2000, see chapter 29 in *Panorama,* in which 123 texts from this period are included by writers from the Dunblane gatherings, the Jubilate Group, the Iona Community, and many others.

27 For more extensive coverage of hymns from Australia and New Zealand, see twenty-nine representative hymn texts in *Panorama,* entries 875-904.

28 *Sing Alleluia: A Supplement to the Australian Hymn Book* (1987), and the *All Together* series, beginning in 1980. In New Zealand came *Alleluia Aotearoa* (1991), *Carol Our Christmas* (1996), and *Faith Forever Singing* (2000).

29 C. Michael Hawn, "Congregational Singing Down Under: An Introduction to Current Australian Hymnals." *The Hymn,* Vol. 56.2 (Summer, 2005), 18.

30 *Panorama,* 447.

31 For more information about these two Australian writers, see "Congregational Singing from Down Under: An Interview with Australian Robin Mann," and "Congregational Singing Down Under: The Hymns of Elizabeth Joyce Smith, Melbourne, Australia," by C. Michael Hawn, *The Hymn,* Vol. 56.4 (Fall, 2005), 8–18.

32 Her published collections are *Every Day in Your Spirit* (1996) *Faith Makes the Song* (2003), and *In Every Corner Sing* (1992) (Carol Stream: Hope Publishing Co.). *Sing for Peace* (2004) (Nashville: Abingdon Press), and *Touch the Earth Lightly* (2008) (Carol Stream: Hope Publishing Co.).

33 For a recent discussion of Murray's hymns, see Deborah Carlton Loftis, "'For Everyone Born, A Place at the Table': Hospitality and Justice in the Hymns of Shirley Erena Murray," *Hearts and Minds in Praise of God: Hymns and Essays in Church Music in Honor of Hugh T. McElrath*, eds. J. Michael Raley and Deborah Carlton Loftis (Franklin, TN: Providence House Publications, 2006), 237–250.

34 That story is told by George Shorney in "The Hymnal Explosion in North America" (Carol Stream: Hope Publishing Company), a publication of an address to the Hymn Society of Great Britain and Ireland on July 26, 1988.

35 Quoted in "Acts and Letters: Song Search Results," by Emily R. Brink, in *Reformed Worship* 79 (March, 2006), p. 28. Available online at www.reformedworship.org.

36 Some texts may be set to gospel-style music as is the case with "God, the Sculptor of the Mountains" by John Thornburg (b. 1954) paired with JENNINGS-HOUSTON, a black-gospel style setting by Amanda Husberg (b. 1940). Carlton Young (b. 1926) wrote NEW BEGINNINGS for Brian Wren's "This is the Day of New Beginnings" in what he calls a "Broadway" style. Hal H. Hopson (b. 1933) adapted an English folk song, "O Waly Waly," for GIFT OF LOVE, a tune set to his own text.

37 *Reformed Worship* 70 (December, 2003), pp. 30–31. Available online at www.reformedworship.org.

38 Single-author and composer collections of the texts of hymn writers and hymn tunes of composers mentioned in this chapter, as well as more recent ones, are available from the Hymn Society Book Service. See "Author and Composer Collections" at www.thehymnsociety.org.

—Stream Three—
African-American Congregational Song

Chapter 3
If It Had Not Been for the Lord on My Side: Hymnody in African-American Churches

James Abbington

In his enduring classic *The Souls of Black Folk*, published in 1903, W. E. B. DuBois (1868–1963) declared, "Three things characterized this religion of the slave—the Preacher, the Music, and the Frenzy. The Preacher is the most unique personality developed by the Negro on American soil." He continued,

> The Music of Negro religion is that plaintive, rhythmic melody, with its touching minor cadences, which, despite caricature and defilement, still remain the most original and beautiful expression of human life and longing yet born on American soil.... Finally, 'the Frenzy' or 'Shouting,' when the Spirit of the Lord passed by, and seizing the devotee, made him mad with supernatural joy, was the last essential of Negro religion and the more devoutly believed in than all the rest.[1]

In a work published in 1984, titled *Soul of Black Worship*, Wyatt Tee Walker (b. 1929) set forth three primary support systems that are always operative in the African-American religious experience: *Preaching, Praying,* and *Singing.*[2]

One need only to visit an African-American church worship experience to witness the significance and reality of DuBois's and Walker's assertions in the twenty-first century.

For certain, the sermon, or more accurately, the *preaching*, and the music, or more precisely, the *singing*, are the focal points of worship in the black church as magnets of attraction and primary vehicles for spiritual transport and formation. All other activities find their place in some subsidiary relationship. C. Eric Lincoln (1924–2000) and Lawrence Mamiya concluded in their critical study *The Black Church in the African-American Experience*:

> [I]n the Black Church, good preaching and good singing are almost invariably the minimum conditions of a successful ministry. Both activities trace their roots back to Africa where music and religion and life itself were all one holistic enterprise.... First of all, music served the important function of convoking the cultus, that is, assembling the faithful to a common place and a common experience of worship. Once this was accomplished it functioned to transcend or to reduce to insignificance those social, cultural, or economic barriers [that] separated individuals in their secular interests in order that genuine corporate worship might take place.[3]

A balanced study of African-American church history must keep in full perspective two unquestionable elements. One, African-Americans felt the need to be converted, to "get religion," and to know God for themselves—that is, on their own terms. This strong, consistent pattern of religious involvement has long been criticized as being pious, otherworldly, a flight from reality. The second element has been the struggle for survival and eventual liberation. It is this position that critics of the former emphasis declare ought to be the church's full agendum. Gayraud Wilmore's study, *Black Religion and Black Radicalism* (third ed., 1998), remains the best historical overview of the involvement of black religious groups and individuals in black-oriented efforts in political and social change in the United States. As Wilmore, C. Eric Lincoln, and others have pointed out, the mere fact of black survival in a total system of dehumanization and exclusion is by itself a significant political act.

Before the enslaved Africans in the United States learned to read or write, they sang songs, told stories, listened and responded to sermons, and expressed their hopes, fears, trials, tribulations, and sorrows through the medium of an oral tradition that had characterized the West-African culture from which their ancestors had come. As the enslaved heard sermons of the slave preacher based upon the Bible, they created songs in response to them. Spirituals grew out of the experiences of slavery and the covert religious practices of enslaved Africans, and were referred to as the invisible institution. Gospel music is a post-emancipation development and a product of the early twentieth century and the concerns of the Great Migration. The musical genres of African-American congregations have developed from folk spirituals, to black-meter music, to prayer and praise hymns, improvised Euro-American hymns, hymns by African-American hymn writers, traditional and contemporary gospel music, and today to praise and worship music and Holy Hip-Hop.

Political and Economic Influences on African-American Congregational Song

Since the Second Vatican Council (1962–1965), a number of social, political, and economic reforms significantly influenced and shaped congregational singing in African-American churches. During this time the Civil Rights Movement, led by the Reverend Dr. Martin Luther King, Jr. was at its peak, having experienced the Montgomery, Alabama, bus protest (1955–1956), the Sit-In Movement (1960) in Greensboro, North Carolina, the Freedom Ride (1961), demonstrations in Albany, Georgia, (1961–1962) and Birmingham, Alabama, (1963), the march from Selma to Montgomery (1965), Chicago race riots (1966), anti-Vietnam protests (1967), the Poor People's Campaign (1968), and the assassination of Dr. King on April 4, 1968, in Memphis, Tennessee. The Reverend Dr. Wyatt Tee Walker's article, "The Soulful Journey of the Negro Spiritual; Freedom Songs" (1963) demonstrated the direct transference of the Negro Spiritual form to the then developing "freedom song." Walker's example "The Birth of Freedom Songs" included in *Negro Digest* provides a clear insight into this phenomenon:

The Birth of the Freedom Song[4]

Refrain: I want Jesus to walk with me, Yes, I want Jesus to walk with me; All along *my pilgrim* journey, Lord, I want Jesus to walk with me. Stanza: When I'm in trouble, Lord, walk with me; When I'm in trouble, Lord, walk with me. All along *my pilgrim* journey, Lord, I want Jesus to walk with me.	I want Jesus to walk with me, Yes, I want Jesus to walk with me; All along *this Freedom* journey, Lord, I want Jesus to walk with me. *Down in the jailhouse,* Lord, walk with me; *Down in the jailhouse,* Lord, walk with me. All along *this Freedom* journey, Lord, I want Jesus to walk with me.

Woke up this mornin' with my mind
    Stayed on Jesus;
Woke up this mornin' with my mind
    Stayed on Jesus;
Woke up this mornin' with my mind
    Stayed on Jesus;
Hal-le-lu, Hal-le-lu, Hal-le-lu-jah!
	Woke up this mornin' with my mind
	    Stayed on *Freedom*;
	Woke up this mornin' with my mind
	    Stayed on *Freedom*;
	Woke up this mornin' with my mind
	    Stayed on *Freedom*;
	Hal-le-lu (Hal-le-lu), Hal-le-lu (Hal-le-lu), Hal-le-lu-jah!

Oh, Freedom! Oh, Freedom! Oh, Freedom over me; And befo'ah I'd be a slave I'd be buried in my grave And go home to my Lord and be free.	(This spiritual hymn's refrain is sung in its exact original form.)
No more weeping, etc. No more moaning (mourning), etc. No more dyin' etc.	No more segregation, etc. No more Jim Crow, etc.

These songs were not only sung in freedom marches and rallies but also were regularly sung as congregational songs in worship, especially in churches throughout the South.

In the late 1930s, the term *gospel* eventually came to identify contemporary religious music that was being performed in Chicago. Thomas A. Dorsey (1899–1993) is considered the "Father of Gospel Music," and it was he who gave it its name—*gospel* music—in contradistinction to the gospel hymns used in the crusades of Dwight L. Moody and Ira D. Sankey. In his essay on Dorsey, Horace C. Boyer (1935–2009) is explicit about this distinction:

A cursory glance at these songs will show that they are in fact 'gospel hymns': strictly organized, standard Protestant hymns of eight bars to the stanza and eight bars to the chorus, with no provisions for the improvisation so much a part of Prof. Dorsey's song, nor the textual attention given to such matters as blessings, sorrows, woes, and the joys of the 'after-life,' nor the Africanisms, which really constitute gospel music—the altered scale degrees and the intricate rhythm [that] separates this music from all others.[5]

Although many African-American churches did not readily embrace gospel music, it began to find its way into churches throughout the United States and first introduced by choirs, ensembles, and soloists, and later embraced by the congregation as its song. Wyatt Tee Walker offers a critical insight:

Gospel music, at bottom, is religious folk music that is clearly identifiable with the social circumstances of the Black community in America. The authenticity of folkways and folk expressions (including music) can be gauged by how closely they mirror the experience of the group. Gospel music, then, is an individual expression of a collective predicament within a religious context.[6]

Gospel music has been generally accepted by most African-American churches, but there are still some prominent segments within elite African-American Baptists, Methodists, and other main-line majority denominations who customarily express annoyance with, or outright rejection of gospel music, both in terms of its often problematic theology and because of its alleged secularity. Lincoln and Mamiya observed:

The problem begins with the fact that gospel choirs often select their repertoires based on what is popular on the radio or television, despite the fact that not all gospel packaged commercially is ideal for worship. Because commercialization presupposes secularization, it is inevitable that many metaphors and musical embellishments acceptable for secular performances are considered unacceptable in a worship setting.[7]

Other concerns about gospel music and its influence upon congregational song include the perception that gospel songwriters compose their songs based upon their personal theology and experiences, or without consideration of broader theological implications rather than with any official theological canon in mind. However, in William B. McClain's (b. 1938) preface to *Songs of Zion*, he asserts:

> The gospel song expresses theology. Not the theology of the academy or the university, not formalistic theology or the theology of the seminary, but a *theology of experience*—the theology of a God who sends the sunshine and the rain, the theology of a God who is very much alive and active and who has not forsaken those who are poor and oppressed and unemployed. It is a *theology of imagination*—it grew out of the fire shut up in the bones, of words painted on the canvas of the mind. Fear is turned into hope in the sanctuary and storefronts, and burst forth in songs of celebration. It is a *theology of grace* that allows the faithful to see the sunshine of His face—even through their tears. Even the words of an ex-slave trader became a song of liberation and an expression of God's amazing grace. It is a *theology of survival* that allows a people to celebrate the ability to continue the journey in spite of the insidious tentacles of racism and oppression and to sing, 'It's another day's journey, and I'm glad about it!'[8]

It was in the context of the Civil Rights and Black-Power Movement that Black Theology was born. According to James H. Cone (b. 1939),

> Black Theology is an attempt to show liberation as the central message of the Christian gospel and thereby bring the contemporary black church back to its liberating heritage. Our worship service must be free and liberating, because we believe 'the Lord will make a way somehow.' Therefore, we must fight until freedom comes.[9]
>
> [T]he certainty about God's immediate presence with the weak is the heart of black worship service. Black worship is a series of recitals of what God has done to bring the people out of 'hurt, harm, and danger.' Through sermon, song, prayer, and testimony, the people tell their story of 'how they got over.' God is that divine miracle who enables the people to survive amid wretched conditions. God is holy, personal, and all-powerful. God is everything the people need in order to triumph over terrible circumstances.[10]

Black Theology strongly influenced the worship and congregational song of many African-American congregations throughout the late 1960s and 1970s. In his vintage book, *The Spiritual and the Blues*, James Cone is emphatic when he declares:

> Black music is unity music. It unites the joy and the sorrow, the love and the hate, the hope and the despair of black people; and it moves the people toward the direction of total liberation. It shapes and defines black existence and creates cultural structures for black expression. Black music is unifying because it confronts the individual with the truth of black existence and affirms that black being is possible only in a communal context....
>
> Black music is functional. Its purposes and aims are directly related to the consciousness of the black community. To be functional is to be useful in community definition, style, and movement.... Black music is a living reality. And to understand it, it is necessary to grasp the contradictions inherent in black experience....

Black music is also social and political. It is social because it is *black* and thus articulates the separateness of the black community. It is an artistic rebellion against the humiliating deadness of western culture. Black music is political because in its rejection of white cultural values, it affirms the political 'otherness' of black people. Through song, new political consciousness is continuously created, one antithetical to the values of white society....

Black music is also theological. That is, it tells us about the divine Spirit that moves the people toward unity and self-determination. It is not possible to be black and encounter the Spirit of black emotion and not be moved.[11]

Wyatt Tee Walker is convinced that Black Theology is more clearly ensconced in the music of the African-American religious experience than attempting to fit the theology of African-American Christians into European theological systems. Another quotation by Walker might be helpful in understanding his posture on this point:

Afro-centric Christian theology proceeds from a different center than does traditional Eurocentric theology. The theology of African-American Christians issues from our pain-predicament (which has been pervasive) and thereby, is more experiential than reflective. Ours is a learned and lived theology. This is not to suggest that the religious faith of African Americans is impervious to Continental musings but only that Afro-centricity is dominant.[12]

Walker maintains that the sacred music of African-American Christians reveals the answers to the questions of any Christian theological inquiry: (1) What is the view of God (Jesus)? (2) What is the view of humankind? (3) What is the view of [the] Judgment? (4) What is the view of salvation?, and (5) What is the view of justice?[13] The thesis of his major work, *Somebody's Calling My Name: Black Sacred Music and Social Change* is that a survey of the musical content of the black religious tradition can serve as a commentary of what was happening to the black community and its response to those conditions. Simply put, what black people are singing religiously will provide a clue to what is happening to them sociologically.

However, that major body of congregational song sung in most mainline African-American churches is almost exclusively Euro-American with the exception of a few hymns by Charles A. Tindley (1851–1933), Charles P. Jones (1865–1949), Thomas A. Dorsey (1899–1993), Lucie E. Campbell (1885–1963), Kenneth Morris (1917–1988), Andraé Crouch (b. 1942), Doris Akers (1923–1995), and Margaret Douroux (b. 1941).

Table 1 provides a list of the most commonly sung hymns in African-American churches by Anglo-Americans and British text writers taken from numerous surveys across the country from music directors and church musicians, denominational conferences, the annual Hampton University Ministers' Conference & Choir Directors' and Organists' Guild Workshop, the Jackson State University Church Music Workshop, to name a few.

Table 1
Anglo-American and British Hymns
Commonly Sung in African-American Churches

"Amazing Grace"	John Newton (1725–1807)
At the Cross	Isaac Watts (1674–1748)
"Blessed Assurance"	Fanny J. Crosby (1820–1915)
Blessed Be the Name	William H. Clark (1854–1925)
Blessed Quietness	Manie P. Ferguson (1850–1932)
Count Your Blessings	Johnson Oatman, Jr. (1856–1922)
"Down at the Cross" (*Glory to His Name*)	Elisha A. Hoffman (1839–1929)
Farther Along	W. B. Stevens (1862–1940)
God Will Take Care of You	Civilla D. Martin (1869–1948)
"Guide Me, O Thou Great Jehovah"	William Williams (1717–1791)
Higher Ground	Johnson Oatman, Jr. (1856–1922)
"Holy, Holy, Holy"	Reginald Heber (1783–1826)
"How Firm a Foundation"	"K" in Rippon's *Selection of Hymns* (1787)
"I Am Thine, O Lord"	Fanny J. Crosby (1820–1915)
"I Must Tell Jesus"	Elisha A. Hoffman (1839–1929)
"I Need Thee Every Hour"	Annie S. Hawks (1835–1918)

I'll Fly Away	Albert E. Brumley (1905–1977)
In the Garden	C. Austin Miles (1868–1946)
Is Your All on the Altar?	Elisha A. Hoffman (1839–1929)
It Is Well with My Soul	Horatio G. Spafford (1828–1888)
"Jesus Is All the World to Me"	Will L. Thompson (1847–1909)
"Jesus, Keep Me Near the Cross"	Fanny J. Crosby (1820–1915)
Keep Me Every Day	F. L. Eiland (1860–1909)
Lead Me to Calvary	Jennie E. Hussey (1874–1958)
Lift Him Up	Johnson Oatman, Jr. (1856–1922)
"Must Jesus Bear the Cross Alone"	Thomas Shepherd (1665–1739)
"My Faith Looks Up to Thee"	Ray Palmer (1808–1887)
"My Hope Is Built On Nothing Less"	Edward Mote (1797–1874)
"Nearer My God to Thee"	Sarah F. Adams (1805–1848)
No, Not One	Johnson Oatman, Jr. (1856–1922)
O How I Love Jesus	Frederick Whitfield (1829–1904)
"Pass Me Not, O Gentle Savior"	Fanny J. Crosby (1820–1915)
"Praise Him, Praise Him"	Fanny J. Crosby
"Savior, More Than Life to Me"	Fanny J. Crosby
"Softly and Tenderly Jesus is Calling"	Will L. Thompson (1847–1909)
"Standing On the Promises"	R. Kelso Carter (1849–1926)
"There Is a Fountain Filled with Blood"	William Cowper (1731–1800)
"'Tis So Sweet to Trust in Jesus"	Louisa M. R. Stead (1850–1917)
Trust and Obey	John H. Sammis (1846–1919)
We're Marching to Zion	Isaac Watts (1674–1748)
"What a Fellowship"	Elisha A. Hoffman (1839–1929)
"What a Friend We Have in Jesus"	Joseph M. Scriven (1819–1886)
When We All Get to Heaven	Eliza E. Hewitt (1851–1920)
"Yield Not to Temptation"	Horatio R. Palmer (1834–1907)

These hymns, and others, have been maintained, preserved in, and perpetuated by the canon of the African-American religious experience, primarily because of their texts and musical accessibility. The texts and music were relevant, applicable, conforming, and unimpeachable with their expressions of praise, adoration, thanksgiving, struggle, pain, hope, joy, aspirations, faith, admonition, pilgrimage, salvation, tribulations; in short, the total religious journey. Referring to an extensive list of "Hymns of Improvisation" in *Somebody's Calling My Name*, Walker offers an excellent analysis of many of these hymns.

> About one-half of the hymns listed have 'Jesus themes,' mirroring the centrality of Jesus in the Black religious experience.... Admittedly, the Jesus umbrella includes such topics as 'Trust and Confidence,' 'Cross and Resurrection,' 'Praise and Adoration,' but the fixation on the Black religious community on Jesus is widely known. As in the music of spirituals, the Jesus emphasis transmits a quality of intimacy and companionship that leaps the barrier of God's transcendence. The commonality of this theme—Jesus emphasis—runs throughout Black hymnody. One-fourth of the hymns thematically expresses 'Dependence on God' one-tenth 'Praise and Adoration' and one-tenth 'Death and Immortality.' The remaining five percent is variously divided among other religious themes.[14]

It is interesting to observe that the influences of the Civil Rights Movement, Black Theology, Black Nationalism, and Afro-centrism—all post-Vatican II movements—critically contributed to the increase and urgency of African-American hymnals published by various denominations. At the same time, the rapid development of gospel choirs and smaller ensembles tended to dominate the worship services and congregational singing was significantly reduced to accommodate these special selections. Table II provides a chronological listing of African-American denominational hymnals and African-American hymnals and supplements published by Anglo-majority denominations since Vatican II.

Table II
African-American Hymnals and Hymnal Supplements
Published Since Vatican II[15]

1977: *The New National Baptist Hymnal*. Chair, Editorial Committee: Ruth Lomax Davis (Nashville: National Baptist Publishing Board).	According to the Foreword, this hymnal "was conceived and published to serve a two-fold purpose; that of enhancing all aspects of [their] worship services, and for the preservation of [their] great religious heritage and musical taste for generations to come."
1977: *His Fullness Songs*, (Jackson, Mississippi: National Publishing Board of the Church of Christ [Holiness] USA).	A large number of the hymns in this hymnal (the first edition was published in 1906) were composed by the founder and bishop of this church, Charles P. Jones, Sr.
1981: *Songs of Zion*. Eds. Verogla Nix and J. Jefferson Cleveland (Nashville: Discipleship Resources).	This collection was published by The United Methodist Church as a supplemental worship resource for African American congregations. *Come Sunday: The Liturgy of Zion* by William B. McClain is a companion to *Songs of Zion*.
1981: *Lift Every Voice and Sing: A Collection of Afro-American Spirituals and Other Songs*. Chair, Ed., Irene V. Jackson. (New York: The Church Hymnal Corp).	This hymnal was published by the Episcopal Church (USA) in conjunction with the Episcopal Commission for Black Ministries.
1982: *Yes, Lord!* Chair, Editorial Committee, Norman N. Quick (Memphis: Church of God in Christ Publishing Board).	This hymnal was the first official hymnal of the COGIC.
1982: *The New Progressive National Baptist Hymnal*, Ed. D. F. King (Washington, D.C.: Progressive National Baptist Convention, Inc.).	This hymnal was a special edition of *The New National Baptist Convention* with adaptations and approximately thirty-five new hymns.
1984: *A.M.E.C. Bicentennial Hymnal*, Ed. Robert O. Hoffelt (Nashville: The African Methodist Episcopal Church).	This is a completely revised edition of the 1954 hymnal which included African-American spirituals for the first time and songs from the AME Church in Africa.
1987: *Lead Me, Guide Me: The African American Catholic Hymnal*, Project Coordinator, James P. Lyke, O.F.M. (Chicago: GIA Publications, Inc.).	According to the Foreword, this hymnal was "born of the needs and aspirations of Black Catholics for music that reflected both [an] African American heritage and [their] Catholic faith." Contains a ten-page introduction to the history of African-American song.
1987: *The Hymnal of the Christian Methodist Episcopal Church*, Chairperson, Othal Hawthorne Lakey (Memphis: CME Publishing House).	The CME Church was founded in 1870. This hymnal is a duplication of *The New National Baptist Hymnal* (1977) with adaptations and additions by the Commission for the Hymnal.

1993: *Lift Every Voice and Sing II: An African American Hymnal*, Ed., Horace Clarence Boyer (New York: Church Pension Fund).	This hymnal was prepared by the Episcopal Commission for Black Ministries in collaboration with the Standing Committee on Church Music under the aegis of the Church Hymnal Corporation. The hymnal contains eleven pages of performance notes at the beginning.
1996: *The A.M.E. Zion. Bicentennial Hymnal*, (New York: The African American Episcopal Church).	This hymnal was published by the African Methodist Episcopal Zion Church.
1999: *This Far By Faith: An African American Resource for Worship*, Project Managers, Bryant Clancy and Karen M. Ward (Minneapolis: Augsburg Fortress Press).	This resource was developed by a cooperative inter-church process involving the Evangelical Lutheran Church in America and the Lutheran Church—Missouri Synod.
2000: *The Hymnal of The Christian Methodist Episcopal Church Discipleship 2000 Edition*, Volume IV, William E. George, General Secretary (CME Publishing House).	This hymnal is a revised and edited version of the 1987 hymnal.
2001: *The African American Heritage Hymnal*, Eds. Delores Carpenter and Nolan B. Williams (Chicago: GIA Publications, Inc.).	Prompted in part by the success of *Lead Me, Guide Me*, a hymnal intended primarily for African-American Catholics, GIA created a similar edition for African American Protestant congregations.
2001: *The New National Baptist Hymnal 21st Century Edition*, (National: National Baptist Convention of America, Inc.).	This hymnal was a revision of the 1977 that includes additional hymns and "Glossary of Musical Terms."
2006: *Beams of Heaven: Hymns of Charles Albert Tindley*, Eds. S T Kimbrough, Jr. and Carlton R. Young (New York: General Board of Global Ministries, GBGMusik).	This collection of forty-six hymns by Charles A. Tindley was published by the General Board of Global Ministries of The United Methodist Church.
2007: *Zion Still Sings! For Every Generation*, Eds. Myron F. McCoy and Marilyn E. Thornton (Nashville: Abingdon Press).	This supplement is a complete revision and updating of *Songs of Zion* with a separate and extensive accompaniment edition.
2007: *New Wine in Old Wineskins*, Volume 1, Ed. James Abbington (Chicago: GIA Publications, Inc.).	This contemporary congregational supplement reflects the marriage of new hymn texts by modern writers to time-honored tune from many different traditions. It also contains twenty-three lesser-known hymns by African-American hymnwriters Charles P. Jones, Charles A. Tindley, G. T. Haywood, Margaret Pleasant Douroux, Charles Watkins, Laymon T. Hunter, Eli Wilson, Jr. and others.

2010: *New Wine in Old Wineskins,* Volume 2, Ed. James Abbington (Chicago: GIA Publications, Inc.).	A second compilation of contemporary congregational hymnody reflects the marriage of new texts by modern writers and to time-honored tunes from many traditions. It contains eighteen lesser-known hymns by African American hymn writers Glenn Burleigh, Charles H. Nicks, Jr., Stephen Key, V. Michael McKay, Jimmy Dowell, Oliver J. Owens, David Frazier, and others.
2011: *Total Praise:Songs and Other Worship Resources for Every Generation.* (Chicago: GIA Publications, Inc. and Nashville: Sunday School Publishing Board).	This hymnal was co-published by the Sunday School Publishing Board of the National Baptist Convention, USA and GIA Publication and is an expanded and revised edition of the *African American Heritage Hymnal.*
2012: *Lead Me, Guide Me* Second Edition. (Chicago: GIA Publications, Inc.).	This hymnal includes the full breadth of African-American church music that is suitable for Catholic worship, along with a broader mix of common Catholic repertoire. It includes a comprehensive array of ritual music, mass settings, and Lectionary psalms written by some of today's finest African-American composers.

In spite of the plethora of hymnals available today, the repertoire of hymns sung by main-line African-American church congregations consists of fewer than fifty hymns, including Christmas carols and Easter hymns. In some cases, it is fewer than twenty-five and in others, no hymns are sung at all and no hymnal is used.[16]

Given the extensive list of hymns in Table I Anglo-American and British text writers sung in African-American churches, it is even more astonishing and bewildering that the representation of hymns by African-American hymn writers such as Charles A. Tindley (1851–1933), Charles P. Jones (1865–1949), James Weldon Randolph (1842–unknown), Thomas A. Dorsey (1899–1993), Lucie E. Campbell (1885–1963), Doris Akers (1922–1995), Garfield T. Haywood (1880–1931), Robert C. Lawson (1883–1961), Roberta Martin (1907–1969), Kenneth Morris (1917–1988), Margaret Douroux (b. 1941), Andraé Crouch (b. 1942), Albert A. Goodson (b. 1933) and others, are very few. The theological themes of the African-American church focus on tribulation, comfort, holding on, consolation, assurance, judgment, and eschatology. Furthermore, many of the hymns listed in Table 1 articulate these themes, indicating that African-Americans took their primary theology from any place they could find it. Until more recently, hymns of praise are not as common in the African-American tradition and, consequently, have been borrowed and adapted from Anglo-American and British authors.[17]

Table III is a list of some of the most commonly sung hymns in African American churches by African-American hymn writers provided by respondents in national surveys found in many of the aforementioned hymnals.

Table III
African-American Hymns Most Commonly Sung in African-American Churches

A Praying Spirit (1980)	Elbernita "Twinkie" Clark (b. 1955)
Bless His Holy Name (1973)	Andraé Crouch (b. 1942)
Can't Nobody Do Me Like Jesus (1982)	Andraé Crouch (b. 1942)
"Deeper, Deeper" (1900)	Charles P. Jones (1865–1949)
"Give Me a Clean Heart" (1970)	Margaret Douroux (b. 1941)
"God Has Smiled on Me" (1973)	Isaiah Jones, Jr. (1940–2008)
He'll Understand and Say "Well Done"	Lucie E. Campbell (1885–1963)
"I Don't Feel No Ways Tired" (1978)	Curtis Burrell (twentieth cent.)
"If It Had Not Been for the Lord" (1980)	Margaret Douroux (b. 1941)
"Jesus, You're the Center of My Joy" (1987)	Richard Smallwood (b. 1948) (in collaboration with William and Gloria Gaither)
Just a Little Talk with Jesus (1937)	Cleavant Derricks (1910–1977)
"Lead Me, Guide Me" (1953)	Doris Akers (1923–1995)
Leave It There (c. 1906)	Charles A. Tindley (1851–1933)
"Lord, Help Me to Hold Out" (1974)	James Cleveland (1932–1991)
My Tribute ("How Can I Give Thanks") (1971)	Andraé Crouch (b. 1942)
"Oh, To Be Kept By Jesus" (1966)	Thurston Frazier (twentieth cent.)
Praise Him ("From the Rising of the Sun") (1986)	Donnie Harper (twentieth cent.)
"Precious Lord, Take My Hand" (1932)	Thomas A. Dorsey (1899–1993)
"Sign Me Up for the Christian Jubilee" (1979)	Kevin Yancy/Jerome Metcalfe (twentieth cent.)
"Something Within" (1919)	Lucie E. Campbell (1885–1963)
"Soon and Very Soon" (1978)	Andraé Crouch (b. 1942)
Sweet, Sweet Spirit (1962)	Doris Akers (1923–1995)

"The Lord is My Light" (1980)	Lillian Bouknight (20th cent.)
This Day	Edwin Hawkins (b. 1943)
Total Praise (1996)	Richard Smallwood (b. 1948)
"Touch Me, Lord Jesus"	Lucie E. Campbell (1922–1995)
Walking Up the King's Highway (1940)	Mary Gardner and Thomas A. Dorsey (1899–1993)
We'll Understand It Better By and By (c. 1906)	Charles A. Tindley (1851–1933)
"We've Come This Far By Faith" (1956)	Albert A. Goodson (b. 1933)
Where Shall I Be?	Charles P. Jones (1865–1949)
Yes, God Is Real (1944)	Kenneth Morris (1917–1988)
"You Can't Beat God's Giving"	Doris Akers (1923–1993)

In her essay, "Hymnals of the Black Church," Eileen Southern (1920–2002) declared:

> The year 1921 brought a milestone in the history of Black church hymnody. In my opinion, *Gospel Pearls*, published that year by the Sunday School Publishing Board of The National Baptist Convention, USA, ranks with Richard Allen's hymnal [*A Collection of Spiritual Songs and Hymns, Selected from Various Authors*] of 1801 in terms of its historical importance. Like the Allen hymnal, it is an anthology of the most popular Black church music of its time. The Music Committee that compiled the hymnal, under the direction of Willa Townsend, included some of the nation's outstanding composers and performers of religious music—among them, John W. Work [Jr., 1871–1925], Frederick J. Work [1879–1942], Lucie Campbell [1885–1963] and W. M. Nix—and the resulting product was truly a 'soul-stirring, message-bearing' songbook.[18]

Recent Significant African-American Hymnals

Since the Second Vatican Council, there have been, in my opinion, seven hymnals and supplemental worship resources in particular that continue that rich legacy and historical importance. They are *His Fullness Songs* (1977), *Songs of Zion* (1981), *Yes, Lord!* (1982), *African American Heritage Hymnal* (2001), and *Zion Still Sings! For Every Generation* (2007), *Total*

Praise: Songs and Other Worship Resources for Every Generation (2011), and *Lead Me, Guide Me, Second Edition: An African American Catholic Hymnal* (2012).

His Fullness Songs (1977) is the official hymnal of the Church of Christ (Holiness) USA, and is a revision of earlier hymnals from the turn of the twentieth century (1899– *Jesus Only, No.1*; 1901—*Jesus Only, No.1* revised and *No. 2*; and 1906—*His Fullness Songs*). Over 350 of the 512 songs in the hymnal were written or co-written by the founder and Bishop Charles Price Jones.

Yes, Lord! (1982), Bishop Charles H. Mason in Memphis, Tennessee, founded the first official hymnal of the Church of God in Christ, in 1897. The title "Yes, Lord" is taken from a praise chant that was often sung by Bishop Mason to gather the congregation in spiritual unity during an outpouring of the Holy Spirit in worship. It is significant. According to Eileen Southern, "*Yes, Lord!* makes a sharp break with the past. In its collection of fifty songs, the handling of accompaniment, in particular, reflects the importance given to instruments and polyphonic textures in the Pentecostal tradition."[19] It contains a wide variety of standard hymns, gospel hymns, spirituals, gospel songs, and songs by some of the denominations most outstanding hymn writers such as Mattie Moss Clark, Andraé Crouch, and Iris Stevenson, among others.

Songs of Zion grew out of the Consultation on the Black Church in Atlanta, Georgia, in 1973, sponsored by the Board of Discipleship to develop a songbook from the black religious tradition to be made available to United Methodist churches. This supplemental worship resource edited by J. Jefferson Cleveland (1937–1988) and Verogla Nix [-Allen] (b. 1933), chaired by William B. McClain (b. 1938) contained the largest number of Negro spirituals and black gospel songs with "Keys to Musical Interpretation, Performance, and Meaningful Worship," "A Historical Account of the Hymn in the Black Worship Experience," "A Historical Account of the Negro Spiritual," "A Historical Account of the Black Gospel" and "Songs for Special Occasions." This was an anthology of the most popular black church music of that time.

Come Sunday: The Liturgy of Zion: A Companion to Songs of Zion by William B. McClain was published by Abingdon Press in 1990. It begins with a discussion of the importance of Sunday in the black experience that explores the meaning and rich tradition of Sunday within the black community from the time of slavery to the present day. It is divided into two parts. The first part helps readers to understand the spiritual response of black people, the singular nature of worship in the black experience, and the importance of fellowship and community. The second part includes a survey of the different types of songs contained in *Songs of Zion*. It also includes chapters devoted to Negro spirituals, hymns, and gospel songs, in addition to a discussion of liturgy and a topical/scriptural index.

The *African American Heritage Hymnal* published by GIA Publications, Inc. in 2001 was a much-needed and long-awaited worship resource and practical anthology of the rich musical diversity of the African-American church. It is the most inclusive compilation of musical and liturgical significance for African-American Protestant churches in the twenty-first century. Wyatt Walker said of the hymnal that it "is probably the most important addition to Protestant hymnody within the past century."[20] It contains 582 hymns, spirituals, meter hymns, African music, and Gospel songs. In addition it has fifty-two Litany Prayers for the Black Church Year and fifty-two Biblical Responsive Readings from the Old and New Testaments based upon a large array of topics. The most significant feature of the hymnal is that the musical notations follow very closely the performance practices and idiomatic treatments of the unique African-Americans genres.

Zion Still Sings! For Every Generation published by Abingdon Press was a revision of *Songs of Zion*. The work of this project began during the 2000–2004 quadrennial with the positing of such as idea to Neil Alexander, President and Publisher of The United Methodist Publishing House. Following the widespread acceptance across ecumenical lines and continuing sales of *Songs of Zion* more than twenty years after its first printing, the project to contemporize and expand musical offerings in a new songbook was met with a great degree of interest and support.

In the spirit of honoring and preserving the richness and inclusiveness of the African-American musical heritage in worship, *Zion Still Sings*: (1)

celebrates the diversity of styles, genres, and performance practices that are rendered in praise to God; (2) offers up new music that will inspire and challenge persons to see God with new eyes; (3) seeks to motivate those outside the church to come to know God; (4) does not compromise the theological and biblical integrity of the church; and (5) in the spirit of Matthew 28:19, serves as a motivating force for persons to "do" the gospel.

The songbook has two editions, Pew and Accompaniment. The Pew Edition has all vocals needed for congregational participation with specific instructions concerning songs that may be linked in medleys. The Accompaniment Edition includes piano accompaniment, synthesizer, and percussion parts. Some songs are exactly the same in both editions, usually four-part hymn style.

Total Praise: Songs and Other Worship Resources for Every Generation (2011) is a co-publication of GIA Publications and the Sunday School Publishing Board of the National Baptist Convention, USA, Inc. The predecessor to this long awaited hymnal was *The Baptist Standard Hymnal with Responsive Readings* published in 1961, an updated edition of the hymnal of 1924 with responsive readings and "A New Book for All Services." *Total Praise* is a multi-faceted worship tool that contains 569 traditional and contemporary songs, fifty-two Responsive Readings, one for every Sunday of the year, forty-six Litanies designed for special days through the year such as Church Anniversaries, Advent, Singles Ministry, Martin Luther King, Jr. Day, Rites of Passage for Youth, Health and Wellness, Racial Reconciliation, and Elder Saints, to name a few.

This hymnal is substantive in content, containing hymnody of all styles, including praise and worship music from the first decade of the twenty-first century by composers such as Kurt Carr, Deon Kipping, Israel and Meleasa Houghton, Martha Munizzi, Kirk Franklin, Steven Hurd, Joseph Pace II, and others. In addition, it includes contemporary writers such as Mary Louise Bringle, Adam Tice, Brian Wren, Herman Stuempfle, Jr., Ruth Duck, Shirley Erena Murray, Delores Dufner, and others. It also includes traditional Black gospel hymnody not found in other hymnals and worship resources by hymn writers such as Charles H. Nicks, Jr., Glenn Burleigh, Norris O. Garner, Walter Hawkins, Robert J. Fryson, Eddie Robinson, Stephen Key, Gale Jones

Murphy, Harrison Johnson, Leonard Burks, and others. It also has selections from two historic publications of the Sunday School Publishing Board, *Gospel Pearls* (1921) and *Spirituals Triumphant Old and New* (1927) edited and arranged by Edward Boatner and Willa A. Townsend.

Finally, eight years in the making, the second edition of *Lead Me, Guide Me: An African American Catholic Hymnal* (2012), is an expanded and enhanced version of its predecessor. The hymnal includes the full breadth of African-American church music that is suitable for Catholic worship, along with a broader mix of common Catholic repertoire. There are an extensive variety of music styles, including a representative selection of music from Africa and the Caribbean. Following the success of GIA Publication's, Inc. *African American Heritage Hymnal* and *Total Praise*, the music notation attempts to reflect the performance practices in the African-American church communities. Also included is a comprehensive array of ritual music, mass settings, and Lectionary psalms written by some of today's finest African-American composers such as M. Roger Holland II, Kenneth W. Louis, Norah Ducan IV, Rawn Harbor, Richard Cheri, and others. The Most Reverend Wilton D. Gregory, SLD, Archbishop of Atlanta summarizes it best in his Forward to the hymnal:

> *Lead Me, Guide Me* is a compilation of a generous selection of that music arranged for use within the celebration of the Roman Catholic liturgy. As Catholics now prepare to receive the third edition of the *Roman Missal* for the English-speaking world, it is most appropriate for a new edition of *Lead Me, Guide Me* to be issued to accompany that new book of Catholic prayer. Those blessed original collaborators have today been joined by a new generation of very capable colleagues in preparing this new text. They build on a solid foundation for faith and now present a worthy successor to that first effort. While *Lead Me, Guide Me* was specifically developed with the particular liturgical needs of the African-American Catholic community in mind, it was never envisioned to be used exclusively in those parish communities. Other Catholics

throughout our nation and beyond have made very effective use of this liturgical resource, and we anticipate that they, too, will welcome this newest edition. Music has a unique capacity to transcend cultures and races and provide a bridge to understanding other people through the vehicle of its combined words and melodies....[21]

Current Trends in African-American Congregational Song

A discussion of congregational song in the late twentieth and early twenty-first century African-American churches would not be complete without examining the new trends in music and worship, which now includes Holy, or Christian Hip Hop. As previously mentioned, rapid development of gospel choirs and ensembles reduced congregational song between the mid-1960s and 1980s. Congregational singing in the 1990s and early twenty-first century is dominated by praise and worship. This period of time, usually at the beginning of worship services, which varies in length from fifteen minutes to one hour, is now essential to the worship of most African-American churches in the United States.

Holiness-Pentecostal, or Sanctified Worship has been historically characterized by hand capping, holy dancing, and the distinctive sound of musical instruments such as the Hammond organ, piano, keyboard synthesizers, drums, tambourines, electric bass and lead guitars, and saxophones. Most main-line and non-denominational African-American congregations adopted and adapted these instruments into their regular worship services.

Cheryl Sanders's *Saints in Exile: The Holiness-Pentecostal Experience in African-American Religion and Culture*, a ground-breaking book written from an insider's perspective, studies the worship practices and social ethics of the African-American family of Holiness, Pentecostal, and Apostolic churches known collectively as the Sanctified Church. After reviewing four, written descriptive narratives of black Pentecostal worship based upon participant observation, Sanders identifies at least eight basic elements in common, with some variation in order: (1) call to worship, (2) songs and hymns, (3) prayer, (4) offering, (5) Scripture reading, (6) preaching, (7) altar call, and (8) benediction.[22] Additionally, Sanders detects that:

The singing of some combination of songs, hymns, choruses, and Negro spirituals is a vital part of all these worship services. It is difficult to denote the role music plays in worship with any degree of precision because music tends to undergird everything else that is done. Unlike some of the other elements of worship, music is interspersed throughout the service and not at just one or two points in the order of worship. In the composite outline, however, the singing of songs and hymns represents a major component of congregational involvement in the worship experience. The sacred repertoire is inclusive of hymns of the mainline evangelical Protestant church, gospel songs, praise choruses, and Negro spirituals.[23]

The Church of God in Christ, commonly referred to by its acronym, COGIC, was formed in 1897 by a group of excommunicated Baptists most notably, Charles Price Jones (1865–1949) and Charles Harrison Mason (1866–1961). It has long been held as the birthplace of leading gospel recording artists such as Andraé Crouch, The Winans, the Clark sisters, and many others. Known for their vibrant and fervent music in worship, The West Angeles Church of God in Christ in Los Angeles, CA, Bishop Charles E. Blake, senior pastor, began a series of recordings that captured the congregational music of the COGIC. The first, and probably most popular was *Saints in Praise: Volume 1* released in 1989 by The West Angeles Church of God in Christ Mass Choir, which became the model for African-American church praise and worship music across denominations. *The Celebration Medley* which contained "This Is the Day" / "I Will Enter His Gates" / *He Has Made Me Glad* / *We Come To Glorify His Name* / and *Victory Is Mine* remains one of the most sung selections in Praise and Worship services.[24] Recordings helped to make these songs popular. In 1990, *Saints in Praise: Volume 2* was released and *Saints in Praise: Volume 3* in 1992. *Yes Lord! Saints in Praise* with Judy McAllister was released in 2002 and *Bishop Charles E. Blake and The West Angeles COGIC Mass Choir* in 2007.

Another significant recording project began in 1995 entitled *Carlton Pearson Live at Azusa*. *Live at Azusa, Volume 2: Precious Memories [Live]* was released in 1997 and *Carlton Pearson Live at Azusa 3* followed in 1999. *Carlton Pearson: Azusa Praise Jubilee* released in 2000 was the last in that series of the historic and contemporary praise and worship music of The Church of God in Christ.

In 2005, another CD/DVD project of congregational singing from the Church of God in Christ tradition was released. The late presiding bishop of the Church of God in Christ was Bishop G. E. Patterson of Memphis, Tennessee. He produced and led his congregation, Temple of Deliverance Church of God in Christ Cathedral of Bountiful Blessings, in an award-winning recording project titled *Bishop G. E. Patterson & Congregation Singing the Old Time Way*, Volume 1 in 2005 and Volume 2 in 2006. When Bishop Patterson passed away in March 2007, he left behind another monumental recording *Having Church with the Saints* which also captures the best of congregational song in The Church of God in Christ. These records not only chronicled the gems of that denomination, but also provided helpful insight and direction for the performance practices of that repertoire.

In her book, *When the Church Becomes Your Party: Contemporary Gospel Music*, Deborah Smith Pollard notes during the 1970s, the youth of many black churches were not active participants in "traditional devotional services; a similar level of disengagement was running through the white Protestant church. For many on each side of the Christian church's racial divide, the praise and worship movement would be the sound that drew them back."[25] Pollard points out that praise and worship music arose within the white Evangelical church because of a remarkable set of circumstances.[26]

Since 1970, seeker services and praise and worship services are becoming increasingly influential among main-line churches. They attract mainliners with their potential to stimulate evangelism and spiritual growth. The seeker-service strategy raises important questions about the relationship of worship and evangelism and the place of popular culture, multimedia technology, and the arts in worship. In addition, Praise and Worship services challenge mainliners to rethink the range of physical and emotional expression in worship and to think differently about the role of music in worship. Certainly, in African-American churches we can already see the convergence of elements from these two approaches and from historic liturgies that are custom-fitted to meet the needs of individual congregations.

According to Robb Redman, two major influences shaped what he calls the "sweeping changes in Christian worship" during the latter part of the twentieth century. The first, the evangelical seeker-service movement, was launched by those who, after reviewing research on the habits of the baby boomer generation, "set to create a 'non-religious' environment for services, an alternative setting for connotations." The second is the charismatic praise and worship movement. He outlines this worship experience stating, "a typical service begins with twenty- to thirty-minutes or more of congregational singing, led by a worship leader, a band with a small ensemble of singers, and often a choir as well, modeling on the gospel choir in African-American churches. Leaders encourage a wide range of physical expressions through clapping, raising hands, swaying, and even dancing."[27]

From these seeker services and praise and worship service movements emerged the popular praise and worship musical genre that not only reflects these influences but also mirrors the fact that a generation that defines its youth by music—rock and roll and Motown—seeks to do so during its religious life as well. As a result, Michael S. Hamilton states that, "thousands of individuals select their churches, or at least the services they attend within a given church, not on the doctrine preached, but on the music that is performed."[28]

Some of the leading African-American composers of praise and worship music most widely sung in churches today include: Stephen Hurd, Byron Cage, Israel Houghton, Chester Baldwin, Donald Lawrence, Fred Hammond, Hezekiah Walker, Jean Eggleston, Joe Pace, John P. Kee, Joshua's Troop, Judith McAllister, Kurt Carr, Norman Hutchins, Norris Garner, Smokie Norful, Terrance Daye, Tony Griffin, and many others. Fortunately, music scores, as well as DVDs and CDs of their compositions can be found today in many religious music stores and bookstores.[29]

In his book *The Black Church in the Post-Civil Rights Era*, Anthony Pinn makes this observation:

> [C]omplaints by black churches point to contemporary gospel's attempt to reach the unchurched, to draw them in by avoiding a message of repentance and salvation that is too confrontational. Christians interested in the music have come to terms with a more subtle message of Jesus Christ and merits of salvation, a form of the Christian message with a new set of influences ranging from post-civil rights politics to the aesthetics of R & B and hip hop culture.[30]

Alan Light has noted that :

> [H]istorically most R & B singers have grown up singing in the church; still today, artist from Cordozar Calvin Broadus (known as "Snoop") to Kimberly Denise Jones (known as "Lil' Kim") have sung in the choir as kids. And the two genres have met in the middle any number of times, from the Teddy Riley who produced "Return" by the Winans (1990), to L. L. Cool J's track "The Power of God." Light continues by pointing out that 'The Edwin Hawkins Singers' 'Oh, Happy Day' was a chart smash in 1972, and the Clark Sisters' 'You Brought the Sunshine' lit up discos in 1982. And, who could forget M. C. Hammer's 1990 'Pray.'[31]

Historically, the black community's most celebrated secular artists have deep roots in the black church such as James Brown, Ruth Brown, Sam Cooke, Debarge, Roberta Flack, Aretha Franklin, Marvin Gaye, Whitney Houston, Louis Jordan, B. B. King, Gladys Knight, Jackie Wilson, Tina Turner, Dinah Washington, and Stevie Wonder. They represent but a fraction of the list of major artists who grew up in the black church singing, praising, preaching, praying, and shouting long before they took to the secular stage and commercial industry.

The most widely discussed and debated artist, yet probably the most popular of the late twentieth century, is probably Kirk Franklin (b. 1970), founder of Kirk Franklin and the Family as well as God's Property. As with Andraé Crouch during the 1970s and 1980s, Franklin developed an exceptional musical form that combines current musical trends—both sacred and secular—and blends them with the message of the gospel worded in slang. His most popular selections, "(The Reason) Why We Sing" and "Now Behold the Lamb" now appear in hymnals and congregational song supplements across denominations. Presently, Franklin reportedly sold ten to twelve million recordings, making him the most successful gospel artist to date.[32] The most famous example of Franklin's style for many years was his 1997 recording of "Stomp" with the group God's Property. According to Horace C. Boyer, "his excursion into rap, hip hop, and rhythm and blues, and the success that his adventures brought to gospel music brought millions of new listeners to gospel, created a record-buying frenzy for gospel music, and even helped other gospel singers gain attention."[33]

The historical struggle of the black church with the appropriation of the sacred and the secular, the culture, and the integrity of God's church began with Thomas A. Dorsey and his leadership in the development of gospel music when he took the feel of the blues and blended it into church music. The black church also faced this struggle and challenge with the advent of James Cleveland, Edwin Hawkins, and Andraé Crouch as it had to deal with the next wave of gospel music. There was the great upheaval and uproar regarding the song "Oh Happy Day" by Edwin Hawkins and then came Kirk Franklin with "Stomp," and yet another struggle emerged. The conflict over the influence and use of new music styles and popular culture is not new to the black church.

Deborah Smith-Pollard asserts, "given the importance of speech throughout the African diaspora in general and within African-American culture in particular, gospel and rap were bound to converge. Holy hip hop, then, can be seen as a logical continuation of Black Church speech patterns."[34] "Indeed," writes Horace C. Boyer, "many gospel music lovers insist that African-American preachers were the first rappers and that gospel rappers have been long overdue."[35]

In their book, *The Hip-Hop Church: Connecting with the Movement Shaping Our Culture*, Efrem Smith and Phil Jackson declare:

> Holy Hip-Hop is rap music created specifically to glorify Jesus Christ and bring the good news of Jesus Christ to those who are living in and influenced by the hip-hop culture. Now this is just a definition that I am offering; you may hear others as you venture further into this music genre, subculture, and ministry opportunity. Some involved in Holy Hip-Hop probably have yet to define what it is that they are doing. Many likely started out loving hip-hop, became Christian, and now are simply putting Jesus lyrics with their artistic gift and passion. In any case, the existence of Holy Hip-Hop is a great opportunity for the church to embrace the emerging generation and create new ministry methods for advancing the church's Mission....
>
> This style of rap music ought to be embraced by the church for a couple of reasons. One, Holy Hip-Hop can be used as an evangelism and outreach tool. Second, young people who are gifted in the arts, especially those with gifts of dance, spoken word or art with the spray can, ought to be nurtured within the church so that they realize how to use their God-given gifts to glorify the Gift Giver.[36]

In *Zion Still Sings: For Every Generation*, four rap selections appear with complete texts and are rhythmically notated by Frederick Burchwell, Craig Watkins, and Kyle Lovett: "God Made Me," "I Remember," "He's My Foundation," and "Never Been Scared."[37] To the knowledge of this writer, this is a first for Holy Hip-Hop being included in a major denominational congregational song supplement.

Conclusion

In *The Black Church in the African-American Experience*, C. Eric Lincoln and Lawrence Mamiya declare that,

> Congregational singing is a well-known device for the temporary reduction of social alienation and for the accomplishment of an *ad interim* sense of community. In the Black church, singing together is not so much as effort to find, or to establish, a transitory community as it is the reaffirmation of a common bond that, while inviolate, has suffered the pain of separation since the last occasion of togetherness.[38]

In a published conversation about music between David Day and my former professor, the late Dr. Wendell P. Whalum, Sr. (1931–1987), entitled "Why Sing?" conducted by The National Humanities Faculty Series in 1972, Day asked Dr. Whalum "[I]n what ways are children going to be better off, and society better off, if they do have opportunities to express themselves creatively, musically, to make music, to learn to enjoy music making, to learn to appreciate the music that other people make?" Dr. Whalum responded:

> [I] think music helps to order a person's life. It brings him to participation with art. That's unity. If it's singing, group singing, it brings the principle of organization and strength even closer. I think, though, it has another dimension. A human being is better off in recognizing the joy associating with other human beings and realizing the worth of such exposure. If he's properly taught, properly encouraged, he may not know all the history, but he will know that music just isn't something that's out there; it's part of 'in there' and it comes out of him as he participates. That's it. That may be the greater value. He's better because he's able to recognize the beauty, the aesthetics. He's able to recognize the subjectivity and the creativity of his existence.[39]

This interview dealt with singing in general, but there are some most appropriate applications and admonishments for the future of congregational singing in church in general and in African-American congregations specifically. Regardless of the style or genre of congregational music, the Christian church must sing in order to be the Christian church. It must be a purposeful act, never merely a time filler or matter of routine. It must be done enthusiastically, not with tentative sighs and spasmodic mumbling, shamefacedly with an ill grace. If it is contemporary, and one fears the obvious root in the word "temporary," it should be biblically based, theologically based, and relevant to the culture of the congregation. And, most important, each member should depart the sanctuary worship vowed to say and mean, in the words of Thomas A Dorsey, "I'm Going to Live the Life I Sing About in My Song," as the African-American church continues to "Lift Every Voice and Sing!" remembering and affirming that "If It Had Not Been for the Lord on My Side, Where Would I be?"

Notes —

1 W. E. B. DuBois, *The Souls of Black Folk* (New York: Dover Publications, Inc., 1903, 1994), 116.
2 Wyatt Tee Walker, *The Soul of Black Worship: A Trilogy—Preaching, Praying, Singing* (New York: Martin Luther King, Jr. Fellows Press, 1984).
3 C. Eric Lincoln and Lawrence H. Mamiya, *The Black Church in the African American Experience* (Durham, NC: Duke University Press, 1990), 346–347.
4 Wyatt Tee Walker, "The Soulful Journey of the Negro Spiritual," *Negro Digest* (July, 1963), 93.
5 Horace C. Boyer, "An Analysis of His Contributions: Thomas A Dorsey: 'Father of Gospel Music,'" *Black World* 23:9 (July, 1974), 21–22.
6 Wyatt Tee Walker, *Somebody's Calling My Name: Black Sacred Music and Social Change* (Valley Forge, PA: Judson Press, 1979), 128.
7 C. Eric Lincoln and Lawrence H. Mamiya, *The Black Church in the African-American Experience*, 377.
8 William B. McClain, "Preface," *The Songs of Zion*, eds. J. Jefferson Cleveland and Verolga Nix (Nashville: Abingdon Press, 1981), x.
9 James H. Cone, *Speaking the Truth: Ecumenism, Liberation, and Black Theology* (Grand Rapids, MI: William B. Eerdmans Publishing Co., 1986), 137.
10 James H. Cone, *Speaking the Truth*, 139–140.
11 James H. Cone, *The Spiritual and the Blues* (Maryknoll, NY: Orbis Books, 1972), 5–6.
12 Wyatt Tee Walker, *Spirits That Dwell in Deep Woods III* (New York: Martin Luther King Fellows Press, 1991), 37.
13 Walker, *Somebody's Calling My Name*, 15–17.

14 Wyatt Tee Walker, *Somebody's Calling My Name*, Chapter 6 "What a Friend We Have in Jesus: Hymns of Improvisation," 110–119.

15 For a list of African American hymnals before 1977, see Melva Wilson Costen, "Published Hymnals in the Afro-American Tradition," *The Hymn* 40:1 (January 1989), 7–13. Also published in *Readings in African American Church Music and Worship*, ed. James Abbington, Jr. (Chicago: GIA Publications, 2001), 153–165.

16 James Abbington, *Let Mt. Zion Rejoice! Music in the African American Church* (Valley Forge: Judson Press, 2001), 58–63.

17 Until the publication of the *African American Heritage Hymnal* (Chicago: GIA Publications, Inc., 2001), the ethnicity of a hymn writer has not always been apparent. See the "Black History Index", 692–693.

18 Eileen Southern, "Hymnals of the Black Church" in *Readings in African American Church Music and Worship*, ed. James Abbington (Chicago: GIA Publications, Inc. 2001), 146.

19 Eileen Southern, "Hymnals of the Black Church," 149.

20 "Introduction" to *African American Heritage Hymnal*, no page number given.

21 "Preface," *Lead Me, Guide Me, Second Edition: An African American Catholic Hymnal* (Chicago: GIA Publishing, Inc., 2012), no page number given.

22 Cheryl J. Sanders, *Saints in Exile: The Holiness-Pentecostal Experience in African-American Religion and Culture* (New York: Oxford University Press, 1996), 53.

23 Sanders, 54.

24 While the initial songs are usually the same, there are a number of variations to *The Celebration Medley*.

25 Deborah Smith Pollard, *When the Church Becomes Your Party: Contemporary Gospel Music* (Detroit: Wayne State University Press, 2008), 24.

26 This is confirmed by Robb Redman who most convincingly examines this claim in his book *The Great Worship Awakening: Singing a New Song in the Postmodern Church* (San Francisco: Jossey-Bass, 2002), 3–92.

27 Robert L. Redman. "Welcoming to the Worship Awakening," *Theology Today* 58:3 (October 2001), 369–383.

28 Michael S. Hamilton. "The Triumph of the Praise Songs," *Christianity Today* 43, no. 8 (July 12, 1999), 29.

29 I highly recommend NTIMEMUSIC.COM in Charlotte, NC for the most up-to-date and comprehensive collection of this music. The address is NTIMEMUSIC.COM, 4913 Albemarle Road, Charlotte, NC 28205, telephone: (704) 531.8961. Visit their website at www.ntimemusic.com, accessed March 18, 2013.

30 Anthony B. Pinn, *The Black Church in the Post-Civil Rights Era* (Maryknoll, New York: Orbis Books, 2002), 55.

31 Alan Light, "Say Amen, Somebody!" *Vibe Magazine* (October 1997), 92.

32 This designation does not include artists such as Aretha Franklin and Amy Grant who sing both secular and gospel. In an e-mail to Deborah Smith Pollard dated December 24, 2004, Vice President Tracey Artis of GospoCentric Records explains that Franklin sold twelve million units as of February 2005.

33 Horace C. Boyer. "African-American Gospel Music" in *African Americans and The Bible: Sacred Texts and Social Textures*, ed. Vincent L. Wimbush (New York: Continuum, 2000), 484.

34 Smith-Pollard, *When the Church Becomes Your Party*, 140.

35 Horace C. Boyer. "African American Gospel Music," 486.
36 Efrem Smith and Phil Jackson, *The Hip-Hop Church: Connecting with the Movement Shaping Our Culture* (Downers Grove, IL: InterVarsity Press, 2005), 131–132.
37 See *Zion Still Sings: For Every Generation* (Nashville: Abingdon Press, 2007), 17, 126, 181, 185.
38 C. Eric Lincoln and Lawrence Mamiya, *The Black Church in the African-American Experience* (Durham, NC: Duke University Press, 1990), 347.
39 *Why Sing? A Conversation about Music with Wendell Whalum conducted by David Day* (San Francisco: Chandler & Sharp Publishers, 1975), 22.

—Stream Four—
Gospel and Revival Song

Chapter 4
I Sing for I Cannot Be Silent:
Gospel and Revival Hymnody in the Twentieth Century

David W. Music

The Roots of Revival Hymnody

The roots of revival hymnody can be traced to the Second Great Awakening of the early nineteenth century. In the countryside, the Awakening took the form of camp meetings in which people from a particular area met at a central location, camping out for several days or weeks of preaching. Attended mainly by Methodists, Presbyterians, and Baptists, these meetings were interdenominational—and, to some degree, interracial—in character; thus, the use of a denominational hymnal was out of the question. Many people would not be able to afford a hymnal or tune book, and some perhaps could not read it if they did have one. Furthermore, the usual hymnody of the time would not have been satisfactory, for it did not reflect the emotional fervor experienced in the camp meeting.

This circumstance gave rise to a new type of congregational song that was more informal and improvisatory in nature than the regular church hymns. The words often consisted of a hymn by Isaac Watts or another eighteenth-century British hymn writer to which a chorus that had no textual connection with the stanzas was attached. Newly written lyrics were sometimes merely a chorus that could be repeated several times, slightly varied on each repetition by the use of family words such as "father," "mother," "sister," "brother," etc. Textual themes included heaven and longing to be there, love for and praise of Jesus, rejection of the world, forgiveness/grace/repentance/atonement, and final things.[1] The musical style was that of the contemporary folk hymn, with modal melodies, gapped scales, or contrafacted, centonized, or parodied from secular folk songs that had been passed down from earlier generations of American settlers.[2] On the whole, the emphasis in these songs was on ease of learning, memorability, and emotional expression.

The Awakening also impacted America's cities through the revival meetings of such figures as Lyman Beecher (1775–1863), Asahel Nettleton (1783–1844), and Charles G. Finney (1792–1875). These urban evangelistic efforts used a type of song that was similar in many respects to that of the camp meeting; in fact, some of the same songs were used in both environments. Two basic types of urban revival hymnody developed, one marked by the "scientific" approach of Thomas Hastings (1784–1872) and Lowell Mason (1792–1872) as found in *Spiritual Songs for Social Worship* (1832)—with its emphasis on musical correctness and purity, i.e., no secular connotations—and the other, exemplified by Joshua Leavitt's *The Christian Lyre* (1831), making use of folk hymns and *contrafacta* of secular melodies. The former style had a significant impact but it was the lighter, less sophisticated type represented by Leavitt (1794–1873) that was to become characteristic of revival hymnody.[3]

The fervor of the Second Great Awakening began to wane somewhat in the mid-1830s, but revival hymnody continued to prosper. Much of the energy of the authors, composers, and publishers of revival hymnody was turned to the production of Sunday school songs. These borrowed many of the characteristics of early nineteenth-century revival hymns—particularly the emphasis upon simplicity and the use of a chorus or refrain—but were geared primarily toward children.[4]

The Gospel Song

The classic form of revival hymnody was achieved during the last thirty years of the nineteenth century when earlier revival hymnody, the Sunday school song, and popular secular musical styles coalesced into the gospel hymn.[5]

Philip Phillips (1834–1895), Philip P. Bliss (1838–1876), and others provided early exemplars of the form, and the type reached an early peak of popularity in England through the pages of *Sacred Songs and Solos* (1873) by Ira D. Sankey (1840–1908) and in America through the six volumes of *Gospel Hymns* (1875–1891) by Sankey, Bliss, James McGranahan (1840–1907), and George C. Stebbins (1846–1945).[6]

The emphasis of both words and music in gospel songs was on subjective emotional appeal and simplicity. The need for repentance, the call to salvation or service, personal testimony, God's love and grace, and the death and resurrection of Jesus were typical themes. The songs were usually person-directed rather than God-directed and made much use of personal pronouns (I, me, and my). As with their secular counterpart, contemporary parlor songs, the texts of gospel songs were sometimes sentimental in emphasis ("Where is my wand'ring boy tonight," Robert Lowry [1826–1899]) but they could also have a strongly biblical content (*The Ninety and Nine*, Elizabeth Clephane [1830–1869]). The message of the stanzas was usually summed up in a refrain, which became a distinct characteristic of gospel songs, though not universally present.[7] Paul Gaarder Kaatrud has aptly summarized another important similarity between the gospel song and contemporary secular music.

> The Gospel Songs, as with the popular parlor songs, maintained a familiarity of language that allowed everyone, no matter how limited in education, to appropriate the expression as his own. Yet, similar to the same secular songs, they avoided all coarseness and vulgarity and maintained at least a modest level of gentility and respectability as poetry.[8]

The music of gospel hymns generally featured major keys, harmonizations using mainly the primary chords (I-IV-V), and the unquestioned dominance of the melody. Many of the songs suggest that they were conceived as vocal solos with simple accompaniment—in fact, some are known to have originated as improvised solos[9]—though the accompaniment was written in four-part hymn style and could easily be sung by congregations.

Early gospel song composers often drew upon nineteenth-century popular secular idioms. This was the age of John Philip Sousa, Johann Strauss, Jr., Stephen C. Foster, and Gilbert and Sullivan, and gospel song composers made full use of the march, waltz, parlor and minstrel show tune, and operetta in their music. "Gospel marches" featured dotted-eighth and sixteenth-note motion in quadruple or duple meter (*When We All Get to Heaven*), while "gospel waltzes" employed lyrical melodies over *oom-pah-pah* accompaniments (*The Glory Song*). The tender plaintiveness of *Jeannie with the Light Brown Hair* was reflected in songs such as *Near to the Heart of God*, and "gospel patter songs" set rapidly reiterated eighth notes over simple harmonic backgrounds (*Count Your Blessings*) in the manner of "The Modern Major General" from Gilbert and Sullivan's *The Pirates of Penzance*.[10] As with the texts, the tunes of gospel songs were simple and attractive enough for almost anyone to understand and appreciate, but their forms and harmonizations usually stayed within the bounds of good taste.

The early period of gospel song development may be said to have ended with the publication of *Gospel Hymns Nos. 1-6 Complete* (1895). During the last decade of the nineteenth century and first decade of the twentieth century, the chief influence on the gospel song centered on Moody Bible Institute in Chicago, where Daniel B. Towner (1850–1919) was the music chair and chief influence. One of Towner's students, Charles M. Alexander (1867–1920), became the best-known revival musician of the period 1900–1910, working principally with evangelists Reuben A. Torrey and J. Wilbur Chapman, and pianists Robert Harkness and Henry Barraclough. Alexander set the prototype of the revival music leader who also served as master of ceremonies for the meeting, joking with the crowd, telling stories, making announcements, etc. It was also largely through his influence that the piano became the principal accompanying instrument for revival services, and thus for gospel hymnody. Alexander was one of the first prominent revival music leaders who was not a prolific writer of gospel songs; as if by way of compensation he acquired the copyrights to numerous songs written by others.[11]

Many aspects of Alexander's example were followed by the music leader for the flamboyant evangelist Billy Sunday, Homer Rodeheaver

(1880–1955). Rodeheaver served as master of ceremonies at the meetings, sometimes leading the singing by playing his trombone, established a publishing company, and—as with Alexander—began acquiring copyrights.[12] Both Alexander and Rodeheaver were serious in their desire to see people accept Christ, but their more entertainment-oriented approach to the service of song represented a departure from earlier traditions of gospel hymnody as represented by Sankey, who had typically led the singing (or sung solos) while seated at a reed organ.

Musically, the gospel songs written during the Alexander/Rodeheaver era maintained many of the characteristics of earlier songs but their largely diatonic nature was beginning to give way to chromatic alterations of the melody, as exemplified in Charles H. Gabriel's (1856–1932) *Brighten the Corner Where You Are* (1913, to a text by Ina Ogden [1872–1964]) and *The Old Rugged Cross* (1912–1913) by George Bennard (1873–1958).[13]

Southern Gospel

Mass evangelism crusades became less frequent during the 1920s and 1930s, and many of the denominations that had been heavily influenced by gospel hymnody began to weed them out of their hymnals, particularly in the North. For some groups, however, the nineteenth-century gospel song continued to be the chief musical fare. This music was especially characteristic of churches in the South and those with a rural orientation.

Along with these classic gospel song expressions authors, composers, and publishers in the South developed their own distinctive style of gospel music. Building upon earlier patterns of seven-shaped shape-note hymnody established by Southerners Ephraim Ruebush (1833–1924), Aldine S. Kieffer (1840–1904), James D. Vaughan (1864–1941), and others, the Stamps-Baxter Music Company (founded in 1926)[14] promulgated a type of gospel hymnody that became known as "Southern" or "country" gospel—and, in fact, many of the songs have the flavor of secular country and western music.

The texts of these songs were frequently light hearted, tended toward the homely, and were sometimes only marginally religious in nature, e.g., "Ain't It a Shame"; many of them contained verbal allusions to earlier gospel songs and hymns (*The Blood That Stained the Old Rugged Cross*).

The music retained the chromatic inflections of the Alexander/Rodeheaver era—often in the context of a hexatonic melody—and added echo effects and syncopations, the latter perhaps influenced by jazz and western swing. In many songs, the melody appeared at least partly in the bass, tenor, or alto voices, reflecting the appropriateness of the pieces as works for vocal quartet rather than solos or congregational songs ("On the Jericho Road"). Publishing companies often sponsored quartets, usually composed of male voices, to perform songs from their latest collection at singing conventions as a marketing device. In time, the quartets became independent of the publishing companies, thanks, in part, to the development of an important new promotional medium: radio, which often featured both traditional and new gospel hymnody in broadcasts of religious programming.[16]

The books in which these songs appeared were not designed as church hymnals but as material for singing conventions, fifth-Sunday sings, and so on. The collections were decidedly ephemeral, being produced inexpensively and designed to wear out quickly to be replaced the following year by a new book.[17]

A related development was the rise of the gospel chorus. Gospel choruses had been written throughout the history of gospel hymnody, but they became particularly prominent—and some of the best-known examples originated—during the 1940s and 1950s. A gospel chorus might be described as a gospel hymn refrain without the stanzas. As with Southern gospel, the gospel chorus was often semi-sacred in nature and was frequently more an expression of the sheer joy of singing than of profound theological truths (*Do Lord,* "Deep and Wide").[18] Gospel choruses were widely used among young people in fellowship settings and in organizations such as Youth for Christ.

Of course, some Southerners continued in the congregational/solo idiom of earlier gospel song composition rather than the newer quartet-dominated style of Southern gospel. Among these were Baylus Benjamin McKinney (1886–1952), a Southern Baptist who became the most beloved songwriter in this large and prominent denomination, and Lloyd O. Sanderson (1901–1992), a member of the Churches of Christ. The works of these two men sought a middle ground between the enthusiasm of Southern gospel and the relatively more refined northern examples from the previous century.[19]

Some Common Features of Revival Hymnody

Before proceeding to a discussion of revival hymnody in the second half of the twentieth century, it will be useful to point out a few aspects that have been characteristic of the genre throughout its history and still remain generally operative. Some of these features have already been mentioned and others are introduced here.

1. Revival hymns usually include a refrain. This serves both as a summary of the stanzas and as an easily memorized unit.

2. The words and music of revival hymns are often by the same person. Certainly, revival hymnody has had its share of persons who write only texts or tunes (Fanny Crosby is a familiar example). Nevertheless, the combination of text and tune writer in one person is more typical of revival hymnody than most other historic types of congregational song.

3. The words and music of revival hymnody generally form an integral unit. Gospel hymn tunes are usually "proper" to a specific text. This is the case not only because the same person frequently writes them, but also because the tune is designed to fit the emotional character of a particular text. Furthermore, revival lyrics and melodies are often in unusual hymnic meters, making it difficult to "mix and match" them with standard hymnic literature.

4. The prominence of the refrain and the close association between revival texts and tunes means that such songs are generally known by a title that describes the song as a whole rather than by a first line and tune name. For example, a familiar gospel song by James M. Black (1856–1938) is popularly known as *When the Roll Is Called Up Yonder* not as "When the trumpet of the Lord shall sound, and time shall be no more"/ROLL CALL. Indeed, revival hymn composers have seldom given names to their tunes, the title of the song generally being sufficient to identify it. Where tune names for revival hymns are present in a congregational song collection these have generally been added by a hymnal committee or editor.

5. Revival hymns almost invariably borrow from popular secular musical and literary styles. These styles may be contemporary with the creation of the revival hymn or they may be those of a previous generation. For example, when Ira D. Sankey wrote *The Ninety and Nine,* he used the style of the parlor ballad that was current at the time. However, when Southern Baptist gospel songwriter B. B. McKinney wrote *Wherever He Leads I'll Go* some sixty years later, he was not using the popular style of the 1930s but that of the 1870s.

6. Revival hymns are most often couched in personal (I, me, and my) rather than corporate terms. The focus is typically on the individual's relationship with Jesus.

7. The songs seldom emphasize doctrinal propositions. Their theological purpose is usually to call for some sort of action on the part of the singer, though the desired response may be internal rather than external: "cherish the old rugged cross," "trust and obey," "sing the wondrous love of Jesus," etc. The songs may also be affirmations of personal faith *(I Know Whom I Have Believed),* offer praise and thanks for salvation ("To God Be the Glory"), or serve as personal testimony *(Victory in Jesus).*

THE LATE TWENTIETH CENTURY

During the second half of the twentieth century, the use of revival hymns by American churches was characterized by considerable diversity, with some congregations and denominations employing them almost exclusively and others hardly at all. Still, other groups made what may be called moderate use of revival hymnody as part of a varied repertoire.

Revival hymnody is most characteristic of churches that hold to a conservative evangelical faith, particularly those with evangelistic, fundamentalist, or charismatic leanings such as Southern Baptists, Churches of Christ, the Church of the Nazarene, or the Assemblies of God. The congregations that are least likely to sing revival hymns are those with a liberal theological bent or a ritualistic or liturgical service order,[20] including the

Roman Catholic, Episcopal, and Lutheran communions. United Methodists and the Presbyterian Church, U.S.A., are examples of denominations in which revival hymnody plays an important but far from central role, though it appears that the number and variety of gospel songs in the most recent hymnals of these communions has increased somewhat, perhaps as a result of the same movement that has produced more examples of world hymnody, shape-note folk hymns, and other song styles.

It will be recognized, of course, that the statements above are generalizations that do not hold true in all cases. There are examples of Southern Baptist churches in which revival hymns hardly figure at all and Lutheran churches that sing them every week. Nevertheless, such generalizations can at least serve as a useful guide to the principal employment of these songs.

1950–1980

During the 1950s, 1960s, and 1970s, churches that availed themselves of gospel hymnody used it in much the same way it had been employed in the nineteenth and early twentieth centuries: as the basic congregational/vocal solo/choral fare for revival meetings. Occasionally, the songs were chosen to fit the theme of the preacher's sermon but, just as often, they were selected in more or less random fashion, the purpose in the first instance being to reinforce the homily and in the second to create a suitably receptive emotional mood for hearing the message. Sometimes a particular song was chosen as a theme song to be sung at every meeting of the revival; often this was a new or recent song, and its frequent use in the revival served to add it to the congregation's permanent repertory. Another means of introducing new gospel songs was to have them sung as solos, usually by the guest music leader—often called the "singer,"—or as choral items.

A key feature of these meetings was the singing of an "invitation" (altar call) hymn after the sermon. The ultimate goal of the invitation and its accompanying hymn was to provide a means of physical and spiritual response to the sermon. During the singing of the hymn, persons who wished to make a public statement of their acceptance of Jesus as Savior, rededicate their lives, devote themselves to ministerial service, or simply receive additional counseling, made their way to the front of the worship space, where they were greeted by the pastor of the church, the evangelist, or other people designated for that purpose. Persons who were committed Christians and did not need to "walk the aisle" were expected to support those who did by praying and keeping the singing going; they were also expected to examine their own lives and make their own rededication without necessarily going to the front. The purposes of the invitation hymn were accomplished partly by the text—which often urged the sinner to repent, testified to God's mercy and grace, or expressed the unconverted singer's desire to know Jesus—and partly by the mood established by the tune, which was more often tender than triumphant in tone and was frequently sung slowly and expressively.

However, the use of revival music was not limited to evangelistic meetings but was a major factor in the Sunday-by-Sunday services. Many churches in this tradition had both a Sunday morning and evening service. These were viewed essentially as single services of a revival meeting, the primary purpose of which was to bring souls into the kingdom of God. The Sunday morning service was sometimes more "formal" than the Sunday night service or revival meeting and frequently used other types of hymnody as well as gospel songs. Sunday evening services tended to be oriented more toward the family of faith and were typically less formal in character than Sunday morning. Nevertheless, the same service elements (including the invitation) in much the same order were found in all of these meetings, and revival hymnody was characteristic of each.

During the 1950s and 1960s, the most important influences on revival hymnody were the Billy Graham crusades and the work of John W. Peterson (1921–2006). Relying as they did principally on gospel songs from the nineteenth and early twentieth centuries, the Billy Graham crusades were one of the few revival movements in history that did not spawn a new type of Christian song. The crusades did introduce some "old" songs that had previously been overlooked, including *How Great Thou Art* (Boberg/Hine/Swedish melody) and "To God Be the Glory" (Crosby/Doane). A few new songs became popular through the crusades, including George Beverly Shea's "I'd Rather Have Jesus" and *The Wonder of It All*. Shea (1909–2013) was the principal soloist for the Graham meetings and both of these songs were used primarily as solos though they have subsequently appeared in hymnals and been sung enthusiastically by congregations. The extensive use of these and older gospel songs undoubtedly had a significant impact on the hymnic repertory of churches that participated in the meetings.[21]

John W. Peterson's influence among evangelical churches was far-reaching during the third quarter of the twentieth century.[22] In the 1950s and 1960s, he was known principally as a writer of vocal solos *(It Took a Miracle)* and seasonal cantatas such as *Love Transcending*, *Born a King*, and *No Greater Love*. His cantatas were perennial best sellers and appealed particularly to smaller evangelical church choirs that otherwise would have had little in the way of major works to sing for the Christmas and Easter seasons.[23]

As with many gospel composers before him, Peterson wrote both the words and music to many of his songs, though this was by no means his invariable practice.[24] As with Sankey and other early gospel song composers, the distinction between Peterson's songs for soloists and for congregation was often negligible.

Peterson compiled a number of hymnals and songbooks for Singspiration Music, a non-denominational company that specialized in gospel music and published most of his works. These volumes were aimed principally at the non-denominational market and at evangelical churches that may have been dissatisfied for some reason with their denomination's hymnal. One such collection, *Praise! Our Songs and Hymns* (Grand Rapids: Singspiration Music, 1982), compiled in association with and edited by Norman Johnson (1928–1983), included forty-five pieces with words and/or music by Peterson, some co-written with others, and serves as a useful compendium of his gospel songs for congregations.

Some of the Peterson pieces in *Praise* are in what might be called "traditional hymn style": a text that extols God's attributes set to a diatonic melody in straightforward rhythm with a harmonization featuring the primary chords and few or no chromatic alterations e.g., "All Glory to Jesus," #75. Others are in Victorian part-song hymn style, such as "Near to Thy Heart" (#387).

More characteristic are the works in the traditional (*Isn't the Love of Jesus Something Wonderful*, #553) and Southern gospel (*Show a Little Bit of Love and Kindness*, #511) idioms, and those that show the influence of popular secular music.[25] Examples of the latter include *Who Will Tell Them* (#514), the last two lines of which are reminiscent of the traditional song "Reuben, Reuben," and "Shepherd of Love" (#448), the middle section of which is similar to portions of the popular Christmas song "It's the Most Wonderful Time of the Year." This is not to suggest that Peterson was consciously copying from these pieces, but to illustrate that he employed the basic style that was prevalent in contemporary popular music of his time.

Peterson made use of the Broadway show-tune idiom in pieces such as *It Took a Miracle* (#518), with its added note (seventh and ninth) chords, its chromatic alterations of both melody and harmony, and its dramatic *bravura* refrain.[26] Not surprisingly, this was one of his most popular songs during the 1950s and 1960s, though it appeared in few hymnals because of its essentially solo style.

During the 1970s, a handful of Peterson's songs that had become familiar as solos or "choir specials"—the way they were usually performed during the 1950s and 1960s, and the manner in which revival hymnody is often introduced—began to appear as congregational fare in denominational and independent hymnals. Few of his works have penetrated the confines of main-line denominational hymnals, but many of Peterson's songs have continued to be popular in non-denominational collections and in the minds and hearts of evangelical church members.[27]

Generally speaking, John W. Peterson exemplified an urban style of gospel hymnody in the 1950s and 1960s. Representative of the Southern gospel tradition at this time were Mosie Lister (b. 1921) and Ira F. Stanphill (1914–1993). Lister's songs have been little used in denominational and main-line independent hymnals, perhaps because many of them were written with gospel quartet in mind; one song that has seen a modest amount of use is *'Til the Storm Passes By*.[28] Stanphill worked mainly outside the usual distribution channels of gospel hymnody.[29] His works followed traditional patterns in blurring the line between vocal solo and congregational music. The songs ranged from the cheery *Happiness Is The Lord* and "Mansion Over The Hilltop" to the more introspective *I Know Who Holds Tomorrow* and *Room At The Cross For You*, the last-named being the one most widely found in denominational and standard non-denominational hymnals.

The most popular successors to these figures in congregational gospel hymnody have been the husband/wife team of William J. (Bill) and Gloria Gaither. The attributions of their songs suggest that Gloria (b. 1942) is the primary "words" person and Bill (b. 1936) the principal "music" part of the team, but both their names are attached to some texts and tunes while others were apparently written completely by the husband.

The Gaithers began their song-writing career in the 1960s, but it was in the 1970s that they began to achieve spectacular success, particularly with the release of the musical *Alleluia: A Praise Gathering for Believers* in 1973. This work was composed primarily of Gaither songs arranged for choral and group singing by Ronn Huff (b. 1938), and in some cases it was exposure to *Alleluia* that first introduced the Gaithers' music to congregations, especially to main-line evangelical churches in urban areas.

Ultimately, the Gaithers founded their own publishing firm, Gaither Music Company, and issued a hymnal, *Worship His Majesty* (1987), edited by Fred Bock (1939–1998). This hymnal contained forty-nine songs with words and/or music by one or both of the Gaithers and serves as a good summary of their style.[30]

The Gaithers' song-writing manner might be characterized as an extension of the Southern gospel style. The textual and musical background is that of the Stamps-Baxter idiom but with a veneer of sophistication that makes their songs attractive to persons who are outside the gospel quartet tradition.[31]

As might be expected from their position in the gospel music tradition, the texts of the Gaithers's songs tend toward informality and immediacy. Sometimes the words reflect the idiosyncracies of modern casual speech ("Let's *Just* Praise the Lord," #45; *Getting Used to the Family of God,* #345). The themes of the texts are often the ones traditionally found in gospel hymnody: the need for salvation and praise for its provision (*Sinner Saved By Grace* #666), heaven and the Second Coming (*The King Is Coming,* #280), the need to tell the Christian story ("Get All Excited," #647), and love for the Savior (*There's Something About That Name,"* #175). Many of the texts consist of a single stanza only—essentially they are gospel choruses. A significant number of the lyrics are irregular in their hymnic meter, perhaps reflecting their origins as solo rather than congregational songs.

Several musical features appear so frequently in the tunes of Bill Gaither as to be fingerprints of his style. Tunes almost invariably begin on the third or fifth degrees of the scale, seldom on the tonic. Chromaticism figures significantly in both the melodies and the harmony parts though a few melodies contain no chromatic alterations whatsoever. The tunes often employ raised seconds that function as neighboring tones to the third degree of the scale and are frequently accompanied by raised fourths in the tenor or alto (see, for example, "Let's Just Praise the Lord," #45; *Because He Lives,* #260; "Something Beautiful," #655). Three-note ascending or descending chromatic melody passages are also common (*I Could Never Outlove the Lord,* #103; *There's Something About That Name,* #175; *Because He Lives,* #260). The added-note harmonies of Southern gospel are used in profusion, sometimes creating chains of dissonance. Only the first two notes in the second phrase of *There's Something About That Name* (#175), for example, are accompanied by consonant chords.

The Scotch snap, which is a short note sung on the beat, followed by a dotted note, is a rhythmic characteristic of many Gaither songs ("Let's Just Praise the Lord," #45; *He Touched Me,* #632; *Praise Be to Jesus,* #66). A related figure is the use of a quarter note followed by a half note or dotted quarter and eighth in 3/4 meter, found in *There's Something About That Name* (#175), *Jesus Is Lord of All* (#185), and other songs. In fact, Gaither seems particularly drawn to 3/4 meter, with more than fifty percent of the tunes attributed to him being cast in that signature (twenty-five of forty-six tunes; an additional tune is in 6/4). The tunes in 4/4, in addition to being fewer in number, often begin on the second or third beat of a measure ("Let's Just Praise the Lord," #45; *Because He Lives,* #260). Even the keys are fairly predictable, with fully a quarter of the tunes appearing in F major (twelve of forty-six).

Perhaps not the most popular of the Gaithers's songs, *Getting Used to the Family of God* (#345) nevertheless seems to sum up the general style of their songs. The song is in 3/4 and is set in F major. The melody begins on the third of the tonic chord and features several raised seconds, always paired with raised fourths in the tenor, and other chromatic alterations. The quarter-/dotted-quarter/eighth-note rhythm figures prominently and there are a number of added-note chords, particularly in the refrain.

Gaither songs are widely known in evangelical congregations but their works have not received significant publication in standard hymnals. Their songs are in many senses quite simple, but also sometimes difficult for congregations to sing because of certain features of their style, chiefly the irregular hymnic meters and the way the melodies often seem to come to a halt just as they get going (e.g., *Because He Lives,* #260). These features are irrelevant when soloists or even choirs and ensembles sing the songs, but they may become barriers when a congregation attempts them. Popular performing artists and church soloists have exacerbated this circumstance, even for the songs that do not have the characteristics noted above, by the variant rhythmic versions that have been sung. Since the principal medium for learning or teaching revival hymnody has frequently been the vocal solo—and gospel soloists are notorious for adding embellishments and fermatas, hurrying or lengthening rhythms, and making other alterations—there is often no standardized version of the song. Some soloists will try to sing it as indicated in the printed version, others will do it according to a recorded performance, and still others will reflect the local usage of a previous church. The Gaither songs that have figured most prominently in denominational and standard non-denominational hymnals are *Because He Lives* and *There's Just Something About That Name.* The refrain of *The Family of God* has been used in many churches as a welcome song though it has seldom appeared in hymnals.[32]

One hymn writer of the same period whose works inhabited a sort of middle ground between the standard hymn and the gospel song was the Canadian Margaret Clarkson (1915–2008). As with Fanny Crosby exclusively a writer of texts, Clarkson began writing hymns at an early age. In 1938, she wrote one of her most widely distributed texts, "So Send I You," which John W. Peterson set to music in 1954. Clarkson subsequently concluded that her original text—which emphasized the trials and difficulties of missionary service—was inadequate, and in 1962 she wrote an alternative text with the same title. The second version of "So Send I You," as with the first, reflects the typical revival hymn theme of personal surrender to missionary and evangelistic work.

Another hymn by Clarkson, "Sing Praise to the Father" (1964–1965), better illustrates the combination of features from revival and standard hymnody in her work. The theme of the text is a typical one for gospel songs—praise to God for redemption—and the hymn is full of characteristically revivalist words: mercy, love, grace, atonement, new life, salvation, and redemption. Jesus is described as "Redeemer and Friend," and the doctrine of substitutionary atonement is implied in the phrase "died in our stead." Another revival hymn element is the presence of a refrain.

On the other hand, the text employs trinitarian hymn structure, with one stanza focusing on each person of the Trinity and a final stanza expressing the unity of the Godhead. Such an objective theological emphasis is unusual in revival hymnody. Also atypical is the corporate nature of the text ("us," "our"; the fourth stanza does include one "my"). Clarkson's texts differ from those usually written or set by Peterson, the Gaithers, and others because they seem to be geared more toward performance by a congregation than a soloist.[33]

Gospel hymnody of the period 1960–1980 may have been dominated by Peterson, the Gaithers, and Clarkson but songs that were published in hymnals and sung in the churches during and after that period were also contributed by many other authors and composers. Table 1 lists a number of these writers, a representative song, and a source for each named song.[34]

Some of these recent songs were in traditional gospel styles, such as *All to Thee* by Richard D. Baker (1927–2011) and *Jesus Is Lord of All* by LeRoy McClard (b. 1926). Other songs represented in Table 1 included elements that linked them with the emerging popular Christian music idiom or other types of song. Examples of these include "Greater Is He That Is in Me" by Lanny Wolfe (b. 1942), with its rhythmic syncopations and worship chorus form, and *Share His Love* by William J. Reynolds (1920–2009), which features a recitative-like melody, Mixolydian harmonic and melodic tendencies, augmented triads, and strings of dissonant chords.

1980–2000 and Beyond

Gospel hymnody pervaded American evangelistic churches until about the beginning of the 1980s. From this point to the end of the twentieth century, a number of factors combined to lessen the impact of gospel hymns on these congregations.

One of these elements was the substitution of a different musical idiom for the role once held by gospel hymnody. The coming of age of the "baby boom" generation led many church leaders to advocate use of the music that was most closely associated with this group, rock music. "Jesus music" had originated during the 1960s as an attempt to appeal to youth, and in the 1970s it became big business. Until the late 1970s, this existed mainly outside the walls of the church as a sort of spiritual entertainment but by the mid-1980s Contemporary Christian Music (as it was now called) was making its way into the churches and quickly became the dominant musical style in some congregations.

Another factor that contributed to a lessening of the influence of gospel hymnody in the 1980s and 1990s was that the arenas in which it had principally been nurtured—the revival meeting and the Sunday night service—began to fall out of favor. Busy baby boomers were not interested in going to the church night after night for an extended series of meetings. The revival meeting, which by the 1960s had typically become a weeklong affair, was gradually reduced in most churches to half a week, a weekend, one day (Sunday), and then was finally eliminated altogether. The same fate befell the Sunday evening service, which was phased out in many places during the last two decades of the century. Thus, two of the principal venues for introducing and learning new gospel songs and performing older ones were no longer available.

Another blow that was struck at gospel hymnody in the 1980s and 1990s was a renewed emphasis upon worship. Since the introduction of the revival meeting in the nineteenth century, evangelistic evangelical churches had focused their attention on the conversion of the lost almost to the exclusion of the Christians meeting their God in a corporate setting.[35] Though thinly disguised by being called a "worship service," the Sunday morning meeting had mainly been geared toward reaching the unconverted.

By 1980, however, the renewal of worship that began with the reforms of Vatican II had begun to trickle down to evangelistic churches in the United States. Evangelistic churches discovered and adopted practices that hitherto had been foreign to them such as observing the Christian Year (previously characteristic only of liturgical churches) or singing medleys of praise choruses (adopted by non-tongues speaking churches from their charismatic cousins). This new emphasis on worship was perfectly suited to the individualistic narcissism of the baby boom generation, which sought to "get something" out of worship and, in part, served as an antidote to it.

Perhaps the most important indication of the changed status of gospel hymnody at the beginning of the twenty-first century was the publication of Hope Publishing Company's hymnal *Worship & Rejoice* (2001). This company had been founded in the nineteenth century as an independent publisher of gospel songs. The firm's emphasis broadened significantly over the years to include other types of hymnody and church music, but it remained true to its historical roots as a central source for gospel songs. However, while *Worship & Rejoice* included many gospel songs of historic vintage and numerous hymns authored or composed between 1980 and 2000, it contained only a very few pieces written during the last two decades of the twentieth century that fit the classic subject matter, form, and style of the gospel song.[36]

An analysis of other hymnals issued by evangelistic denominations and independent publishers in the last decade of the century yields much the same result: a substantial number of historic gospel hymns and a fair sampling of gospel songs written between 1950 and 1980, but hardly any pieces of this type from the last twenty years of the century. Table 2 lists some of the songs copyrighted between 1980 and 2000 that might be considered to fall into the gospel hymn orbit, though even some of these exhibit crossover tendencies with other styles.[37]

But, if the use and composition of gospel hymns seems to be on the decline, this is not the same as saying that recent revival hymnody is absent from the hymnals and the churches. It is merely that the central focus of revival hymnody has moved away from the gospel song to other types of hymns. In a sense, the place of gospel hymnody has been—or is being—taken by certain types of worship choruses and Contemporary Christian songs.

Though different in musical and textual style, and to some degree in purpose as well, these songs fulfill much the same function that gospel hymnody historically held, that of providing an emotional response or testimony to the Good News of the gospel. Similar to gospel songs of previous generations, the new songs are based largely upon secular musical and textual idioms, the principal difference being that the Contemporary Christian songs draw on more recent popular styles.

Four songs from the late twentieth century will serve to illustrate this suggestion: *Here I Am, Lord* by Dan Schutte (b. 1947), *Shine, Jesus, Shine* by Graham Kendrick (b. 1950), "There Is a Redeemer" by Melody Green (b. 1946), and *People Need the Lord* by Greg Nelson (b. 1948) and Phill McHugh (b. 1951). The first three all use the stock stanza/refrain form that is familiar from both gospel hymnody and pop/rock music. Personal pronouns figure prominently in the texts, which focus upon the singer's surrender to do God's work in the world, the call for personal and communal revival, and testimony that Jesus (the Son of God) is the redeemer of humanity (compare the historic gospel songs "Take My Life and Let It Be," *Revive Us Again,* and "Redeemed, How I Love to Proclaim It"). *People Need the Lord* differs from the first three in its brevity, but it seems to inhabit a middle ground between the traditional gospel chorus and the more recent worship chorus: its text places it squarely in the gospel song tradition but it is musically more closely related to easy listening music than to historic gospel style. Thus, the song functions in much the same way as the traditional gospel chorus though it is more serious than the early exemplars of this form.

In a sense, it is ironic to contemplate the displacement of gospel hymnody by worship choruses and Contemporary Christian Music in the favor of many churches, for this is exactly what gospel hymnody did to other types of congregational song almost exactly 100 years before. However, to use an arboreal metaphor, the roots of revival hymnody are still healthy. Many of its older branches are still alive, though they may no longer bud as they once did, and the trunk is in the process of sending out new branches that will perhaps serve to revitalize the entire tree.

Key to Table

Baptist =	Wesley L. Forbis, ed., *The Baptist Hymnal* (Nashville: Convention Press, 1991).
Celebration =	Tom Fettke, ed., *The Celebration Hymnal* (N.pl.: Word Music/Integrity Music, 1997).
Family =	Fred Bock, ed., *Hymns for the Family of God* (Nashville: Paragon Associates, 1976).
Worship =	*Worship & Rejoice* (Carol Stream, IL: Hope Publishing Company, 2001).
Worshiping =	Donald P. Hustad, ed., *The Worshiping Church* (Carol Stream, IL: Hope Publishing Company, 1990).

Table I
Representative Gospel Song Writers of the Period 1960–1980

Author/Composer	Representative Song	Source
Richard D. Baker	*All to Thee*	Baptist, 482
Gene Bartlett	"Set My Soul Afire"	Baptist, 573
A. L. Butler	"Redeemed"	Baptist, 531
Ralph Carmichael	*Like a Lamb Who Needs the Shepherd*	Family, 61
Marian Wood Chaplin	*I Have Come From the Darkness*	Baptist, 532
David Danner	*Jesus Is the Song*	Baptist, 552
Barbara Fowler Gaultney	*My Lord Is Near Me All the Time*	Baptist, 59
Tom Fettke/Linda Lee Johnson	*Be Strong in the Lord*	Celebration, 734
Mylon R. LeFevre	*Without Him*	Celebration, 504
LeRoy McClard	*Jesus Is Lord of All*	Baptist, 296
Carol Owens	*Freely, Freely*	Celebration, 436
Squire E. Parsons, Jr.	*Sweet Beulah Land*	Celebration, 776
Dottie Rambo	*If That Isn't Love*	Family, 224
R. Maines Rawls	"Take My Life, Lead Me, Lord"	Baptist, 287
William J. Reynolds	*Share His Love*	Baptist, 567
Marsha Stevens	*For Those Tears I Died*	Family, 436
Kathleen Thomerson	"I Want to Walk as a Child of the Light"	Worship, 248
Lanny Wolfe	"Greater Is He That Is in Me"	Baptist, 437
Don Wyrtzen	"Love Was When"	Family, 28

Table II
Representative Gospel Song Writers of the Period 1980–2000

Author/Composer	Representative Song	Source
Fanny Crosby/John Ness Beck	*Lord, Here Am I*	Baptist, 486
Mark Blankenship/Terry York	"Worthy of Worship"	Baptist, 3
J. Phillip Landgrave	*He Is Coming Soon*	Worshiping, 281
Greg Nelson/Phill McHugh	*Lamb of Glory*	Celebration, 109
Rae Whitney	*O What a Wonder It Is*	Baptist, 548

Notes —

1. Ellen Jane Lorenz, *Glory, Hallelujah! The Story of the Campmeeting Spiritual* (Nashville: Abingdon, 1978), 56.
2. A *contrafactum* is a song in which the words have been changed (usually from secular to sacred) while leaving the music essentially intact. *Centonization* involves constructing a new song from phrases of pre-existing songs. *Parody* in this context means merely replacing a word or two to make the song sacred.
3. For a thorough discussion of urban revival music in the early nineteenth century see Paul Garnett Hammond, "Music in Urban Revivalism in the Northern United States, 1800–1835" (DMA dissertation, Southern Baptist Theological Seminary, 1974).
4. Revival hymnody in the middle third of the nineteenth century is discussed in Paul Gaarder Kaatrud, "Revivalism and the Popular Spiritual Song in Mid-nineteenth Century America: 1830–1870" (PhD dissertation, University of Minnesota, 1977). The standard history of the early Sunday school song is Virginia Ann Cross, "The Development of Sunday School Hymnody in the United States of America, 1816–1869" (DMA dissertation, New Orleans Baptist Theological Seminary, 1985).
5. The present chapter discusses only white gospel hymnody. Black gospel song is discussed in chapter three.
6. Significant resources on the contents of the *Gospel Hymns* series include Esther Heidi Rothenbusch, "The Role of *Gospel Hymns Nos. 1 to 6* (1875–1894) in American Revivalism" (PhD dissertation, University of Michigan, 1991), especially chapter four, and Melvin Ross Wilhoit, "A Guide to the Principal Authors and Composers of Gospel Song of the Nineteenth Century" (DMA dissertation, Southern Baptist Theological Seminary, 1982).
7. Unlike the choruses of earlier camp meeting songs the refrain of a gospel song was usually related to the theme of the stanzas. (The term "chorus" is generally employed for a refrain that is not organically connected with the stanzas). Elizabeth Clephane's *The Ninety and Nine* (with music by Ira Sankey) was perhaps the best-known example of a gospel song without a refrain.
8. Kaatrud, "Revivalism and the Popular Spiritual Song," 297–298.
9. The most famous example is *The Ninety and Nine*, the melody and harmony of which Sankey improvised during a revival meeting in Scotland. See Mel R. Wilhoit, "Sing Me a Sankey: Ira D. Sankey and Congregational Song," *The Hymn* 42 (January 1991), 16-17,

and Mel R. Wilhoit, "The Birth of a Classic: Sankey's 'The Ninety and Nine,'" in David W. Music, ed., *We'll Shout and Sing Hosanna: Essays on Church Music in Honor of William J. Reynolds* (Fort Worth, TX: School of Church Music, Southwestern Baptist Theological Seminary, 1998), 229–253.

10 For recent publications of the gospel songs mentioned in this paragraph see *The Baptist Hymnal* (Nashville: Convention Press, 1991), #s 514, 520, 295, 644.

11 Mel R. Wilhoit, "Alexander the Great: Or, Just Plain *Charlie*," *The Hymn* 46 (April 1995): 20–28.

12 See Thomas Henry Porter, "Homer Alvan Rodeheaver (1880–1955): Evangelistic Singer and Publisher" (EdD dissertation, New Orleans Baptist Theological Seminary, 1981).

13 Gabriel was the most prolific and successful composer of gospel songs during the early twentieth century. See Terry W. York, "Charles Hutchinson Gabriel (1856–1932): Composer, Author, and Editor in the Gospel Tradition" (DMA dissertation, New Orleans Baptist Theological Seminary, 1985). The chromatically altered tones of the melody often included raising the second and/or fourth degrees of the scale (with the latter not forming a secondary dominant but serving simply as a neighboring tone).

14 The company moved its headquarters to Dallas, Texas, in 1929 and was renamed the Stamps-Baxter Music and Printing Company.

15 The Southern gospel songs mentioned in this section are found in Luther G. Presley, comp., *Heavenly Highway Hymns* (Dallas: Stamps-Baxter Music and Printing Company, 1956).

16 See Donald P. Hustad, *Jubilate II: Church Music in Worship and Renewal* (Carol Stream: Hope Publishing Company, 1993), 251–252.

17 For important surveys of Southern gospel hymnody, see James R. Goff, Jr., *Close Harmony: A History of Southern Gospel* (Chapel Hill & London: University of North Carolina Press, 2002), especially chapters 1–4; Jo Lee Fleming, "James D. Vaughan, Music Publisher, Lawrenceburg, Tennessee, 1912–1964" (SMD dissertation, Union Theological Seminary, 1972); and Shirley L. Beary, "The Stamps-Baxter Music and Printing Company: A Continuing American Tradition, 1926–1976" (DMA dissertation, Southwestern Baptist Theological Seminary, 1977).

18 Both *Do Lord* and "Deep and Wide" appeared in *Youth Sings: A Praise Book of Hymns and Choruses* (Mound, MN: Pariase Book Pub. 1951). *Do Lord* was also found in *Heavenly Highway Hymns*.

19 On McKinney see William J. Reynolds, "The Contributions of B. B. McKinney to Southern Baptist Church Music," *Baptist History and Heritage* 21 (July 1986), 41–49 (particularly p. 48). On Sanderson see Jim Mankin, "L. O. Sanderson, Church of Christ Hymn Writer," *The Hymn* 46 (January 1995), 27–31.

20 In this context, "liturgical" is used to mean a planned, logical order of worship that is not necessarily the same every time, thus not "ritualistic."

21 For a thorough study of the music of the Graham crusades through 1970, see George William Stansbury, Jr., "The Music of the Billy Graham Crusades 1947–1970: An Analysis and Evaluation" (DMA dissertation, Southern Baptist Theological Seminary, 1971).

22 Peterson's autobiography (co-written with Richard Engquist) was published in 1976 under the title *The Miracle Goes On* (Grand Rapids: Zondervan Publishing House).

23 Thurston J. Dox, *American Oratorios and Cantatas: A Catalog of Works Written in the United States from Colonial Times to 1985* (Metuchen, NJ: Scarecrow Press, 1986), lists

nineteen works by Peterson (pp. 868–872). By the beginning of the 1980s, Peterson's cantatas were beginning to lose favor and as of this writing, they have almost entirely disappeared from the repertoire of evangelical churches.

24 One of his most successful tunes for the lyrics of another poet was "So Send I You" to words by Margaret Clarkson.

25 See Stansbury, "The Music of the Billy Graham Crusades," 216.

26 Stylistically, the solo is reminiscent of "Climb Every Mountain" from Rogers and Hammerstein's *The Sound of Music* and Mitch Leigh's "The Impossible Dream" ("The Quest") from *Man of LaMancha*. Another "inspirational" song from approximately the same era that exhibits similar traits is "I Believe" (Shirl/Graham/Drake/Stillman).

27 The *Baptist Hymnal* 1991 included three Peterson songs, more than practically any other denominational hymnal of the late twentieth century: *Heaven Came Down* (#438), "So Send I You" (#565), and "Surely Goodness and Mercy" (#422).

28 See *Hymns for the Family of God* (Nashville: Paragon Associates, 1976), #501.

29 Many of Stanphill's songs were self-published, especially early in his career, and the principal advertising they received was his own singing of them in revivals for which he was the featured musician.

30 This figure does not include prose writings found in the hymnal (many of them by Gloria Gaither) and omits pieces in which their role was minimal e.g., the alteration of a single stanza in "O Happy Day," #649. A number of the Gaithers's songs were co-written with other authors and composers. Hymn numbers in the following discussion refer to this collection.

31 The importance of the Southern gospel tradition in the work of Bill Gaither is well defined in his autobiography (written with Ken Abraham), *It's More Than the Music: Life Lessons for Loving God, Loving Each Other* (N.pl.: Warner Faith, 2003), particularly chapter two.

32 For a recent study of the Southern gospel tradition and the role of the Gaithers, see Douglas Harrison, *Then Sings my Soul: The Culture of Southern Gospel Music* (Champaign, IL: Univeristy of Illinois Press, 2012).

33 A collection of Clarkson's texts was issued by Hope Publishing Company in 1987 under the title *A Singing Heart*.

34 The dates are derived principally from the copyrights of the songs. Some songs that were written and copyrighted before 1980 did not appear in hymnals for another decade or so e.g., David Danner's *Jesus Is the Song*.

35 "Evangelistic" and "evangelical" are not synonyms. An evangelical church is one that claims that salvation comes by grace through faith. An evangelistic church is geared toward spreading that message to others. Thus, all evangelistic churches may be termed "evangelical," but not all evangelical churches are "evangelistic."

36 See *Rain Down* (#444). The hymnal did contain several texts by Margaret Clarkson that had been written in the 1980s but these showed few characteristics of revival hymnody (for example, only one of them contained a refrain [#142]).

37 For example, the tune BECK ("Lord, Here Am I") by John Ness Beck (1930–1987) is most assuredly in gospel style, but the composer was known primarily as a composer of anthem literature in a musically sophisticated idiom, not as a writer of gospel hymns.

38 All four are found in *Worship & Rejoice* (Carol Stream, IL: Hope Publishing Company, 2001), #s 559, 319, 117, and 568, respectively.

Stream Five
Folk Hymnody

Chapter 5

Dance then Wherever You May Be: Folk Hymnody

Deborah Carlton Loftis

Folk music has long been incorporated into congregational singing. From the medieval carol to Ralph Vaughan Williams's (1872–1958) reharmonizations of English folk melodies, anonymous words and melodies passed down through generations of aural transmission have strengthened Christian worship. By definition, folk music is music "of the people"—that is, words and melodies whose original composers are unknown. Indeed, the process of transmission often shapes the song with changes or additions in the text and melody over time. Individuals, both the original composer and subsequent "editors," are unimportant for folk music; rather, folk music is the expression of a particular culture. A song's survival over time, transmitted by one singer teaching another, attests to its value to that culture. In the late twentieth century, however, the concept of folk song expanded to include works by a known author that were composed in the *style* of earlier traditional folk songs. These songs, although often still passed from one singer to another, appeared in print right from the beginning so that the composer's name remains associated with the song.

A description of the style of folk hymns includes consideration of textual and musical characteristics. The texts are often narrative, telling a story, as with the ballads of secular folk songs. The narrative can be a biblical story or a retelling of a believer's experience. Folk hymns can also center on social concerns, challenging the status quo of religion and advocating for justice and peace making. The language is simple and direct, even conversational, in tone and lacking sophisticated, finely crafted poetic devices. Repetitions of phrases or entire lines of text aid the memory and allow for improvisatory added stanzas. Many folk songs incorporate a refrain or chorus.

The melodies of folk songs are also simple in structure: tonal and diatonic with little chromaticism. Despite their simplicity, these melodies are strong and durable. John Ylvisaker, (b. 1937) in describing his process of the ways tunes can be adapted to encourage congregational singing, offers an accurate description of what happens naturally over time with folk tunes:

> We have examined several ways of altering tunes, such as changing meter, changing rhythm, adding pick-up notes to the beginning of each phrase, adding a chorus where there was none, simplifying an ornate melody, weaving a familiar tune into an original composition, and cutting a tune in half. It may seem like cruel and unusual punishment, but have no fear, these tunes are indestructible. That is why they are still being sung.[1]

These indestructible tunes are conceived vocally and can be sung unaccompanied without depending on harmonization for interest. The melodic contours are predictable but satisfying and fall comfortably within the vocal range of most singers, often using a "gapped" scale of five or six tones (pentatonic and hexatonic). Melodies usually can be harmonized with just tonic, dominant, and subdominant chords, although other diatonic chords can be (and usually are) added for color and variety. Though hymnals may provide keyboard accompaniments, songs in the folk tradition are flexible. They are often accompanied by guitar, but a variety of instruments, or no instrumentation, could be used. As Ylvisaker concludes, "The beauty of folk music (and folk-like music) is that it sounds good with any sort of accompaniment. Whatever a church group has in terms in instruments, that is what works. It always seems to be just fine."[2] Given the broad range of possible instrumentation, the folk style is essentially an acoustic idiom that is accessible not only to highly proficient musicians, but also to those with basic musical skills. The genre focuses on group participation rather than requiring a polished solo performance.

The folk stream in twentieth-century congregational singing includes texts set to traditional folk melodies as well as recently composed works by known composers. The words and melodies of hymns in this folk-like style are most often composed together by one author/composer. This circumstance would set them apart from classical hymn writing in which the words and tunes are usually composed separately and subsequently paired together.

Historical Antecedents

Before examining the current folk-song style in congregational singing, let us look at some historical examples of traditional folk music incorporated into the church's worship. These traditional folk styles continue to be used and they influence the "composed" folk songs in current usage.

The Carol

The medieval carol developed in village life and not as a part of the church's liturgy. They were devotional and often joyous in nature and may at first have been associated with dancing.[3] Only gradually did the songs move into the corporate worship setting of English-speaking congregations, largely due to the work of John Mason Neale (1818–866), Thomas Helmore (1811–1890) and other leaders of the Oxford Movement in the nineteenth century. Their interest in historical research and reverence for things ancient led to the translation and adoption of many old carols for congregational use in England.[4] The text, "Oh love, how deep, how broad, how high" [*Panorama*: 167B] attributed to Thomas á Kempis, was translated by Neale and paired with the ancient English tune for "The Agincourt Song" (DEO GRACIAS), which celebrated the victory of King Henry V. "In dulci jubilo" known to us through Neale's translation, "Good Christian Men (Friends) Rejoice," is a macaronic carol, a mixture of two languages, from fourteenth-century Germany. *Christmas Carols New and Old,* by H. R. Bramley and John Stainer (1871 and enlarged in 1878) included a number of traditional carols, among them, "God Rest You Merry Gentlemen," "I Saw Three Ships," "The Angel Gabriel," and "A Virgin Unspotted." This book of carols, with both traditional and newly composed carols, held popular sway for fifty years until the *Oxford Book of Carols* appeared in 1928.[5] European carols came into British use largely through *Piae Cantiones,* printed in Finland in 1562. G. J. R. Gordon, working for the British government in Stockholm, brought the rare volume to England in 1853 and gave it to John Mason Neale.[6] The collection is the source for several popular tunes, including DIVINUM MYSTERIUM (in a rhythmic dance mode)[7] with "Of the Father's love begotten" [*Panorama*: 155B] and TEMPUS ADEST FLORIDIUM with "Good King Wenceslas" and "Gentle Mary Laid Her Child."

Wesley's Use of Folk Tunes

Charles's hymn texts used quite a few different poetic meters, so John Wesley looked for good hymn tunes wherever he could find them. Because singing was such a vital part of the Wesleys' evangelical reforms, John favored simple melodies that could easily be sung by the people, avoiding complex fuging tunes and anthems favored by some. Not only did he use tunes by Handel and other professional composers, John Wesley (1703–1791) incorporated folk tunes, but also often adapted them for hymn tunes by amateur Methodist musicians, in his three major collections of music, known popularly as the *Foundery Collection* (1742), *Sacred Melody* (1761) and *Sacred Harmony* (1780).[8] Charles Wesley (1707–1788) also used folk songs as a basis for his texts as is revealed in a well-known account of his hymn, "The True Use of Musik." The story goes that a group of rowdy sailors and soldiers interrupted the outdoor service by singing a lewd song, "Nancy Dawson." At the next meeting, Wesley had composed a new text for the tune that the gathered group sang in response to the earlier interruption. As the story is related in several sources, it is plausible that the event may have occurred in Plymouth in 1746.[9] The hymn was published in 1749 in

Hymns and Sacred Poems and appeared in America in Jeremiah Ingalls's (1764–1838) *Christian Harmony* (1805) as "Innocent Sounds."[10]

American Folk Hymnody in the Eighteenth and Nineteenth Centuries

Folk hymnody appeared early in the United States. Joshua Smith's (1760–1795) *Divine Hymns or Spiritual Songs,* published around 1784 with later editions from 1791, contained a number of anonymous folk hymn texts interspersed among works by British writers. These anonymous texts fell into two groups: either patterned after John Cennick (1718–1755), John Newton (1725–1807), and the Wesleys, or in the style of secular folk ballads. Similar collections followed, notably those by Josiah Goddard (1813–1854) in New Hampshire, Andrew Broaddus (1789–1848) in Virginia and Jesse Mercer (1769–1841) in Georgia. These books show that a body of folk hymn texts was circulating prior to the beginning of the Second Great Awakening.[11]

It was during the Second Great Awakening, however, that the most important flowering of folk hymnody took place. Starting in 1800, the frontier camp meeting was at the center of a religious revival, attracting thousands for protracted meetings of preaching and singing. During those gatherings, song leaders depended on short improvised songs, a call-and-response style of singing, and familiar tunes. These techniques enabled the crowds to sing together, overcoming the barriers of widespread illiteracy and the lack of sufficient numbers of hymnals or songbooks. The improvised choruses and added refrains place camp-meeting songs in the folk genre because they were taught and passed on orally before ever being collected in printed collections. It was during these camp meetings that folk tunes, many of which can be traced to "families" of British secular folk tunes, were paired with both folk texts and standard British hymn texts. Several types of folk hymns emerged from the camp meeting.[12]

Improvised Songs and Spirituals

These songs were often ephemeral, used in the moment and not preserved. Some enjoyed a brief life span in camp-meeting "songsters" published in the early decades of the century. One group of songs, however, that did survive is the spiritual. Both black and white Christians were present at the camp meetings and spirituals arose from both groups, likely mingling and influencing each other in style. Spiritual texts often incorporated a significant amount of textual repetition within a form that allowed for new stanzas to be added at will. Two very common forms were *aaba* ("Were You There When They Crucified My Lord?" [*Panorama*: 394]) and *aaab* ("Where Are the Hebrew Children?" [*Panorama*: 401]). New stanzas can be easily added and all singers can quickly join in because of the template structure of the stanza.

Call-and-response style also allowed for great flexibility in adding stanzas and easy participation from the crowds. In the spiritual, *Certainly, Lord,* the leader asks a question to which the group replies, "certainly, Lord." The leader can continue to insert new questions as long as the group's enthusiasm holds.

> Have you got good religion? *Certainly, Lord!*
> Have you got good religion? *Certainly, Lord!*
> Have you got good religion? *Certainly, Lord!*
> *Certainly, certainly, certainly, Lord!*

Repetitions are also important in white spirituals. The predictability of the repetitions allow singers to participate, even as they are first learning the hymn.

> What wondrous love is this, oh, my soul, oh my soul?
> What wondrous love is this, oh my soul?
> What wondrous love is this that caused the Lord of bliss
> To lay aside his crown for my soul, for my soul
> To lay aside his crown for my soul. [See *Panorama*: 399 for entire text]

Additions to a Pre-Existent or "Mother" Hymn

During the spirited singing at the camp meeting, there was little thought for the integrity of authorship. Liberties were taken with standard hymn texts, altering them and adding new text. A chorus, whose words typified the spirit of the camp meeting was added to Robert Robinson's (1735–1790) text, "Come, Thou Fount of Every Blessing."

> Come, thou fount of every blessing,
> Tune my heart to sing Thy grace;
> Streams of mercy, never ceasing,
> Call for songs of loudest praise.
> *I am bound for the kingdom,*
> *Will you go to glory with me?*
> *Hallelujah, praise the Lord.*

In Charles Wesley's classic text, "O for a thousand tongues to sing" [See *Panorama*: 60 for complete text], the second and fourth phrases of each stanza are omitted and an interrupting refrain is substituted. To this revised stanza, a chorus of repeated phrases is added.[13]

> O for a thousand tongues to sing, *Blessed be the name of the Lord!*
> The glories of my God and King, *Blessed be the name of the Lord!*
> *Blessed be the name, Blessed be the name, Blessed be the name of the Lord!*
> *Blessed be the name, Blessed be the name, Blessed be the name of the Lord!*

Occasionally, entire stanzas were added to standard hymns. The best-known example is the last stanza of "Amazing Grace" as it is commonly sung today. John Newton's text does not include the familiar words, "When we've been there ten thousand years…." Those words comprised the closing stanza for the very popular anonymous text, "Jerusalem, my happy home"[14] [*Panorama*: 410] In 1910 E. O. Excell (1851–1921) published Newton's three stanzas with this anonymous fourth stanza.[15] With his keen sense of marketability, always looking for popular songs to publish, Excell must have known that the hymn was already being sung with the added stanza. Because of Excell's prominence in the publishing of congregational song, his version most likely influenced the subsequent printings of the hymn.

Use of Folk Melodies

Perhaps the most important folk legacy from the camp-meeting era is the pairing of folk tunes with standard hymn texts. Many of these melodies have been traced to secular folk song origins.[16] The texts and tunes of the revival hymnody were published primarily in shape-note tune books. Tunebook compilers were always looking for popular tunes in order to make the latest edition of their tune book appealing and increase sales. Two of the earliest tune books containing a significant body of folk hymnody were John Wyeth's (1770–1858) *Repository of Sacred Music, Part Second* (Harrisburg, PA, 1813) and Ananias Davisson's (1780–1857) *Supplement to the Kentucky Harmony* (Harrisonburg, VA, 1820). In 1831 James P. Carrell (1757–1854) and David L. Clayton (1801–1854) published *The Virginia Harmony*. Though Carrell deplored his contemporaries' use of "light airs" for sacred music, his tune book included a significant number of folk hymns, including the current tune for "Amazing grace, how sweet the sound," though set to a different text. That folk tune appeared in a number of publications, variously known as NEW BRITAIN, and HARMONY GROVE. Of wider circulation and longer lasting influence, however, were William Walker's (1809–1875) *Southern Harmony and Musical Companion* (Spartanburg, SC; printed in New Haven, CT, 1835) and Benjamin Franklin White (1800–1879) and E. J. King's (c. 1821–1844) *The Sacred Harp* (Hamilton, GA; printed in Philadelphia, 1844). *The Southern Harmony* first published the folk hymn "What wondrous love is this" cited earlier and is also the earliest publication linking "Amazing grace, how sweet the sound" with its now well-known folk tune.

In current hymnals, editors have mined these nineteenth-century tune books for their treasure of strong, singable folk tunes, using these melodies for newly written hymn texts. Twelve of the most frequently used tunes are discussed by Harry Eskew and Hugh T. McElrath in *Sing with Understanding* and include BEACH SPRING, BOURBON, CONSOLATION (MORNING SONG), DETROIT, FOUNDATION, HOLY MANNA, KEDRON, NETTLETON, NEW BRITAIN (AMAZING GRACE), RESTORATION, TWENTY-FOURTH (DUNLAP'S CREEK), WONDROUS LOVE.[17] The trend toward using tunes from the shape-note tradition continues. One of the most recently published hymnals, *Worship & Rejoice* (Hope, 2001), includes twelve tunes, though not exactly the twelve above. Another indication of the popularity and strength of these tunes is their inclusion in hymnals published outside the United States. The Australian hymnal, *Together in Song* (HarperCollins, 1999) includes five tunes and the newest edition of the Church of Scotland's *Church Hymnary*, fourth edition (Canterbury Press, 2005) includes thirteen.

British Folk Hymnody in the Twentieth Century

In the first half of the twentieth century, several collections were published that underscored a renewed interest in English folk songs. *The English Hymnal* (London, 1906), the first of these works, was widely used for decades. Edited by Percy Dearmer (1867–1936), it was a notable hymnal in a number of ways, but the musical editor, Ralph Vaughan Williams, made a significant contribution through the fine quality of tunes he included. Paul Westermeyer describes Vaughan Williams and his work in this way:

> [A] rare first-rate composer who understood and supported congregational song. No other composer of his stature lavished such effort on hymn tunes. He was the musical editor for a remarkable hymnal, mined folk song for its hymnic possibilities, and wrote and arranged tunes in which congregations have delighted.[18]

In the introduction to the 1933 edition of the hymnal with tunes, Vaughan Williams outlined the broad range of sources for the tunes. Traditional, or folk, melodies figure significantly, coming from all over Europe (German, French, Swiss, Italian, Spanish, Flemish, Dutch), America, and the British Isles.[19] Among the English traditional melodies, KINGSFOLD, KING'S LYNN, and FOREST GREEN continue to be used in current hymnals.

Dearmer, along with musical editors Vaughan Williams and Martin Shaw, (1875–1958) also produced *Songs of Praise*, first published in 1925, with an enlarged edition following in 1931. In addition to the tunes listed above from the American shape-note tradition, the 1931 edition includes

ES IST EIN' ROS ENTSPRUNGEN from Germany, all of which remain in widespread use. It was during this period as well that *The Oxford Book of Carols* (London, 1928) was first published, bringing even more attention to folk melodies that had gone unnoticed for generations.[20]

Twentieth-Century Influences on the Current Folk Style of Congregational Song

In order to understand the stream of folk hymnody flourishing in the late twentieth and into the twenty-first century, it is necessary to step back and explore how traditional folk music gained prestige and popularity through scholarly research. In the last decades of the nineteenth century, Harvard professor Francis James Child's (1825–1896) brilliant and thorough five-volume compilation *The English and Scottish Popular Ballads* provided full texts (not music) and commentary on 305 ballads, with one-third of the variants coming from American sources. Child showed that these ballads were not dusty old relics, but a living expression of the people.[21] Just a few years later, Cecil Sharp (1859–1924) focused on the musical tradition and produced *English Folk Song: Some Conclusions* (1907) and *Folk Songs of the Southern Appalachians* (1917).[22] By 1928, Robert Winslow Gordon had engineered the establishment of the Archive of American Folk Song at the Library of Congress in Washington, D.C. Gordon's successor, John A. Lomax (1867–1948), and his son, Alan Lomax (1915–2002), became advocates for the music of the common people. In their estimation, the purity of transmission of the folk songs was endangered because of the rapid exploitation of the music for commercial purposes. Radio and phonograph recordings, even printed music, pushed the transmission of folk songs beyond the geographic confines of oral transmission. In order to capture the folk songs in their most pristine forms, the Lomaxes traveled to many isolated places and amassed large numbers of field recordings. In 1941, Alan Lomax began to release a series of these field recordings through the Archive of American Folk Song, and produced nationally syndicated radio shows for CBS. Perhaps one of Alan Lomax's greatest contributions to folk song was his "discovery" of Woody Guthrie (1912–1967). Lomax invited Guthrie to Washington, D. C. to record some of his huge repertory. Without the benefit (or hindrance, perhaps) of formal schooling, Guthrie wrote and sang over a thousand songs, accompanying himself on guitar. Of his style, Lomax said that he was,

> [S]omeone who understood the power and integrity of the traditional forms and sang the old songs in an old-fashioned way, his voice droning and nasal and high-pitched. At the same time, and even more miraculously, he was a political radical . . . those were political songs he was singing in traditional fashion. . . . His songs had the beautiful, easy-to-remember simplicity of the best of folk art....[23]

At the Archive, Guthrie met Pete Seeger and they formed, with several others, "The Almanacs," described as the first urban folk-singing group.[24] Other folk-singing groups proliferated through the fifties and early sixties: The Weavers, the Kingston Trio, the New Christy Minstrels, and the Brothers Four, to cite just a few examples. As they sang on college campuses and made commercial recordings, folk music became even more a part of the cultural fabric of young Americans.

By the early 1960s, as societal shifts focused on civil rights and on protests against the war in Vietnam, folk singers were positioned to voice the concerns of young adults. Bob Dylan (b. 1941) provided the link to the political heritage of the 1930s when he modeled himself after Woody Guthrie. He sang Guthrie's songs, listened to his albums and even made a poignant pilgrimage to seek out the aging Guthrie.[25] Dylan was not the only folk singer concerned about social travails. Richard Crawford succinctly summed up the situation as he described the closing of the Newport Folk Festival of 1963.

> The evening concert ended with Dylan, Baez, Pete Seeger, Theodore Bikel, the folk trio Peter, Paul, and Mary, and the Freedom Singers, an African-American group from the South featuring Cordell Reagon and Bernice Johnson, joining together for a grand finale on *We Shall Overcome*, the anthem

of the Civil Rights Movement. In August of that year, the same group of performers cemented the folk revival's link with the Civil Rights Movement as they gathered to sing during a march on Washington, which culminated in the Reverend Martin Luther King's historic "I Have a Dream" speech on the steps of the Lincoln Memorial.[26]

Whether singing protests against the war with Dylan's "Blowing in the Wind," or Pete Seeger's (b. 1919) "Where Have All the Flowers Gone?" or extolling the bravery of fighting forces with songs such as Sgt. Barry Sadler's (1940–1989) "Ballad of the Green Berets," songs in the folk style helped Americans express their sentiments about U.S. involvement in Vietnam.

Within the Church, Vatican II changes in Catholic liturgy emphasized vernacular languages rather than Latin leading to a scramble to provide songs in English for the new English liturgy. Church leaders, both Catholic and Protestant, expressed a hope that a new style of song would attract young people and encourage them to return to worship. Simple folk songs, accompanied by guitars, provided an appealing solution. Over time, what started, perhaps, as a temporary measure was refined by Catholic musicians and blossomed into the lyric forms described in the Catholic Liturgical Renewal stream in chapter one. One of the earliest expressions of the new style was Geoffrey Beaumont's (1903–1970) *Twentieth-Century Folk Mass* (1960). A member of the Light Music Group of the Church of England, Beaumont believed that worship should include popular styles of the day. In the United States, Ray Repp has been described as "the person most responsible for introducing folk music and the guitar into Christian Churches." His *Mass for Young Americans* made a significant impact on congregations when it was introduced in 1965 and his subsequent collections of songs continue to influence congregational singing.[27]

In evangelical Churches, the advent in the late sixties of folk musicals such as *Good News, Tell It Like It Is,* and *Purpose*[28] began to attract large numbers of teenagers with their catchy tunes and instrumental accompaniments provided by guitars, keyboards, and drums. As will be shown shortly, some individual songs from these musicals shifted into the repertoire of congregational song. The church, once again, incorporated the appealing style of folk music. We turn now to explore the composers who combine these threads of folk music and create songs in a folk style for the twenty-first century.

Twenty-First Century Folk Hymnody: Representative Composers and Works

In discussing the hymns in this section, references to sources will be given in brackets following the title. Inclusion of that hymn in Routley's *English Speaking Hymnal Guide* [ESHG] and *Panorama of Christian Hymnody* [PCH] will be noted first. In addition to the hymnals referenced in the *Hymnal Guide*, several additional hymnals and denominational supplements are included here to expand the reader's access to full text and tune. The key to these abbreviations may be found at the end of the chapter.

Sydney Bertram Carter (1915–2004) was one of the most influential figures in British folk music. Born in London and educated at Balliol College, Oxford, Carter began his career as poet and folk singer in the 1950s in the secular realm of television and cabaret. The most complete collection of his songs, *Green Print for Song* (1963), containing comments and explanations is out of print but still available are *Songs of Sydney Carter: In the Present Tense* (5 vols.) and *Lord of the Dance* and other songs and poems (with companion CD). After his death, his publisher, Stainer & Bell, posted this statement on their Web site:

> By nature a radical, Sydney was no stranger to controversy, and for a long period after joining the Stainer & Bell 'family' he remained a marginal figure, outside the theological establishment. That his work now belongs firmly in the mainstream of worship material used in churches and schools worldwide is a potent symbol both of evolving attitudes in society and of the integrity and scope of his vision.[29]

Carter's songs continue to be sung around the globe, especially "One More Step," [ESHG689], which, in 1996, was determined to be the most frequently sung copyright song in school assemblies in the UK,[30] along with his best known, "I danced in the morning" (*Lord of the Dance*) [ESHG385, WR118, WOVNZ183]

In 1963, Carter composed *Lord of the Dance*, his carol about the death and resurrection of Jesus, adapting the melody of American Shaker tune, SIMPLE GIFTS ("Tis the gift to be simple"). Published first in *9 Carols or Ballads* (1964), it was based upon the Cornish carol, "Tomorrow Shall be My Dancing Day,"[31] one of the folk songs that gained popularity through the publishing efforts of the Oxford Movement described earlier.

Written in 1959, but first published in *9 Carols or Ballads*, "It Was on a Friday Morning" [*Panorama*: 523] reveals Carter as a man standing at the edges of faith, lashing out at the shocking injustice of the crucifixion, expressing doubts about the nature of God's goodness. Written as the voice of one of those crucified beside Jesus, the ironic words are harsh:

> To hell with Jehovah,
> > to the carpenter I said,
> I wish that a carpenter
> > had made the world instead.

The refrain adds to the bitterness:

> "It's God they ought to crucify
> > instead of you and me."
> I said to the carpenter
> > a-hanging on the tree.

Though some were offended by its tone, Erik Routley defended Carter: "he is a folk poet in that he expresses the unexpressed thoughts of ordinary human beings about Jesus, about grief, about the church, and even about the cross. He exposes them as alarmingly as this."[32] The crucified thief dares to wonder if evil is a part of God's plan and judges that God is idly watching this cruel execution. More than forty-five years after its creation, this hymn's dark tone still disturbs.

Kurt Frederic Kaiser (b. 1934), composer, arranger, and recording artist, is credited with 200 copyrighted songs. Educated at the American Conservatory of Music and Northwestern University, he has been honored by the American Society of Composers, Authors, and Publishers (ASCAP) and the Gospel Music Hall of Fame. Since 1959, Kaiser has been associated with Word Publishing Company, first as Director of Artists and Repertoire and later as Vice President and Director of Music. Kaiser was involved in the youth folk musical movement from the beginning. In collaboration with Ralph Carmichael (b. 1927), Kaiser produced *Tell It Like It Is* (1969), *Natural High* (1969), and *I'm Here, God's Here, Now We Can Start* (1973).[33]

In this writer's experience "It Only Takes a Spark," commonly known as *Pass It On* [ESHG430] was the emotional peak in *Tell It Like It Is*. At that point in the musical, an altar call was often given and streams of young people came forward to accept Christ or rededicate their lives. Reminiscent of large evangelical rallies, the song usually had to be sung more than once to allow for the large response. The song quickly moved outside the bounds of the musical to be sung in youth retreats and worship settings. By the mid-1970s, *Pass It On* was included in two new hymnals: *Hymns for the Living Church* (Hope, 1974) and *Baptist Hymnal* (Convention, 1975). That song, along with "Oh, how he loves you and me," a short chorus written in a matter of moments in 1975,[34] continue to used in evangelical settings.[35]

The composing team of Avery & Marsh made a significant impact as contemporary worship specialists in the 1960s. Richard Kinsey Avery (b. 1934) received his B.A. from the University of Redlands and his divinity degree from Union Theological Seminary in New York.[36] Donald Stuart Marsh (b. 1923) attended Western Maryland University, the University of Houston and Theodora Irvine School of Drama. In 1960, both men joined the ministerial staff of the First Presbyterian Church in Port Jervis, New York, Avery as pastor and Marsh as choirmaster and Director of Arts in Christian Education.[37] Working together, the two men published 150 hymn texts and tunes. In addition to completely original hymns, Avery and Marsh also reset traditional texts with contemporary tunes.[38] "Praise God from whom all blessings flow" [PH 593], and "Glory be to the Father" [PH577, WOVNZ675] were published first in *Hymns Hot and Carols Cool*.[39]

Regarding their setting of the traditional Doxology, Donald Hustad relates that the writers "'felt the need for a merry, lively tune' for these classic words", to be sung when "events in history or in our personal and corporate life inspire light-hearted and over-flowing joy. The calypso style of Spanish cultures seems a good style for expression of these feelings."[40]

Their best-known original text and tune, "We Are the Church" [CH204, UMH558, WR550,], acknowledges that the church is comprised of all believers, in all times and all places. The genius of the songs of Avery and Marsh was that they were simple and groups of singers could join in immediately. Their technique is demonstrated in the tune for "We Are the Church," which uses phrases repeated exactly and phrases in sequence (repeating a melodic motif but starting a step higher or lower) to help singers pick up the tune quickly.

Another important early contribution to the folk genre was made by Karen Lafferty, (b. 1948). Born in Alamagordo, New Mexico, and educated at Eastern New Mexico University, Lafferty became worship leader and concert artist at Calvary Chapel, Costa Mesa, California, in 1971.[41] Although she soon migrated to a more electronic sound in her work with Maranatha! Music (her contribution to Contemporary Christian Music is discussed more fully in stream six), her first and most popular song, "Seek Ye First" [ESHG744, CH641, WOVL783] belongs to the folk tradition. Written in 1971 following a Bible study on Mathew 6:33, the text is taken directly from the King James Version of scripture. The short, simple melody is stated twice to accommodate the text and an "alleluia" descant adds a sense of ethereal tranquility. Carlton Young states that the song was shared informally and soon became a standard song of the "Jesus movement." True to the genre's propensity for variation and accretions, an anonymous second stanza and the descant first appeared in print in 1980.[42]

John Ylvisaker (b. 1937) is a native of Moorhead, Minnesota, and a graduate of Concordia College in his hometown. A prolific composer of 1000 songs, writer on worship, and highly sought after conference leader, Ylvisaker has also directed church choirs and produced a weekly radio program sponsored by the Evangelical Lutheran Church in America. In his collection, *Borning Cry* (2 vols. 2000, 2003) Ylvisaker offers 900 hymns and songs in a wide variety of musical styles. He advocates using traditional song, both American and songs from other cultures, blended with new words and adapted in its accompaniment as an approach to ending the recent "worship wars" over musical style in congregations. This approach, Ylvisaker argues, has been used effectively by the church for generations and offers rich possibilities for future congregational singing.[43] His ballad-like hymn, "I was there to hear your borning cry" [CHAL75; FWS2051; NCeH351; VU644; WOVL770; WR680] celebrates the presence of God through all the stages of life from birth to baptism, from rebellious youth to midlife and old age. There is even an eschatological reassurance that at the end, God will still be present with "just one more surprise." The melody has a lilting motion, one stanza flowing seamlessly into the next, which summons the image of a parent rocking and crooning to a beloved child.

Jim Strathdee (b. 1941) and his wife, Jean, are active concert artists and worship leaders. Together they have written 400 songs, hymns, and anthems. Their work blends concert touring alongside serving for many years as Directors of Music at St. Mark's United Methodist Church in Sacramento, California. They tour not only the United States and Canada on a regular basis, but also have "a longtime connection to churches in Central America, and have done several tours there, singing their songs in Spanish translation."[44] Among current hymnals, the most selections by Strathdee (10) may be found in *Voices United*. *Chalice Hymnal*, along with its complementary volume, *Chalice Praise*, includes nine compositions. The two most commonly included works are the lively hymn, "I am the light of the world" [CHAL469; NCeH584; WOVNZ669; VU87] and a short setting of Micah 6:8, "What does the Lord require of you?" [CHAL661; FWS2174; TIS751; VU701]. In 1969, in response to a Christmas poem by twentieth-century writer, theologian, and teacher Howard Thurman,[45] Strathdee wrote "I Am the Light of the World." Though the text begins with Christmas, the hymn calls us to look at the year-long task of following Jesus. Through each repetition of the refrain, singers are reminded of Jesus' imperative, "You people come and follow me!" Through that journey, Jesus' followers learn to "do and be."

In his setting of Micah 6:8, Strathdee provides a lovely three-part texture with the calm repetitions of a Taizé-like chant and replete with possibilities for improvisation. The first eight bars are sung by all and the congregation continues to repeat this short passage as the other two parts enter at eight-measure intervals. Parts two and three can be sung by groups within the congregation or by soloists or by the choir, making the performance of this song very adaptable to the musical expertise of the congregation.

Example 5:1

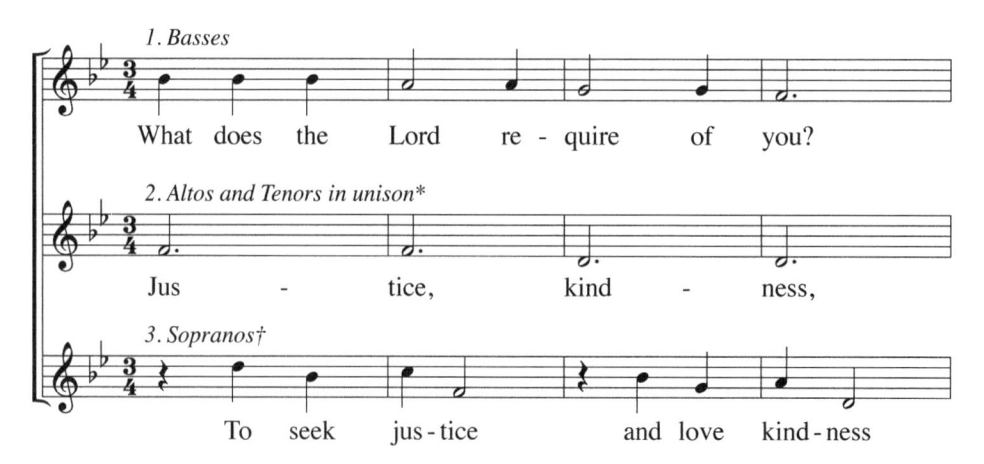

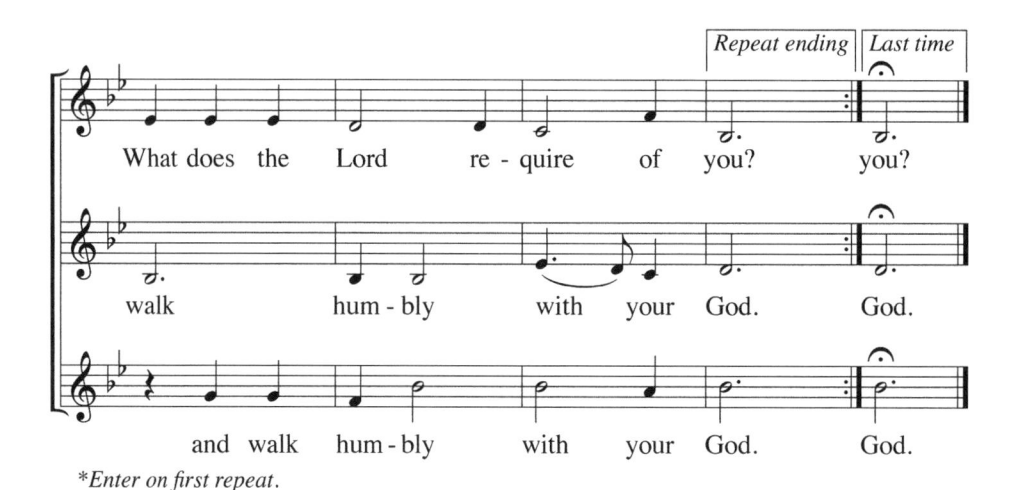

*Enter on first repeat.
†Enter on second repeat.

© 1986 Desert Flower Music

Gordon Light (b. 1944) was born in Alberta, Canada, and raised in Ontario. An Anglican bishop, he is married to an Anglican priest. In the mid-1980s in Winnipeg, Light, along with Bob Wallace, Jim Uhrich, and Ian Macdonald, all clergy in neighboring parishes, formed a music and ministry group, The Common Cup Company.[46] On the Common Cup Web site that is liberally sprinkled with humor, members of the group related their memories of the early days of singing together. Ian Macdonald remembered:

> It felt important to get together, to sing. Which is why we did a (first) concert in 1987 in Kamloops. And, that wound up getting "She Flies On" into the green book (Songs for a Gospel People), and that really surprised us. Gord had already given up on the song. We did it that once, and that was the time Ralph Milton was in the audience. He came running up on stage to get it. He grabbed the sheet right off Gordon's stand.[47]

Though the men are quick to joke, they are quite serious about the songs they write and sing. Gordon Light described something of his process of writing:

> Sometimes I write to push myself over the brink, to go past a margin that's been there for me. So "Draw the Circle Wide" is a very important song for me. It pushes me to take some personal responsibility.... To write and sing "She Flies On" pushed me to say it was okay to use feminine imagery for God. After that, I didn't feel uncomfortable.... I think sometimes that to put something new down and to sing it, I've said something to myself. It's allowed me to go further in my own faith than I've gone before....[48]

"She Comes Sailing on the Wind" (*She Flies On*) [VU380; FWS2122] recounts the work of the Holy Spirit in creation, in the life of the prophets, and in the birth, ministry, and resurrection of Jesus. "Draw the Circle Wide" [SA16] is a song about the inclusive community of Christ. The words of the refrain sum up Light's intention: "Let this be our song, no one stands alone, standing side by side."

"Joy Comes with the Dawn" [FWS2210; VU166] takes its inspiration from Psalm 30, especially verse 5: "Weeping may linger for the night, but joy comes with the morning." [NRSV] In the melody, Light incorporates a rest on the downbeat at the beginning of each phrase, bringing the voices in on beat two. This technique, used often in pop styles, along with the guitar-like broken-chord accompaniment, contributes to the rolling nature of the tune. (See Example 5:2, page 151)

Another Canadian, Ron Klusmeier (b. 1946), has also recently made several contributions to this stream. A United Church of Canada minister from Vancouver, he has contributed folk-style musical settings to the texts of several prominent twentieth-century (stream two) hymn writers such as Ruth Duck, Walter Farquharson, Fred Kaan, Shirley Erena Murray, and Brian Wren in the current United Church hymnals, *Voices United* (1996) and *More Voices* (2007).

Three musicians that are closely associated with the Roman Catholic Liturgical Renewal stream also warrant discussion as a part of this folk stream. Marty Haugen (b. 1950), a Protestant, has worked closely within Catholic circles to produce liturgical music for the Mass and other services as well as numerous hymns. His name appears frequently on the pages of *Gather*, *Worship* (3d edition), and *Ritual Song*, recent hymnals published by GIA Publications, Inc.. Many of his hymns have also found a home within Protestant congregations and are included in a wide range of hymnals. "Awake! Awake, and Greet the New Morn" [ESHG66, WR160, WOVL633] is a lilting carol for Advent. The text reassures that despite the cheerless winter and despairing darkness, Christ comes as warm and gentle morning light. The coming of the baby will restore wholeness and peace to us all:

> Then shall the silent join in song,
> the tired shall leap in wonder,
> the weak be raised above the strong,
> and weapons be broken asunder.[49]

Example 5:2

New Songs of Celebration Render ◆ Hawn

Verses

1. Weep-ing may come; weep-ing may come in the night, when dark shad-ows cloud our sight.
2. Sor-row will turn, sor-row will turn in-to song, and God's laugh-ter makes us strong.
3. We will re-joice, we will re-joice, and give praise, to the One who brings us grace.

Words and Music by Gordon Light © 1985 Common Cup Company

152

The melody, in 6/8 meter, opens with a rising fourth (from dominant to tonic) that is immediately repeated—surely an attention-getting clarion call. This motive is repeated through the tune, echoing the call to "awake" and contributing to the buoyancy of the melody.

"Healer of Our Every Ill" [ESHG337, FWS2213, WR630, WOVL738] is a prayer for wholeness. The stanzas outline the ways in which God's presence is needed in particular difficult situations and the refrain summarizes the gifts God offers: light, peace, and hope. The tune for the stanzas uses a dotted-rhythmic figure, repeated on four consecutive measures, subtly underscoring the halting pleas we make to God. The refrain, in contrast, uses a very even rhythm that confidently attests to God's response.

Perhaps one of Haugen's best-known hymns is "Here in This Place," (*Gather Us In*) [*Panorama*: 809, ESHG344, CH623, FWS2236, W&R649, WOVL718]. In this hymn about the church at worship, Haugen reminds us of the church's mission: "called to be light to the whole human race," and "call us anew to be salt for the earth." He also recalls the role of baptism and Eucharist as part of our worship experience, but the overarching theme of the hymn is the recognition that, through worship, God is the one who brings us together—the young and the old, male and female, rich and powerful, or lost and forsaken:

> Gather us in and hold us forever;
> > gather us in and make us your own;
> > gather us in, all peoples together,
> > > fire of love in our flesh and our bone.[50]

Each stanza is divided into halves: the first half describes something of the worship experience, the second half petitions God in various ways ("Gather us in," "Give us to drink," "Call to us now"). Haugen's melody aptly supports the text's construction. There is a sustained note at the end of the first half of the tune before launching into the second half, which opens with a very different melody—repeated tones for the words, "Gather us in." The form of the entire melody could be described as ABAB¹/CC¹AB¹. The combination of melodic repetition and variation make the tune engaging and memorable.

Cesáreo Gabaráin (1936–1991) was one of Spain's most prolific and liturgical composers. He was first a parish priest in Antzuola, near his birthplace, before working in Madrid with music and youth ministries in the parish of Our Lady of Sorrows. In addition, he served as Spanish chaplain to Pope Paul VI. In 1990, he traveled to the United States, where he led workshops in twenty-two cities. His many works and recordings are available from Oregon Catholic Press. Raquel Martínez, writing about Hispanic hymnody assessed Gabaráin's contribution to congregational singing:

> Gabaráin truly felt that the ministry of music is one of the noblest and most effective ministries in the life of the church. He enjoyed working with youth, causing his pastoral music styles to reflect a modern and youthful tone. Furthermore, he always sought to create texts that would enrich the faith of those who would sing them.[51]

"Tú Has Venido a la Orilla" (*Pescador de hombres*) [*Panorama*: 918, ESHG553, CH532, WR347, WOVL784] is certainly Gabaráin's best-known hymn. It has been translated into eighty languages. In English, the hymn is translated with several variants: "Lord, you have come to the lakeshore," "Lord, you have come to the seashore," or "You have come down to the lakeshore." Most hymnals provide both the original Spanish and an English translation. The text is based upon Jesus' call to Peter and Andrew to leave their fishing nets and become fishers of men, but is written in the first person so that the text becomes an acknowledgement that Jesus invites each of us to leave lesser pursuits behind and follow him.

"Una Espiga," in translation known as ["Sheaves of Summer"] or ["Grains of Wheat"] [*Panorama*: 917, ESHG749, WOVL708] is a communion hymn that stresses our unity as Christ's body. Just as individual grains of wheat and separate bunches of grapes are combined to create the bread and wine of the Eucharist, so are we bound together by God's love. The tune is bright and confident in character, each phrase beginning with a rising melodic line. The even rhythm and melodic repetition in the first half of the tune is balanced nicely with gentle syncopation, a dotted rhythm, and contrasting melodic material in the second half of the tune.

Suzanne Toolan, RSM (b. 1927) was born in Lansing, Michigan, and is a Sister of Mercy. She earned a masters degree in humanities and has enjoyed a career in teaching. In addition to her academic work, she has held various liturgy and music director positions in California, where she now resides. Currently, she leads the monthly Taizé evening prayer around the cross at Mercy Center, a retreat facility in Burlingame, though most Catholics know her as the composer of "I Am the Bread of Life" [ESHG376, WOV Lu703, WR703]. At GIA Publications, Inc. website, a story is told about the creation of that well-loved hymn written in 1966:

> A while back, she constructed some sketches for a eucharistic piece to be used at an upcoming archdiocesan event. Disappointed with the results, she tore up the manuscript and threw it into the waste can. Leaving the room, she encountered a freshman student who asked what she was playing. The student thought it was beautiful. Sister Suzanne rescued the shred and reworked it. The item was "I Am the Bread of Life," and it has certainly enjoyed a life of its own. It appears now in more hymnals and collections than any other title in the GIA catalog and has been translated into at least ten other languages.[52]

Based upon John 6, "I am the Bread of Life" features declamatory prose verses echoing the scripture passage that are best sung by a cantor or choir. The basic melodic shape remains constant, but the rhythm for each stanza varies slightly to accommodate the text as is the practice in chanting the psalms. The congregation joins on the rhythmically regular and tuneful refrain. Toolan's use of increasingly larger intervals leaping upward on the repeated phrase "And I will raise" creates within the singers a stirring hope to be raised up "on the last day." In keeping with the nature of folk transmission, there are variants in the settings, not only in the rhythmic outlines of the stanzas, but also in the wording of the refrain. In some cases, the refrain appears as:

> And I will raise you up, and I will raise you up,
> And I will raise you up on the last day.[53]

Other hymnals use the pronoun "them" in place of "you" throughout the refrain, and in one source, "them" is used except on stanza three in which "you" is specified.

Another of Toolan's hymns that is less widely published, but worthy of consideration is "Two Fishermen" [*Panorama*: 815, FWS2101, WC654, WSHP633]. The hymn tells the story of Jesus calling his disciples, naming not only the fishermen, "Simon Peter, Andrew, James, and John," but also women, "Susanna, Mary, Magdalene." Her text concludes by moving away from the biblical narrative to call present-day Christians to "leave behind what keeps you bound to trappings of our day." The folk-like character of the tune is reflected in its melodic structure. In a minor key and 6/8 meter, the melody opens on the upbeat with a rising dominant-tonic figure that continues then in a step-wise motion and includes the lowered seventh degree of the natural minor mode (5-1-2-3-2-1-7-1). The closing melodic figure of both the verse and the refrain also reflects a stock folk motif: (1-3-2-7-1). Overall, two phrases of melody, gently rising and falling in a stepwise motion, set the first half of the stanza and is then repeated for the second half. The short refrain departs from the established rhythmic pattern (quarter/eighth) momentarily but then returns to it, repeating the closing figure of the stanza.

Example 5:3

Verses

1. Two fish-er-men, who lived a-long / The Sea of Gal-i-lee, / Stood by the shore to / cast their nets In-to an age-less sea. / Now Je-sus watched them from a-far, / Then called them each by name. / It changed their lives, these sim-ple men; / They'd

2. And as he walked a-long the shore / 'Twas James and John he'd find, / And these two sons of / Zeb-e-dee Would leave their boats be-hind. / Their work and all they held so dear / They left be-side their / nets. Their names they'd heard as Je-sus called; / They

3. O Si-mon Pe-ter, An-drew, James, / And John be-lov-ed one, / You heard Christ's call to / speak good news Re-vealed to God's own Son. / Su-san-na, Mar-y, Mag-da-lene / Who trav-eled with your / Lord, You min-is-tered to him with joy / For

4. And you, good Chris-tians, one and all / Who'd fol-low Jesus' way, / Come leave be-hind what / keeps you bound To trap-pings of our day, / And lis-ten as he calls your name / To come and fol-low / near; For still he speaks in var-ied ways / To

[Sheet music]

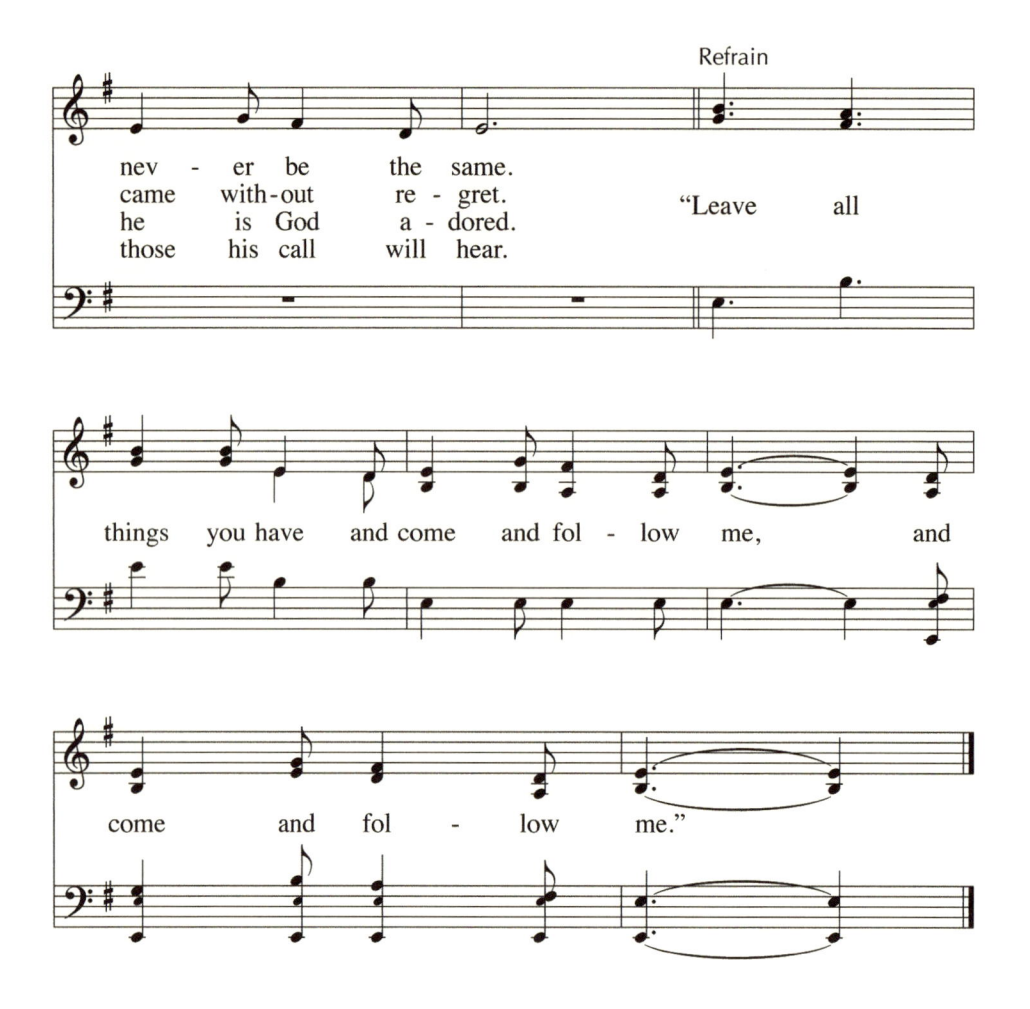

nev - er be the same.
came with-out re - gret.
he is God a - dored.
those his call will hear.

"Leave all things you have and come and fol - low me, and come and fol - low me."

Words © 1986; Music © 1970 GIA Publications, Inc.

Felicia Edgecombe (b. 1945) has been associated with Titahi Bay Gospel Chapel outside Wellington, New Zealand, for thirty years. This independent evangelical congregation has a broad vision for ministry and a progressive attitude toward music as a part of that ministry. In the seventies, the congregation began increasingly to move toward a folk-like style of singing as initially found in Dave and Dale Garrett's *Scripture In Song*.[54] Felicia had been organist but began to focus on composing in response to the stimulus of the church and also of the Festival Singers.[55] The publication of *Servant Songs*[56] in 1987 was a milestone in that development. Three of Edgecombe's hymns are published in *Alleluia Aotearoa* [AA], an ecumenical hymnal published in 1993 by the New Zealand Hymn Book Trust to provide new texts and tunes for worship. The ballad-like "God gave to man the woman" [AA46] was written for the wedding of friends. The refrain, "God Gave to Man the Woman, and to the woman gave the man, that they together both should live in love and friendship as he planned," underscores the gift of mutuality in marriage that God intended.

"Just a Cup of Water" [AA83] explores the gifts we give others. The author is careful to stress that we do not give out of our own strength, but must be strengthened by God for those tasks. Edgecombe uses a low, melodic register, syncopation, downward motion, and minor mode to provide a plaintive, introspective quality to the stanzas, brightening to the relative major mode at the refrain. The melody reaches its highest point during the refrain at the phrase, "Jesus' words *come* to us and they *will not* go away." [italics added where highest notes fall]. The hymn was written in the 1980s for a doctor and his wife when they went abroad to work in a refugee hospital in a dangerous situation.[57]

"O He is Born" [AA107] is a rollicking, joyful Christmas song. Constructed in a refrain/stanza pattern, the refrain is sung twice before each stanza and concludes the song after the last stanza. The repetition, of course, enables the congregation to pick up the tune quickly and join in heartily. The stanzas may be sung by soloists or the choir when the hymn is new to the congregation. The brisk tempo, syncopation, and leaps upward contribute to the energy that bursts from the refrain each time it returns.

Example 5:4

[Musical notation with lyrics: "vis-it from the Lord. The Ho-ly Spir-it came up-on her, prom-is-ing her a child. O he is"]

© Felicia Edgecombe

Robin Mann (b. 1949) has helped to shape the sung theology of many Australian Christians through his contributions to congregational song. He was a parish layworker in the Lutheran Church for twenty years and since 1995 has been a freelance composer and performer.[58] One of his significant achievements is the compiling and editing of the five volume series, *All Together Now*,[59] which contains 509 hymns in a wide range of styles. For most of Mann's eighty or so compositions in these volumes, he wrote both the text and tune. When asked about the influences on his hymn writing, Mann acknowledged, among other musicians, the importance of folk singers such as Bob Dylan, Paul Simon, and Peter, Paul and Mary. He sees his songs as part of his Lutheran heritage "as they [chorales] have melodies rooted in folk songs and are designed to be singable."[60] In addition to being a resource for introducing new music from other parts of the world to Australians, e.g., Taizé, Iona, and global repertoires, Mann's collections featured the Christian folk songs of other Australian composers Digby Hannah (b. 1949) and Leigh Newton.

His best-known song is "Father Welcomes All His Children,"[61] written in 1973 for the baptism of his daughter, Kristin. Mann says of this song, "The experience of having a child, of being a parent, led to a joy that completely took me by surprise. Mixed with other ingredients—the parable of the prodigal son and the sacrament of baptism—that joy was transformed into this song."[62]

Sorrowing Song [TIS689] is one of several songs based upon the psalms of lament. As with many by Sydney Carter, these songs that "complain" to God have a prophetic edge and do not shy away from asking hard questions. In his notes on the song, Mann says, "The psalms are full of complaints and questions, people asking why, wondering about God's wisdom. Yet so few of the contemporary Christian songs argue with God. . . . Honesty, reality, anger–God can stand a little more of that from us. God is big enough."[63]

The minor-mode melody, harmonized largely in thirds with a broken-chord accompaniment, is reminiscent of traditional melodies from central Europe. A four-measure interlude after each stanza offers a moment of reflection for the singer.

Example 5:5

1. Lord, hear my praying, listen to me;
   you know there's evil in what I see.
   I know I'm part of all that is wrong:
   still, won't you hear my sorrowing song?

2. Children are crying, hungry for food,
   sick from diseases— God, are you good?
   People are homeless, lost and alone:
   God, are you hiding? Where have you gone?

3. Why do the rich ones steal from the poor?
   Why do they build their weapons of war?
   How can you stand the torture and pain,
   hope disappearing, freedom in chains?

4. Jesus, remind us that you are found
   with those who cry, with those who are bound;
   where there is suff'ring, you will be there—
   help us to follow: Lord, hear my prayer.

Words and Music: Robin Mann © 1986
www.robinmann.com.au

The folk influence is present in much of the music of the Iona Community. John L. Bell (b. 1949) and Graham Maule (b. 1958), the primary song writers for the Community will be discussed in stream seven more extensively, but they also warrant mention here because of their use of traditional folk melodies and newly composed melodies in the folk style. "Jesus Calls Us Here to Meet Mim" [ESHG436, CH510] is set to a Gaelic air adapted by Bell and "Will You Come and Follow Me" (*The Summons*) [*Panorama*: 702, ESHG959, CH533, WR350] is set to a Scottish melody, KELVIN GROVE. Of the sixty-seven songs in the *Iona Abbey Music Book*,[64] twenty-one are set to traditional melodies. The folk style permeates many of John Bell's original compositions. His tune for *Enemy of Apathy*, also known as "She Sits like a Bird," [*Panorama*: 706, CH593, CHAL255, TIS418], is cast in the folk mold with a haunting melody that is propelled by its eighth-note motion. The rise and fall of the mostly stepwise melody evokes a sense of the waters over which the Spirit broods. Because the Hebrew word for Spirit is *ruach*, a feminine noun, Bell and Maule use feminine images throughout the text, challenging the singer to image the work of the Holy Spirit in new ways: "She sits like a bird, brooding on the waters . . . she sighs and she sings, mothering creation, waiting to give birth to all the Word will say."[65]

Songs with a strong Celtic folk influence are emerging from the Northumbria Community, a network of diverse and dispersed people who are exploring new ways of living the Christian faith. Drawing from the spiritual tradition of monasticism, but also actively engaged in mission, members of the Northumbria Community meet in ecumenical groups around the United Kingdom for prayer and hospitality. That their ethos is rooted in the history and spiritual heritage of Celtic Northumbria is clearly evident in the music developing in their midst. Musicians Nick and Anita Haigh have produced several compact discs of their compositions for the Community.[66] In their songs, the Haighs blend a variety of acoustical instruments with Anita's voice gently embellishing the melody in authentic Celtic fashion. Nick's performances on violin and bodhran reveal his Irish roots.

"Kyrie Eleison" tropes the ancient text after each phrase of the Haigh's original poetry. The entire Kyrie becomes a closing refrain for each stanza.

> Empty, broken, here I stand – Kyrie eleison
> Touch me with your healing hand – Kyrie eleison
> Take my arrogance and pride – Kyrie eleison
> Wash me in your mercy's tide – Kyrie eleison
> Kyrie eleison, Christe eleison, Kyrie eleison.[67]

The format of this song underscores the continuity of folk techniques of composition across time and place. Though the context is quite different, this Kyrie uses the same format of interrupting refrain and chorus as "Blessed be the Name," discussed earlier in the camp-meeting tradition.

Captivate Me expresses a longing for true spirituality and oneness with God. The Haighs draw on patterns of traditional Celtic prayers and songs, such as those in *Carmina Gaedelica*,[68] which depend on repeated phrases and a similar structure from one stanza to the next. By looking at the first two stanzas, one may clearly see the pattern:

> Speak to me, speak to me, fill my heart with passion.
> Speak to me, speak to me, let my heart rejoice.
> Speak to me, speak to me, stir again my first love.
> Speak to me, speak to me, let me hear your voice.
> Captivate me, captivate me, captivate me, let me hear your voice.
> Captivate me, captivate me, captivate me, let me hear your voice.
>
> Cover me, cover me, comfort for this aching.
> Cover me, cover me, mercy for my sin.
> Cover me, cover me, vision for this blindness.
> Cover me, cover me, be my clothing.
> Captivate me, captivate me, captivate me, be my clothing.
> Captivate me, captivate me, captivate me, be my clothing.[69]

Another style of Celtic poetry is found in *Open to You*, set to a traditional Irish melody. There is no repeated phrase as in the earlier examples, but rather a listing technique is employed.

> My eyes be open to your presence,
> My ears to hear your call.
> My heart be open to your love
> And in your arms to fall.
> My mind be open to your word,
> My soul to heaven's cure
> That I be open to you Lord
> This day and evermore.[70]

The music of Nick and Anita Haigh, along with other musicians from the Northumbria Community, offers new songs for congregations wishing to include Celtic elements in their worship services.

Themes and Theological Perspectives in Folk Hymnody

One may find songs in the folk tradition across the spectrum of the church's life and worship. As seen in the examples above, there is a strong element of storytelling, as in the ballad style of secular folk songs. The narrative may be based upon the writer's own experiences of faith, but more frequently is based upon biblical stories. In addition to simply telling the biblical story, writers, such as Suzanne Toolan, often move the narrative into the present, applying the truth of the story to the lives of believers today. In this way, the songs offer a guide for living one's faith in light of scriptural examples. Folk songs offer a broad range of emotional response in our communication with God: songs of inward devotion, joyful praise, lament, penitence, and songs that voice doubts and fears. Writers such as Sydney Carter and Robin Mann reassure us that God will not reject our honest questions or anger at the frustrations of life.

Social concerns figure prominently in folk hymnody. Perhaps because the role of folk music in the protest songs of the 1960s, hymns that advocate peace-making, justice for all persons, and the responsibility of all Christians to care for those in need seem to find full voice in the folk tradition. Strathdee's "What Does the Lord Require of You?" makes the point simply by quoting Micah 6:8. Other songs such as Marty Haugen's "Awake! Awake to Greet the New Morn" offer the poet's hope for a world changed by Christ's presence. Gordon Light's "Draw the Circle Wide" emphasizes that all people have a place in the Body of Christ. The questions posed by Jesus in John Bell's "Will You Come and Follow Me" underscore the reality that following Jesus results in attitudes and lives that are thoroughly changed. In addition to challenging singers about the way Christians should live in relation to others, writers in the folk style also challenge believers to stretch their understanding of the nature of God. Both John Bell and Gordon Light wrote about the Holy Spirit using feminine imagery; Sydney Carter described Jesus' life and ministry in terms of dance.

The writers of folk hymns remind us that in whatever condition we find ourselves, whether confident or full of doubt, joyful or angry, energetically working for the Kingdom or standing back at the fringes, we may offer our lives to God in songs that are simple and direct.

Liturgical Uses

The nature of folk song is flexibility; these hymns are easily adaptable to the needs of particular groups and circumstances. It is possible, perhaps even desirable, to vary the manner of their performance. Many can be sung as call-and-response with a soloist or choir alternating with the entire body. The accompaniment can vary from the sensitive use of piano or organ in large corporate settings to guitars and other folk instruments. There is room for improvisation in harmonization and the use of counter-melodies. As John Ylvisaker attests, whatever instruments are at hand will work just fine. Because the folk style uses mostly primary chords, musicians with basic skills can successfully accompany the singing. Additionally, because the intent of the style is group singing, soloists and accompaniments play a secondary role. Instrumental accompaniment is not always necessary, however, as folk hymns often are effective as unaccompanied song.

The informal character of folk hymns is well-suited to small group settings, such as house worship and retreats, where there is more intimate interaction. Different age groups, from young children to senior adults, relate well to the folk style, making these songs useful for intergenerational gatherings. Because the structure (repetitions, refrain, call-and-response format) allows people to join in immediately, folk hymns can be helpful in situations in which people who don't have a common repertoire of song are gathered for worship. There are times when worship is focused on a ritual action such as Communion or baptism. At these points, the cyclical, open-ended nature of many folk songs, allowing new stanzas to be created as needed, frees the congregation to sing and participate without depending upon the printed text.[71]

Folk hymns are available for all seasons and celebrations of the Christian year. Just the few examples above include selections appropriate for Advent, Christmas, Easter, and Pentecost. There are also choices for Communion, baptism, weddings, and funerals. These folk hymns connect us to the liturgical cycle celebrating the life of Christ and the church and mark significant moments in the life of the congregation. They voice our prayers, proclaim the Gospel, challenge us to a new ethic, and remind us of our calling in Christ. The accessible style of the folk tradition has proven its durability and appeal through generations of believers. Clearly, this stream of hymnody will continue to flow in the lives and worship of believers.

Key to Hymn Source Abbreviations

ESHG	Routley, Erik. *An English-Speaking Hymnal Guide*, edited and expanded by Peter W. Cutts. Chicago: GIA, 2005.
PCH	Routley, Erik. *A Panorama of Christian Hymnody*, edited and expanded by Paul A. Richardson. Chicago: GIA, 2005.
AA	*Alleluia Aotearoa* (interdenominational, New Zealand) Raumati: New Zealand Hymn Book Trust, 1993.
BH	*The Baptist Hymnal*. (Southern Baptist, USA) Nashville, Convention Press, 1991.
CH	*Church Hymnary*, 4 ed. (Church of Scotland) Norwich, England: Canterbury Press, 2005.

CHAL   *Chalice Hymnal.* (Disciples of Christ, USA) St. Louis: Chalice Press, 1995.

FWS   *The Faith We Sing* (United Methodist, USA) Nashville: Abingdon, 2000.

NCeH   *The New Century Hymnal* (UCC USA) Cleveland: Pilgrim Press, 1995.

PH   *Presbyterian Hymnal* (USA) Louisville: Westminster/John Knox, 1990.

SA   *Spirit Anew: Singing Prayer & Praise* (interdenominational, Canada) Kelowna, British Columbia: Wood Lake Books, 1999.

TIS   *Together in Song* (interdenominational, Australia) Sydney: HarperCollins*Religious*, 1999.

UMH   *The United Methodist Hymnal* (USA) Nashville: The United Methodist Publishing House, 1989.

VU   *Voices United* (United Church of Canada) Etobicoke, Ontario: United Church Publishing House, 1996.

WC   *The Worshipping Church* (interdenominational, USA) Carol Stream, IL: Hope, 1990.

WOVL   *With One Voice: A Lutheran Resource for Worship* (USA) Minneapolis: Augsburg Fortress, 1995.

WOVNZ   *With One Voice: A Hymn Book for All the Churches with New Zealand Supplement* (interdenominational) London: Collins Liturgical Publications, 1982.

WSHP   *Worship*, 3d ed. (Roman Catholic, USA) Chicago: GIA, 1986.

Notes —

1   John Ylvisaker, *What Song Shall We Sing?* (Minneapolis: Augsburg Fortress, 2005), 57.
2   Ylvisaker, 90.
3   Willi Apel, *Harvard Dictionary of Music*, 2nd ed. (Cambridge, MA: Belknap Press of Harvard Univ. Press, 1969), 136. The name is thought to be derived from the medieval French word *carole*, a round dance. See also Erik Routley, *The English Carol* (New York: Oxford University Press, 1959), 26.
4   Harry Eskew and Hugh T. McElrath, *Sing with Understanding: An Introduction to Christian Hymnology*, 2d ed. (Nashville: Church Street Press, 1995), 158.
5   Routley, *The English Carol*, 181.
6   Routley, *The English Carol*, 191.

7   Routley, *The English Carol*, 193. Routley asserts that Helmore, the musical transcriber, was mistaken in his interpretation of the tune as plainsong. See also Routley's hymn collection, *Rejoice in the Lord* 191, for the rhythmic version of the tune.
8   Carlton R. Young, *Music of the Heart: John & Charles Wesley on Music and Musicians* (Carol Stream, IL: Hope, 1995), 91, 103.
9   Frank Baker, *Representative Verse of Charles Wesley* (Nashville: Abingdon, 1962), 117.
10 Young, *Music of the Heart*, 170.
11 Paul C. Echols, "Hymnody," in *The New Grove Dictionary of American Music*, ed. H. Wiley Hitchcock and Stanley Sadie, 4 vols (London: Macmillan, 1986) 2:448
12 See Ellen Jane Lorenz, *Gory Hallelujah: the story of the Campmeeting Spiritual* (Nashville: Abingdon, 1980) for an excellent description of both the camp meeting and its music.
13 Hugh T. McElrath, "O for a thousand tongues to sing," in *Handbook to the Baptist Hymnal* (Nashville: Convention Press, 1992), 200. Ralph Hudson (1843-1901) adapted the text and arranged the anonymous tune for *Songs for the Ransomed,* first published in Ohio in 1887. In 1909, Baptist Robert H. Coleman included the hymn in his collection *The Evangel* and the text and tune have been included in all subsequent Southern Baptist hymnals.
14 Carlton R. Young, *Companion to the United Methodist Hymnal* (Nashville: Abingdon, 1993), 207.
15 E. O. Excell, *Coronation Hymns* (Chicago, 1910), no. 282.
16 George Pullen Jackson analyzed many folk hymn tunes and showed their relationship to pre-existent British folk sources in four seminal monographs: *White Spirituals in the Southern Uplands* (Chapel Hill,: University of North Carolina Press, 1933); *Spiritual Folk-Songs of Early America* (New York: J. J. Augustin, 1937); *Down East Spirituals and Others* (New York: J. J. Augustin, 1943); and *Another Sheaf of White Spirituals* (Gainesville: University of Florida Press, 1952).
17 Harry Eskew and Hugh T. McElrath, *Sing With Understanding: An Introduction to Christian Hymnology*, 2 ed. (Nashville: Church Street Press, 1995), 182-185.
18 Paul Westermeyer, *Let the People Sing: Hymn Tunes in Perspective* (Chicago: GIA, 2005), 355.
19 *The English Hymnal with Tunes* (London: Oxford University Press,1933), xiv-xv.
20 A new edition was recently published: *The New Oxford Book of Carols*, ed. Hugh Keyte and Andrew Parrott (Oxford and New York: Oxford University Press, 1992).
21 Richard Crawford, *America's Musical Life: A History* (New York: W. W. Norton, 2001), 597.
22 Crawford, 599.
23 Joe Klein, *Woody Guthrie: A Life* (New York, Knopf, 1980), 149-150. As quoted in Crawford, 613.
24 Crawford, 617.
25 Dylan's own memories and video clips regarding his relationship to Guthrie are documented in the DVD, *No Direction Home: Bob Dylan,* a Martin Scorsese picture, Spitfire Pictures / Paramount Pictures, ©2005. ISBN: 1-4157-1389-8.
26 Crawford, 789.
27 Repp's music is available from Oregon Catholic Press.

28 Bob Oldenburg, *Good News: A Christian Folk Musical* (Nashville: Broadman, 1967); Kurt Kaiser and Ralph Carmichael, *Tell It Like It Is* (Waco, TX: Lexicon, 1969); Phillip Landgrave, *Purpose* (Nashville: Broadman, 1968).

29 http://www.stainer.co.uk/carter.html.

30 As posted on the Stainer & Bell Web site, the ranking was based upon CCLI statistics, an organization offering copyright permissions by subscription, and published in an interview with Carter in *The Times* (London) in August 1996.

31 Routley, *The English Carol*, 83.

32 Erik Routley, *A Panorama of Christian Hymnody*, ed. and expanded by Paul A. Richardson (Chicago: GIA, 2005), 420.

33 William J. Reynolds, *Companion to Baptist Hymnal* (Nashville: Broadman, 1976), 348.

34 *Handbook to The Baptist Hymnal* (1992), 203.

35 The most recent publication of these two songs in a major hymnal is *Worship and Rejoice* (Hope, 2001).

36 Hustad, *Dictionary-Handbook*, 199.

37 Hustad, *Dictionary-Handbook*, 282.

38 "Donald S. Marsh" Composer Listing, Hope Publishing Company website: http://www.hopepublishing.com.

39 Richard Avery and Don Marsh, *Hymns Hot and Carols Cool* (Port Jervic, NY: Proclamation Productions, 1963).

40 Hustad, *Dictionary-Handbook*, 188.

41 Carlton R. Young, "Lafferty, Karen," *Companion to the United Methodist Hymnal* (Nashville: Abingdon, 1993), 784.

42 Young, 578. The informal sharing disseminated the song rapidly across the country. This writer can attest to its popularity—with the second stanza and descant—among Baptist young people in Virginia by 1973.

43 John Ylvisaker, *What Song Shall We Sing?* (Minneapolis: Augsburg Fortress, 2005).

44 www.strathdeemusic.com.

45 "I Am the Light of the World" *Chalice Hymnal* (St. Louis: Chalice Press, 1995) hymn number 469.

46 The group has now scattered geographically and has also expanded to include Scott McDonald and Richard Betts. The Common Cup Company produced a new collection of songs on CD in 2003, *Like Water Through Rock*.

47 Ian Macdonald, "On Ministry and Song." The Common Cup Company Interviewed. http://www.commoncup.com/mainpage/index.htm

48 Gordon Light. "On Justice and Song." The Common Cup Company Interviewed. http://www.commoncup.com/mainpage/index.htm

49 Marty Haugen, "Awake! Awake, and greet the new morn," [GREET THE NEW MORN] (Chicago: GIA, 1983), stanza 2.

50 Marty Haugen, "Gather Us In" (Chicago: GIA, 1982), stanza 4.

51 Raquel Mora Martínez, "A Survey of Hispanic Hymnody as Represented in *The New Century Hymnal*," *The New Century Hymnal Companion*, ed. Kristen Forman (Cleveland: Pilgrim Press, 1998), 161.

52 "Suzanne Toolan, RSM" GIA Sacred Music. http://www.giamusic.com/artists/Toolan-Suzanne.cfm.

53 Suzanne Toolan, "I Am the Bread of Life" (GIA,©1966).

54 David and Dale Garratt, *Scripture in Song*, 2 vols. (Auckland, NZ, Costa Mesa, CA: Scripture in Song, 1979-1981). Many New Zealanders consider this watershed collection, which at first used a folk style, to mark the beginning of Praise and Worship music.

55 The Festival Singers, a choral ensemble, was formed in Wellington by Guy Jensen. The group makes frequent concert appearances and has released several recordings.

56 Four musicians at Titahi church, Felicia Edgecombe, Rosemary Russell, Jillian Bray and Glynnis Chiaroni produced *Servant Songs,* published first in Australia by Albatross Books in 1987. It is available in a 1993 reprint edition from Festivity Productions, Box 1325, Wellington, NZ.

57 Felicia Edgecombe, interview with the author, Parameta, New Zealand, November 24, 2005.

58 C. Michael Hawn, "Congregational Singing from Down Under: An Interview with Australian Robin Mann," *The Hymn* (Autumn 2005), 56:4, 10.

59 The *All Together* Series includes *All Together Now* (1980), *All Together Again* (1983), *All Together Everybody* (1991), *All Together OK* (1996), and *All Together Whatever* (2001), published in Adelaide by Openbook Publishers.

60 Hawn, "Congregational Singing from Down Under," 10.

61 Robin Mann, *Let's Sing It Again: 20 of Robin Mann's Best Community Songs* (Adelaide: Openbook Publishers, 1999), 12-13.

62 Robin Mann, as cited in Hawn, "Congregational Singing from Down Under," 11.

63 Mann, *Let's Sing It Again*, 24-25.

64 The Iona Community, *Iona Abbey Music Book: Songs from the Iona Abbey Worship Book* (Glasgow: Wild Goose Publications, 2003). This collection does not contain all the songs by Bell and Maule, but it is representative of the Iona Community's reliance on traditional folk melodies.

65 John Bell and Graham Maule, "Enemy of Apathy," (Wild Goose Resource Group, Iona Community, ©1988)

66 *Celtic Roots and Rhythms: Heartcry* (Sussex, England: ICC Records, 2000). This recording and others are available from Cloisters, the trading arm of the Community, at their Web site, http://www.northumbriacommunity.org.

67 Nick and Anita Haigh, "Kyrie Eleison," ©Break of Day Music/Daybreak Music, 2000.

68 Alexander Carmichael and others collected and edited the six volumes of the *Carmina Gadelica*, originally published by the Scottish Academic Press between 1900-1928. A new edition in one volume was published in 1992 by Floris Books.

69 Nick and Anita Haigh, "Captivate Me" ©Break of Day Music/Daybreak Music, 2000.

70 Words, Nick and Anita Haigh, "Open To You," ©Break of Day Music/Daybreak Music, 2000.

71 For a description of cyclical versus sequential hymnody, see C. Michael Hawn, *Gather Into One* (Grand Rapids: Eerdmans, 2003), 224-240.

—Stream Six—
Praise and Worship Music

Chapter 6
Shout to the Lord:
Praise and Worship from Jesus People to Gen X

Greg Scheer

> Preacher isn't talkin' 'bout religion no more
> He just wants to praise the Lord
> People aren't as stuffy as they were before
> They just want to praise the Lord
> and it's very plain to see
> it's not the way it used to be.[1]

Even the casual observer of American Christianity will have noticed that today's worship is not the way it used to be.[2] Projection screens, drum sets, people raising their hands as they sing, an explosion of new publications and recordings, and a multi-million dollar worship industry. All these have one common denominator: a genre of congregational song called praise & worship.[3] From its renegade roots in the Jesus movement in the early 1970s until its storming of the religious and commercial establishment in recent years, it has changed dramatically. But, through each era the praise & worship genre continues to bear three primary traits: it is a product of American Evangelicalism, its aesthetic is drawn from pop culture, and it has a personal and ecstatic spiritual orientation.

Praise & Worship is a Product of American Evangelicals

Evangelicals are often defined by their core beliefs: a personal conversion experience (being "born again"), a high regard for the Bible (trumping other forms of spiritual authority such as tradition, creeds, or church authority), the centrality of Christ's sacrifice and the need to tell others about the faith (evangelism).[4] Evangelicals are also a distinctive social group with their own cultural identity. A symbiotic relationship has formed between Evangelicals and praise & worship in which the musical style has reflected and supported the Evangelical group identity while Evangelical churches have given the music a place to grow and Evangelical beliefs have informed that growth. Without Evangelicals, praise & worship would not have been possible.

Praise & worship Draws its Aesthetic From Pop Culture

Evangelicals have a tradition of using secular culture as a tool in the service of evangelism. From the theatrics of Aimee Semple McPherson (1890–1944) to Christian "boy bands," Evangelicals have not been shy about using worldly means for a spiritual end. Musical style is often considered secondary to the timeless message of the gospel,[5] so music is chosen for its ability to appeal to the masses rather than for any intrinsic aesthetic value. As pop music has become one of the chief conduits of contemporary culture, Evangelicals have used pop music styles liberally. Praise & worship doesn't mimic musical trends as closely as music with specifically evangelistic goals, but it is clear that it is marching to the drum of pop music style. As Andy Crouch posits: "contemporary worship has two distinctives: a near-total lack of conventional liturgical forms and an enthusiastic embrace of contemporary culture, especially pop and rock music."[6] Along with praise & worship's orientation to pop culture comes an involvement with youth culture and the techniques of mass marketing.

Praise & Worship Has a Personal and Ecstatic Spiritual Orientation

American Evangelicals have an intensely individualistic view of the faith that carries over into praise & worship. The music supports the goal of intimacy between Jesus and the individual worshiper, as can be seen in the abundance of lyrics written in the first person and addressed directly to Jesus. In fact, Lester Ruth questions whether praise & worship moves away from a traditional understanding of worship—we worship God through Christ in the power of the Holy Spirit—to a model where we worship Jesus in the power of music.[7] The goal of intimacy is heightened by the Pentecostal influence on praise & worship. Though most Evangelicals may not choose to be labeled "Spirit-filled," they draw heavily on the passionate aura of Pentecostal worship and hope to have some form of emotional experience in worship.

PRECURSORS

Why Should the Devil Have All the Good Tunes?[8]

A precedent was established when Martin Luther encouraged the use of the vernacular in worship. Though his primary concern was the reading of scripture in the people's language, he introduced songs in vernacular styles as well.[9] But, while Luther was open to the use of music with vernacular origins, William Booth (1829–1912) was the first to use secular pop tunes outright. This circumstance set a number of precedents. It was the first time that church music was used to appeal to those outside the church, favoring music's evangelical, rather than liturgical, function. It began a stream of worship music that took its stylistic cues from secular culture rather than the churches own musical history. Because popular music styles are often based upon dance forms, it marked a shift away from church music's previous vocal orientation toward strongly rhythmic styles.

After Booth, various American religious movements left their specific marks on the worship landscape, paving the way for today's praise & worship. Frontier revivals contributed evangelical fervor and emotional engagement.

The Methodist Holiness movement lent American Christianity a social conservatism and concern for personal moral standards that is still held by today's Evangelicals. Pentecostals continued a strong focus on emotions while adding a desire for the gifts of the Spirit that permeates praise & worship today. A strong African-American influence is another major mark of the Pentecostal movement. Though today's color lines may not be entirely "washed away in the blood of the lamb" as they were during 1906 Pentecostal revival on Azusa Street, the African-American influence is still felt.

In the middle of the twentieth century, the Evangelical movement came to prominence in American Christianity, popularized in large part by Billy Graham. His crusades continued the lineage of revivalist preaching and reintroduced the song leader/preacher format that started with Moody and Sankey. Graham continued the use of popular music to draw crowds, inviting pop musicians such as Cliff Richard (b. 1940) to perform at his crusades. At the same time as the Evangelical identity was solidifying, the Evangelical interest in youth culture grew through organizations such as Youth for Christ and youth musicals such as *Good News* and *Tell It Like It Is*. This focus on youth and youth culture continues today.

The fifties and sixties set the stage for the Jesus Movement. In England the Twentieth-Century Light Music Group introduced light rock music to the church. In Rome, the Constitution on the Sacred Liturgy revolutionized Catholic worship's relationship to culture. In New Zealand, David and Dale Garrett began to compile the scriptural songs that had been developing in Pentecostal circles. Closer to home, Bill Gaither (b. 1936) carried the gospel hymn and Southern gospel tradition one step further with catchy tunes such as *He Touched Me* that drew from Broadway and Hollywood as much as from the church. The Charismatic movement was brewing beneath the surface in many Episcopal, Catholic, and many main-line churches.

By the late sixties, youth discontent with the establishment had erupted in a counter culture that experimented with drugs, sex, music, and religion. A number of these hippies became Christians. During the height of the movement (1969–1974), these "Jesus People" were outsiders to both the hippy counter culture and the church, but their influence was soon felt in the established church's worship.

SCRIPTURE SONG (1971–1977)

> "I used to be all messed up on drugs. Now I'm all messed up on the Lord."[10]

According to Jesus Music folklore, it all started when a group of enthusiastic converted hippies cornered Pastor Chuck Smith (b. 1927) in the parking lot of Calvary Chapel, Costa Mesa, California. Smith had been reaching out to the hippy culture through Bible studies and "House of Miracles" communal living projects. Some of the recent converts were part of a band called Love Song, who began to express their newfound faith in song. They wanted Pastor Chuck to hear one called "Welcome Back." He liked it enough to have them play it at the following evening's Bible study.

A new music was born. This union of Christianity and pop music resulted in the first Maranatha! Music recording, the 1971 album *The Everlastin' Living Jesus Concert*, made possible by a $2,500 loan from Pastor Chuck. These were heady times. Enthusiastic young musicians shared their faith in churches and coffeehouses, selling albums out of their vans.

At first, there was no distinction between songs for worship and songs for evangelism. It was all just Jesus Music. The rock and roll of Larry Norman (1947–2008) and Randy Stonehill (b. 1952) shared the stage with the country rock of Love Song and the light folk of Karen Lafferty (b. 1948). It wasn't until 1974 when Maranatha! Music released the *Maranatha! Praise* album that worship music and evangelistic music began to split into two distinct branches with their own fledgling markets.

The evangelistic branch became known as Contemporary Christian Music, or CCM. It was hoped that it would reach the lost in a musical language they could understand. Regardless of its intent, the CCM industry clearly grew around Christian youth who wanted an alternative to secular pop music. So CCM soon began to broaden its self-definition to include music that exhorted believers. This young industry mirrored its secular counterpart, focusing on album production, artist development, and radio play. It even had a *bona fide* hit in 1977 with Don Francisco's (b. 1946) *He's*

Alive and its own trade journal by 1978 (*Contemporary Christian Music*). However, it remained a fraction of the overall pop music market.

Maranatha! Music

Worship music from this era remained centered around Maranatha! Music. Encouraged by the sales of *Maranatha! Praise*, they continued to release worship albums until it became their main focus in the 1980s. At first, the songs traveled by word of mouth among youth groups, but in 1983 Maranatha! released *The Praise Book* that became the "bible" of the genre. Subsequent editions continue to sell well today.

The early Maranatha! style is marked by heavy use of scriptural quotations, chord structures that can be played easily on guitar, and simple, singable folk melodies. This era of worship music is often dubbed "scripture song" because many of the lyrics quote scripture verbatim. This is a strength and a weakness. Advocates of early scripture songs argue that songs taken directly from the Bible have a stamp of approval from God. Detractors point out that the passages rarely benefit from a larger scriptural context and often avoid difficult passages.[11] Then there is the issue of the frequent use of the King James translation. Why would songwriters so concerned about reaching mo-dern culture on its own terms write lyrics riddled with "thee" and "ye"?[12] We see evidence of this in three songs from the era, all of which remain on the top 100 list of Christian Copyright License International (CCLI) even today[13]: "Seek Ye First" (Karen Lafferty, 1972), *Glorify Thy Name (*Donna Adkins, 1976), and *I Exalt Thee* (Pete Sanchez, Jr., 1977). "Seek Ye First" and *I Exalt Thee* also provide typical examples of the use of scripture in the genre. "Seek Ye First" extracts portions of Matthew 6:33, 4:4 and 7:7 and artfully weaves them into one theme.[14] *I Exalt Thee* quotes Psalm 97:9 in the verse and provides a response of praise in the chorus. Both songs have endured in part because they allow the worshiper to make a short passage of scripture a sung prayer.

The impact of the guitar on scripture song cannot be underestimated. The guitar was an emblem of hippy culture that naturally transferred to the Jesus Music culture. It was hip, portable, and easy to learn. More important, it took songwriting from the establishment and put it in the hands of the people.

But, its effect went beyond its iconoclastic power. Because of its physical layout, some chords are easier to play on the guitar than others.[15] Therefore, music written at the guitar is more likely to include chords such as G, C, D, A minor and E minor then it is C minor, A^b or C$^\#$7-5, etc. Scripture songs are no exception. The three songs discussed above fit neatly into patterns of "open" chords on the guitar fingerboard.[16] Further, the chords move quite slowly when compared to music that is written at the harmonically agile keyboard.

As with all good congregational songs, the best of the scripture song era have melodies that are quickly learned by groups, yet have classic proportions that wear well on repeated singing. "Seek Ye First" is the song that churches outside of the Jesus Music culture have most readily embraced, as evidenced by the number of hymnals in which it appears.[17] Perhaps it has won the support of so many hymnal committees because of its finely nuanced melody. It starts on the third of the scale, immediately establishing itself as sweet rather than stately. It rises up to the fifth and then floats all the way down to the sixth before returning to the third, never coming to rest on a strong scale degree as, for example, one or five. The use of the pentatonic one, six, one in the second measure lends instability and a folk-like quality. The first phrase is completed with downward motion outlining four, three, and two. The second phrase begins like the first, but it finally comes to completion with a four, three, two, one sequence. This minimal melodic arch creates a subdued tension that is released by the descant. Starting on the high C, it completes the octave span we've been hoping for and then floats down in perfect harmony with the melody. Reductive analysis of the melody and descant shows a textbook example of first species contrapuntal technique:

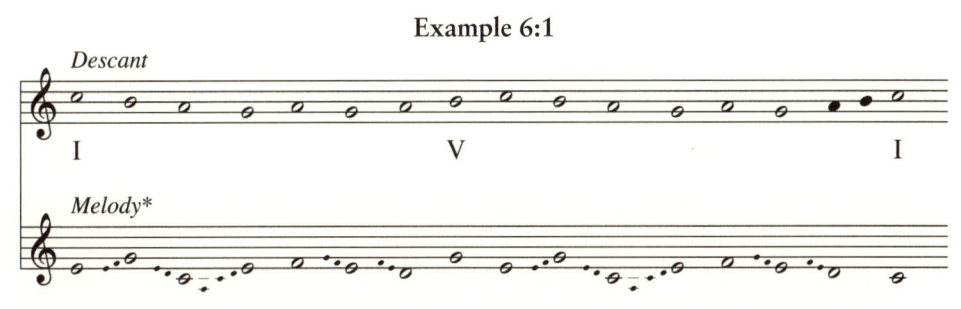

Example 6:1

*Larger notes indicate reductive analysis.

PRAISE CHORUS (1978–1992)

"One word, two chords, three hours."[18]

At the same time that CCM was testing its wings as a young industry and a new generation of hymnals was appearing in main-line denominations, the seeds that had been planted by scripture song were beginning to grow in churches across America.

Jesus People and hippies started families of their own, and they found themselves settling into mainstream American life: houses in the suburbs, minivans, soccer practices, and church. At the same time, kids who grew up in the church expected the "big" church to accommodate them in the way their youth groups had previously with practical sermons and music that catered to their demographic. The "boomers" were a large, demanding generation, and churches that listened to their requests found that they grew by leaps and bounds.[19]

Scripture songs, Gaither hymns, Catholic renewal music and youth musical hits (Kurt Kaiser's [b. 1934] *Pass It On* et al.) were a ubiquitous part of youth gatherings and Bible studies and soon made appearances on Sunday mornings. Some churchgoers were appalled at the idea of the guitar making an appearance in the sanctuary—certainly this symbol of rebellion couldn't be sanctified for worship! New churches sprouted up based upon musical and congregational models pioneered by places such as Calvary Chapel. Many churches sought a middle ground that accommodated a limited number of these "praise choruses" within their Sunday morning service. It was a time of great tension between two ideologies: the established church culture, which held tightly to hymnals, liturgy, and organ, and the youth culture that embraced new music, free-flowing charismatically influenced services and the musical leadership of the "praise band."

Classic Praise Choruses

It is hard to imagine so much division over songs that are so common today. Songs such as "Majesty" (Jack Hayford, 1981), "I Will Call Upon the Lord" (Michael O'Shields, 1981), "Lord, I Lift Your Name on High" (Rick Founds, 1987), and "As the Deer" (Martin Nystrom, 1984), hardly seem threatening by today's standards. In fact, there is much to commend in these songs. "Majesty," though its motivic development is hardly subtle, is a singable song of praise that fits comfortably beside more traditional counterparts such as "All Hail the Power of Jesus' Name" [*Panorama*: 84]. "I Will Call Upon the Lord" harks back to the King James Version quotation of the scripture song era, adding male/female echoes and handclaps that are so characteristic of the praise chorus style. "Lord, I Lift Your Name on High" has endured like no other song from this era, retaining a place in the CCLI charts well into the 2000s. It is simple to perform, has a memorable melody and uses a satisfying miniature pop form. Its chorus is a succinct summary of Christ's work with echoes of the ancient acclamation "Christ has died, Christ has risen, Christ will come again." "As the Deer" has been criticized for its mixed metaphors and for its unwillingness to address the deeper emotions of Psalm 42, from which it culls its initial image.[20] The lyrics have their weaknesses, but the melody is beautiful. The AABA form is enhanced by the melodic jump to the high D and harmonic shift to the relative minor at the start of the B section. Ambiguity is introduced at the end of the B section by a major III chord, not unlike the hymn tune FINLANDIA and the tension is released as the song concludes with a repeat of the A section in the tonic. It is a simple, satisfying melody.

CCM's Contribution

Another source of praise choruses was CCM. The CCM industry now had more marketing savvy, and soon had its first great success story with the album *Age to Age* (1982) by Amy Grant (b. 1960). Though focused outside the walls of the church, CCM often produced songs that crossed over into the sanctuary. These songs tended to be concise, expertly crafted, piano-based pop songs that were catchy enough for commercial appeal and simple enough for group singing. "How Majestic Is Your Name" (1981) and "Great Is the Lord" (1982) by Michael W. Smith (b. 1957) both contain sophisticated harmonic devices such as secondary dominants and inversions. Advanced pop craftsmanship such as this distinguishes this repertoire from the simple harmonies of scripture song. Smith is also known for his mastery of thematic development, form, and range, which make his songs memorable and durable. His lyrics aren't exquisite poetry or deep theology, but, as Robert Bridges pointed out a century earlier, a passable text can be ennobled by fine music whereas the reverse is not true. Twila Paris (b. 1958) penned a number of praise choruses that are still used today. "We Will Glorify" (1982) and "We Bow Down" (1984) have rhyme schemes that are as simple as any nursery rhyme, but they avoid triteness by the balance of a form that pivots on a deceptive cadence. Simple is not always banal. "He Is Exalted" (1985) is one of the best examples of the era. Its exuberant surface lies on a strong foundation of motivic development in which the AABA structure is invigorated by the return of the last section a fourth higher. Melody Green's "There Is a Redeemer" (1982) is a modern hymn that was popularized by her husband Keith. Amy Grant's album *Straight Ahead* introduced "Thy Word" (1984) to the church. Here we see how awkward the transition from stage to sanctuary can be. The chorus of this song is readily singable by a group, but the stanza is more appropriate for a soloist.[21]

Integrity

Founded in 1987, Integrity Music quickly became a major source of praise choruses. In fact, their slick and cheerful signature sound is what people most often associate with this era. Upbeat songs such as Daniel Gardner's "My Life Is In You" and Gary Oliver's "Celebrate Jesus" are high on energy, but low on content. Ballads such as Sondra Corbett's "I Worship You Almighty God" and Lenny LeBlanc's (b. 1951) "There Is None Like You" must have seemed heartfelt in their specific context, but an objective analysis finds them sentimental. All these songs suffer from an egocentric lyrical outlook, a point taken up in Marva Dawn's *Reaching Out without Dumbing Down*. To be fair, Integrity's Hosanna! Music label has produced a series of musical snapshots from interesting communities around the world. It introduced a number of influential worship movements, including Hillsong, the March for Jesus and the Brownsville revival. It has also been pivotal in bringing an African-American influence to contemporary Evangelical worship. Ron Kenoly (b. 1944), the Brooklyn Tabernacle Choir and Israel Houghton

(b. 1972) have all earned gold status bringing their black gospel sound to the primarily white praise & worship market. Integrity's most important contribution, however, was its business savvy. Although Maranatha! Music's timidity had limited its marketing reach, Integrity embraced the business side of publishing with gusto, soon becoming a publicly traded company and forging distribution deals with Sony and Time-Life to extend its reach into secular markets. This approach would bear fruit for Integrity and set the standard for the worship industry in the coming years.

Graham Kendrick

Graham Kendrick (b. 1950) was well known in his native England when such albums as *Make Way for Jesus–Shine, Jesus, Shine* (1988), *Make Way –Crown Him* (1991), and *King of the Nations* (1993) popularized him and "public praise" throughout the world. Kendrick's "March for Jesus" gathered Christians to march through their city's streets singing and chanting praise. From modest beginnings in London, it grew to a worldwide march of ten million people in 1994. Because of the popularity of the March for Jesus, Kendrick is often associated with such triumphant praise choruses as *Shine, Jesus, Shine* (1987) and "Say It Loud" (1995). However, much of his output, including *Amazing Love* (1989), "Meekness and Majesty" (1986) and *Servant King* (1983) go well beyond the theological depth and musical sophistication of the typical praise chorus. Kendrick continues to compose and has become something of a father figure to a new generation of songwriters, even collaborating with Matt Redman (b. 1978) and Martin Smith (b. 1970) on 2001's *What Grace*.

Vineyard

Vineyard was an increasingly influential worship movement in the latter part of this period, due in large part to the worship theology of leader John Wimber (1934–1997). Whereas Maranatha! and Integrity focused on the songs and business, Vineyard emphasized worship as an experience of intimacy "that moves to a climatic point, not unlike physical lovemaking."[22] This theology encouraged an outpouring of "vertical" songs (songs of love sung directly to God) from Vineyard composers. For example, John Barnett's "Holy and Anointed One" (1988) begins as a meditation on the name and attributes of Jesus. In the chorus, the focus shifts as the singer responds with phrases such as "Your name is like honey on my lips." The chorus climaxes on the words "Jesus I love You," set to a melodic turn that is suffused with sensuality. As a whole, the church was not ready for this intimate, almost sexual, approach to worship, but it would become the dominant theology in the years to come.

PRAISE & WORSHIP (1993–1998)

> "I told my therapist that every time I go to church, I get so depressed that I want to kill myself. He suggested that I should stop going to church."[23]

Just as Amy Grant's *Age to Age* had opened new commercial vistas for the CCM industry in 1982, the worship industry entered a new era with the breakout success of Darlene Zschech's (b. 1965) *Shout to the Lord* (1993) and Martin Smith's *I Could Sing of Your Love Forever* (1994).[24] Some dubbed this new era the "worship explosion," but the moniker that has lasted is "praise & worship." This is also the phrase most commonly used to describe the genre as a whole.[25]

Strangely, Grant may have had something to do with the emergence of the praise & worship era. Her number one single "Baby, Baby" (1991) brought CCM's identity crisis to a head: was CCM evangelism, entertainment, music about Christ, or music by Christians?[26] The secular conglomerates that were gobbling up CCM labels didn't care much for these deeper questions. They were more interested in the new SoundScan statistics that proved CCM was outselling jazz and classical combined. But, evangelical Christians did care. As CCM became broader lyrically and more adventurous stylistically, many fans gravitated to the clear-cut, God-directed message of the new pop praise. Perhaps the appearance of CCM in top forty lists and Wal-Mart bins made Evangelicals seek an alternative that was more distinctively "not of this world." The new praise & worship reinforced Evangelical identity, rallying the faithful like nothing had since the early days of CCM.[27]

Marketing gurus found that praise & worship albums sold well even without airplay, creating hits with unusual staying power. As one record executive put it "the church is our radio station."[28] Of course, it didn't hurt that the new recordings had much higher production values and there was a significant shift to performer-based albums rather than the song-based praise chorus albums of the past. Performers moved away from the generic light rock style and smooth vocal harmonies that had previously marked praise chorus recordings, creating specific signature sounds. Likewise, church praise teams began to move away from the "wall of singer" approach, embracing the standard rock band configuration: lead vocal, one or two backing vocals, guitar, piano, bass, and drums.

The new praise & worship also found an audience in the massive Evangelical gatherings that were popular during this time. The March for Jesus popularized many of Graham Kendrick's songs. Promise Keepers introduced songs such as "I See the Lord" (Chris Falson, 1992) and *Knowing You* (Graham Kendrick, 1993) to crowds of men who brought the songs home to their local churches. Megachurches, somewhere between church and stadium, also served to introduce new songs to local churches that were aspiring to greater things by attending church growth conferences. A final rallying point for the new praise & worship explosion was the formation of *Worship Leader* magazine in 1992. Since its inception, it has been the publication most closely aligned with the praise & worship genre, similar to the relationship between *Christianity Today* and Evangelicals. But, *Worship Leader* not only reflects the genre. Since 1997, its *SongDiscovery* service has significantly shaped the genre's repertoire by introducing new songs in CD and leadsheet format.[29]

Hillsong

Two distinct styles emerged during this period. The first was the slick, radio-ready pop style forged by Darlene Zschech (b. 1965) and Hillsong,[30] marketed in large part by Integrity Music. *Shout to the Lord* (1993) was the first of this style. Something about this song captured the ears of congregations throughout the world. Perhaps it was the song's Psalm-like language. The lyrics are lofty enough to be singular and inspiring, yet common enough to be a universal expression of praise. The music is competently composed, with a satisfying form and a soaring chorus. However, the song's extreme range points out one of the problems of the new performer orientation of the period. Music that flatters a performer's voice is often at odds with the technical limitations of the group voice. From this period forward, the needs of the performer generally trumped the needs of the congregation. Hillsong followed *Shout to the Lord* with a string of popular praise hits including *My Redeemer Lives* (Reuben Morgan, 1998) and *Hear Our Praises* (Reuben Morgan, 1998), all of which are high-energy, well-crafted pop gems. Along the same stylistic lines, Tommy Walker contributed *He Knows My Name* (1996) and other infectiously melodic praise & worship songs. Interestingly, both Zschech and Walker come from Pentecostal congregations.[31] This could account for the nuances of black gospel heard in their style. Vestiges of Pentecostalism's multiracial roots are still apparent in the songs and their performance.[32]

The "Delirious" Style

A second style that emerged during this period was heartfelt, guitar-driven rock. Martin Smith and his band Delirious pioneered this sound with their hit *I Could Sing of Your Love Forever* (1994). The simple open-chord guitar patterns made the song a favorite among guitarists who had been waiting for guitar-friendly worship music since the early days of scripture songs. *I Could Sing of Your Love Forever* fit the guitar perfectly, but it was awkward for the voice. The song's composition evidently started with a chord sequence, squeezing the melody in later.[33] The result was a melody that had few of the sweeping arches normally associated with classic melodies. The style sounded similar to secular singer-songwriters of the day (The Proclaimers, R.E.M., Duncan Sheik). This speech-like effect[34] could be quite beautiful, but it was very difficult for group singing. However, it seemed that worshipers were content to move to a paradigm in which they sang along with a leader rather than carrying the melody as a group.

A number of hits followed in the same style: Martin Smith's *Shout to the North* (1995), Matt Redman's *Heart of Worship* (1997) which became the anthem of the era, Paul Baloche's (b. 1962) "Open the Eyes of My Heart" (1997) and Chris Tomlin's (b. 1972) "We Fall Down" (1998). All these songs followed a similar pattern: speech-like stanzas center around a single note (similar to a chant formula) then rise to a chorus that is in a higher *tessitura* and uses longer notes, often with a greater sense of melodic arch. Many of the songs also include a "bridge" in their formal structure. The bridge is common in pop music, providing relief to the stanza (A) and chorus (B) with a fresh C section. It had rarely been used in congregational song previously because it significantly increases the complexity of a song. This was another sign that the balance was shifting in favor of the performer rather than the assembly. Another common denominator in this style is an orientation toward guitar-friendly keys and chords. Songs in the key of G or D remained common, but by the end of this era the key of E had come into vogue.[35] Especially popular were songs such as "Open the Eyes of My Heart" that let the guitar's B and E strings ring while chords change beneath them, creating a ringing, harp-like sound.

During this period there was a blossoming of interest in worship and worship theology. People were no longer content simply to sing songs that sounded modern and relevant to culture. They wanted music that led them to greater intimacy with Jesus. Vineyard worship theology provided this framework. John Wimber's writings talked about five phases of worship: call to worship, engagement, expression, visitation, and giving of substance.[36] The first three stages were escalating foreplay leading to visitation—an intimate encounter between the individual worshiper and Jesus. This nearly sexual approach to worship theology had an enormous influence on the genre. Unlike the psalms that link God's greatness to God's deeds, songwriters of this era cut to the chase with first-person love songs to God. In fact, the whole genre earned the title "praise & worship" from the idea that there are two types of worship songs: "praise" songs talk *about* God whereas "worship" songs are sung directly *to* God.

Vineyard

Though these ideas permeated the whole genre, Vineyard song writers, in particular, fleshed out this worship theology with a number of popular "Jesus is my girlfriend"[37] songs. "Draw Me Close" (Kelly Carpenter, 1994) has a beautiful melody with interesting intervals in the stanza that stretch toward a chorus that explodes with yearning on the words "You're all I want. You're all I've ever needed." For all its musical finesse, the lyrics never actually mention a deity as the object of affection. Given its context as a Christian worship song, we can surmise that the song is directed to Jesus. However, the combination of a first-rate romantic pop ballad with love lyrics like "nothing else could take Your place/To feel the warmth of Your embrace" causes many to question the appropriateness of the song's use in congregational worship. The faster tempo of "In the Secret" (Andy Park, 1995) keeps it from dripping with romanticism such as "Draw Me Close to You," but the romantic overtones are still there when the song culminates in the words of the chorus: "I want to touch You/I want to see Your face/I want to know You more." It also has an intensely first-person outlook much like the oft-criticized *In the Garden*. Yes, he does "walk with us and talk with us" and meet us "in the secret, in the quiet place," but should we emphasize an exclusive relationship that is just "Jesus and me?" *Breathe* (Marie Barnett, 1995) continues the Vineyard tradition of mixing romance and religion. Though Barnett specifically mentions the Holy Spirit, it is in the context of pop ballad clichés such as "I'm desperate for you." These mixed messages carry over into the recording that made the song popular. The vocal delivery has a sultry edge that make the lyrics sound more like pillow talk than God talk.[38] Not every church embraced a full-blown Vineyard worship theology, but there was an overall shift from using praise & worship as a way to reach out to the world to using it as a vehicle for intimacy with God in worship.

By the end of this era, praise & worship had become the dominant worship style in the American Evangelical church. *Christianity Today* declared the "Triumph of the Praise Song" on the cover of its July 1999 issue. Indeed, many lamented the decline of the organ, hymnal, and choir in churches across America. Meanwhile, the praise & worship industry continued to expand and praise & worship became the new "traditional" church music.

EMERGING WORSHIP (1999–PRESENT)

> "Worshiping God is fun and all. The only thing that makes people think it's boring is church."[39]

By 1999, praise & worship was no longer the renegade youth worship knocking at the door of the Church. It was the establishment.[40] Not only was it the dominant repertoire within the church walls, but also it was a commercial success outside as well. Two commercial high points for the praise industry were the double-platinum status of the first *WoW Worship* album[41] and the *Songs 4 Worship* series in which Time-Life partnered with Integrity Music. Time-Life invested $30 million in the project's marketing campaign, yielding their most successful venture to date.

As is true of any pop music idiom, by the time a movement meets acceptance of one generation, the next generation has to break away and create a new genre that relates specifically (perhaps only) to their generation. Praise & worship was no different. Young worshipers complained that the established praise & worship was too slick, too happy, and too tame. They wanted music that was more up-to-date and edgy, something that felt authentic to their youth culture.

SonicFlood

They found what they were looking for in the release of SonicFlood's self-titled debut. Though SonicFlood didn't break much new ground with the songs,[42] they performed and recorded in a style more like alternative radio regulars such as U2 than the praise & worship tradition. The success of the album (certified gold by 2001) proved there was a market for "wall of sound" alternative worship. Though SonicFlood's original line up of musicians soon disbanded, the stage had been set for a new generation of worship.

SonicFlood's debut was not the only disruption to the status quo of Evangelical church and contemporary worship. PostModernism, which had been discussed in academia since the 1960s, began to affect the thinking of churches. The path had been forged as early as 1986 by alternative worship

AN OVERVIEW OF SONGS CITED

Song Title Composed	Composer	Publisher	Year
SCRIPTURE SONG (1971-1977)			
Seek Ye First	Lafferty, Karen	CCCM Music/Maranatha! Music	1972
Glorify Thy Name	Adkins, Donna	CCCM Music/Maranatha! Music	1976
Exalt Thee	Sanchez, Pete, Jr.	Sanchez, Pete Jr.	1977
PRAISE CHORUS (1978-1992)			
Majesty	Hayford, Jack	Rocksmith Music	1981
I Will Call Upon The Lord	O'Shields, Michael	Sound III, Inc.	1981
How Majestic Is Your Name	Smith, Michael W.	Meadowgreen Music Company/EMI	1981
Great Is The Lord	Smith, Michael W.\Smith,	Meadowgreen Music Company/EMI	1982
There Is A Redeemer	Green-Sievright, Melody	Ears To Hear\BMG	1982
We Will Glorify	Paris, Twila	Singspiration Music/Brentwood-Benson	1982
As The Deer	Nystrom, Martin	Maranatha Praise, Inc.	1984
Thy Word	Grant, Amy\Smith, Michael	Meadowgreen/Word	1984
We Bow Down	Paris, Twila	Singspiration Music/Brentwood-Benson	1984
He Is Exalted	Paris, Twila	Straightway Music/Mountain Spring	1985
Shine Jesus Shine	Kendrick, Graham	Make Way Music	1987
Lord I Lift Your Name On High	Founds, Rick	Maranatha Praise, Inc.	1987
Celebrate Jesus	Oliver, Gary	Integrity's Hosanna! Music	1988
Holy And Anointed One	Barnett, John	Mercy / Vineyard Publishing	1988
Jesus Draw Me Close	Founds, Rick	Maranatha Praise, Inc.	1990
You Are My All In All	Jernigan, Dennis	Shepherd's Heart Music, Inc./Word	1991
Ancient Of Days	Harvill, Jamie\Sadler, Ga	Integrity's Hosanna! Music	1992

PRAISE & WORSHIP (1993-1998)

Song	Author	Publisher	Year
Knowing You	Kendrick, Graham	Make Way Music	1993
Shout To The Lord	Zschech, Darlene	Hillsong Publishing/Integrity	1993
I Could Sing Of Your Love Forever	Smith, Martin	Curious? Music UK/EMI	1994
Draw Me Close	Carpenter, Kelly	Mercy / Vineyard Publishing	1994
In The Secret	Park, Andy	Mercy / Vineyard Publishing	1995
Breathe	Barnett, Marie	Mercy / Vineyard Publishing	1995
The Heart Of Worship	Redman, Matt	ThankYou Music/EMI	1997
Open The Eyes Of My Heart	Baloche, Paul	Integrity's Hosanna! Music	1997
Come Now Is The Time To Worship	Doerksen, Brian	Vineyard Songs (UK/Eire)	1998
We Fall Down	Tomlin, Chris	worshiptogether.com songs/EMI	1998

EMERGING WORSHIP (1999 – present)

Song	Author	Publisher	Year
Give Us Clean Hands	Hall, Charlie	worshiptogether.com songs/sixstep/EMI	2000
Forever	Tomlin, Chris	worshiptogether.com songs/sixstep/EMI	2001
In Christ Alone	Townend, Stuart\Getty, Keith	ThankYou Music/EMI	2001
Blessed Be Your Name	Redman, Beth\Redman, Matt	ThankYou Music/EMI	2002

TWENTY-FIRST CENTURY PRAISE & WORSHIP SONGS (some examples) with CCLI ranking for songs in the top twenty-five as of February 2013

Song	Author	Publisher	Year
God of Wonders	Tomlin, Chris (Passion)	Meaux Music/Storm Boy Music	2000
You Are Good	Houghton, Israel	Integrity's Praise! Music	2001
Revelation Song (7)	Riddle, Jennie Lee	Gateway Create Publishing	2004
Here I Am to Worship (10)	Hughes, Tim	Warner/Chappell Music	2005
Holy Is the Lord (20)	Tomlin, Chris and Louie Giglio	Universal Music Publishing Group	2003
Your Grace Is Enough (15)	Maher, Matt	spirit.com	2004
Love the Lord	Brewster, Lincoln	Integrity Music	2005
The Stand (12)	Houston, Joel	Hillsong Publishing	2005
Mighty to Save (3)	Fielding, Ben and Reuben Morgan	Hillsong Publishing	2006
God of This City	Tomlin, Chris	Songs/sixsteps music	2006
How Great You Are	Posthuma, Phil	Phil Posthuma	2006
Forever Reign (8)	Morgan, Reuben and Jason Ingram	Reuben Morgan/Shout!	2009
Our God (1)	Redman, Matt, Jonas Myrin, Chris Tomlin, Jesse Reeves	Thankyou Music	2010
10,000 Reasons (Bless the Lord) (4)	Myrin, Jonas and Matt Redman	Shout! Publishing	2011

gatherings such as The Nine O'clock Service in Sheffield. It soon appeared elsewhere in the UK, New Zealand, and Australia, eventually finding its way to America. The idea of ministering to and in a PostModern culture was brought to the attention of the broader Christian community through the writings of Leonard Sweet, Brian McLaren, and Dan Kimball.[43] Soon PostModern and Gen X were buzzwords bantered about by church leaders eager to ride the next wave of ministry.

It may have looked at first like a fad from the fringe, but it soon became clear that there was an undeniable shift away from the passive consumer orientation of the Boomers' faith and worship. Gen Xers, and later Millennials, were interested in participating rather than observing, experiencing rather than just hearing, and they were open to non-linear modes of thought and art. They were also much more interested in being a part of a community and living out their faith in tangible ways (political activism, volunteering for Habitat for Humanity, for example) than the previous generation. Even churches such as Willow Creek that had their seeker services honed to a science, had to adjust their methods for this new generation of seekers. Once the dust had settled, "emerging" was the moniker that described the Evangelical churches, church plants and worship services that attempted to minister in this new PostModern context, breaking out of what they considered a business-as-usual way of doing church.

Passion

This young generation of worshipers found its focal point in Passion. Two thousand college students attended the first Passion gathering in 1997. By 2000, this number had grown to 40,000 students who attended the Passion-sponsored "OneDay" gathering. Passion continued some themes from the previous generation of worship music—passionate songs of intimate worship, high production standards and a rock concert setting—and added a student-orientation, a focus on an emotion-filled worship experience and exhortation to live one's whole life for God. Passion also added volume. As one pastor put it, "the music seems like it's made not so much to attract young people as to repel older folks."

Passion and its affiliates[44] have a symbiotic relationship with a small stable of musicians, most notably David Crowder, Charlie Hall (b. 1973), Chris Tomlin, and Matt Redman. David Crowder is the maverick of the group. Music and Arts Pastor at University Baptist Church in Waco, Texas, his band's 2002 release *Can You Hear Us?* Blindsided, the praise & worship establishment with a daring combination of acoustic guitar, pre-recorded loops and bone-crushing rhythm section. The songs vacillated between the bravado of *Our Love Is Loud* to the tender "I Need Words." It remains one of the few—perhaps only—praise & worship projects that is not derivative of a secular style. Charlie Hall is known for his up-to-date and skillfully written worship songs such as *Give Us Clean Hands* that rally young, sincere worshipers with lyrics such as "We bow our hearts, we bend our knees/O Spirit come make us humble/We turn our eyes from evil things/O Lord we cast down our idols/Give us clean hands/Give us pure hearts/Let us not lift our souls to another/God let us be a generation that seeks/That seeks Your face oh God of Jacob." Chris Tomlin has been the most successful of the Passion artists with the release of his *Arriving* CD. His *Arriving* CD won the 2004 Gospel Music Association award for Praise & Worship album and set the unprecedented feat of having three simultaneous Top thirty hits in 2005. It's no wonder that Tomlin has been so successful, given his expansive U2-like praise anthems. Matt Redman became popular in a previous era, but continues to relate to today's students with heartfelt releases such as *Facedown*.

CCM Crossover

As praise & worship became "a driving force in Christian music,"[45] more and more mainstream CCM performers began to release worship albums. Third Day had an unexpected hit with its 2000 *Offerings: A Worship Album* that went gold within a year. Third Day may have "helped redefine modern worship with its guitar-driven *Offerings* album,"[46] but one has to ask how far this new definition moved worship music away from a context that included the local congregation. Songs such as "Consuming Fire" work well on a recording or in a live rock concert, but they are hardly crafted for group singing—especially in an intergenerational context led by amateur musicians. Another CCM performer who crossed over into worship to great success was Michael W. Smith. He reignited his career with *Worship* (2001). It went platinum within a year without the radio play or marketing that normally accompanies a hit album. Third Day and Smith caused a stir when they teamed up with Chevrolet for their 2002 "Come Together and Worship" tour. For many, this was exactly the kind of commercialism they were hoping to avoid when they embraced praise & worship rather than the broader CCM industry—it was an example of Christian artists being "unequally yoked" with the world.[47] Perhaps these artists weren't merely cashing in on the latest fad, but praise & worship had certainly become the industry's hottest trend. *Billboard* posted praise & worship sales at 4.5 million units in 2002[48] and *Campus Life* related anecdotally that "every other CD that arrived here came with this label (or something like it): *praise & worship* music."[49]

Though it had commercial aspects, in general emerging worship tried to avoid the superficial pop veneer of the previous generation. In their search for worship that was authentic and rooted, many worshipers discovered the Church's history, theology, and liturgy. Hip college-aged Christians began to use the Book of Common Prayer and historic creeds in their worship. They used icons and candles and drew on modern liturgical movements such as Taizé. Song writers such as Matt Redman became more intentional about the theology of their lyrics, even including lament such as "And blessed be Your name on the road marked with suffering/Though there's pain in the offering/Blessed be Your name."[50] Granted, all of these historical elements are layered on top of an ever-present backbeat. Still, it is more connected to the universal Church than the previous generation that had attempted to sever all ties with anything but itself.

A Hymn Revival

Along with this interest in tradition came a surge of activity with historic hymns. Even *Worship Leader*, the primary magazine of the praise & worship movement is expressing interest in recovering hymns in worship.[51] Unlike previous eras of praise & worship in which hymns were led by praise bands in an attempt to blend "contemporary" and "traditional" music, emerging worship musicians intentionally sought out obscure or ancient hymns specifically for their exotic appeal. This trend seems to have been initiated by the folk-rock settings of hymn texts that circulated in Reformed University Fellowship circles as early as the 1990s. The RUF involvement in hymns was fostered by Kevin Twit and resulted in a series of *Indelible Grace* CDs beginning in 2000.[52] Four types of new hymns emerged. Most worship leaders kept the lyrics and music intact, merely rearranging them for a praise band context. David Crowder's *Illuminate* CD contains a rendition of "All Creatures of Our God and King," which recasts the hymn in an introspective light. This may not seem a particularly obscure choice of hymn to those steeped in hymnody, but many of Crowder's fans would be hearing the song for the first time. If they were brought up in the church in the 90s, it is likely that they would be more familiar with Darlene Zschech than St. Francis. Some emerging leaders followed the lead of RUF, writing new music for old texts. One example of this is "God Will Lift Up Your Head" that appears on Jars of Clay's CD *Redemption Songs* (2005). The song matches Paul Gerhardt's text "Give to the Winds Thy Fears" (trans. John Wesley) with energetic rock music that has all the trimmings—whispered stanzas, full-throated choruses, a driving beat and slick production. Another approach is to add a new chorus to hymn stanzas. Chris Tomlin does this in his song *The Wonderful Cross*.[53] He retains the melody HAMBURG and Isaac Watts's text "When I Survey the Wondrous Cross" and adds his own exclamation of dedication in the chorus: "O the wonderful cross, O the wonderful cross/ Bids me come and die and find that I may truly live/O the wonderful cross, O the wonderful cross/All who gather here by grace draw near and bless Your name" Finally, some songwriters have begun to break with the praise & worship tradition of using succinct, repetitive forms, opting instead for the thicker, developmental approach used by hymn writers of the past. Graham Kendrick has taken this approach for years, but a song that has recently been embraced by both young and old is Stuart Townend (b. 1963) and Keith Getty's (b. 1974) "In Christ Alone" (ThankYou Music/EMI, 2001). The text is weighty theology expressed in vivid poetry. The music has a slightly Celtic feel, giving it a timeless quality that will help it to transcend its immediate context.

THE FRINGE

As with any movement, emerging worship has a fringe that takes various aspects of the movement to extremes. Whereas most emerging churches remain unmistakably Evangelical—simply adding edgy music, historic ritual, and multimedia to their worship as a way of connecting with the younger generation—there are some churches who take PostModern culture so seriously that they have revamped the very foundations of their fellowship and worship. For example, Seattle's Church of the Apostles[54] meets in a church under restoration that includes a coffee shop. The coffee shop serves as an outpost for involvement in the neighborhood during the week. Churches such as this take community so seriously that they rarely look outside their own fellowship for music. It makes for some interesting combinations—music written last week combined with liturgy from the early Church; Orthodox icons projected from a laptop; candles, and lattes. One worship project that picks up on the communal aspect of PostModern culture is *Enter the Worship Circle* (1999). Recorded live without amplification or overdubs, the CD has a sincerity that harks back to the early days of the Jesus Movement. Though the recording sounds fresh and authentic, many of the songs have theology that is weak or overly romanticized. In a similar vein, the International House of Prayer (IHOP) has developed a singular form of worship and music making. This "harp and bowl" worship goes on seven days a week, twenty-four hours a day with music leaders taking shifts. This form of prophetic praise is largely improvised. One vocalist will begin singing a scripture or meditative phrase, and soon the rest of the musicians and worshipers will join in. The ebb and flow of songs is quite beautiful in a similar way to Pentecostal Spirit singing. Though one may be generally enthusiastic at such whole-hearted and participatory worship, this is somewhat diminished by IHOP's focus on spiritual warfare and imagery from Song of Songs as applied to the relationship between Jesus and the worshiper.

THE CYCLE BEGINS AGAIN

And so, praise & worship has come full circle. The songs that seemed so revolutionary in the late 1960s found their way into the church in the 1970s, became an industry in the 1980s and established themselves as tradition in the 1990s. By the new millennium, a new generation began a new cycle of rejecting their parents' way of "doing church and worship," creating their own revolution.

But, the apple doesn't fall far from the tree. For all the revolutionary trappings of the new music, it still shares family traits with the old.

Praise & worship remains largely an American Evangelical phenomenon. The genre simultaneously borrows from American pop culture and reinforces the Evangelical identity as a sub- or counterculture. The music has become so intertwined with Evangelical identity that it has in many instances become the world's introduction to the Evangelical faith. For better or for worse, praise & worship is the unofficial world ambassador for American Evangelical Christianity.

As the Evangelical culture from which it springs, praise & worship remains theologically conservative. From the early days of King James-riddled scripture song, praise & worship has always reflected and reinforced Evangelicals' high view of scripture, a personal relationship with Christ and a conservative moral code. It has rarely addressed themes that have been taken up by other branches of modern hymnody: social justice, the Christian's relation to the environment, gender-neutral language and so on.

New praise & worship continues to be closely tied to pop culture and current music trends. From Love Song to Third Day, it would be difficult to think of any praise & worship music style that had no precedent in pop music. This is, in fact, a selling point for some. As far back as William Booth, Evangelicals have sought to remain relevant to secular culture by becoming fluent in current musical vocabulary. Praise & worship styles have changed dramatically in the last forty years, but they have never lagged far behind secular musical trends. Similar to the secular industry from which it takes its cues, praise & worship has become a mass-marketed consumer product. This doesn't imply that the praise & worship industry is more interested financial gain than spiritual results, but as one record executive put it, "if we don't make money, we don't make a profit, and then we have no ministry."[55]

Praise & worship continues to be tethered to youth culture. As is true of American culture at large, the college-aged population sets cultural trends.

Over and over again, a new worship trend has sprouted up from the college-age demographic only to be replaced by the next generation of college students. The once-shocking long hair of Larry Norman has been replaced by the now-shocking goatee and dark glasses of David Crowder. The guitar and projection screen that once caused such rage upon entering the sanctuary have become commonplace; now we worry at the younger generation's use of the candles and iPods in worship. It seems that the American and Evangelical dedication to youth and youth culture has committed the church to endless cycles of youth worship revolutions that eventually grow into the mainstream.

Finally, the praise & worship context is still driven largely by the goal of intimacy. This is a legacy of the movement's Pentecostal and Charismatic roots that was fine tuned by John Wimber and furthered by today's emerging worship leaders. Unlike other worship contexts in which the focus is on preaching or the sacraments, the primary focus of praise & worship is on personal intimacy with Jesus. Accordingly, many of the songs' lyrics address the attributes of Jesus or the worshiper's passion. Some are love songs sung directly to Jesus. Even the name of one of today's most influential worship movements—Passion—reveals the weight that is given to personal, ecstatic worship experienced with music as a primary conduit.

As praise & worship begins a new cycle of its life, a number of questions loom on the horizon. Will the current influence of the pop *milieu* cause a performer orientation to permeate the church's worship, or will local congregations craft a new and more group-oriented musical style? Will praise & worship become more or less of a commercial commodity? Will the Internet neutralize or invigorate the current mass market context of praise & worship? Will the historical worship elements currently being used by the emerging church eventually have an effect on the theology of the Evangelical Church? Will today's goals of worship intimacy become primarily a narcissistic ritual, or will it be the spark that motivates people to serve God outside the walls of the church? Will the PostModern desire for community encourage them to look beyond their own demographic to embrace intergenerational church life?

It will be interesting to see a hymnal (or its digital equivalent?) forty years from now. Given the previous forty years, we can probably expect each new worship movement to contribute its particular perspective and add a few songs to the Church's repertoire. Or as Terry York predicts:

> We know that hymnody not only withstands the threats of its challengers, it conscripts the best of their ranks. Religious folk songs, gospel songs, and praise choruses, each in their turn, challenged mainstream hymnody. These contenders sought to usurp hymnody by popular demand and acclamation. Yet, hymnody marched ever forward absorbing into its hymnals the best along the way. Given that history, we can expect *modern worship song* to eventually surrender the best of its genre to the ever-expanding working definition of hymnody.[56]

Praise & worship is a little less than the worship utopia proponents predicted, but a little better than the erosion of foundations that detractors expected. Time will winnow the wheat from the chaff.[57]

Notes—

1 "Little Country Church" by Love Song, from the *Everlastin' Living Jesus Music Concert* album released in 1971 by Maranatha! Records.

2 For example: Donald E. Miller, *Reinventing American Protestantism: Christianity in the New Millennium* (Berkeley and Los Angeles, CA: University of California Press, 1997); Arian Campo-Flores, "Get Your Praise On," *Newsweek*. April 19, 2004, 56–57; and "Church Music," *All Things Considered*. Dec 10, 2001.

3 Elsewhere, the genre has been called "contemporary Christian worship," "contemporary worship music" or subsumed under the umbrella of "contemporary Christian music" (CCM). Most practitioners refer to the music as "Praise & Worship," and that label will be used here.

4 See Larry Eskridge, "Defining the Term in Contemporary Times," <http://www.wheaton.edu/isae/defining_evangelicalism.html> Accessed March 20, 2013.

5 One of the most influential champions of the neutrality of musical style has been Harold M. Best, *Music Through The Eyes of Faith* (New York: HarperCollins, 1993). See, for example, chapter 2, "What Does Music Mean?" Here he portrays music as "morally relative and inherently incapable of articulating, for want of a better term, truth speech" (page 42), whereas "word-deeded art forms are bound more closely to moral content and response than others" (page 60).

6 Andy Crouch, "A Humbling Experience: Contemporary Worship's Simple Aesthetic," *re:generation quarterly*, 3.1 (Winter 1997), 11–13.

7 Lester Ruth, "Lex Amandi, Lex Orandi: The Trinity in the Most Used Contemporary Christian Worship Songs," Manuscript, 2005.

8 Attributed variously to Martin Luther, Charles Wesley, Rowland Hill and William Booth. See Chris Armstrong, "Christian History Corner: From Oratorios to Elvis, Pop culture has been coming to a church near you for hundreds of years, *Christianity Today* (January 1, 2003). See <http://www.christianitytoday.com/ct/2003/januaryweb-only/1-6-53.0.html >Accessed March 20, 2013.

9 His relationship to "bar tunes" was not as proactive as many proponents of praise & worship claim. [See "Did Martin Luther Really Use Tavern Tunes in Church?" <http://www.elca.org/Growing-In-Faith/Worship/Learning-Center/FAQs/Tavern-Tunes.aspx> However, the simultaneous introduction of vernacular language and folk music seems to indicate that Luther considered both "languages" that could be either more or less intelligible to worshipers.

10 A line from a Cheech and Chong sketch.

11 An example of the former is John M. Frame, *Contemporary Worship Music, A Biblical Defense* (Phillipsburg, NJ: Presbyterian & Reformed Publishing, 1997). An example of the latter is Cornelius Plantinga, Jr., "Theological Particularities of Recent Hymnody" *The Hymn*, 52 (October 2001), 8– 5.

12 This points out the tension of the *milieu*: though they tried to position themselves at the cutting edge of popular culture, the Jesus People generally had their roots in an Evangelical culture that was reluctant to let go of conservative traditions such as the use of the King James. This tension continues today.

13 Christian Copyright Licensing International monitors use of worship songs in churches, distributing royalties to songwriters and publishers. It is the most accurate source of statistics for congregational use of praise and worship.

14 According to Phil Christensen and Shari MacDonald. *Our God Reigns: The Stories Behind Your Favorite Praise and Worship Songs*, (Grand Rapids, MI: Kregel Publications, 2000), 132, Lafferty originally wrote only the verse based upon Matthew 6:33. The other verses were added later. This is a testament to the dissemination of early scripture songs. Similar to traditional folk music, they traveled by word of mouth, changing slightly along the way.

15 This is especially true of the steel string acoustic guitar most often used in 60s folk and rock. The thick, steel strings maximize volume, but require more finger pressure than other guitars. Players gravitate toward "open" chords which include some open strings, rather than "barre" chords in which the player must press down all the strings at the same time.

16 For example, both "Seek Ye First" and *Glorify Thy Name* are written in the key of C, a "guitar-friendly" key. "Seek Ye First" never moves out of the comfortable chords of the key. This and its initial C – G – Am – Em-chord sequence make it sound similar to folk songs of its day—*Streets of London* and *Puff the Magic Dragon*—though singular in its own right. *Glorify Thy Name* contains only one chord that moves outside of the key—a V of vi chord (E) that is also easy to play on guitar. *I Exalt Thee* is written in the key of F—a somewhat difficult key for guitar—but is played on the guitar with the help of a capo. (The capo is a device that wraps around the fingerboard of the guitar, raising the key.) With a capo on the third fret, the ii – V – I patterns off *I Exalt Thee* fall into easy D-chord formations while sounding in the key of F.

17 Proof of the song's universality is found in the diversity of hymnals in which it appears: the *Episcopal Hymnal 1982* (1985), *This Far by Faith* (1999), the *Psalter Hymnal* (1987), *The United Methodist Hymnal* (1989), *Celebremos su Gloria* (1992), *The Presbyterian Hymnal* (1990) and *RitualSong* (1996) to name a few.

18 A derisive definition of the praise chorus that circulated among its detractors. Another is "7-11 songs" (seven words sung eleven times).

19 Willow Creek is the most celebrated example of boomer growth. For more on the way the Jesus Movement, evangelist outreach, and youth ministry changed the American church, see Terry W. York, *America's Worship War* (Peabody, MA: Hendrickson Publishers, Inc, 2003).

20 Bert Polman, "The Praise and Worship hit parade: a brief analysis of some of the most-sung choruses of 1990," *Reformed Worship*, 20 (June 1991): 33–35.

21 Some of the songs of this era are analyzed and evaluated in Dori Erwin Collins and Scott C. Weidler, *Sound Decisions: Evaluating Contemporary Music for Lutheran Worship* (Minneapolis: Augsburg Fortress Press, 1997).

22 John and Carol Wimber, "Worship: Intimacy with God." http://renaissanceofasoul.com/?page_id=1656 Accessed March 20, 2013.

23 This was a conversation with a friend during the height of the praise & worship era. I assume that his reaction had something to do with the overly enthusiastic aura of most Evangelical churches at the time. Everything was so upbeat and celebratory during this period it gave some people the impression that they were the only ones having problems.

24 Praise & worship's "second wave" is traced to these two songs in Brian Mansfield, "Praise Hymn with an Upbeat," *USA Today*. October 19, 2001, Friday, FINAL EDITION, LIFE, Pg. 1E. Ted Olsen questions this assessment in "Weblog: Praisin' Worship Music," <http://www.christianitytoday.com/ct/2001/143/12.0.html> posted 10/22/01, accessed 9/17/05, saying "Huh? As popular as those songs were, they weren't the 'Rock Around the Clock' of worship music." However, the songs were pivotal in reinvigorating the praise & worship industry during that time and they introduced non-American worship to the genre. Proof of these songs importance is seen in their continued popularity on today's CCLI charts: "Shout to the Lord" is as of 2005 #4 and "I Could Sing of Your Love Forever" is #19.

25 This is similar to the way the title of one period of Western art music—classical—has become the most common name for western art music as a whole.

26 See William D. Romanowski, "Where's the Gospel?" *Christianity Today*, 41:14 (December 8, 1997), 44, for an overview of how Grant's career has shaped CCM identity, at times causing an identity crisis.

27 See Jay R. Howard and John M. Streck, *Apostles of Rock: The Splintered World of Contemporary Christian Music* (Lexington, KY: The University Press of Kentucky, 1999), 60–64, where worship is given as one of the justifications of CCM. Throughout this book Howard and Streck make a strong case for the role CCM plays in reinforcing and reflecting the Evangelical identity.

28 Danny McGuffey, chief marketing officer for Integrity Media, as quoted in Deborah Evans Price, "Praise & Worship: Thank Heavens for the Music!" *Billboard*. April 24, 2004. Accessed 9/17/2005 via LexisNexis.

29 By 2002, *Worship Leader* had 50,000 paid subscribers, and *SongDiscovery* had 20,000. (Email with *SongDiscovery* editor Trish Carlson, 8/5/02).

30 For a more in-depth look at Hillsong worship, see C. Michael Hawn, "Congregational Singing from Down Under: Experiencing Hillsong's 'Shout to the Lord,'" *The Hymn* 57:2 (Spring 2006), 15–24.

31 Zschech led worship at the Assemblies of God Hillsong Church, Sydney, Australia from the beginnings of the church in c. 1986 until January 2011 when Mark and Darlene Zschech accepted the role as Senior Pastors of Church Unlimited on the Central Coast of New South Wales, north of Sydney. Tommy Walker leads music at Christian Assembly Church in Los Angeles.

32 In fact, the affinity with Black Gospel is strong enough that Zschech has invited singers such as Ron Kenoly to participate in her worship conferences. See the video *Shout to the Lord 2000* (Hosanna! Music, 2000).

33 In the words of John Mortensen: "Most contemporary worship melodies come into being as a by-product of noodling around with chords on a guitar or piano (I speak from experience here). This is a natural result of the fact that many songwriters think of music mainly as chords. In this mindset, to write new music is to play some familiar chords in a different order and try to find a tune that fits." (from "A POSTSCRIPT to Brian McLaren's "Open Letter to Worship Songwriters" http://brianmclaren.net/archives/blog/open-letter-to-worship-songwrite.html Accessed March 20, 2013.

34 This vocal style is likely inspired by the burgeoning popularity of rap during this time.

35 As some guitarists joke, "E is the new G."

36 John and Carol Wimber, "Worship: Intimacy with God." http://renaissanceofasoul.com/?page_id=1656 Accessed March 20, 2013.

37 Though romantic overtones have always existed to some extent in hymnody ("Jesus, the Very Thought of Thee," "My Jesus, I Love You" and *In the Garden*, for example), it has become a dominant theme in the praise & worship genre. Detractors of this theology use the phrase "Jesus is my girlfriend" to point out what they feel to be the inappropriate mixing of romantic yearnings and worship. It is also the title of a dissertation that explores the issue: Sam Hargreaves, *Jesus Is My Girlfriend?* Dissertation, London Bible College, May 2001.

38 To be fair, this is a dominant vocal style for modern pop vocalists.

39 Brendan Dean, age 11, quoted in Kenda Creasy Dean, "Moshing for Jesus: Adolescence as a Cultural Context for Worship" in Brian K. Blount and Leonora Tubbs Tisdale, eds., *Making Room at the Table: An Invitation to Multicultural Worship* (Louisville, KY: Westminster John Knox Press, 2001), 131.

40 John C. LaRue reported that "in 1993, the majority of American church worship services featured traditional music, with half of all churches classifying themselves as primarily traditional in worship style." By 2001, "only a third (thirty-five percent) of churches [said] more than 75 percent of their worship music could be termed traditional." ("Worship Style Synthesis." *Your Church* [Nov/Dec 2001], 72.) The same series of surveys showed that churches identifying themselves as primarily contemporary rose from thirteen percent in 1993 to thirty-two percent in 2004, passing the thirty-one percent traditional churches. The remaining churches in all of these surveys identified themselves as blended. "Worship Music Trends" http://www.christianitytoday.com/le/2001/september-online-only/cln10926.html Accessed March 30, 2013.

41 The WoW Worship albums were a joint effort of Maranatha!, Integrity and Vineyard which featured many of the hits from the praise & worship era. A double-platinum status indicates more than two million units sold, as verified by the Recording Industry Association of America. This line of CDs continues to sell well.

42 The album included such praise & worship standards as "I Could Sing of Your Love Forever" and even resurrected Bill Gaither's *There's Something About That Name*.

43 See Leonard Sweet, *SoulTsunami* (Zondervan, 1999) and *Post-Modern Pilgrims* (Nashville, TN: Broadman & Holman Publishers, 2000), Brian McLaren, *A Generous Orthodoxy* (Grand Rapids. MI: Zondervan, 2004) and Dan Kimball, *The Emerging Church* (Grand Rapids, MI: Zondervan, 2003).

44 Passion, OneDay, 268generation, sixsteprecords, Thirsty.

45 Debra Akins, "Praise and Worship Tours on the Rise," *Billboard,* 116:17 (April 24, 2004), 20.

46 Deborah Evans Price, "Praise and Worship Genre Blessed with Global Growth." *Billboard.* February 15, 2003, 1.

47 http://www.christianitytoday.com/ct/2002/143/42.0.html.

48 Deborah Evans Price, "Praise and Worship Genre Blessed with Global Growth," *Billboard.* February 15, 2003, 1.

49 Mark Moring, "I Could Sing of Your Love Forever." *Campus Life*, 59:6 (January 2001), 20-22.

50 "Blessed Be Your Name" by Beth and Matt Redman © 2002 ThankYou Music/EMI

51 As an example of the changing views toward hymns by praise & worship movement, Michael Hawn was asked by *Worship Leader Magazine* editor, Jeremy Armstrong to write an article on hymnals. See "Shaping Up: The Role of the Hymnal in Faith Formation," *Worship Leader* (January 2013), http://worshipleader.com/shapingup/ Accessed March 20, 2013.

52 See www.igracemusic.com for hymns. Accessed March 20, 2013.

53 *The Wonderful Cross* by Jess Reeves and Chris Tomlin © 2000 WorshipTogether.com/sixsteprecords/EMI.

54 http://www.apostlechurch.org/.

55 Candi Cushman, "Salt or Sugar?" *World.* May 13, 2000, 23.

56 Terry W. York, "Add One Hymn," *The Hymn: A Journal of Congregational Song,* 55:3 (July 2004), 29-33.

57 For those leading praise and worship music in local congregations, see also Greg Scheer, *The Art of Worship: A Musician's Guide to Leading Modern Worship* (Grand Rapids: Baker Books, 2006), a resource that includes discussion of choosing music, planning services, and leading worship bands.

—Stream Seven—
Ecumenical and Global Stream

Chapter 7
Through Every Land, by Every Tongue: The Rise of Ecumenical Global Song

C. Michael Hawn

From all that dwell below the skies,
Let the Creator's praise arise;
Let the Redeemer's name be sung,
Through every land, by every tongue. (Isaac Watts, 1719)

Part I
Historical Perspectives, Issues in and Dissemination of Ecumenical Global Song

Isaac Watts's paraphrase of Psalm 117 indicated an emerging, though ethnocentric, early eighteenth-century global consciousness. The British Empire was taking shape and with it, the expansion of the modern missionary movement.[1] Though Christian song has been transmitted across language groups and cultures since the apostolic era, the first wave of global song in the modern era[2] was the hymns that accompanied the European, and later the North American missionaries to the ends of the earth, translated into many languages and accepted broadly by the peoples of the world as sung expressions of the Christian faith.

By the end of the nineteenth century, John Julian's *A Dictionary of Hymnology: Setting for the Origin and History of Christian Hymns of All Ages and Nations* (1st ed., 1892) bore witness to the effects of the mission movement in an extensive entry by W. R. Stevenson (1823-1889), editor of the *Baptist Hymnal,* titled "Foreign Missions." Though the examples of hymnody beyond the Western world cited in Stevenson's article are anecdotal at best, this twenty-page summary is amazing for its day and provides some substance for the ambitious subtitle of Julian's *Dictionary—Christian Hymns of All Ages and Nations.*[3]

Erik Routley (1917–1982) provided a mid-twentieth-century perspective in 1959, just prior to the Second Vatican Council, in his short monograph titled *Ecumenical Hymnody*. Routley had been asked to address the Council of British Missionary Societies on what was called "Ecumenical and Missionary Hymnody." Routley noted the observation of the Council "that there was some disquiet among those who are especially concerned about the overseas and ecumenical work of the church for the paucity and the indifferent quality of our 'missionary' hymns."[4] Although Routley would edit the fifth edition of *Cantate Domino* in 1980 for the World Council of Churches twenty-one years later, he confesses in 1959 that he is "virtually ignorant of the musical traditions which prevail among most of the non-European races among whom Christian missionary work is carried on."[5] His anecdotal evidence being limited to a few hymnal collections that he had acquired from South Africa and China, Routley laments the general quality of European hymns that have found their way into these hymnals. The focus of Routley's essay moves from hymns in Christian missions to ecumenical hymnody.

Riding the ecumenical wave of the World Council of Churches formed in 1948, Routley set the stage for a discussion of global congregational song:

> [T]he note which in these present times we wish to sound, if we are not to accept with passive resignation the prevalent tendency to think of missionary work as one thing and the ecumenical movement another, is the conception of missionary work as partnership. If we look far enough ahead we can see

> ... that it can hardly be the Lord's will that missionary work should always mean preaching the Gospel to dark-skinned people while ecumenical work should always be study groups to see how far Methodists and Presbyterians can agree about church order.[6]

Continuing this line of thought, Routley challenges the church "to attend to the need for a truly ecumenical hymnody which will have little to do ... with the processes of missionary work, but will provide a vehicle for the praises of a growing world-church."[7] Desiring to free the world church of hymns specifically focused on a paternalistic sense of Christian missions, he was not aware at this point of hymns that spoke to the ecumenical concerns of the entire church other than those from Europe and North America. The Second Vatican Council (1962–1965) provided an impetus to include voices beyond the Euro-North American sphere in English-language hymnals. At the cusp of the twenty-first century, I suggest that the time has come to move beyond provincial definitions that focus only on inter-confessional dialogue, but rather on the original meaning of the word from the Greek οἰκουμένη [oikoumene], "the whole inhabited earth."

Questions, Terminology, and Definitions

Unlike other streams of congregational song discussed in this book, the stream of ecumenical global hymnody requires that we ask specific questions and, perhaps, challenge conventional assumptions based on Western hymn practice. Philip Bohlman acknowledges that any discussion of world music begs the ontological question, "What is music?"[8]

From the perspective of Western hymnology, the study of global congregational song raises an analogous ontological question, "What is a hymn?" This is more than an academic question.

Many of the songs cited in this chapter will not meet a strict definition of a hymn according to historical Western practice.[9] Ecumenical global hymnody takes a variety of forms. This chapter references only a sampling of global hymns that are most accessible to Christians in the northern world and appear in current hymnals.[10] The diversity and complexity of ecumenical global congregational song challenges many Western ontological assumptions about the nature of a hymn and the experience of congregational singing. Though not specific to this stream of congregational song, singing with the world church often encourages us to look beyond the printed page and incorporate improvisatory oral-tradition practices. Songs from the Southern Hemisphere often invite us to join in with our bodies as we sing. Many songs are through-composed rather than in a classic Western stanza form. Numerous songs have few words. Some press us to sing in languages we do not speak. A number are group compositions that come from the experience of a community with no recognizable single composer. In most cases, music and text are composed by the same person or community and are inextricably linked. Instruments that are not often available to Western congregations accompany many compositions. Yet, countless other songs that come from the world church sound almost identical to classic Western hymns. When looking at ecumenical global hymns, our ontological assumptions may be challenged.

What is "Global Hymnody"?

Global hymnody is often used interchangeably with world, ethnic, international, or multicultural music. "Third-World music" has been used occasionally, but is inaccurate (Japan, for example, is not a third-world country) and, more importantly, carries vestiges of colonialism. The term "global hymnody," however, also presents some difficulties. The first relates to perspective: What hymnody is global and what hymnody is not? If this book were being written on another continent, for example, Africa, Australia, Europe, or South America, the physical location and cultural orientation of the authors would change the perspective and, in varying degrees, the streams of song that would emerge. "Global," though seemingly a universal term, is still subject to a specific social location.

As mentioned earlier, the Western hymns introduced by missionaries during the eighteenth, nineteenth, and first half of the twentieth centuries became the global musical currency of the church universal. Late in the twentieth century, European and North American churches became aware of music produced by Christians from non-Western cultures. Interest in global music today reflects a demographic shift between 1950 and the turn of the twenty-first century. Where once seventy percent of baptized Christians lived in the Northern Hemisphere, now only thirty to thirty-five percent of Christians do. The remaining sixty to seventy-five percent of Christians lives in the Southern Hemisphere.[11] This second wave of global hymnody from the two-thirds Christian world is the primary subject of this chapter.

The second difficulty with the term "global hymnody" is the political nature of globalization. As an economic strategy, globalization is often associated with the spread of Western economic approaches and cultural values around the world, especially those from the United States. This connection of globalization—and by association, global—with cultural assimilation is unfortunate.[12] For the most part, those who promote the use of global music within Euro-North American worship have the opposite intent; they strive to bring the authentic musical voice of Christians from the far reaches of the globe into Western liturgy as a reminder that the church, though gathered locally, is a part of the universal body of Christ.[13]

Closely aligned with the negative aspects of globalization is the problem of exoticism or, according to Timothy D. Taylor, "manifestations of awareness of racial, ethnic, and cultural others captured in sound."[14] Taylor points out that exoticism has a long history in Western music, going back to at least the seventeenth century, and tends to "fetishlike form and style" rather than to appreciate the cultural context from which the music comes. The nineteenth century, according to Taylor, led to "the classical music ideology" promoting the twin concepts of individual genius and masterpiece—notions that a composer's works, though of a particular time and place, "are thought to speak directly to the listener."[15] Taylor continues:

> That musicology is primarily based on the study of individuals and their works betrays a usually unacknowledged Enlightenment notion of the individual—and the later idea of genius—so that musicians are not usually viewed as subjects inhabiting a particular historical moment and a particular place, but instead are viewed unproblematically as total agents: things happen in a musical work because a composer makes them happen.[16]

Whether one agrees with Taylor's assumptions, his premise helps to clarify the intent of the authors of this chapter. Though summary in nature, this chapter attempts to identify not only individual contributions to ecumenical global hymnody, but also some insight into the cultural, theological, and liturgical context from which their music springs. Of course, the composers in this chapter display creativity, but they are definitely children of specific times and places in the world. The study of world music offers scholars a methodology to view the masterpieces of the Western canon as more than supra-cultural feat by geniuses—an inherently racist notion as this privilege is rarely extended to those beyond the Western world—but as a product of a specific time and place. This is an essential assumption of this chapter because it is the alterity or "otherness" of ecumenical global hymnody that displays the manifold face of Christ not bound by one culture or one age, but for all cultures and ages.

For the purpose of this chapter, ecumenical global hymnody will signify Christian songs originating beyond Euro-North American cultural contexts with the exception of the influential European ecumenical communities of Iona and Taizé whose ecumenical song has become global. Since the late twentieth-century, hymnals produced in the United States, Canada, and some countries in Europe include Christian songs primarily from sub-Saharan Africa, Asia (especially eastern Asia), Latin America (Spanish-speaking countries), Portuguese speaking countries, and the Caribbean. Christian music from the Middle East, Eastern Europe, the former Soviet Republics, and the Polynesian islands has been less widely disseminated except in ecumenical international collections and worship resources. Christian music created by African-Americans (discussed in stream three) and Native Americans—co-cultures in North America—is beyond the scope of this chapter. Though global hymnody often makes use of instrumental and dance structures, the focus here is upon congregational songs. For the sake of convenience, the term used in this chapter will be "global" hymnody or "global" song with the understanding that this is also ecumenical hymnody in the broadest sense of that term.

How Have These Songs Come to North American Hymnals?

The transmission of global song reflects the migrations of our age, the frequency of international confessional and ecumenical gatherings, the relative ease and proliferation of publications, and the desire of many to experience ways of singing and praying beyond their cultural context. This migration often reflects the struggles and crises of particular members of the world church.[17] The body of Christ comprises those who are near and dear and the church universal.

What Is the Best Way to Organize the Information?

This chapter will consider global song from the perspective of broad continental regions of the world—Africa, Asia, and Latin/South America, with a European addendum.[18] This approach contrasts with the way many ethnomusicologists present their findings.

Ethnomusicologists usually explore the music of a specific ethnic group or tribal context in detail. The wide variety of musical styles and the integral relationship of any particular music to its cultural context make it difficult for ethnomusicologists to make universal assertions about the meaning of their area of research in the broader global arena. Because of the number, variety and complexity of various world musical systems, ethnomusicologists speak of world *musics*.[19] Music making is a universal phenomenon, but it is not a universal language.[20]

The focus of this chapter is primarily on global congregational song, most of which has been composed since the mid-1960s, and on songs that have been included in hymnals and hymnal supplements published in the United States, Canada and Western Europe since the late 1980s. The broad survey of selected continents undertaken in this chapter runs the risk of superficiality and may give the impression that music from a given continent is monolithic in style. The opposite is true. The musics of Africa, Asian, and Latin America are extremely varied in language, instruments, vocal styles, and rhythmic complexity. The examples that appear in North American hymnals are but brief glimpses of what is happening in the world Christian church. Furthermore, the selection of global materials by North American hymnal committees by its nature affects this survey because usually only the most accessible music from other cultures is chosen by a hymnal committee.[21] Moreover, by the time a given song appears in print in a North American hymnal, the sending culture may have moved on newer songs. Therefore, a survey such as this will be limited in scope and current relevance by issues of accessibility to receiving cultures and availability to hymnal committees.

INFLUENCES OF VATICAN II

With some few exceptions, congregations beyond the European and North American context primarily sang Western hymns in translation before the liturgical reforms of the Second Vatican Council (1962–1965). Although folk tunes from "native" cultures appeared occasionally in Western collections, these tunes were often domesticated by eliminating intervals difficult for Western singers and by adding keyboard harmonizations that were usually incompatible with the original musical style. Even original compositions by non-Western composers were regularly composed in Western musical styles. Colonial missionaries and their converts often assumed that indigenous cultural forms were technically and aesthetically inadequate or even inherently evil, incapable of conveying sound Christian theology. Admittedly, specific melodies, musical instruments, and rhythmic patterns are often associated with non-Christian cultural practices. In many cultures, however, indigenous musical resources have been wedded with the gospel to produce musical expressions that are liturgically faithful and culturally relevant.

One primary method of dissemination of global song is through the collections produced for the international assemblies such as those of the World Lutheran Federation and the ecumenical gatherings of the World Student Christian Federation.[22] These collections foreshadowed to a degree liturgical inculturation—the examination of the reciprocal relationship between worship and culture and the conscious incorporation of cultural elements within liturgy—encouraged by Vatican II.[23] This view may be seen in the difference between compilations produced before and after Vatican II. Four hymnals—all editions of *Laudamus* with the exception of the first assembly that used a small collection entitled *Hymnal for the Assembly*—were used in assemblies of the World Lutheran Federation (WLF) before

Vatican II: Lund, 1947 (thirty-six hymns), Hanover, 1952 (seventy-one hymns), Minneapolis, 1957 (seventy-four hymns), and Helsinki, 1963 (108) hymns. English, German and Spanish were the normative languages for each entry with the exception of four Latin hymns. The major cultural expansion in collections during this period was the broader inclusion of Scandinavian hymnody (Norway, Finland, Denmark, and Sweden)[24] from three hymns in 1947 to eighteen hymns, including hymns in Norwegian, Danish and Swedish languages, in 1963. WLF Assembly collections since the 1970 assembly in Evian have incorporated many more hymns and languages from the two-thirds world.

Cantate Domino was the hymnal of the World Student Christian Federation from its first edition in 1924 edited by Suzanne Bidgrain (1879–1961) to the fourth edition in 1951 edited by R. C. Mackie. French, German, and English dominate the languages and the countries of origin. One African selection, a hymn from South Africa by the Xhosa prophet Ntsikana (c. 1780–1821), appears in the second (1930) and third (1938) editions. Between five and seven hymns from Asian sources appear in the various editions. Eastern European and Scandinavian hymns (often in the original languages) appear in more abundance in these collections. *Cantate Domino* did not demonstrate greater inclusion of hymns from the two-thirds world until it became a hymnal for the World Council of Churches in 1974. The impact of Vatican II was profound on these international and ecumenical hymnals.

Sacrosanctum Concilium (*Constitution on the Sacred Liturgy,* 1963) produced by Vatican II promoted liturgy inculturated in the linguistic patterns, metaphors, dance, and music of individual cultures while sharing a common historical liturgical shape throughout the world. Roman Catholic Mass settings based upon specific musical/cultural idioms began to appear in the 1960s. This document acknowledged that the "Church respects and fosters the genius and talents of the various races and peoples." (par. 37) Ecclesiastical control of the incorporation of cultural elements was given in part to knowledgeable persons in specific regions, especially in the areas of the "administration of the sacraments, sacramentals, processions, liturgical language, sacred music, and the arts" as long as these practices were carried out within the norms established by *Sacrosanctum Concilium*. (par. 39)[25]

Because of the context of the reforms within the Roman Catholic Church, incorporation of local cultural musical styles often took place within the ordinary of the Mass rather than in specific hymns, since congregational singing was an anomaly in the Mass before Vatican II.[26] While the reforms provided in *Sacrosanctum Concilium* gave a great impetus to the liturgical inculturation movement, there were notable exceptions that predate Vatican II, especially in Africa.

> ### Missa Luba, A Case Study for Musical Inculturation
>
> A case study of musical liturgical inculturation comes from an African perspective. *Missa Luba*, a Congolese Mass, was the result of encouragement provided by Fr. Guido Haazen (1921–2004), a Franciscan priest from Belgium. Establishing a choir among the students in the mission at Kamina in 1953 in the Belgian Congo (later Zaïre, now the Democratic Republic of the Congo), Haazen laid the ground work for a Mass setting in a Congolese musical style. He noted:
>
> > Soon I discovered the unbelievable musicality of the Africans. Their songs, their dances and their profound sense of rhythm was [sic] a revelation to me. But to my great disappointment I noticed that in our missionary church they only sang the old European hymns and songs that they had learned from our missionary priests! It surprised me greatly because I had already noticed that the Africans could express their feelings of joy and sorrow by singing and dancing.[27]
>
> Haazen's positive response to the culture and music of his students became a great source of pride for them. Rather than composing a setting of the Mass, he worked through a local musician who inspired a group creative oral process. Marc Foster notes that, "Haazen, because of his early church studies and interest in the music of the church, was quite familiar with the concept of a parody Mass. However, the idea for the creation of an African Mass using

> African music, but with Latin text and *improvised collectively*, was unparalleled at the time. Indeed, of all the African Masses written from 1900-1965, none has a similar process of creation."[28] Though *Missa Luba* was first performed in 1958, it was not transcribed by Haazen until 1964 and finally engraved in a performing edition in 1969.[29]
>
> Though not containing congregational song, the background of *Missa Luba* is helpful in understanding the formation of much global song. In many world music traditions, song is conceived, shared, and sung long before it is written down. Where oral tradition is normative in a culture, the transcription of the music is an afterthought rather than integral to the creative process. In many cases the music is through-composed to fit the text rather than conceived in the more conventional method of writing in stanzas that recycle the music with a metrical text. In Africa and beyond, congregational song depends on a leader who inspires the singing of the people, prompts changes in text, and improvises over the congregation's part. Even Western hymnody is often modified to fit this call-response style of performance in countries where oral tradition is common.[30]

African Mass settings near the time of Vatican II include the Congolese *Missa Luba* (1958) transcribed by Fr. Guido Haazen, *Missa Baba Yetu* [*Mass of Our Father*] by Fr. Stephen B. G. Mbunga (1927–1982)[31] composed in 1959 based on traditional music of the Tanzania's Lake Malawi region, and *Missa 1* (c. 1965), a Xhosa Mass setting from South Africa by Benjamin John Peter Tyamzashe (1890-1978).[32]

Eventually, ritual songs supporting various elements of the Mass were added to the ordinary and have become a part of the world song found in recent hymnals. Stephen Cuthbert Molefe (1917–1987) composed his "Masithi—Amen" ("Amen siakudumisa") as part of a series of composition workshops conducted by South African Catholic priest, David Dargie (b. 1938) in 1977. This was one of fifty-three new church songs that Dargie collected in his composition workshops on various parts of the Mass.

Conceived as the Great Amen at the end of the Great Thanksgiving, it was immediately popular during Holy Week that year and incorporated into a Xhosa Catholic hymnal, *Bongan' iNkosi* [*Praise the Lord*], (c. 1978) by Oswald Hirmer, a missionary priest. The text exhorts the people "Let us say 'Amen, we praise you'"—the congregation's response to the Eucharist at the conclusion of the Great Thanksgiving, extending the celebrant's prayer with a burst of joy. Its cyclic construction allows the choir to improvise over the congregational refrain above and is often supported by marimbas playing in a 3+3+2 rhythm. The brief text would not qualify as a hymn in the Western sense, but it is a vibrant congregational song that has spread broadly around the world.[33] (see example 7.1 on page 221)

Spanish language Masses followed a similar course. Early Masses included *Misa Criolla* (Ariel Ramírez, 1921–2010), an Argentine Mass based on indigenous folk rhythms, and several Central American Masses including the collaborations between Archbishop Oscar Romero (1917–1980) and composer Guillermo Cuéllar (b. 1955) in El Salvador resulting in *La Nueva Misa Mesoamericana* and *Misa Popular Salvadoreña*. Folk Masses from Nicaragua include *Misa Popular Nicaragüense* and Carlos Godoy's (b. 1943) *Misa Campesina Nicaragüense*.[34] These Central American Masses added entrance songs and other ritual music to the ordinary of the Mass, several that have been incorporated into recent hymnals. The music from these Masses will be covered below in the section on Latin American and Caribbean hymns.

By composing in vernacular styles, these Masses paved the way for reinforcing cultural identity through congregational music. Even though the forms of the Mass are set, composers find ways to contextualize them for their own situations. In performance, the *estribillos* [refrains] are often used to engage the community directly allowing them to move and observe the ritual action while singing. Cantors or choirs often sing the stanzas, freeing the congregation to sing without written music if they choose. Some are not hymns in the classic sense (perhaps more properly they may be called ritual music), and these congregational acclamations provide a way for the people to sing as a part of the liturgy. The insertion of words beyond the texts of the ordinary of the Mass blurs the distinction between a hymn and ritual song.

Example 7:1: Amen Siakudumisa (excerpt)

Music transcription © 1983 David Dargle, administered by Choristers Guild

Ecumenical Gatherings:
Contributions of the World Council of Churches

The World Council of Churches' (WCC) publications, international assemblies, and church music symposia are important sources for global song. Initial efforts centered on *Cantate Domino* (melody edition, 1974; full-harmony edition, 1980), published by the WCC and edited by Erik Routley. This version, containing 202 selections in thirteen languages with participation by Roman Catholics and, for the first time, Orthodox Christians, was a radical departure from the four earlier editions published by the World Student Christian Federation. Texts appear in the original language and, usually, in English, French, and German. In spite of the broader global perspective of the fifth edition, the collection retained the feel of a European hymnal and many of the songs were harmonized without regard to the culture of origin. Later more culturally focused publications such as *African Songs of Worship* (1986), edited by Taiwanese ethnomusicologist I-to Loh (b. 1936), and *Brazilian Songs of Worship* (1989), edited by Brazilian theologian and composer Jaci Maraschin (1929–2009), avoid some of the pitfalls of *Cantate Domino*.[35]

The sixth General Assembly in Vancouver (1983) was a turning point for integrating global song into the shared ecumenical liturgies of the WCC. The diversity of the music from around the world became the primary means for embodying an ecumenical and global faith. Liturgical/musical *animateurs* [animators] from most continents provided leadership for assembly worship. Publications of songs from this assembly and subsequent events in Canberra (1991), Harare (1998), and Porto Alegre (2006)[36] have become important sources for disseminating global song throughout the world. Some of the primary *animateurs* include I-to Loh (Presbyterian, Taiwan), Patrick Matsikenyiri (b. 1937, United Methodist, Zimbabwe), Simei Monteiro (b. 1943, Methodist, Brazil), George Mxadana (South Africa), Pablo Sosa (b. 1933, Methodist, Argentina), Per Harling (b. 1948, Lutheran, Sweden), Dinah Reindorf (b. 1927, Ghana), and Terry MacArthur (b. 1949, United Methodist, USA). In addition to leading global song in a wide variety of venues around the world, WCC *animateurs* were often composers, editors, or translators, greatly enhancing the dissemination of global resources.[37]

MacArthur served as the Worship Consultant for the WCC during both the Canberra and Harare Assemblies. From this position he brought together international musicians and prepared ecumenical liturgies that reflected a breadth of world Christian song heretofore unachieved. MacArthur's commitment to collecting global songs and other worship materials, engaging global *animateurs*, and producing global worship resources place him at the forefront of this movement.[38]

The tenth assembly of the WCC, held in Busan, South Korea, October 30 – November 8, 2013, under the leadership of Canadian Andrew Donaldson (b. 1951) continued this tradition by using song enliveners and music from around the world.

Other Disseminators of Global Song

Global resources have been disseminated through an increasing number of publications. From Germany, *Thuma Mina: Internationales oekumenishches Liederbuch* (1995), edited by Dieter Trautwein (1928-2002) and endorsed by the Association of Protestant Churches and Mission in Germany, reflects the spirit of the WCC gatherings. Trautwein coordinated worship for the Vancouver Assembly.[39]

Scotland's Iona Community has also been at the forefront of promoting global song. John Bell (b. 1949), a minister of the Church of Scotland (Reformed), and the members of the Wild Goose Resource Group (WGRG) edited two global collections, *Many and Great: Songs of the World Church* (1990) and *Sent by the Lord* (1991). Subsequent publications by the WGRG usually include global songs among their varied contents, providing a sung complement to the prophetic message of justice and peace for which the Community is known. These global efforts complement Bell's musical contextualization on a local level as he often matches Scottish and Irish melodies with texts composed by himself and the WGRG.[40]

Geoff Weaver (b. 1943) is one of the leading musicians in the Anglican Church in the dissemination of Christian global song. He taught in the United Kingdom before working under the auspices of the Church Mission Society (CMS) for eight years in Hong Kong. After serving as Director of Music at Bradford Cathedral, he was on the staff of the CMS Training College in

Selly Oak, Birmingham. For eight years Weaver served as Director of Studies/Outreach for the Royal School of Church Music. A composer and arranger, his most notable publications in global song include three editions of *World Praise* (1993, 1995, 2000) prepared for congresses of the Baptist World Alliance, edited with David Peacock (b. 1949).[41] In his capacity as music director for the 1998 and 2008 Lambeth Conferences, Weaver has included an unprecedented amount of global song in the liturgy of the international gatherings of the Anglican community.[42] According to Peacock, these volumes represent significant stylistic "compromises" for "making music transfer to other cultures" in order to provide repertoire for a worship journey. In the future, he would prefer, for example, to "set African music in a more traditional manner, providing model recordings for most songs in a downloadable format" with additional notes such as accompaniment rhythms on the page in order to encourage more faithful representations of the music and performance.[43]

The focus on culture and worship by the World Lutheran Federation (WLF) and its Assemblies (the tenth was in 2003) has set the stage for incorporating global song into liturgy. *Laudamus*, with six editions from 1952-1990, was a collection used in these gatherings. The 1990 Supplement was the first to focus on global song. *Agape: Songs of Hope and Reconciliation* (2003), compiled by Maggie Hamilton and Päivi Jussila for the assembly in Winnipeg, is the most diverse to date with 111 entries in forty languages. Fifty selections are from the Southern Hemisphere. Gerhard Cartford (b. 1923) and Mark P. Bangert (b. 1938), participants in WLF consultations on worship, have been among the foremost proponents of global song for the Lutheran (ELCA) Church in the United States.[44]

From Sweden, Per Harling (b. 1948) has promoted global song and liturgy both for the WCC (See *Worshipping Ecumenically*, 1995), through a series of ten documentaries entitled "The Whole World Sings" for Swedish television and his own collection of global song *Hela världen sjunger* [*The Whole World Sings*] (1997) that introduce songs from many parts of the two-thirds world to Swedes. A minister in the [Lutheran] Church of Sweden, Harling has also explored the folk song roots of his own country. His folk Mass, *Träd in i dansen: Mässa i Viston* [*Come, Join the Dance: A Mass in*

Song] (1993) provides a Swedish contextualization of the liturgy. Harling's most widely sung hymn is "Du är helig" ["You are holy"] is an adaptation of the *Sanctus* and *Benedictus* from his folk mass. "För livets skull" ["For sake of life"], also from the folk mass, is found in *Panorama*: 915.

Global song collections for specific events include *Aleluya: Let the Whole World Sing*, edited by Corean Bakke and Tony Payne, for the Lausanne II Congress on World Evangelization (Manila, 1989), and *World Praise* and *World Praise 2*, edited by David Peacock and Geoff Weaver, for the Baptist World Alliance Congresses (Buenos Aires, 1995; Melbourne, 2000). The latter volume contains 117 songs from approximately fifty countries.

In the United States, a Lutheran-based ensemble, Bread for the Journey, has published three collections of global songs: *Global Songs: Local Voices* (1995), *Global Songs 2* (1997), and *Pave the Way: Global Songs 3* (2004) along with recordings. Their programs are participatory and have helped to disseminate world Christian song throughout the USA.[45]

The United Methodist Global Praise Project (GPP) has made significant contributions to the dissemination of global song.[46] Begun in 1993 through the General Board of Global Ministries, the GPP was led by S T Kimbrough, Jr. (b. 1936), general editor, until 2006 with Carlton R. Young (b. 1926) serving as musical editor. The GPP has brought together leading church musicians and composers from around the world to share songs, plan publications, and design conferences that encourage the singing of global songs by local congregations. In addition to WCC animateurs Harling, Loh, Matsikenyiri, Monteiro, and Sosa, other GPP leaders have included Raquel Guitierrez-Achón (Cuban-American), Tomas Boström (Sweden), Tom Colvin (Scotland/Africa), Melva Costen (African-American), Ludmilla Garbouzova (Russia), Hartmut Handt (Germany), Ivor Jones (England), Jorge Lockward (Dominican Republic/USA), George Mulrain (Trinidad and Tobago), and Lim Swee Hong (Singapore).

Global Praise I (1996, rev. 1997), *Global Praise II* (2000), and *Global Praise III* (2004), timed to appear at the quadrennial General Conferences of the United Methodist Church, are collections with a broad diversity of world song. Additional focused collections include *Africa Praise Songbook* (1998) compiled by Matsikenyiri, *Russian Praise* (1999) compiled by Garbuzova,

Caribbean Praise (2000) compiled by Mulrain, and *Tenemos Esperanza/Temos Esperança/We Have Hope* (2002) edited by Lockward. *Songs for the World: Contemporary Settings of Charles Wesley Hymns from Five Continents* (2001) and *Songs of Love and Praise: The Hymns of John Wesley* (2003) provide fresh settings of the Wesleys' hymns by composers around the world. Each collection is accompanied by a recording that is helpful in learning the musical styles of the songs. The *Companion to Songbooks Global Praise 1 and Global Praise 2: Worship Leaders Guide*, ed. S T Kimbrough, Jr. (2005), provides needed biographical background and performance practice suggestions.

Through his position with the General Board of Global Ministries of the United Methodist Church, Kimbrough, with the musical assistance of Carlton R. Young, has also initiated hymnals for congregations in other parts of the world. These collaborative efforts have taken place in countries ranging from Lithuania in northern Europe to Cambodia.[47] The GPP continues under the leadership of Jorge Lockward producing collections for the North American audience and local settings around the world such a the United Methodist Church in Cameroon.

Mennonite congregations have been exposed to global song through Mennonite World Assemblies' song collections produced for these events, and their primary hymnal, *Hymnal: A Worship Book* (1992), a joint publication for congregations in the Believers Church Tradition. Mary Oyer (b. 1923), a primary proponent for global song among Mennonites, studied music extensively in Africa and taught with I-to Loh in Taiwan.[48] A tradition with a strong sense of world missions, Mennonites use global song as a symbol of partnership in mission with Christians around the world.

Recently, the International Council of Ethnodoxologists (ICE) has been formed by Evangelicals to promote global Christian music. Founders of ICE include ethnomusicologists Frank Fortunato (b. 1946), Robin Harris (b. 1961), Roberta King (b. 1949), and Paul Neeley (b. 1958). According to Robin Harris, "The ICE network exists to encourage and equip Christ-followers in every culture to express their faith through their own heart music and other arts. ICE facilitates online networking and provides resources for the development of culturally appropriate Christian worship, utilizing insights from ethnomusicology, missiology, worship studies and the arts."[49]

ICE was a sponsor of GCoMM 2006 (Global Consultation on Music and Missions) which drew several hundred participants. *EthnoDoxology*, a journal begun in 2002, edited by Paul Neeley, is "devoted to the multifaceted music, arts and worship of every tribe, tongue, and nation."[50]

Recent Scholarship in Global Hymnody

Another tributary to the global stream is the availability of scholarship in major musical dictionaries and encyclopedias. Three deserve special mention here.

The Garland Encyclopedia of World Music[51] is the most complete recent research tool in this area. This ten-volume work approaches music from a comprehensive cultural perspective and touches virtually every corner of the globe. Each volume contains an extensive index and bibliography and is arranged by topic, region, or by ethnic group according to the material covered. Especially helpful are the recordings that accompany each volume. Though much broader in scope, the development of church music, both colonial and indigenous, receives ample attention.

The various editions of *Grove's Dictionary of Music and Musicians*[52] throughout the twentieth century have made significant contributions to musicology. Grove Music Online www.grovemusic.com, published simultaneously with the print version, *The New Grove Dictionary of Music and Musicians*, offers a convenient resource for specific information. During the last quarter of the twentieth century, editions have increasingly incorporated composers, musical terminology, works and forms beyond the Euro-North American sphere. The online version has the advantage of constant updates and new articles.

Oxford University Press's Global Music Series consists of more than fifteen handy volumes with compact discs. Series general editors, Bonnie C. Wade and Patricia Shehan Campbell, have developed these resources since 2003 under the rubric "Experiencing Music, Expressing Culture."

In addition, the *Canterbury Dictionary of Hymnology,*[53] successor of John Julian's *Dictionary of Hymnology* 1892, 1907, under the general editorship of J. Richard Watson (b. 1934) includes extensive entries on hymns and hymn writers beyond the Euro-North American context.

Perhaps the best indicator of current congregational song repertoire and practice in various regions of the world is through recordings produced locally. These recordings offer current glimpses into local congregational song styles and are usually much more current than print collections. YouTube also provides video clips of world music performances for those who search carefully. By means of the Internet, recordings are more accessible than ever before, but travel directly to the countries is still the best way to secure them.

PART II
Regional Perspectives: An Introduction to African Hymnody

This stream of global hymnody is actually a great river with many tributaries. Some of the tributaries that have contributed to this swelling river have been discussed above: the Second Vatican Council; international and ecumenical assemblies such as those by the World Council of Churches; confessional contributions to global song, especially from European and North American collections. In this section, global congregational song will be examined from three broad continental regions—Africa, Latin America/Caribbean, and Asian (contributed by Lim Swee Hong) with a European addendum. A comprehensive approach will not be possible. Examples will be limited for the most part to those that have appeared with some regularity in North American hymnals.

An Introduction to African Hymnody

"Music might be considered as one of the best ways to educate Christian people. A beautiful hymn, well understood and lived, has the value of a good sermon."[54] In this quotation, Father Ntahokaja expresses the importance of hymnody in African worship. Christian missionaries also began to recognize the importance of hymnody at this same time, though they were unprepared for the most part to understand how to work with indigenous music.[55] The purpose of this section is to document the expansion of African indigenous hymnody into the twenty-first century.

African songs began to appear in Western hymnals during the late 1980s, though there were sporadic examples in earlier collections, and continue with growing interest in the twenty-first century. This discussion will focus on selected missionary pioneers of sub-Saharan African indigenous song leading up to and following the Second Vatican Council (1962–1965) and the processes they used to encourage compositions by Africans. Representative examples of African hymns will be drawn from those that are in common usage or, at least, appear in denominational hymnals and ecumenical song collections in the United States, Canada, and Europe.

The major African national independence movements of the early 1960s coincided with the liturgical reforms of the Second Vatican Council. This resulted in extensive efforts to inculturate the Roman Catholic Mass, including the music sung by the assembly.[56] The role of *Missa Luba*, a Congolese Mass composed in an oral tradition, combining liturgical Latin with indigenous folk melodies, has been referred to above under "Influences of Vatican II." With the recognition by Pope John Paul II of the "Zaïrian Rite" (now the Democratic Republic of Congo) of the Mass in 1988, composers of African Christian music since the Second Vatican Council have been encouraged to continue their efforts toward musical inculturation.

In the 1960s and 1970s Protestant missions began to send missionaries who incorporated anthropological and ethnomusicological approaches in their work. These included John Kaemmer and Robert Kauffman in Zimbabwe serving under the American United Methodist Church, Olof Axelsson in Zimbabwe with the Church of Sweden Mission (Lutheran), Roberta King, Conservative Baptist in Kenya, Howard Olson, American Lutheran in Tanzania, and Nathan Corbitt, Southern Baptist in Kenya and Zimbabwe.[57] These people were representative of many who developed a significant expertise in particular styles of African music, nurtured African musicians in the compositional process, and incorporated African musical styles into worship where previously Western hymns in translation had been the norm.[58]

Hugh Tracey : The Mentor of Missionaries

No discussion of African church music should omit the contributions of Hugh Tracey (1903–1977) to African music research. Axelsson, Kaemmer, Kauffman, and Olson were just a few who studied directly with Tracey in the formative years of their research. Tracey, an Englishman who settled with his brother in Southern Rhodesia (now Zimbabwe) on a tobacco farm in 1920, heard the African workers singing their songs in the fields. Upon the advice of Gustav Holst and Ralph Vaughan Williams, he began to record and collect songs from his workers, viewing African music, in the words of Ghanaian ethnomusicologist J. H. Kwabena Nketia (b. 1921), as "an artistic heritage to be shared, preserved, and promoted."[59]

Nketia further states that, "No single individual has collected as much African music over such a vast territory as did Hugh Tracey."[60] Tracey's travels throughout much of Africa convinced him that "Westerners visiting or residing in Africa—educators, social workers, missionaries, administrative officers, choreographers, musicians, linguists, and other scholars specializing in African studies" could make contributions in the collection of factual data.[61] Though not professing to be a Christian, he was open to missionaries on the basis of the need to gather knowledge about African culture from many disciplines.

Tracey was the co-founder with Winifred Hoernle of the African Music Society in 1945. He served as secretary and edited its newsletter (1948–1953) and *African Music*, the annual journal of the society, from (1955–1971). After twenty-five years of recording African music, Tracey founded the International Library of African Music (ILAM) near Johannesburg, South Africa in 1954 with a grant from the Nuffield Foundation.[62] Shortly after his death, ILAM moved to Rhodes University in Grahamstown in 1979. Tracey helped missionaries learn to record music, and his "Sound of Africa" series, consisting of 210 LP albums, provided them with recordings of traditional music. His son, Andrew Tracey, (b. 1936) himself a noted ethnomusicologist and

> African musician fluent in many styles, joined his father in his work in 1969 and continued as director of ILAM following his father's death. *African Music: Journal of the African Music Society*, edited by Andrew Tracey and published by ILAM since 1954, has been a further source of information for missionaries seeking to nourish the development of indigenous African congregational song.[63]

Characteristics of Traditional African Music.[64] In order to better appreciate African Christian hymns, it is helpful to understand the foundations of traditional African music making. The ontological question—What is music for a given culture?—confronts the African ethnomusicologist and ethno hymnologist. John Kaemmer notes, for example, that, "many peoples in Southern Africa define music in terms of the presence of metered rhythm. That means that drumming alone is also considered music, and chanting or speaking words is singing, so long as it is metrical."[65] Vocalization without rhythm is not usually considered music. Africans think of themselves as inherently musical. Although some are recognized for their special musical abilities, e.g., dancer, singer, or drummer, virtually everyone is a singer. As a Zimbabwean pastor noted, "only a few of us were born with weak beats."[66] The role of African music, however, extends beyond individual musicality to social structure. Music is an important symbol of political power throughout the continent, including the sponsorship of royal musicians in many tribes.[67] Songs for work, celebration, and traditional religious rituals are integral to the social fabric of African life. African musicologist Nketia notes, "A village that has no organized music or neglects community singing, drumming, or dancing is said to be dead."[68]

The characteristics of traditional African music making are more than a point of comparison between Western and African ontological world-views. Incorporating African hymns in worship is part of the formation of corporate identity. Stephen Mbunga recognized this in his treatise on African music in liturgy in 1963: "It is a great pity that modern Africans are consistently losing their art which their forefathers invented for them. We cannot be disinterested spectators while the heritage of our tribes shatters into dust. If anything is worth retaining, it is our African music which binds together the elements of our social organization."[69]

Essential to an understanding of African congregational song is the process of oral tradition. Traditional African society uses songs abundantly to enliven social events, protest acts of injustice, ease the drudgery of labor, and to enhance religious rituals such as soliciting the aid of ancestors. In most circumstances any singer may interject a song into an occasion spontaneously and the group will participate in a leader (call)-response fashion. The leader is free to improvise a text, contextualizing the song to fit the situation. Traditional songs are often cyclic in structure. Cyclic musical structures often involve a shorter text, at least by the standards of Western classical hymnody, that may be repeated by the group while leaders provide textual variety. It is common for the leader to sing either between the group's responses or over the ends of phrases, bridging the cycle together in a continuous line. African songs maintain a steady beat once they begin. This is essential because dance usually accompanies singing.[70]

Oral tradition within a culture does not presume illiteracy. Many parishioners bring their own hymnals along with their Bibles to worship. In the rural areas where some people may either not be literate or able to afford hymnals, an African style of "lining out" the hymns facilitates everyone's participation. The hymn proceeds at the given tempo while the leader speaks the next phrase as the people sing the preceding one. Because of African skills in call-response techniques, the congregation is able to maintain the pace at a regular tempo, often accompanied by a drum ensemble. It is also common for Western hymn tunes to be slightly altered by Africans. This is probably due to the difficulty of a specific ethnic group to cognitively process a given Western hymn in light of the natural tones and rhythms of the African vernacular language. Another possibility is that the hymn was not learned as printed when first taught and spread through a deep-rooted practice of oral tradition to other groups in the altered form. One can observe these same practices at work in reverse when Western congregations attempt African songs.

Judith Bangsund describes the role of hymnals within oral cultures from the perspective of her work as a Lutheran church musician and missionary in Tanzania. While the literacy rate varies from region to region, the experience of this author in western, eastern and southern Africa suggests that her observations have a broader application.

> Hymns are learned by ear. They are sung wherever Christians meet: at church gatherings, youth conventions, religion classes at school, and so on. In some areas local instruments may be used, mostly as percussive accompaniment. Very few Western instruments are used country-wide; in larger churches found in cities, or where there have been mission stations, some organs, pianos, brass instruments and guitars may be found. Church singing is largely *a cappella*. It is therefore common for the same hymns to be sung over and over in a given parish, and pastors complain that every year the number of hymns that the congregations know is fewer. Unfamiliar hymns may be learned from visitors, from cassette tapes, or from the radio. Increasingly, as music education enters the school system, there may be one person in a parish who has learned to read staff notation or Tonic sol-fa, and can teach a choir a new hymn. It may be said that congregations, especially outside the towns, still inhabit an 'oral culture,' but that in towns and cities, a 'print culture' is slowly growing. Books are seen to be very important, and the people are asking for more hymnbooks, more books with staff notation. [Nearly two-thirds of the] people can read Swahili in this country. But very few can read standard staff notation.[71]

Tonal inflections, characteristic of many African languages, usually shape melodies in traditional African singing. The melody of songs generally corresponds to the tonal shape of the words so that a sung text makes sense.[72] An example of this is "Wa Wa Wa," a song from the *aladura* movement (Yoruba language for "owners of prayer"), an overarching designation for a syncretistic group of African Initiated Churches[73] that began in the 1920s. Christopher Brooks notes that *aladura* hymns come from at least three sources: (1) Western hymnals with a Yoruba text substituted (not translated) for the English one, a kind of *contrafactum* that is a widespread practice in Africa, though "Western melodies [do] not always meet the linguistic demands of African languages." (2) Original compositions affected by both indigenous and Western musical styles. (3) Hymns that use "holy words," a form of glossolalia understood by the speaker but not always to other Yoruba speakers.[74]

Among the Yoruba (Nigeria) there are three tones—low, medium and high. Note several characteristics of African compositional style in this original *aladura* song:

Example 7:2

© 1986 World Council of Churches and The Asian Institute for Liturgy and Music

The melody follows the general shape of the tones of the spoken text (e.g., "E-mi-mi-mo" – _ _ – or "A-lag-ba-ra" – ¯ _ _) "Wa" is the imperative form of the verb "to come". An "o" on the end of the verb, such as "wao", doubles its intensity—"come NOW!" The phrases are linked together by a leader. The harmony also follows the natural tones of the words resulting in parallel movement similar to organum in Western medieval music. Rather than the contrary motion characteristic of part writing at the time of Bach, harmony in traditional music is more responsive to the tonal inflection of the words and not vertical harmonic structures.[75] This well-known West African song is accompanied by various sizes of drums, *sekere* (rattle gourd), and a double bell gong (two-toned cowbell sound). Since it is an invocation to the Holy Spirit, a choir might sing this in a dancing procession at the beginning of worship with the congregation joining them in singing and dancing. Furthermore, the congregation may provide additional percussion by clapping cross-rhythms or by beating on hymn books or pews.

Dance is indispensable to the musical process.[76] In many African languages, the word for "music" includes singing, dancing and playing drums.[77] Rhythm is as foundational to most African music as melody and harmony are in most Western styles. Kofi Agawu notes that the Ewe language (Ghana) lacks a single word for "rhythm" and that this "suggests that rhythm refers to a binding together of different dimensional processes, a joining rather than a separating, an across the dimensions instead of a within-the dimension phenomenon."[78] In other words, rhythm merges so completely with the total processes of Ghanaian music making that it does not need a specific word. Rather than recurring metrical patterns of Western hymns, the rhythm of many traditional songs is additive—driven by a regular pulse in groups of threes and twos but not subject to the predictability of meter.[79]

When considering musical instruments in Africa, variety is the key word.[80] Drumming is integral to musical experiences throughout Africa, but the complexity, instruments themselves, and ways of playing them vary widely throughout the continent. Some tribes are known for instruments other than drums. In southern Africa, especially in Mozambique, Zimbabwe, and more recently among the Xhosa people of South Africa, xylophones are common. Traditional Xhosa music uses a variety of bows that are either plucked or bowed and produce overtones through various means. Though rare in churches, the *mbira* (so-called "thumb" piano) of the Shona people (Zimbabwe) provides a mellow buzz, much more intimate in contrast to drumming.[81]

Western instruments, especially guitars, electronic keyboards and band instruments are common, particularly in urban churches. These instruments are often adapted to African musical styles and played in ways idiomatic to local African practice. Other general African music features are more difficult to ascertain. Vocal music is dominant, but the presence of the Salvation Army and British marching bands in some regions has opened the way to some instrumental music without voices.

A key concept of African music making is that of repetition versus variation—a characteristic of cyclic musical structures. Western notation of African music usually provides only the part that is repeated, often leading Western-trained musicians to think that "there isn't much content in African music." This assumption is based upon a lack of understanding that much of what takes place in African musical performance cannot be easily notated. Learning music conceived in oral musical tradition from a written score is often frustrating to an African. Much of an African musical performance is improvisatory—including dancer, vocalists and instrumentalists. Variations come in very subtle ways—slight changes in drumming patterns, variations in dance steps, and vocal improvisations by the leader.

Cyclic musical structures are tied closely to an African sense of time. In classic Western hymnody, one can estimate the time that it will take for the hymn to be sung, depending on the tempo and number of stanzas. In African music, the musical experience continues until the performers, which may include the audience, tire of it or the song has served its ritual purpose. Traditional African music often accompanies a social or ritual occasion. Cyclic structures may be extended at the pleasure of the performers, allowing the length of the music to fit the occasion. African musicians are not in a hurry. They take as much time as needed to involve as many in the community as possible in music making. Music serves a primary purpose of building and experiencing community rather than just communicating information.

In many African liturgies it is difficult to tell the difference between the choir and the congregation if a song is being embraced by the entire worshipping community.[82] S.C. Molefe's "Masithi-Amen, Siakudumisa", cited above, is an example of many of these African musical characteristics.

Africans freely mix styles of music from neighboring tribes with their own. Urban musical styles tend to differ from more traditional rural styles. Church music styles are often a fusion of western hymns with traditional oral performance techniques, instruments and dance.

In summary, Thomas Turino, speaking specifically from the context of the Ewe people of Ghana, offers the following musical principles and aesthetic values that are generally common in sub-Saharan Africa:

> call-and-response, interlock, ostinato organization, improvised variation based on stock formulaic patterns, and density in the resulting sound of the entire ensemble. The drum ensemble accompanies both the dancing and the singing, and it is the songs themselves that are considered particularly important ... for expressing the distinctive identity of the [group].... [I]n Africa, the dance steps performed can be considered integral to the polyrhythmic fabric of the total performance.[83]

Current Congregational Song Practice in Africa
—Two Examples—

In 2008, I participated in African worship in Methodist contexts in South Africa and Côte d'Ivoire. Although these experiences are anecdotal at best, they do offer a glimpse of the variety and genres of congregational songs present in worship.

I participated in Good Friday and Easter Sunday worship among Xhosa speakers in a Methodist township congregation outside of Grahamstown, South Africa.[86] The services incorporated two choirs. The women's choir led psalm singing in an Anglican chant style (Psalm

150 and the *Te Deum*) and Western-style hymns, for example, an Easter hymn text to the tune of STUTTGART. The men's chorus led congregational song in the Western Gospel song style and the *makwaya* style of the Freedom Songs (see page 260 for further discussion of this style). All music in the service was *a cappella* though a leather hand pillow that was used to keep a basic beat, holding the more than 500 worshippers together, usually accompanied the music of the men's chorus. Dance also accompanied the music led by the men's chorus. The music led by the women's chorus usually was sung without rhythmic accompaniment or movement. The leadership of the two choirs came together in the seven stanzas sung to STUTTGART. The women's chorus began the hymn in a steady stately manner. However, each stanza took on more African compositional techniques as the men's chorus improvised vocal links between stanzas and across phrase endings, added hand percussion on the back of pews in front of them, and increasingly swayed. This congregation incorporated genres two, three, four, and six regularly into all worship experiences.

I visited several United Methodist congregations in August of 2008 in urban settings in or near Abidjan, Côte d'Ivoire. As with the South African congregation, the denominational heritage came from the British Methodist evangelism. While the colonial language of French was dominant, selective songs incorporated local tribal languages from time to time. Each of the choirs—mixed chorus, men's choir, women's choir and youth choir—had the responsibility of leading different styles. The mixed chorus led songs that were based primarily upon Western hymn styles. The men's and women's choirs focused more on traditional or local styles. The youth choir sang a wider range of styles including more popular Western forms. The range of musical styles depended somewhat on what choir was leading worship on a given day. In one large urban congregation in Abidjan, I witnessed a similar diversity of musical styles found in the South African congregation. An electronic keyboard using a variety of sounds, a drummer playing a trap set, electric guitars, and a jazz-style

> trumpet accompanied virtually all music. The *Te Deum* was sung in French in an Anglican Chant style. Hymns were largely from the Western repertoire, but the addition of a jazz trumpeter and trap set added a more up-beat quality to the performance. Some prayer hymns or responses were sung unaccompanied. A brass band accompanied some songs giving a quasi-Dixieland feel to the congregational singing. In other venues beyond Sunday morning, the practice of polyrhythmic handclapping and African drums on Western hymns was common. Some songs that were more local in origin incorporated stylized hand and body gestures that interpreted the song. Generally, much of the music was drawn from genres two and three with use of genres of four and six, depending on the choir leading the service.
>
> Other experiences in Nigeria, Zimbabwe, and Kenya generally reveal a wide variety of the genres described above in a single service though the exact mix depends upon the denominational heritage, setting in an urban or rural environment, tribal influences, and colonial history.

Varieties of African Hymnody

African congregational singing draws upon a diverse repertoire of songs. It is impossible to define an African hymn in a single, concise manner. Several genres exist and may appear within a single liturgy. Genres include:

1. Western hymns taken directly from European or North American hymnals, sung in a colonial language, and accompanied on organ or piano;
2. Western hymns translated into a vernacular African language, often with some melodic and/or rhythmic alterations to accommodate the African vernacular;
3. Western hymns sung with African oral tradition performance techniques such as leader-response and use of percussion;
4. blending of Western hymns with traditional compositional tech-niques including improvised harmonies, parallel harmonic progressions, and, in some areas multipart improvisatory vocal

singing, as well as increased use of percussion and dance, further disguising the Western origins of the hymn;

5. African melodies with texts written by Western missionaries or in collaboration with Africans;
6. congregational song compositions by Africans in western or blended idioms; and
7. congregational songs composed by Africans in thoroughly traditional musical styles.[85]

At the time of the writing of Julian's *Dictionary of Hymnology*[96] there was strong evidence of hymns in the first genre of African hymnody above, Western hymns from European or North American hymnals. *Hymns Ancient and Modern* (1st ed., 1861) "and other well-known hymnals of our own country" (p. 756) were available for English residents and had their influence on translations to African languages. Different denominations held sway in the various regions of the continent, influencing the hymnic repertoire ranging from Latin Hymns such as *Te Deum* and "Veni Creator Spiritus" among Roman Catholics, to Heber's "Holy, Holy, Holy! Lord God almighty" among Anglicans, and Ira D. Sankey's *Sacred Songs and Solos* (1873) among Baptists and other evangelical groups. Though much less prominent now, colonial hymnals may still be found, especially in churches where expatriates attend and in seminaries where, because of the presence of many tribal languages among the students, English is the linguistic currency. This is largely an urban phenomenon, however, with rural areas singing in their vernacular.

With regard to the second genre above— Western hymns in translation— it was not uncommon in the nineteenth century to have a single translator render almost all of the hymns in an African language often with mixed results. Writing in Julian's *Dictionary*, Stevenson noted several cases of this in his entry on "Foreign Missions" including the hymnal *Sechuana* (1873) shared with six missionary societies. Of the 327 hymns in the collection, 250 were "translated or composed by Dr. Moffat." Many missionaries took on this task and, occasionally, a "native teacher" such as "Morolong" in

Matabeleland (p.756), a province in current Zimbabwe. Julian also notes that efforts to improve hymn singing in Africa were made through teaching the [British] Tonic Sol-fa system and the preparation of tune books and school songbooks. (p.755)

The examples cited in this chapter are drawn primarily from the fifth, sixth and seventh genres outlined above—original African hymns with texts by Western missionaries, hymns by Africans using Western or blended musical idioms, and original hymns in thoroughly indigenous styles. Two features included in this chapter differ from a discussion of Western hymn repertoire: (1) In contrast to a discussion of Western hymns, it is impossible to consider texts and tunes separately, as they are generally composed together by the same person and integrally linked; and (2) these illustrations will present not only the most notable examples of African hymns found in Western hymnals, but will also include representative processes used by missionaries to encourage the development of African hymns. The self-conscious, intentional compositional processes developed by Western missionaries to encourage the development of hymns by African Christians are as much a part of the story of the expansion of African hymnology as the hymns and African composers. The hymns included reflect no more than the minutest portion of a vast African repertoire, of which these examples are admittedly ones most accessible to Westerners theologically and musically. With that delimitation, hymns cited in this article are representative of African genres only in the most general terms.

Composing an African Hymn — A Case Study

A primary example of a hymn written in an indigenous African idiom and found in several North American hymnals is "Jesus, We Want to Meet" by **A. T. Olajida Olude** (1908-c. 1986). A Nigerian Methodist minister, Olude was educated at Wesley College, Ibadan, and at the Mindola training school. He was awarded the Order of Niger and, from the University of Nigeria, the Mus.D. degree.[87]

A.M. Jones describes Olude as "profoundly upset by the way European-type hymns murdered his language."[88] Jones also notes that

Olude built up a collection of at least seventy-seven hymns whose melodies followed precisely the speech tones of the Yoruba language "in every verse"—an astounding poetic feat.

While in a Mission School in the 1940s, Olude learned a text by Elizabeth Parsons (1812–1873), "Jesus, We Love to Meet," dating from 1840. He based his Yoruba translation ["Jesu a fe pade"] on Parsons' text and composed his own melody in 1949. Olude presented the song in Abeokuta, Nigeria in 1949 at a service designed to popularize indigenous Yoruba music in Christian worship—a clear reaction against the exclusive use of colonial hymnody.[89]

Austin C. Lovelace's (1910–2010) versification of Biodun Adebesin's (b. 1928) translation is the version most commonly found ("Jesus, We Want to Meet"). This version appeared initially in the *Methodist Hymnal* (1966) and then in Erik Routley's fifth edition of *Cantate Domino* (1974) and several hymnals since that time. It is the West African hymn most frequently found in Western hymnals. Some hymnals (See the *Psalter Hymnal*, 1987) have paired Olude's tune with the original English-language poem by Parsons.

Though a harmonization has been added in some hymnals, this hymn is more successful in its original monophonic form.[90] The call-and-response pattern makes it relatively easy for congregations to sing because their short sung response is the same virtually throughout the entire hymn. The angular melody, best sung by a solo leader, reflects the Yoruba tonal language. The additive rhythms alternate between what feels like 3/4 and 6/8 to Westerners. The drum pattern provided in many hymnals as "optional" is a basic Yoruba beat found in many traditional songs and should be used if at all possible.

More recently Godwin Sadoh (b. 1965) has published a collection of short Nigerian compositions, some original and many transmitted through oral tradition. On the page they appear more in the style of short praise choruses (stream six), but in the Nigerian context they come to life with a vocal music leader, drums, dance and polyrhythmic handclapping.[91]

Missionary Contributions to the Development of African Hymnody

The interaction between Western missionaries and African musicians, especially since the general independence movements of the 1960s, has been an essential dynamic in the development of an "African" hymnody. The following section details the specific contributions of selected missionaries, the techniques they used to bridge the gap between Western and African styles, and their close collaboration with and cultivation of African church musicians.

Arthur Morris Jones (1889–1980), a Roman Catholic missionary and ethnomusicologist from Great Britain, was an example of a missionary with an abiding interest in African music before Vatican II and the wave of nationalism and independence that swept over much of Africa beginning in the early 1960s. His theological study was at Oxford and he served from 1923-1952 as a missionary in Africa, most of it as principal of St Mark's College (1929–1950), Mapanza, Northern Rhodesia (now Zambia). Upon returning to England he was appointed a lecturer in African music at the School of Oriental and African Studies, University of London, where he taught until his retirement in 1966. Morris was a prolific author and researcher. His publications were standard reading for those researching African music, especially his studies of African rhythms.[92] Jones's *African Music* (1943), published in an abridged form as *African Music in Northern Rhodesia and Some Other Places* (1949), and *Studies in African Music*, Vol. 2 (1959, reprinted 1962) were significant collections representing some of the most important research.[93]

Jones's slim volume, *African Hymnody in Christian Worship: a Contribution to the History of its Development*, (Zimbabwe, 1976) is his major contribution to church music. He edited a number of collections of hymns for schools in Africa as well. Though not all of Jones's scholarship stands up to the scrutiny of today's standards, he was a missionary devoted to the music of Africa, its people, and the work of the church.

Lutheran **Howard S. Olson** (1922–2010) had a long ministry (1946-88) as a pastor, linguist and seminary professor with the American Lutheran Church (ELCA) that produced significant results in Tanzania. In addition to editing the *Africa Theological Journal*, writing *The Phonology and Morphology of the Rimi Language*, and *Jufunze Kiyuani*, a text for teaching Koine Greek in Swahili, he also edited *Tumshangilie Mungu* [*Let Us Praise God*]—150 songs in six editions 1968–1987 with translations of selected songs in English, German and French for international use. Some songs appear in the USA in *Lead Us, Lord* (1977) and *Set Free* (1993). In the first collection of twenty songs, Olson encouraged choirs to sing the predominately unison music as presented in the collection, and to avoid "the temptation to harmonize these [songs] according to Western standards…. The music is written [in this collection] as it has been traditionally sung, harmonized according to what is considered harmonic in each particular local African setting."[94] By the time that the thirty songs in *Set Free* were published 16 years later, Olson noted that "Culture is never static, and has changed since my original observation. Now worshippers in African congregations often sing the hymns in parts."[95] Rather than transcribing harmonies sung by Tanzanian congregations, however, arrangements by notable Western composers such as Richard Hillert, Egil Hovland and Austin Lovelace were used. While appropriately understated with simple chord progressions, these arrangements avoid the parallel fifths and octaves so typical of African oral harmonic practice. Eight songs are published in a bilingual format—English and Swahili.

Though not primarily a musician, Olson encouraged his students to compose in their own musical styles.

> At first I got together with musicians from the tribe and started working on a hymnal. I listened to and recorded traditional music using a wire recorder and then put into staff notation the folk songs I heard. I kept the same genre when putting an English text to the traditional tune: A song of praise to the chief became praise to the Deity or Christ; a war song became a song of victory over death and sin; a wedding song became a song for a Christian wedding; a harvest song was enriched and put in a Christian direction; a lullaby became a Christmas song for the infant Jesus.

Later, I started each of my classes at Lutheran Theological Seminary in Makumira with Psalms. In my classes there were 30 students or so with several different tribes present. I asked the students to do a paraphrase of the Psalm text to a popular folk melody. Then I had the class choose the five best. This indicated the songs that had crossed tribal differences the best. Then I transcribed the five best songs for broader use. When a hymnal produced by Tanzanian ministers was published in 1988, *Mwimbieni Bwana* [*Sing to the Lord*], 45 songs from *Tumshangilie Mungu* were chosen. Some songs were picked for political reasons and ethnic balance, so not all of the best ones made it into this hymnal.[96]

Olson's translations of "Njoo kwetu, Roho mwema" ["Gracious Spirit"] by Wilson Niwaglia (b. 1940) appears in several collections. In addition to the Olson's collections cited above, several of Olson's translations from Swahili are available in *Panorama*: 922, 923, 924, 925, 926.

The most prominent missionary associated with the development of indigenous hymnody in Malawi is **Thomas S. Colvin** (1925–2000). He was a pastoral missionary for the Church of Scotland in Ghana from 1958-1964 and Nyasaland (Malawi) from 1954-1958 and 1964-1974. Trained as an engineer before studying theology at Trinity College in Glasgow, he was an active member of the Iona Community for nearly fifty years.[97]

Colvin introduced his hymns first to the Iona Community and then beyond in two collections, *Free to Serve* (1969) and *Leap My Soul* (1976). These collections were brought together in a single volume, *Fill Us with Your Love* (1983). A last volume, *Come, Let Us Walk This Road Together*, was added in 1997. Although Howard Olson's process straddles genres five, six and seven Colvin's texts set to African melodies clearly reflect genre five. Though the arrangements published in the collections in the United States seem highly western in nature, Colvin provides a helpful introduction to African performance practice in the Preface to his last collection:

> In Africa, particularly in churches in rural areas, hymns are sung without instrumental accompaniments, except in cases where drums or other percussion instruments can be used. This means that the leader has a very important part to play. He or she must pitch the song, give a lead in rhythm and tempo as well as introducing the words in each verse [stanza], often creating verses as the song proceeds. Since the hymns are usually interlined in Tonic Sol-fa notation, teaching the group to read music is still another task for the leader. If and when the music is written down, it is more of an outline of the melody than a definitive and final form to be followed. Singers are creative in forming their own version of the song by improvising harmonies, overlapping or repeating phrases and by other means as they are led by the Spirit.[98]

Africans understand the "art-form" of embellishing a simple melody and each leader seems to have her or his own version. One need provide the "melody only, the rest being left to the singers to create."[99]

Justice issues such as Christian service committees, refugee resettlement, and community development projects—issues consistent with his commitment to the Iona Community—were the focus of Colvin's ministry rather than the development of indigenous congregational song. Members of the Iona Community around the world have spread the songs collected by Colvin. Several of his texts set to African melodies have found a home in Western hymnals including "Yesu, Yesu, [Jesu, Jesu] Fill Us With Your Love" [*Panorama*: 928], "God Sends Us the Spirit" [*Panorama*: 929], and "That Boy-Child of Mary" [*Panorama*: 930].

As an example, "That Boy-Child of Mary" captures the essence of an African baby-naming ceremony with stanzas that alternate between questions and responses. Like many African melodies, this one begins higher, in this case with a falling minor third, and gradually descends. Western hymnal editors, in an unnecessary attempt to make the incipit easier, have often taken the first note down the octave, making the initial interval a rising major sixth. This has the effect of obscuring the natural descending line of the melody.

Colvin's modesty comes through as he expresses his role in the larger process of assisting Africans in developing their own hymnody: "I see myself as a rather inadequate scribbler of words and I hope that I will soon be replaced by African hymn-writers.... I pray that they will soon provide us with songs from Africa that will undoubtedly be more authentic than mine."[100]

In Zimbabwe the interaction between missionaries and African musicians yielded hymnody that captured the spirit of the country's churches. **Robert Kauffman** (b. 1929) arrived in Africa in 1960. A Mennonite under appointment with the Methodist Church, he studied briefly in Ghana and Nigeria initially during a time of strong nationalism and emerging independence. British Prime Minister Harold Macmillan made his famous "Winds of Change" speech to the South African parliament in February 1960, distancing himself from the apartheid regime of Hendrik Verwoerd. Kauffman then proceeded to South Africa to study field-recording techniques with Hugh Tracey, and was there during the Sharpeville Massacre on March 21, 1960. These events helped to orient his thinking toward the development of African church music.

Describing his early efforts, Kauffman notes:

> My wife and I would go out for one month for recording and then come back and transcribe and process the music. I was looking for songs that were appropriate for vocal music for the church. Praise songs (to the local Chief) and work songs seemed the most appropriate. Then I had workshops with choir directors and played the songs, e.g., a hunting song, and changed the words to 'Let us praise the Creator.' The local musicians added the words. I was not satisfied with this process, however, because the tones of the new words didn't work with the old melody.[101]

During Shona language study in Southern Rhodesia (now Zimbabwe) in 1961, Kauffman organized the concept of Arts Workshops. He met an mbira player, Baba Mtambenengewe, who continued playing the instrument after becoming a Christian in spite of its association with ancestor worship.

Kauffman describes the creative process that followed:

> While the drums were beating and the mbira was being played the group began humming. Suddenly some words came from one section of the group. A little later another section had a counter theme. These two melodies were repeated over and over with growing intensity—the drums growing louder and more agitated—a cross beat handclap added and the music climaxing with the words "Ndaiwe Bofu, Zvino Ndaakuona" ["I was blind, but now I see"]. In the meantime the drama group was working on an English dramatization of the story written by Mrs. Find. The music and the drama groups joined forces for our final worship service.[102]

The song on the text of blind Barthemaeus was affirmed by other Christians in the group composition workshop as a truly African church music expression in the spirit of rising African nationalism. This first arts workshop at Nyakatsapa, "The Use of Art, Music and Drama in the Life and Worship of the Church," was broad in scope, incorporating all kinds of African artistic expressions—not just religious art. These workshops became annual events, nurturing some of Zimbabwe's leading church musicians.

In a lecture given in South Africa, Swedish missionary Olof Axelsson summarized Kauffman's three-step approach to developing African church music: (1) collect extensive recordings of traditional Shona music on tape and analyze the music for its salient features, techniques and forms; (2) find Shona composers who had some theoretical musical training to compose music for the church; and (3) modify the traditional musical styles and forms to some degree "in order to get away from the accusations of being too traditional . . . being diplomatic so that the new music wouldn't indicate too much of the traditional African worship."[103]

Kauffman gave birth to the *All African Church Music Journal*, an organ of the All Africa Church Music Association formed in Kitwe, Northern Rhodesia (now Zambia) in January 1963. Because of the *Journal* a more complete record of some of the church musicians from this region exists than is available in many other parts of Africa. The *Journal* records the contributions of two prominent church musicians, Abraham Dumisani Maraire (1943-2000) and Patrick Matsikenyiri (b. 1937).[104] Recordings produced by Kauffman made African hymns available to a broader audience.[105]

John Kaemmer (1928–2011), also a Methodist missionary with musical training, arrived in 1963 and continued the arts workshop tradition. Taking a broader anthropological perspective,[106] Kaemmer built upon Kauffman's compositional process through recordings and editions of hymnals. He studied mbira with Andrew Tracey, Hugh Tracey's son. From 1965–1968 Kaemmer provided African music in its original form through live performances or recordings for church musicians to hear. Many Africans were composing new texts. Some composed new music, "but it was hard to tell because their compositions might have been some traditional songs in their memories"[107] Kaemmer wanted to help Africans understand why their music was not inferior to European music. "Just because western music had a significant theoretical system did not make it a more important form", he stated. To this end Kaemmer wrote several articles about African musical theory. Among his many publications, he contributed several entries in the volume *Africa* in *The Garland Encyclopedia of World Music* (1998).[108] He retired from the anthropology department of the University of Washington (Seattle).

Olof Axelsson (1934-1993), a prominent church musician in the Church of Sweden, became, upon his arrival in 1966, a collaborator in the arts workshops begun by Kauffman and continued by Kaemmer. Axelsson, following in the footsteps of fellow Swedish cathedral musician Henry Weman (1897–1992),[109] entered enthusiastically into every aspect of church music life in Zimbabwe—composing musical dramas, building marimbas, and directing choirs. Originally sent to Zimbabwe by the Church of Sweden Mission as a school inspector and church musician, Axelsson returned to Sweden occasionally for studies in musicology, completing his Master's thesis in 1971.[110] His contagious spirit also influenced important Zimbabwean musicians. Olof Axelsson was the director for the College of Music at Kwanongoma College in Bulawayo from 1972 to 1981. From 1983-1985 Axelsson devoted himself to the manufacture of marimbas[111] and mbiras, returning to Sweden to finish his doctorate in ethnomusicology, serving as an organist and lecturer in ethnomusicology in the last years of his life. The "Bulawayo marimba" became known throughout southern Africa and in many places around the world.[112] Unafraid of conflict, Axelsson worked in both the church and in secular Zimbabwean music circles. This unorthodox behavior and his interest in African independent churches garnered considerable criticism from the colonial mission church.

Axelsson encouraged compositions that followed some of the general traits of African music in the south of the continent: responsorial singing, a general downward movement of the melody, relationship between spoken tonal patterns and the melody, and both parallel and contrapuntal motion in multipart singing.[113] Stig-Magnus Thorsén summarizes Axelsson's contributions in the following manner:

> Olof Axelsson had a dream of creating a new and African musicology. In that way, he gave himself a new commission. He shifted his professional role and performed new methods and perspectives on the study of music in Africa. [His] research came from being convinced that [the] West has developed a misconception of music and culture in Africa.[114]

The ecumenical church, through its support of musical missionaries like Olof Axelsson, was responsible for the popularity of the marimbas in the schools of Zimbabwe.[115] One of the most colorful Western church musicians to work in Zimbabwe, Maria Minnaar described her father as first, an adventurer, then a lover of people, and finally, a missionary.[116] Axelsson, Kaemmer and Kauffman nurtured two important Zimbabwean composers, Abraham Dumisani Maraire and Patrick Matsikenyiri.

Abraham Dumisani Maraire (1943–2000), a graduate of Kwanongoma College in Bulawayo, was a teacher in one of the primary schools. Robert Kauffman hoped to encourage students to compose original songs for a passion play, using African American spirituals to fill out the musical portions of the drama where original compositions did not materialize. With this in mind, Kauffman suggested that Maraire come to the Methodist mission station where he invited him to write music for Easter Sunday. Because of a misunderstanding, however, Maraire composed ten or fifteen songs for the entire Holy Week story. Maraire recorded each of the parts of the songs and, using the recordings to prompt his memory, taught the people by rote.[117] *Mazuva Ekupedzisa* [*The Last Days*], composed in 1965, was a Holy Week musical drama or passion play. Maraire also composed the majority of the songs in the second edition of *Ndwiyo Dzechechi Dzevu* [*Church Music of the Soil*], a project begun by Kauffman in 1963 with fifteen songs and continued under Kaemmer in 1965 with a total of forty-three songs. Maraire learned marimbas at Kwanongoma College in the early 1960s. After Kauffman left Rhodesia in 1965 and completed his graduate studies in ethnomusicology, he taught at the University of Washington. Maraire was invited to teach mbira at the University by Kauffman and also developed Zimbabwean marimba ensembles, which became very popular in the northwestern United States.[118]

Maraire's Easter "Alleluia" appears in several collections. The syncopated stanzas in a call-response style provide a lively musical setting of the Shona resurrection text.[119]

Example 7:3 (excerpt)

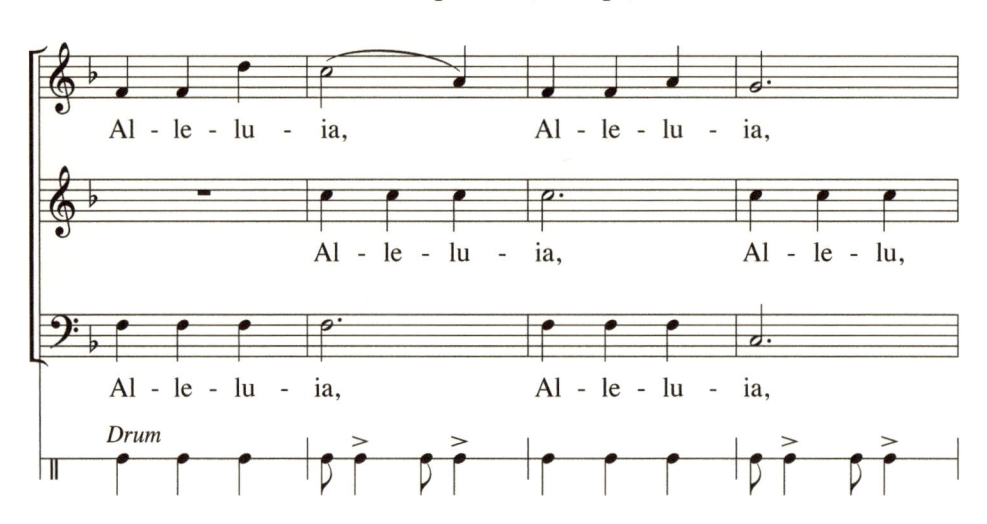

[Musical notation with four staves: three vocal parts singing "Al-le-lu-ia, Al-le-lu-ia," and a Drum part. Second system marked "Sing three times" with "Al-le-lu-ia, Al-le-lu-ia!"]

© Abraham Maraire

Patrick Matsikenyiri (b. 1937) continued the annual ecumenical arts workshops even during the tumultuous days of the war for black majority rule in Zimbabwe in the 1970s. His men's and women's groups (alternating years) prepared Holy Week dramas. Matsikenyiri's work with the United Methodist Church in Zimbabwe is legendary—organizing annual choir competitions, directing Wabvuwi, a Methodist men's group that sings a hybrid style of songs somewhere between Western and traditional music, and composing many songs himself. A headmaster of schools for many years, Matsikenyiri was deeply involved with the leaders of Zimbabwe's movement for black majority rule, composing songs used by the fighters and assisting Canaan Banana, a Methodist minister and Zimbabwe's first state president under black rule. These songs often linked political and spiritual liberation. Matsikenyiri served as Conference Music Director for the United Methodist Church in 1968, a position he held until he left for study in the United States in 1990. Because of his reputation in church music and work as Director of Music in the Mutare District, Matsikenyiri was part of the team that revised the Zimbabwe United Methodist hymnal, *Ngoma*, in 1964, and has continued to make corrections and revisions in succeeding editions.[120]

After completing undergraduate and graduate degrees at Shenandoah Conservatory in the United States, he returned to Mutare, Zimbabwe as a Lecturer in Music in the Faculty of Humanities of the newly opened Africa University in 1993, a post he held until retirement in 2002. He developed a four-year music major beginning in 1996, the only program of its kind in Zimbabwe.

Matsikenyiri was catapulted to international recognition through his work with the World Council of Churches and the United Methodist Church in the United States. In 1979, just before the end of the war for black rule in Zimbabwe, he was invited to the World Council of Churches (WCC) in Geneva to plan music for a Mission and Evangelism Conference held in Melbourne (1980). Continuing on the WCC Worship Committee in 1982, he served as an *animateur* [musical animator or leader] for the sixth Assembly of the WCC in Vancouver. Matsikenyiri has served as member of the Global Praise Working Group of the General Board of Global Ministries of the United Methodist Church in the United States. He has contributed songs to the three volumes of *Global Praise* as well as compiled the *Africa Praise Songbook: Songs from Africa* (1998). In 1998 Matsikenyiri prepared the conference choir for the WCC Eighth Assembly held in Harare and served again as *animateur*.[121] He continues to compile collections of songs from Zimbabwe.[122]

Music composed by Maraire was much more in the African vein. Matsikenyiri's songs are often crafted with African compositional techniques while drawing on some Western hymn influences. An extended song that illustrates Matsikenyiri's style is "Uyai mweya wakachena" ["Come now, come, O Holy Spirit"]. It is a petition for hope and blessing in the time of trials faced by the people of Zimbabwe. Just as the "heroes of Holy Scripture lived with hope," the song asks the Holy Spirit to "grant us life with you forever."[123]

"Jesu, Tawa Pano" is one of Matsikenyiri's best-known songs. It is a gathering often used by the choir during a processional into the sanctuary. It may also be used for gathering at the table during communion. The basic cycle of the congregation's part is standard length for many traditional Shona songs. Many singers, especially the lead-singer, will anticipate the initial pulse of each phrase, diminishing the "squared-off" look the song has in its notational form. The version printed here is based on an oral-tradition recording by Taiwanese ethnomusicologist, I-to Loh.

Example 7:4

Patrick Masikenyiri, arr. I-to Loh, © 1996 Global Praise 1, GBGMusik

South Africa. One of the most fertile areas for a hymnologist in Africa is South Africa. Though the Moravians began the first mission station in South Africa in 1737, it was not until 1800 that a variety of mission societies and denominations pursued the evangelization of this region in earnest. Because of the long contact with Europe, especially with Dutch and British settlers, one can discern a general history of hymnology in this country unlike any other on the continent.

David Dargie (b. 1938) is one of South Africa's leading ethnomusicologists. He studied with Andrew Tracey at Rhodes University in Grahamstown. Dargie is also a foremost encourager of compositions by Africans for the church. Of Scottish descent, Dargie is a third-generation South African raised in the coastal town of East London. Following seminary training in Pretoria and his ordination in 1964, he served in New Brighton as a priest until 1965. In 1977, following the lead of the Second Vatican Council, Dargie was able to build on the work of two of his colleagues at the Lumko Missiological Institute, Fritz Lobinger and Oswald Hirmer, priests who had come to South Africa in the 1950s. They began to encourage the local people to create their own music for the Mass in the spirit of the Vatican II reforms. The Lumko Institute began as a language institute for missionaries in 1962.

Through Dargie's efforts, The Institute also became a promoter of indigenous compositions for the liturgy. After leaving the priesthood in 1989, Dargie lived in Germany for several years where he married. He conducted workshops in Germany on African music and facilitated the appearance of Xhosa traditional musicians in Europe on several occasions. In 1995 he returned to South Africa when he was appointed chair of the music department at Fort Hare University in Alice, one of the few universities opened to black South Africans under apartheid. During apartheid, other universities were designated for "coloureds" [mixed race South Africans or Indians] only. At Fort Hare Dargie established a music major that put African music at the core of requirements for graduation.

As he began his work, Dargie noted that Catholic missionaries were content to follow Protestant models of translation of Western hymns into Xhosa. This practice sometimes led to totally absurd pairings of text and tune such as singing the Latin hymn "Tantum ergo" to the tune of "My

Darling Clementine."[124] Given the tonal nature of African languages, the entire exercise of translating Western texts into Xhosa and joining them to existing Western tunes produced many songs that ranged from humorous to meaningless.

The success of church music composition workshops with African traditional musicians eventually led to the formation of a music department at Lumko in 1979. After conducting over forty workshops and refining the techniques used to facilitate them, the Lumko Institute published a book detailing the process for encouraging the composition of new African church music. *Workshops for Composing Local Church Music* (1983) is a guide accompanied by cassette tapes of actual workshop sessions. This process spread to other regions of South Africa. The Lumko Institute has published more than 100 cassettes of music from these encounters, containing hundreds of new songs for the church.[125]

In Dargie's model, the organizer of the composition workshops serves as a catalyst for the event rather than a performer. As catalyst, the organizer "inspire[s] and encourage[s] the people, tell[ing] them about the needs of the church, their service to the church, and their own people, the value of offering their own music to God, the value of preserving their own musical style which God has especially given to them."[126] The catalyst also provides texts appropriate for the liturgy, enlists local musicians as a source of inspiration, and records the sessions on tape. Following the event, the cassettes and texts are made available to those who attended so that they can learn the music and incorporate it into the liturgy.[127]

In summary, the compositional process proposed by Dargie is communal rather than solitary; inspired by texts appropriate for the liturgy; based on aural/oral transmission rather than notation, derived from traditional musical styles, and includes both the musical layperson and the recognized musician.

South African Hymnody: An Overview

Unlike other countries in sub-Saharan Africa, South Africa has a figure that can be identified as the "Father" of South African indigenous hymnody. **Ntsikana Gaba** (c. 1780-1821) is a legendary Xhosa leader who is generally accepted to be the first Xhosa Christian. His followers joined the first permanent mission at Tyhume near Fort Hare soon after the prophet's death in 1821. Among the legacies of Ntsikana were four hymns that were conceived and taught to his followers. They expressed his conversion in purely Xhosa musical style and cultural images. Through oral tradition, and later notation, these songs have survived for 200 years in Xhosa culture.

Several South African hymn writers are in a direct line from Ntsikana including **John Knox Bokwe** (1855–1922), a descendant of Ntsikana's disciples and a student of William Kobe Ntsikana, Ntsikana's grandson. His transcription of the text of the "Great Hymn" of Ntsikana was published in *Isigidimi sama-Xhosa* [*The Xhosa Messenger*] in November 1876 and again in *Christian Express* in 1878/9. Its first publication in sol-fa may have been in the collection *Amaculo ase Lovedale* [*Lovedale Music*] in 1885. John Knox Bokwe is credited with developing the *makwaya* style of singing. Selborne T. Bokwe, his son, known as a choir leader, recorded versions of Ntskana's four hymns for Hugh Tracey.[128]

Others who contributed to the development of South African hymnody include: **Tiyo Soga** (1829–1871), mentioned in Julian's *Dictionary*: "The Rev. Tiyo Soga, a gifted Kafir missionary educated by the United Presbyterian Church, and early removed by death, compiled a book of hymns, which was printed in Scotland." (p. 757) Soga, who trained for ministry in Scotland on two occasions, was the first Xhosa ordained in the United Presbyterian Church. Returning to South Africa the final time in 1856 with a Scottish wife, Soga worked as an evangelist, catechist, and translator into the Xhosa language, including sections of the New Testament and Part I of John Bunyan's *Pilgrim's Progress*, a work still available today. Soga composed approximately 30 hymns many of which are available in Xhosa hymnals today.[129]

Enoch Mankayi Sontonga (1873–1905), who wrote the text and the music of his most famous hymn and the best known hymn in all of Africa, "Nkosi Sikelel' iAfrika" ["God Bless Africa"], in 1897. "Nkosi" was first sung in public at the ordination of a Methodist minister, Rev. Boweni, in 1899 and included in the Presbyterian Xhosa hymn book, *Incwadi Yamaculo Ase-rabe* (1929). It became integral to the anti-apartheid protests of the

African National Congress, and, on April 20, 1994, just before the election of Nelson Mandela in May, was adopted with "Die Stem van Suid-Afrika" ["The Call of South Africa," the Afrikaans' national anthem], as official anthems of South Africa.

Benjamin Peter John Tyamzashe (1890–1978), the best known Xhosa composer of his day, whose *Missa 1* (c. 1965) incorporated the music of Ntsikana in the "Gloria."

Stephen Cuthbert Molefe (1917–1987), who was one of the key church musicians in Dargie's compostion workshops beginning in 1977, whose "Masithi-Amen Siakudumisa" was discussed above.[130]

South African Freedom Songs[131]

No other genre of African song has been adopted by the Western church and around the world more broadly than South African Freedom Songs. The story of these songs is one born in the struggle for political freedom during the apartheid regime and initially disseminated beyond their borders primarily through the efforts of Anders Nyberg of Sweden.

The anti-apartheid struggle in South Africa captured the attention of the world during the 1980s. News reports from CNN often included singing black South Africans and their supporters singing songs of freedom.

In the decades that followed, right up until the election of Nelson Mandela, any gathering of blacks, especially for funerals of slain black South Africans, was subject to unprovoked violence from police. Even the appearance of white priests and nuns could not guarantee that a black mourner would not be shot during the funeral march. During the "Emergencies" of 1960 and 1986 when all civil rights were suspended for blacks and "coloureds," the threat of violence increased. Although large gatherings of black South Africans were illegal, these funerals were defiantly held in large soccer fields, capable of holding thousands of mourners, under the watchful eye of heavily armed South African Police who were ready to move in at the slightest provocation. Closed caskets were illegally draped in the black, green, and gold flag of the banned African National Congress (ANC). Following angry speeches and the sounds of wailing, Enoch Mankayi Sontonga's anthem "Nkosi Sikelel' iAfrika" ["Lord, Bless Africa"], the anthem of the ANC proscribed by the apartheid government, was sung. The sound of its strains unified the oppressed protestors and gave them the courage to continue their peaceful march in the face of evil. The *toyi-toyi*, a South Africa militant dance performed by a circular group of protesters with high steps, accompanied by chanted slogans and singing, provided a context for the singing of many of the Freedom Songs.

The roots of these songs may be found in a synthesis of traditional African music and the *makwaya* style of singing. "Makwaya," coming from an African distortion of the English "my choir," represents a synthesis of African group singing styles and European choral music. John Knox Bokwe developed "makwaya" as a choral style that blended African music with choral singing as an expression of rising nationalism, both as a way to support himself while studying for the ministry in Scotland and to raise support for South African mission work.

A Case Study: "Siyahamba"

The most famous song in this style in Western collections, "Siyahamba," originated with Amadodana, a Methodist young men's group.[132] Usually translated as "We are marching in the light of God," the simple text contains layers of meaning: "We" may be seen as a word of community, the community of those living and the community of the living dead. "Marching" is an action that unifies the community as they move physically and spiritually in the same direction. It is a physical, kinesthetic response to the Spirit, not a passive acquiescence. "The Light of God" has meaning on several levels. Although it is a symbol of creation and of Jesus Christ, the light of the world, it is also a common refrain in songs of healing or *ngoma* throughout Southern and Central Africa. This refrain, "Let darkness be replaced with light," is coded language for "seeing clearly."[133] God is the source of clear sight in the midst of the struggle, the source of discernment and truth. As we march we can see our way ahead. Our path is clear. Where there is light, there is hope.

> When this message is mediated with the music, the words become embodied in the lives of the community that sing and dance it. The accessibility of the musical form draws all present into the song's cyclic structure immediately. Its portability allows the song to be taken to places of "darkness" where its message can illuminate evil in its myriad forms and offer the singers hope as they see clearly the path ahead. Its flexibility allows for the performer/participants to add to the basic song a message that draws into it the existential reality of the situation. "We" grow in number as we "march," for there are those who join us—literally—on the way. The song accommodates and even facilitates a growing, evolving community of believers. "We are marching," knowing that the living dead are singing with us. If this song is taken into the liturgy as a processional, it brings with it the struggle of the streets and sanctifies it.[134]

Swedish Lutherans deserve special mention in the dissemination of global song from southern Africa. In addition to cathedral musicians Olof Axelsson and Henry Wemen who worked extensively in southern Africa, Anders Nyberg (b. 1955) played a crucial role bringing South African Freedom Songs to the attention of the rest of the world when he took Fjedur, a choir of young people, to South Africa in 1978 to sing and learn songs from the country. He collected three volumes of South African Freedom Songs during apartheid, selections of which were published in Sweden, by the Iona Community in Scotland, and then in the United States as *Freedom is Coming*[135] (Utryck, 1984). Upon return to Sweden, members of Fjedur spread these songs throughout the churches. The Church of Sweden hymnal began to incorporate some of these songs as is reflected in *Den Svenska Psalmboken med Tillägg* (2002). Fjedur sang South African Freedom Songs during the Budapest Assembly of the World Lutheran Federation in 1984; the songs spread rapidly around the world.[136] The publication and recording of these songs has been significant in anti-apartheid awareness in Europe.

In addition to "Siyahamba," other popular Freedom Songs include "Freedom is Coming", "Haleluya! Pelo tsa rona" ["Hallelujah! We sing your praises"], and "Thuma mina" ["Send us, Lord"]. Freedom Songs may appear in liturgies, such as those of black Methodists, alongside translations from Western hymns, South African adaptations of Anglican chant, and songs with more traditional musical roots. They remain an important genre, even in the post-apartheid years since Nelson Mandela's election as president of South Africa in 1994.

Theology of African Hymns

It is impossible to summarize the theology of African hymnody in a few words. The texts often invoke the presence of the Holy Spirit, e.g., "Wa, wa, wa Emimimo" (Yoruba, Nigeria), "God sends us His Spirit" (Tom Colvin, Scotland/Malawi), "Njoo kwetu, Roho mwena" ("Gracious Spirit, head our pleading," Wilson Niwagila/Howard Olson, Tanzania). Songs may call people to worship, e.g., "Uyai mose" (Alexander Gondo, Shona, Zimbabwe) or "Jesu tawa pano" (Patrick Matsikenyiri, Shona, Zimbabwe). They may fit prayers or acclamations suitable for insertion in liturgy, e. g., "Nkosi, Nkosi" (Xhosa, *Kyrie eleison*), Dinah Reindorf's "Kyrie eleison" (Ghana), Abraham Dumisani Maraire's "Alleluia" (Shona, Zimbawe), or S.C. Molefe's "Masithi—Amen Siakudumisa" (Xhosa, South Africa). They may also reflect the political struggles openly such as many South African Freedom Songs. Scriptural allusions abound and they often reflect the power of Christ to overcome evil and death. (See Appendix B for sources for these songs.)

PART III
Regional Perspectives: An Introduction to Caribbean, Central and South American Hymnody[137]

Earlier in this chapter the role of Mass settings from Central and South America were discussed (see "Influences of Vatican II") both as examples of musical/liturgical inculturation and as a source for hymns and congregational acclamations immediately following the Second Vatican Council. Other Catholic Spanish-language hymns from the Iberian Peninsula, especially those of Catholic Priest Cesáreo Gabaráin (1936–1991) have been discussed in Streams one and five. The focus of this section will be Catholic and Protestant contributions to hymnody from Central and South America since Vatican II in the Portuguese and Spanish languages. As in the case of Africa, there has been an explosion of congregational song from this region of the world. These examples provide only an anecdotal look at the most commonly used songs in bilingual and Spanish/Portuguese speaking communities in North America, and in international assemblies.

Not included in this discussion are the wealth of songs—many of which are not in print—that come from the Pentecostal Church in the Southern Hemisphere. Daniel Ramírez discusses early twentieth-century Latino Pentecostal hymnody as a movement that "forged a new aural universe that incorporated as much sensory corporeality as the earlier popular Catholic visual one of saints, candles, gilded stars, and paintings (which had been erased by earlier Latino Protestantism)."[138] Ramírez notes that the Latino Pentecostal movement borrowed heavily from the African-American community in song structures (especially call and response patterns), theology (a "radical monotheistic doctrine"), and ecclesiology (with an episcopal hierarchy).[139] The rise of the Latino Pentecostal movement coincided with the onset of the Great Depression in the United States in the late 1920s and 1930s . Persecution of Latino immigrant groups combined with meager resources led to some unexpected developments: "Solidarity amidst scarcity bred fecundity. Also, the retreat of sponsor denominations under financial duress left wider margins for innovation."[140] Many Latino songs are translations of choruses discussed in stream six while others are original. These *coritos* are an important part of the faith expression of the church in Central and South America as well as Latino worship life in the United States. Because so many of the songs have been transmitted in oral form or in informal collections with words only, very few have found their way into the hymnals that define this study.[141] Therefore, though significant source of indigenous musical expression, Latino Pentecostal song generally falls outside the realm of this study.[142]

Early Songs from Mass Settings

Many early songs were used as entrance and offertory hymns. "Somos pueblo que camina" ["We are people on a journey"] and "Te Ofrecemos Padre Nuestro" ["We offer you our Father"] come from the *Misa Popular Nicaragüense* (1968) as entrance and offertory songs respectively. Appropriate to the context of the Mass, many songs point to the Eucharist. The refrain "Acudamos jubilosos a la cena del Señor" ["Let us come joyfully to the supper of the Lord"] from the entrance song "Somos pueblo" invites the assembly to joyfully gather at the Eucharist table. Another offertory song by Guillermo Cuéllar (b. 1955), "Vamos todos al banquete" ["Let us all go to the banquet"] from *Misa Popular Salvadoreña* (c. 1980) centers on the invitation to the table and relationships that are made there:

Example 7:5

Estribillo: Vamos todos al banquete,	**Refrain:** Let us all go to the banquet,
a la mesa de la creación;	to the table of creation (the universe);
cada cual con su taburete	each one with her/his stool (has a seat)
tiene un puesto y una misión.	has a job (role) and mission (at this table).
Estrofa: Hoy me levanto muy temprano;	**Stanza:** I rise very early today;
ya me espera la comunidad;	the community is already waiting for me.
Voy subiendo alegre la cuesta,	I am happily climbing the hill,
voy en busca de tu amistad.	looking for your friendship (community).[143]

The *Sanctus* during the Great Thanksgiving has inspired several congregational settings that have been incorporated into North American hymnals. Two of the most common are "Santo, santo, santo" also from Cuéllar's *Misa Popular Salvadoreña*. "Le lo le lo lay lo" by Puerto Rican priest William Loperena (1935-1996). While following closely the text of the original *Sanctus*, each makes alterations that contextualize this portion of the Great Thanksgiving for their particular cultural setting. Cuéllar's "Santo" incorporates aspects of liberation theology into this part of the ordinary of the Mass:

Example 7:6

Santo, santo, santo, santo es nuestro Dios,	Holy, holy, holy is our God,
Señor de toda la tierra.	Lord of all the earth.
que acompaña a nuestro pueblo,	who accompanies our people,
que vive en nuestras luchas	who lives in [the midst of] our struggles
del universo entero el único Señor.	as the only Lord of the whole universe.
Benditos los que en su nombre	Blessed are those who in your name
el evangelio anuncian,	announce the gospel,
el buena y gran noticias de la liberación.	the good and grand news of liberation.[144]

The joyful nature of the music also reflects the hope of liberation. Loperena's "Le lo le lo lay lo" maintains the text of the original *Sanctus* in tact, but begins with non-lexical syllables of joy as a refrain adding to the celebrative character of the song.

The Fiesta Spirit

The spirit of fiesta is a central theme of Latin American hymnody. Argentinean composer and pastor Pablo Sosa suggests that the fiesta is much more than a party or celebration:

> Out of oppression, men and women rise up to celebrate, not forgetting their struggle, to be nurtured by the sweet foretaste of the great fiesta of victory and liberation. It is not ordinary fiesta, intended to have people forget about their worries, to alienate them. It is the fiesta, which liberates. For this reason it is said: 'People who have no strength to celebrate, have no strength to liberate themselves.'[145]

The fiesta spirit of much Latin American hymnody may find a more tepid reception in some main-line Protestant Latino congregations, however. Cuban American church musician and Spanish-language hymnal editor Raquel Gutiérrez-Achón (b. 1927) relates an experience that she had in the 1970s. An article by United Methodist pastor Roberto Escamilla (b. 1931) that encouraged Latino congregations to sing more authentic Latin American songs, songs that expressed and encouraged a sense of celebration.[146] After introducing some festive Latino songs with her congregation, Gutiérrez-Achón was surprised at the rather cold reception.

> [These songs] shocked my own mother, who was a very faithful Christian. She was alarmed to the point that one day after we arrived home from a Sunday service, she told me, 'Just to think that after I prayed for years, that whatever talent you had you would dedicate to the Lord, you are the one now to bring the Devil to our services.' It took some very careful explaining on my part to somehow be able to change (to some extent) her way of thinking. One of my strongest arguments was, of course, my growing concern to preserve our cultural heritage in our worship and our music as well.[147]

Latino Protestants in the United States, especially those who are third- or fourth-generation Latino citizens in the USA, may be thoroughly bi-lingual, having often adopted the hymnody of the dominant Anglo main-line church. While this is changing, one cannot assume that all Latinos/as will respond the same way to music that comes from Central and South America.

Musical and Theological Characteristics of Latino Song

Though Latino Christian song reflects extreme stylistic diversity, some general characteristics can be suggested: (1) Hispanic hymns generally employ an *estribillo* [refrain]. Many begin with the refrain and repeat it at the beginning and end.[148] Shorter songs consist only of the refrain, especially *coritos*, usually with scriptural texts or simple ideas. *Coritos* are easily learned and may be accompanied by handclapping, tambourines and other non-pitched percussion as well as guitar and piano. It is difficult for those raised on classical Western hymnody to appreciate the repetitive nature of *coritos*. Jorge Lockward (b. 1965), a church musician from the Dominican Republic, now a U.S. citizen, comments on his own journey to appreciate *coritos*:

"I once attended a church in Higuey (Dominican Republic) where the people repeated the same *corito* maybe eighty times (no joking). The people stood there and just kept singing this one song for what seemed like almost an hour."

> It is easy to look down from a more 'sophisticated' perch and judge that kind of experience. But the truth is that upon a deeper look, great richness can be found in it. The people I saw in the church were tired, exhausted from work. Yet they went to their church that night, and they sang this song, and something in that experience freed them up. It's not just about the song it's about living in community. It's about rhythm, the being together, even the sweat in the air.[149]

(2) Many styles of music are based on local folkloric dance forms. The particular form indicates the spirit of the music. Pablo Sosa's songs, discussed below, often employ various dances forms found in Argentina and Chile. The music of Argentinean composer Ariel Ramírez (1921–2010), especially *Misa Criolla* (1964) and *Navidad Nuestra* (1965), reflects a wide variety of dance forms. Employing dance rhythms, as well as the instruments associated with specific dance forms, is one of the most effective ways to compose in indigenous styles.[150] (3) Countries whose population reflects the African diaspora employ more complex drumming patterns similar to polyrhythmic drumming found in western Africa. These countries include Cuba, the Dominican Republic, and other Caribbean islands, as well as Brazil. African musical influences may also be found in countries where the African presence is not as visible or no longer apparent, such as Argentina.[151] (4) The music of various indigenous populations influences musical style. While in some countries the indigenous population did not survive militant imperialism, e.g., Cuba, many other cultures have rich indigenous musical forms that are reflected in dance, instrumentation, and musical style. (5) Movement cannot be separated from song throughout Latin American and the Caribbean. The strong association of indigenous music with dance has made an impact on Latino church music.[152]

Several theological conclusions may be drawn from these songs that have been inserted into the Central American Masses; (1) The Eucharist (thanksgiving) is the centerpiece of the celebration. (2) The music stresses that this is a joyful feast. The rhythm of the music invites the singer to dance (or at least sway) on the way to the table; (3) *All* (*todos*) are invited to this table where no one is excluded. It is a table of justice, hope and liberation. We are fully in community at the table not only with each other, but also in the cosmic sense; (4) The journey to the table is part of the journey of life. While we encounter many difficulties, struggles, and injustice on the journey of life, we can travel joyfully as we move toward the *gran fiesta* at the table;[153] and (5) This Eucharist is in a post-Vatican II spirit—a table for shaping community, inspiring hope, and engendering justice for all who share the meal—rather than the memorial observances that characterize the manner in which many Protestant congregations participate in the communion meal.

For many Latin American Christians the experience of their indigenous musical idioms in worship symbolizes freedom from oppression—freedom to participate in musical styles and ways of expressing themselves that had been suppressed by church practice influenced by colonial forms of Christianity during the missionary expansion of the ninteeth century. According to Raquel Mora Martínez, (b. 1940) a United Methodist church musician and hymnal editor, the Chicano movement of the Southwest United States, for example, incorporated "the use of the Spanish language along with music, drama and old traditions that had been neglected by Mexican Americans" provided a point of identity that contributed to "demands for justice from employers and from schools and universities."[154] These theological themes are present in the hymns selected for the following overview.

South American Contributions

Pablo David Sosa (b. 1933) has been the leading figure in the development of hymnody from South America both as an *animateur* for the World Council of Churches Assemblies, Base Community gatherings, and numerous international conferences, and as editor of *Cancionero Abierto* [*Open Songbook*]. Begun in 1974, *Cancionero Abierto* was unlike any previous Protestant or evangelical hymnal. Sosa's philosophy was simple:

"If you have a song of praise, we will include it and see if people want to use it."[155] Songs came by individual submission, adaptations from choral works, and even creative group compositions conducted by Sosa with young people and congregations. Six volumes were published, the most recent, an accompaniment edition, in 1994. Sosa prepared early volumes at his kitchen table using a manual music typewriter. *Cancionero Abierto* has been a primary source for dispensing Latin American hymnody around the world. Several of the recent Spanish-language hymnals published in the United States have drawn from its resources. The recordings of the songs in *Cancionero Abierto* prepared by Sosa with his choir in Buenos Aires, *Música para Todos* [Music for All], have been a very important part in disseminating and teaching them, especially in predominately oral cultures.

One hundred and fifty songs have been published in the six volumes. Volumes 1–5 have been collected together in a melody only and accompaniment editions. The authors and composers, while mostly Argentinean, also come from countries throughout Latin America including Bolivia, Brazil, Costa Rica, Chile, Ecuador, Nicaragua, Peru, and Uruguay. There are occasional additional selections from outside Latin America including songs from Cameroon, England, India, Israel, Germany, Spain, Sweden, and the United States.

Sosa's earlier hymnal, *Cantico Nuevo* [*New Song*] published in 1960, reflected virtually only Euro-North American musical traditions. *Cancionero Abierto*, however, encouraged indigenous composition by South Americans. Its informal format with cassette recordings brought new authors and composers to light. This collection has influenced virtually every Spanish language songbook and hymnal published in the United States since the last quarter of the twentieth century.

A Methodist minister, Sosa's earliest songs are the best known. They include "¡Miren, qué bueno!" ["Look, how good it is!"] [*Panorama*: 972] composed in 1970 and "El cielo canta alegría" ["Heaven is singing for joy"] composed in 1958. The music reflects popular dance rhythms from Argentina—*chamarrita* and *carnavalito* respectively—adding not only a festive musical sense but linking them with the culture of the people. Both songs employ refrains with short stanzas. A third song, "Gloria, gloria,

gloria", a setting of Luke 2:14, was composed in 1979 for a Christmas pageant in the style of a *cueca*, a lively partner dance in Chile. Though Sosa could use these songs initially only for church social occasions outside of worship, they now are sung broadly in worship both in by local congregations and at international gatherings. A lesser-known song in the United States, Sosa's "Este momento" ["This is the moment"] captures the energy and urgency of his music making and work in the church.

Sosa also brought to light a simple, effective anonymous chorus, "Santo, santo, santo, mi corazon te adora" ["Holy, holy, holy, my heart adores you"], from Argentina. It appears more often in bilingual hymnals than it does Spanish-language collections and is popular both for its beautiful melody and because it can easily be sung in Spanish, even by Anglos.

It is hard to overstate the significance of *Cancionero Abierto* as a source for encouraging composition and nurturing the development of composers throughout Latin America since the mid 1970s. Several will be discussed below who have had an impact on hymnals in North America. Many of Sosa's songs are available in the United States in the collection, *Este es el Dia / This is the Day*, published by GIA Publications, Inc., 2007, with CD.

Writing Hymns in South America: A Case Study.

Federico José Pagura (b. 1923) May be considered the most famous text writer to emerge from those contributing to *Cancionero Abierto*. An Argentinean who served as Bishop of the Methodist Church in Chile and Argentina, Pagura's hymns reflect both a passion for seeing Christ in the midst of life's struggles and bold cries for justice. He is the most represented author in *Cancionero Abierto* with thirteen contributions, nine original texts and four translations. Pagura's translations include a hymn by Swedish author Anders Frostenson (1906-2006), Peter Scholtes' (1938–2009) "We are one in the spirit," and Sydney Carter's (1915-2004) "Lord of the Dance." Other often-used translations by Pagura include "Fruto del amor divino" ["Fruit of divine love"], commonly known as "Of the Father's love begotten" from the fourth-century Latin hymn by Prudentius, and "Mil voces para celebrar" ["O for a thousand tongues to sing"] by the eighteenth-century hymn writer Charles Wesley.

Pagura had contributed four hymns texts to the earlier European-based *Cantico Nuevo*. Among those was "Bendito el Rey" ["Blessed be the King"] [*Panorama*: 975] for Palm Sunday. Following the Vatican II reforms the atmosphere began to change at the ecumenical seminary in Buenos Aires where Pagura served as chaplain. He started to work with Homero Perera, (b. 1939) a talented young musician who had come from Uruguay in 1958. Perera was a tango musician who studied organ and composition in the music program at the seminary. After *Cantico Nuevo* was published in 1960, Pagura offered a fresh challenge to the students and faculty of his theology school in November 1961:

> The times are ripe that the bosom of the church, in our [South] America, produce a liturgical and musical renovation to make of worship an act of pleasurable and solemn adoration. The times are ripe for our young churches not only to familiarize themselves with the richest of the Christian musical heritage that has come to us, but also to encourage our new musicians and Christian poets to put wings to the gospel, in agreement with our own methods and talents.[156]

Pagura had written his first important religious poem as a seminary student at Union Theological Seminary in Buenos Aires in 1943 for the inauguration of the seminary's chapel. It was entitled, "¿Señor, qué es nuestro templo si tu no estas presente?" ["Lord, what is our temple if you are not present?"]. The provocative, prophetic tone of Pagura's first text was a portent of his future as a hymnwriter and translator. Pagura and Perera collaborated on the *Cantata Folklorico para Pascua de Resurrección* [*Folk Cantata for Easter*] during this time. This work included three provincial folk forms, the *baguala*, *zamba* (not to be confused with the Brazilian *samba*), and *chacarera*, as it traced the events of Holy Week. Pagura notes: "This Cantata grew from the search for elements of expression and communication of the gospel intimately connected to everyday life, particularly in this region of the world. It is an attempt to worship our Lord through music; the music that God gave to our people."[157]

During the mid-1960s, in the midst of the fervor of Vatican II, choral music by Argentinean Ariel Ramírez also added momentum. It was his music that influenced Perera in his composition of *Cantata Folklorico*. Ramírez' *Misa Criolla*, composed in 1964 (*criollos* are the Argentinean-born descendants of Spanish parents), was the first vernacular Spanish-language Mass based upon folk forms. *Navidad Nuestra* (1965), a Christmas cantata based on various Argentinean provincial musical forms, brought the issues of inculturation to a larger public.[158]

However, it was the collaboration between Pagura and Perera on "Solitario" in 1963 that resulted in the first evangelical tango, setting a new course. The tango is in many ways the essence of popular music and dance in the varied cultural milieu of Buenos Aires. The tango is a product of the singular blend of European immigrants and African slaves that constituted life in Argentina, especially Buenos Aires, in the second half of the nineteenth century.

The tango is a melding of the pulsing rhythms of the *candombe* that came to Argentina with the African slaves, the haunting melodies of Andalusia and southern Italy, as well as the Argentinean provincial dance/song, the *milonga*. The tango represents an earthiness and sensuality that is unmistakable, regardless of one's cultural perspective.[159] Sosa notes "The tango, that hybrid birth of nostalgia, the letting go of everything you love, and male ownership, is the essence and explanation of the Argentinean way of being, or at least of a *porteño* [a resident of Buenos Aires] . . . way of being. And, so, it was a good day that Federico would write a tango."[160]

"Solitario," the first evangelical tango, "didn't win any prizes" according to Sosa, but it did help to establish a bond between Pagura and Perera that proved fruitful for the future. Pagura returned to the form in the 1970s when he and Perera wrote a trilogy of "Porque" [Because] hymns: "Porque él venció" [also called *Sursum Corda*], "Porque hay un mundo" [also called *Alegría* or "Joy"], and "Porque él entró en el mundo" [also known as *Tenemos Esperanza* or *We have hope*] [*Panorama*: 974].[161] The first is in the *carnavalito* style of Sosa's "El cielo canta alegría", while the latter two are tangos.[162] By 1969, Pagura had been elected Methodist bishop of Costa Rica and Panama. In 1977 he was elected bishop of Argentina, and then president of Consejo Latinoamericano de Iglesias (CLAI). The visibility of his positions as bishop and president of CLAI (Counsel of Latin American Churches) provided Bishop Pagura with the podium from which he could address *derechos humanos* [human rights] throughout Latin America. Federico Pagura is recognized as one of the leading Protestant voices against political oppression in Latin America for the last half of the twentieth century.

For many within the church, *Tenemos Esperanza* became the South American "Ein feste Burg" during the epidemic of political turmoil and oppression of the 1970s. After overthrowing Salvador Allende, the first elected Socialist president in Latin America, the military regime (1973–1989) of Augusto Pinochet in Chile was especially vicious. As a result of oppression in Chile and Argentina's own "dirty war," people were asking "¿Por qué?" or "Why?" Why is this happening to us? Why has God abandoned us? Pagura's hymns play on the Spanish interrogative "¿Por qué?" and respond by using anaphora, beginning many of the lines of each stanza with "Porque" ["Because"]. In *Tenemos Esperanza* Pagura states that we can have hope *because* Christ came to live among us and suffered with us. Sosa expresses the relationship between the political events of the times and Pagura's hymn this way:

> [In] a time of military dictatorship, the death, the disappearance, the injustice, the horror.... How is it possible to have hope? Someone has to raise up our faith before everything is emptied

> out. It was Federico's turn. He completed the mission of the poet, as he intuited it, to put wings to the gospel. To lift up hope with a song. And Perera accompanied him with a tango, because he needed the male determination (or, perhaps, that determination which many women have, and not all men) to have hope, even in Christ, and especially in Christ in those terrible times.[163]
>
> By using the tango to embody Christ's ministry and hope in a difficult time of persecution and oppression, Pagura had planted the gospel of the incarnation deeply in Latin American soil.

Although space does not permit extensive coverage of all hymn writers, a fuller understanding of this stream will hopefully emerge in the following discussion of additional writers from Central and South America.

Mortimer Arias (b. 1924) is an *Emeritus* Methodist Bishop of Bolivia, now residing in Montevideo, Uruguay. His work as a liberation theologian is widely recognized throughout Latin America and beyond. *Announcing The Reign of God: Evangelization and the Subversive Memory of Jesus* (1984) is one of his most influential books. Like Sosa and Pagura, the music of his hymns often draws upon dance rhythms. Hymns include *Cristo* Vive ("Hoy celebramos") [*Christ lives*] is a buoyant Easter text set to music by Antonio Auza in the spirit of the *cueca*.[164] "En medio de la vida" ["In the middle of life"] [*Panorama*: 976] composed in 1973 speaks of Christ's presence in all aspects of living.

Nicolás Martínez (1917–1972) contributed a powerful Easter text in his hymn "Cristo vive" ["Christ lives"] [*Panorama*: 973]. Born a Roman Catholic, this Argentinean became a Disciples of Christ minister in 1948. Martínez based his hymn on 1 Corinthians 15:12–23. The text was written for *Cántico Nuevo* (1960) a hymnal in which he served as an editor with Pablo Sosa. Sosa's setting CENTRAL, a melody in a contemporary Western art music style, is named for Central Methodist Church in Buenos Aires. Fred Kaan translated it as "Christ is risen, Christ is living" in 1972 for inclusion in *Cantate Domino* (1974), edited by Erik Routley for the World Council of Churches.[165]

Mexican Contributions

Rubén Ruíz's (Avila) (b. 1945) hymn "Mantos y Palmas" ["Cloaks and Palms"] [*Panorama*: 964] is widely sung in the Mexican Protestant church and increasingly in the United States. Ruíz is the son of Bishop Alejandro Ruíz, a beloved bishop in the Methodist Church in Mexico. This hymn was written for one of the largest Methodist churches in Mexico City, La Santíssima Trinidad, where his father once served as pastor, but is now commonly used in Baptist, Presbyterian, and Pentecostal as well as Methodist Churches. The text tells the story of Palm Sunday as a historical event (stanza one), with contemporary applications (stanza two), and with future (eschatological) understanding (stanza three). The refrain builds and all voices join in singing "¡Hosanna al Rey!" The music has the melodic and rhythmic feel of a mariachi celebration, though the accompaniment is rather stagnant due to its use on the pipe organ in the original church.

"Pues si vivimos" ["When we are living"] [*Panorama*: 965] is an anonymous Mexican hymn that is widely used in North America. Collected by Gertrude C. Suppe (1911–2007)[166] from a Mexican woman at La Trinidad United Methodist Church in Los Angeles, California in 1980, the song later appeared in the United Methodist collection *Celebremos II* (1983). Based on Romans 14:7–8 , the first stanza echoes the idea that whether we live or die, we belong to the Lord. Additional stanzas were added by Roberto Escamilla, a member of the *Celebremos* hymnal committee.[167] The slower lilting melody has made this a popular hymn to sing bilingually.

Vicente Mendoza (1875–1955) lived before Vatican II, but his most famous hymn "Jesús es mi Rey soberano" ["O Jesus, my King and my Sovereign"] [*Panorama*: 963] did not appear more widely in English-language hymnals until the mid-1980s. Mendoza was a first-generation Mexican Methodist and a pioneer for Hispanic Methodism in the United States. His hymn, written in a nineteenth-century gospel song style, captures strong Mexican theological values of the paradox of Jesus as *familia* [family] and friend, yet one who is King and Lord. Through this sovereign friend, one finds complete joy. This hymn was written in California in 1921, but first sung that same year at El Gante Iglesia Metodista in Mexico City. It appeared in a revision of *Himnos Selectos*, first published in 1921. It was translated by Esther Frances for inclusion in the *Supplement to the Book of Hymns* (1982) and altered by George Lockwood for *The United Methodist Hymnal* (1989).[168]

Carlos Rosas (b. 1939), Roman Catholic, was born in the state of Nuevo León, Mexico, but served many years as music and liturgy coordinator at San Juan de los Lagos parish in San Antonio, Texas beginning in 1970. "Cantemos al Señor" ["O Sing unto the Lord"] [*Panorama*: 966], written in 1976, is his most famous song ecumenically. The text draws upon Psalm 19 for its images.[169] "En el principio" ["In the Beginning"] [*Panorama*: 967] is a later song (1991) reminding us that humanity is created in the image of God in spite of the greed, oppression, and pain in the world.

Brazilian Contributions

Jaci Correia Maraschin (1929–2009), Anglican, is one of the most influential of Brazilian liturgists, theologians and church musicians. A Professor of Theology at the Ecumenical Institute and the Universidade Metodista de São Paulo, his writings present a challenging view of how to contextualize worship in Brazil. For Maraschin worship is about aesthetics, i.e., is concerned about beauty and the appreciation of beauty (See his *A Beleza da Santidade*). A hindrance to worship is rationalism, which reduces faith to intellectual categories and activism, and diminishes religion to socio-ethical categories. His groundbreaking collection of indigenous Christian song, *O Novo Canto da Terra* (1987) remains a primary source for Brazilian hymns. With his student Simei Monteiro, he published *A Canção do Senhor na Terra Brasileira* (1982), a collection of 70 songs by Brazilian Christian composers and edited *Brazilian Songs of Worship* for World Council of Churches in 1989. "Vem, Jesus nossa esperança" ["Come to be our hope, Lord Jesus"] [*Panorama*: 977] is perhaps his best-known hymn. In Maraschin's own English translation, it parallels many of the ideas of Charles Wesley's "Come, thou long-expected Jesus." Maraschin's invocation of Jesus as our hope speaks well to the Advent season.

Simei Monteiro (b. 1943), Methodist, has been a professor in the Methodist Seminary in São Paulo, Brazil. More recently she has served as the worship coordinator for the World Council of Churches in Geneva, Switzerland, preparing worship for the 2006 Assembly of the World Council of Church in Porto Alegre, Brazil. Her numerous songs draw from the rhythms and modal melodies of various parts of Brazil. They range from musical settings of liturgical texts such as "Alleluia" and "Kyrie eleison" to hymns. Three of her most published songs are "Canção da caminhada" ["If walking is our vocation"], "Tua Palavra na vida" ["Your word in our lives"], and "Tua Palavra é lâmpada" ["Your word is a lamp"], a short scripture song based on Psalm 119:105, "Your word is a lamp unto my feet and a light unto my path." Equally skilled as a poet and composer, Monteiro's hymns have a strong scriptural basis and often have roots in themes on issues of justice. "Um menino" ["A child"] [*Panorama*: 978] appeared first in the 1992 publication *Canções de Rua* [*Songs of the Street*], a collection of songs describing the plight of street children in São Paulo. This particular song invites the singer to see the face of the Christ Child in an unwanted street child. All children are children of God. Shirley Erena Murray (b. 1931) captured the essence of Monteiro's "Vem, Santo Espiritu" ["Come, Creating Spirit"] [*Panorama*: 979] in a translation prepared for the 1999 Vancouver convocation of the Hymn Society in the United States and Canada. In addition to a collection of Brazilian hymns published with her mentor Jaci Maraschin, she has written her own work on song, faith and worship, *O Cântico da Vida* (1991).

Two additional songs from Brazil appear in a number of hymnals. "Cantai ao Senhor"["Sing to the Lord"] is a *vals* (waltz) moving in one beat to the measure. It is known in the United States mostly in its Spanish version "Cantad al Señor." This is a vocal form Brazil that does not use accompanying percussion instruments.

"Momento Novo" ["New Moment"] [*Panorama*: 980] is a collaborative work of six Brazilian authors. Written in 1983, this is an energetic hymn of unity along the journey. The new life that God calls people to is a shared experience and cannot be made alone. The road that we must walk together is not easy, but God "calls for us to work together for justice."[170]

CARIBBEAN CONTRIBUTIONS.[171]

Paschal Jordan, O.S.B. (b. 1944) from the Republic of Guyana, has also been an *animateur* in WCC Assemblies and other international events. "Darkness now enfolds us" is a hymn inspired by the Song of Simeon, *Nunc dimittis*, and written for a new monastery in Guyana in 1988.[172] "How great your name" reflects the more lively Caribbean style.[173]

Richard Ho Lung (b. 1939), a Roman Catholic Priest of Chinese ancestry from Jamaica, composed "Enter into Jerusalem," a song ideal for Christian festivals, especially Palm Sunday. The text includes Jamaican dialect throughout.[174]

George Mulrain (b. 1946) is a Methodist minister from Trinidad and Tobago and former President of the Methodist Church in the Caribbean and the Americas. "The thirsty deer longs for the steam" is a paraphrase of Psalm 42. The text reflects a Caribbean spirit that relies on God regardless of the natural or political difficulties. "There was a man named Jonah" reflects the composer's interest in telling biblical narratives in a calypso style that reaches the people. "Halle, Halle, Hallelujah" [*Panorama*: 969] Many of the "I AM" sayings of Christ have been incorporated by Mulrain into this traditional Caribbean song.

Patrick Prescod (b. 1932), a Methodist minister from Saint Vincent, composed "The right hand of God" for the Inaugural Ceremony of the Caribbean Conference of Churches in 1973 drawing from Psalm 98:1 for the primary image in the title. Noel Dexter (b. 1938) from Jamaica composed the calypso music.[175]

CENTRAL AMERICA

Néstor Jaén, S.J. (b. 1935), from Panama, composed "Arriba los corazones" ["Come, praise God all hearts together"] as a joyful setting and expansion of the *sursum corda* [Lift up your hearts], a spoken dialogue between the minister and the people at the beginning of the Eucharist. Father Jaén's ministry and this text reflect a concern about justice for all.[176] The repeated words, "¡Ven Señor!" ["Come Lord!"], echo the Lord's Prayer, "Venga tu reino en tierra" ["Your kingdom come on earth"]—words of liberation in an unjust world.

Additional contributions from Central America have been discussed in the earlier section on Mass settings.

Table 1

Spanish- and Portuguese-Language Hymnals

In addition to the number of Anglo hymnals including bilingual hymns from Central and South America, denominational hymnals in Spanish and Portuguese have provided valuable resources. See Appendix B for a list of hymns cited in this chapter and their sources.

Baptist

Himnario Bautista, ed. Eduardo Nelson G. (Casa Bautista de Publicaciones, 1978).

Hinário para o Culto Cristao, ed. Joan Larie Sutton (Rio de Janeiro: JUERP, 1990).

Disciples of Christ

Cáliz de Bendiciones: Himnario Discipulos de Cristo, ed. Conchita Delgado (St. Louis: Christian Board of Publications, 1996).

Episcopal

El Himnario, ed. Raquel Gutiérrez-Achón (Church Publishing Corporation, 1998), is a joint publication of the Episcopal church, Presbyterian Church, and the United Church of Christ.

Lutheran Church (ELCA)

Libro de Liturgia y Cántico, ed. Pedro Suarez (Minneapolis: Augsburg Fortress, 1998).

Lutheran Church (LCMS)

¡Cantad al Señor!, eds. Otto Hintza, Carlos Puig (St. Louis: Concordia Publishing House, 1991).

Presbyterian Church (PCUSA)

El Himario Presbiteriano, ed. Raquel Gutiérrez-Achón (Geneva Press, 1999).

United Church of Christ

Himnario Unido, ed. Raquel Gutiérrez-Achón (United Church Resources, 1999).

United Methodist contributions

Celebremos (1979) and Celebremos II (1983), eds. Roberto Escamilla and Elise Shoemaker Eslinger, and *Mil Voces Para Celebrar,* ed. Raquel Mora Martínez (Nashville: The United Methodist Publishing House, 1996).

Roman Catholic

Flor y Canto, ed. Owen Alstott (Portland, Oregon: OCP, 1989, 2001, and 2011).

Oramos Cantando, We Pray in Song, ed. Ronald Krisman (Chicago, Illinois: GIA Publications, Inc., 2013) Bilingual Spanish and English

Independent Hymnals

Cantos de Alabanza y Adoración/Songs of Praise and Worship (El Paso: Editorial Mundo Hispano, 1997). Bilingual Spanish and English.

Celebremos su Gloria, ed. Juan Rojas (Miami: Libros Internacional, 1994.)

Other sources for Spanish-language hymnody cited in this chapter:

Global Praise 1, eds. S T Kimbrough and Carlton Young (New York: GBGMusik, 1996).

Global Praise II, eds. S T Kimbrough and Carlton Young (New York: GBGMusik, 2000).

Global Praise III, eds. S T Kimbrough and Carlton Young (New York: GBGMusik, 2004).

Tenemos Esperanza/Temos Esperança/We Have Hope, ed. Jorge Lockward (New York: GBG Musik, General Board of Global Ministries, 2003).

PART IV
Regional Perspectives:
An Introduction to Asian Hymnody by Lim Swee Hong

> [M]uch is often left unsaid because it is presumed to be familiar to the readers. [Likewise, texts] do not generally deal with accepted and customary things, but only with new, uncertain, or controverted points: everything else will tend either to be passed over in silence, or to receive the briefest of allusions.[177]

An introductory work of Asian hymnody oftentimes risks making the exception the normative and the unique as commonplace. Indeed, one must always remember the abovementioned counsel of early church liturgics scholar, Paul Bradshaw, as we become acquainted with the practice of congregational song in Asia fully recognizing that "much is often left unsaid because they are familiar."[178]

Surely, what is familiar is the ubiquitous influence of Western musical practice in Asia. In fact, wherever mass media is present, it has enabled Western musical influence to seep into the local cultures. Yet, Asian cultures do not merely accept this external influence holistically. In fact, critical studies of the present day Asian church music practices will attest to varying degrees of adaptation and assimilation. This effort of enculturation or contextualization is a natural phenomenon so that external elements may become meaningful and relevant to the host cultures.

It is common knowledge that Asia is not a homogenous entity. Aside from its geographical differences, it cradles a wide variety of cultures, history, and traditions, all of which have a direct significant impact on the practice of church music in this region. More importantly, in being the birthplace and nurturing ground for Buddhism and Hinduism, the relational issue of faith and culture is a critical factor in appreciating the ethos of the Asian church in its praxis of music.[179]

Three Asian hymnals have been particularly influential in Asian congregations in the twentieth century. D. T. Niles (1908–1970), co-founder and first General Secretary of the East Asian Christian Conference, edited the *E.A.C.C. Hymnal* (1963). Niles's volume consisted largely of his own hymns in Western musical idioms. Yet, these songs moved closer to the heart of Asian people. The *E.A.C.C. Hymnal* was more popular in ecumenical than Asian circles with four printings by 1966. The first edition of *Hymns of Universal Praise,* 普天頌讚 *pu tian song tsan,* edited by Bliss Wiant, was published in 1936 in China as a joint project of several denominations.[180] A second edition was published in Hong Kong in 1977. While nineteenth-century Western hymns and Gospel songs have dominated the various editions of this hymnal, the third edition, edited by Angela Tam and published in 2006, includes a generous selection of twentieth-century Western hymn writers and with a significant number of new hymns by Chinese writers and composers.[181] These hymnals were produced out of Hong Kong. The most common hymnal on the Chinese mainland is *The New Hymnal* 赞美诗, *zan mei shi* prepared by the Three-Self Committee and the Chinese Christian Conference (1983).[182] In contrast to hymnals produced in Hong Kong, the percentage of indigenous Chinese materials, texts and tunes, is much greater. The third hymnal is *Sound the Bamboo* edited by Taiwanese composer and ethnomusicologist I-to Loh and published by the Christian Conference of Asia (1990, 2000). Unlike the first two hymnals, this collection is devoted totally to indigenous expressions of Asian Christian song with minimal Western influences.

Special mention should be made of one of the most diverse denominational hymnals in Asia, *Sèng-sí* 聖詩, *sheng shi,* edited by I-to Loh (The Presbyterian Church in Taiwan, 2009), which, though containing many Western hymns, is more inclusive of songs from Asia, Africa and Latin America than any other Asian denominational hymnal. The Loh family has taken responsibility of editing hymnals for The Presbyterian in Taiwan for seventy years. Loh's father, Sian-chhun Loh (1905–1984) edited an earlier version of *Sèng-sí* (1936). This hymnal was followed by I-to Loh's first hymnal in 1964 and the latest in 2009, each becoming more responsive to hymns from the Asian community.[183]

Following is an examination of that branch of Asian hymnody that consciously seeks to co-mingle both Western and local nuances in developing expressions that resonate with local communities. Due to limited hymnological resources in North American hymnals, musical examples will be quoted from *Sound the Bamboo* (STB) and *The United Methodist Hymnal* (UMH).[184] Broadly speaking, we can divide the Asian musical landscape into three regions, namely, East, South, and Southeast.

East Asia

The traditional music of China, Korea, Japan, Taiwan, and Hong Kong typifies the musical characteristics of East Asia.[185] All these countries have their own distinctive musical characteristics, but there appears to be some common features that they share which seem to reflect an underlying Chinese musical influence. These features include the:

- prevalent use of the pentatonic (five-note) scale system;[186]
- preference for monophony in both instrumental and choral music e.g., unison singing;
- use of heterophonic accompaniment;
- appreciation for nasal quality vocal production;
- subtle use of embellishment to accentuate melodic phrase and cadential point; and
- symbiotic relationship between tonal inflections of the spoken language to the melodic line.

"Winter has Passed, the Rain is Over" (STB 71) [*Panorama:* 938], with a text by Weifan Wang (b. 1927) and translated by Ewing W. Carroll, Jr. (b. 1937), was birthed after the long trauma of the Cultural Revolution (1966–1976). This hymn became a source of encouragement for Christians in China.[187] A quick perusal of the arrangement by I-to Loh, who uses his pseudonym Pen-li Chen, clearly attests to many of the abovementioned features.

Example 7:7

1. Winter has passed, the rain is o'er, earth is a-bloom, songs fill the air. Linger no more, why must you wait? "Rise up my love, come follow me."

Refrain
Jesus, my Lord, my love, my all, body and soul forever yours, in dale so dark I long for you, abide with me in spring anew.

© 1990 Christian Conference of Asia, GIA Publications, Inc., agent.

In contrast to the lyrical nature of "Winter has Passed" is "Ohoradiya" (STB 101), a setting of Psalm 150. Well-known South Korean composer, Geonyong Lee (b. 1947), who also composed the popular hymn "O-so-so" ["Come Now, O Prince of Peace"], trans. Marion Pope, (STB 241), crafts the latter. "Ohoradiya" reflects the inherent strength and vigor typical of Korean hymnody and the vibrancy of the Christian faith in a geographical region that is politically divided and threatened by the development of nuclear warfare. In this hymn, the unison singing is heightened by a call-and-response approach marked by changing tempo. Typically accompanied by the use of the *changgo* (a two-headed drum played with sticks), Lee provides a hymn for the local culture to articulate their Christian faith with much integrity and meaning.

Taiwan has experienced significant immigration influx from mainland China in the last two centuries, but there remains a small but vibrant population of indigenous groups and their musical cultures have been studied extensively by both Asian and Western scholars.[188] In fact, these indigenous musical idioms have contributed much to the church's effort of locating its identity within a Taiwanese *milieu*. Chief among the pioneers who have made this possible is I-to Loh.[189] Through him, Taiwanese indigenous works such as "The Rice of Life" (STB 190) are beginning to find a place in the world of congregational song. In this work, Loh incorporates the distinctive "sliding" singing style of the Bunun people of Taiwan, matching it with a text by presently retired United Methodist missionary, Andrew Fowler (b. 1935).

Much more minimalist in approach and typical of North Asian music is the Japanese hymn "Here, O Lord, Your Servants Gather" (STB 242, UMH 552) [*Panorama:* 946] by Tokuo Yamaguchi (1900–1995) with an English translation by Everett M. Stowe (b. 1897). Based upon John 14:6, "I am the way, the truth, and the life," the melody is from the Gagaku tradition, coming from the ancient court music practice of the Japanese emperor. Composed in 1958, only thirteen years after the conclusion of World War II, it would have been unthinkable to use the emperor's melodies in a Christian hymn before the end of the war. In this hymn, unison singing is enhanced by heterophony. Instead of using thirds as the *de facto* harmonic accompaniment as in most hymns, the use of fourths, particularly in parallel motion, creates a sonic quality typically associated with music from the Far East. Carlton Young, in commenting about the tune, points out that the composer of the music, Isao Koizumi (1907-1992), uses traditional scales supported by open parallel harmonies, a compositional approach typical of the school of post-World War II Japanese composers.[190] Indeed, it is this minimalistic aural character that brings forth a focus on the melodic line and its text. This uncanny illumination of the melody clearly reinforces the monophonic nature of Asian hymnic tradition. Accompaniments if used should be typically sparse and non intrusive.

Thus, broadly speaking, music in this region tends to share certain aesthetic traits such as simplicity, meditative, quiet, melancholy, reflective, and convey a sense of mystery. Composers often use timbre and/or rhythm differentiation to create musical interest rather than harmonic devices such as modulations and cadential progressions. However, with the spreading influence of "Praise and Worship," such musical characteristics are being merged with the harmonic practice of Western music. The lack of Western-style harmony in Asian traditional musical practice together with a general fascination with all things Western by the local populace, in my opinion, have inadvertently contributed to the process of assimilation. This has given rise to some polarizing debates within the Church in East Asia seeking to establish its identity.

The Role of Missionaries in the Development of Asian Hymns

Missionary contributions to the development of Asian hymns are many. Two missionary couples must suffice as examples. **Bliss (1895-1975) and Mildred (1898–2001) Wiant**, United States music missionaries of the Methodist Episcopal Church, served in Peking, China where he was head of the music department at Yenching University and later as a professor at Chung Chi College, Chinese University, Hong Kong. He served as musical editor of the first edition of *Hymns of Universal Praise* (1936) and, along with his wife Mildred translated many Chinese hymns into English.[191] Of the more than 400 Western hymns in translation, this hymnal also included sixty-two hymn texts by Chinese Christians and seventy-two tunes of Chinese origin or by Chinese composers.[192] "Rise to Greet the Sun" ["Qing zao qi-lai kan"], a text by Chao Tzu-chen (1888–1979) with a pentatonic tune by Hu Te-ai (STB 155[193]), first appeared in *Hymns of Universal Praise* and is an example of a translation by the Wiants.[194]

Leaving for China in 1923, the Wiants were forced to depart in 1940 to avoid internment by the Japanese, but returned from 1948–1951 until the Communist revolution made a continuation of their work impossible. Bliss Wiant was granted a Master's degree in music composition in 1936 from Boston University and then pursued a PhD, writing on the topic of "The Music of China," the most comprehensive ethnomusicological study on this topic to date in English.[195]

The Wiants promoted Chinese hymnody in the United States especially in the publication of *The Pagoda* in 1946.[196] In addition to the thirteen Chinese folk tunes, five additional original tunes by Chinese composers were included, as well as two tunes of Confusion and Buddhist origins. A lover of Chinese art, the pamphlet also includes several examples of Chinese painting. Seven texts are by the Wiant's close friend T.C. (Tze-chen) Chao (c. 1887–1979), and Episcopalian, Dean of the Yenching University School of Religion from (1925–1950), and a vice president of the World Council of Churches. Wiants translated most of the texts, and Bliss provided all the musical arrangements. Wiant states that the "beautiful melodies of China [have been accompanied] with western harmonic and contrapuntal material so that community singing of the songs may be more easily achieved."[197] The collection contains some folksongs and with their original texts and also illustrates how "folk music has been adapted to modern religious uses."[198]

Mildred Wiant was an essential partner in the couple's work. When Bliss Wiant introduced G. F. Handel's *Messiah* in China very early in their ministry, Mildred was the soprano soloist. Educated in

Boston in opera, Mildred trained some of the leading Chinese opera singers of the day. She was very diligent in her translations, striving to bring as much as possible the full meaning of the Chinese language into the English translation.[199]

The Wiants left a collection of over 500 items including Chinese musical instruments, art, books and other cultural artifacts to Ohio State University who in turn established the "Bliss and Mildred Wiant Professorship in Chinese Literature and Culture" in 1977.[200] Ohio Wesleyan University (Delaware, Ohio) has sponsored The Wiant House since 1967 where male students from various ethnicities, religions and nationalities live together, and awards the Bliss and Mildred Wiant Award for outstanding leadership in inter-cultural understanding on the campus and in the community at its annual baccalaureate service.[201]

Boris (b. 1918) and Clare Anderson (1923–2008) were born in Yorkshire, England. They were Presbyterian missionaries to Taiwan, serving in various capacities at Tainan Theological College (TTC), a seminary for the Presbyterian Church of Taiwan. Both were New Testament scholars and musicians—Clare playing the piano and Boris the flute. Through their work at TTC they promoted indigenous Taiwanese music and culture and supported Taiwan independence. Their love of Formosa (the green isle), the earlier name of Taiwan, may best be illustrated by their English paraphrase of a hymn "Taiwan the Green" by John Jyi-giokk Ti'n, a minister in the Presbyterian Church in Taiwan:

> By Pacific's western shore,
> Beauteous isle, our green Taiwan.
> Once suffered under alien rule,
> Free at last to be its own.
> Here's the basis of our nation:
> Four diverse groups in unity,
> Come to offer all their varied skills,
> For the good of all and a world at peace.

> "God Created Heaven and Earth" ("Chin Chu Siong-te cho thi{n} toe") (STB 173) [*Panorama*: 939] is a representative translation. Based upon Genesis 1:1-5, the Andersons prepared their translation of this popular creation hymn in 1962 for the *E.A.C.C. Hymnal* (1963) edited by D. T. Niles. Niles adapted it for this publication and set it to Pepuhoan tune. The Andersons revised their translation in 1981 for *Hymns from the Four Winds* (1983), edited by Loh I-to where it was set to TOA-SIA, a traditional Taiwanese melody from the Pin-po people. The hymn was then included in two editions of *Sound the Bamboo*.[202]

South Asia

Though this region encompasses several countries including Bangladesh, Nepal, Pakistan, India and Sri Lanka, it is made up of two dominant musical cultures: Hindustani in the North and Carnartic in the South. The latter tends to be more melissmatic in character with complex rhythmic patterns. In this region, a melissma is not merely a decorative element but an essential component of the musical ethos. Broadly speaking, traditional music in this region tends to exhibit one or more of these traits:

- a highly melissmatic and embellished melodic line;
- drone and/or *ostinato* typically accompany the melody;
- unison singing is prevalent. However, multipart singing is evident though usually in leader-chorus or responsorial styles;
- the scale system in this region is equally complex as the scales/modes (ragas) are strictly governed by philosophical rules that predetermined when these ragas can be used; and[203]
- music is typically rhythmically driven and sustained through the use of drone that are "built-in" within the music making process.[204]

"Yellaam Yesuvee" ["Christ is All to Me"] (STB 55) with text and tune by Y. Gnanamani. This song reflects the Indian Diaspora in Southeast Asia and it continues to be an important hymn in the church music corpus of Tamil-speaking churches in Malaysia and Singapore. In looking at the hymn, one cannot help but realize that it is the melissmas and glides between pitches that significantly enable the song to speak with an Indian idiom. Though notated in *Sound the Bamboo* hymnal as a single melody, one must not presume that it is sung unaccompanied. As Loh succinctly points out, "the original [Indian] styles may be simulated by use of a pair of concussion bells, a pair of *tabla* drums, and drones...."[205] Indeed for the Indian church, monophony does not mean unaccompanied but rather accompaniment that is improvisatory.

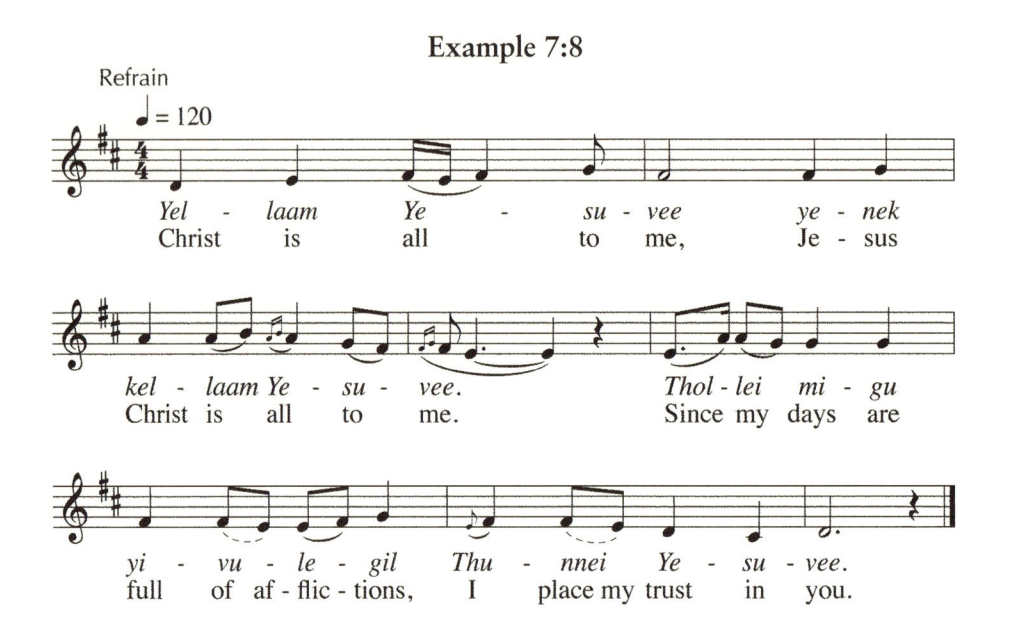

Example 7:8

Refrain
♩ = 120

Yel - laam Ye - su - vee. ye - nek
Christ is all to me, Je - sus

kel - laam Ye - su - vee. Thol - lei mi - gu
Christ is all to me. Since my days are

yi - vu - le - gil Thu - nnei Ye - su - vee.
full of af - flic - tions, I place my trust in you.

© 1990 Christian Conference of Asia, GIA Publications, Inc., agent.

In contrast, "Khudaayaa, raeham kar" ["Have Mercy on Us, Lord"] (STB 120) is a Pakistani work whose melody is hauntingly effective without elaborate accompaniment. Simply accompanied by concussion bell, this monophonic work intuitively draws us into a *milieu* of prayer. Discovered by I-to Loh in the basement of a theological library in Pakistan in one of his many trips to the Indian subcontinent, he subsequently introduced the hymn at various ecumenical gatherings and in time, this work by R. F. Liberius became widely used as a piece of liturgical music, easily replacing traditional Western musical setting of *Kyrie eleison* in ecumenical worship events.

Example 7:9

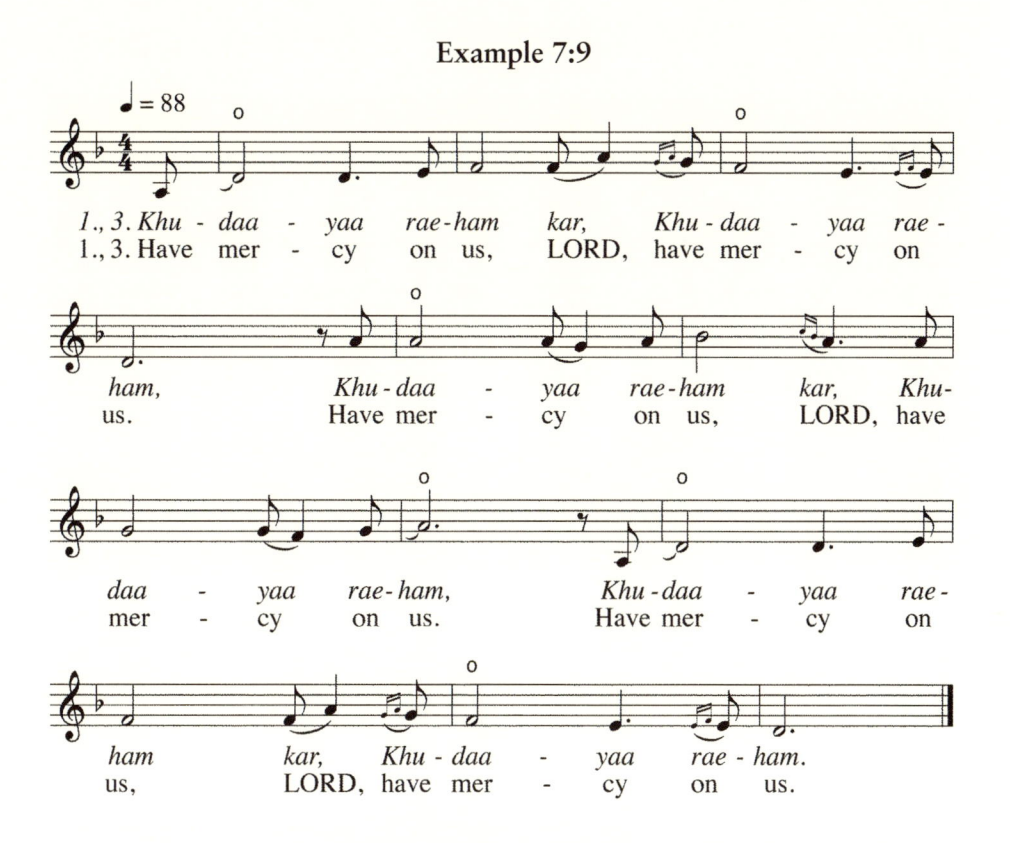

Transcription © 1990, GIA Publications, Inc.

In 1987, Bart Shaha (b. 1946), then General Secretary of the Asia Alliance of YMCAs participated in the Asian Workshop for Liturgy and Music in the Philippines.[206] It was at this event that the delegates became acquainted with the Bangladeshi hymn "Esho hae Probhu" ["Come, Lord Jesus Christ"] (STB 8). Through the editorial effort of I-to Loh, this hymn eventually found its way into several publications including *Sound the Bamboo*. Though simple in form, the melody accentuates the text through its initial descending line invoking a sense of the incarnate Christ dwelling in our midst followed by a sweeping rise in the melody corresponding to the text as it raises a petition for freedom and proclaims total trust in Christ.

Example 7:10

E - sho hae Pro - bhu   Tu - mi dho - ra   yee - sho,
Come, O Je - sus Christ, make your dwell-ing with us.

Am - ra ro - ey - chi   ja - gro - to.
We shall be watch - full through the night;

Bho - rer - a shaye   mo - ra ja - gro - to,
we'll wait with hope for your Day to dawn.

Muk - ti - da - ta   tu - mi dho - ra   yee - sho.
Come, set us free, all our trust is in you;

E - sho hae Pro - bhu   Tu - mi dho - ra   yee - sho.
now, O Je - sus Christ, make your dwell-ing with us.

© 1990 Christian Conference of Asia, GIA Publications, Inc., agent.

The United Methodist Hymnal (1989) is one of the first denominational hymnals in the West to include non-Western hymns extensively in its repertoire. "Saranam, Saranam" ["Refuge"] (UMH 523) from South Asia is one such work. "Saranam" is a word that communicates deep reverence for the God and appears in many Indian Christian hymns across language groups. The word has its origins in Sanskrit—an ancient language no longer spoken, but from which many words in modern Indian languages are derived. This hymn comes to us by way of the *E. A. C. C. Hymnal* (1963), edited by D. T. Niles (1908–1970). Unfortunately, this effort did not incorporate any embellishments owing to different understanding of their function in musical praxis. Although Western hymnologists may view such embellishment as decorative, these embellishments to the Indian church give meaning and character to Indian sacred music, an essential element of Indian musical praxis. Not surprising, in the Asian hymnal, *Sound the Bamboo*, the editor, I-to Loh sought to reinstate these embellishments.[207]

In recent years, music from this region has successfully penetrated the popular music market of Europe in particular in the United Kingdom. In fact, *Bhangra*, in both traditional and fusion forms of reggae, hip-hop, etc., is widely performed in various parts of the world.[208] Might this Punjabi musical form eventually find its way into the practice of church music both in and beyond South Asia?

At the time of this writing, few hymns from India are currently available in North American hymnals due to the complexity of the musical style. Nevertheless, they flourish locally. A popular Tamil language hymnal in southern India is *Christian Hymns, Lyrics and Songs of New Life* (1949)[209] is in its twenty-third edition in May 2007. "Christian hymns" are older Western hymns in Tamil. "Lyrics" are songs from southern India in the classical Carnatic structures of *kriti* (sometimes called keertani in the church community) and *bhajan*. Both are based on the complex rhythmic structures (*talas*) and melodic scales (*ragas*) of the classical tradition. The number of ragas, each with a distinctive performance style and context, are a challenge to Indian Christians to sing in worship and extremely difficult for Western congregations to incorporate into their hymnic repertoire. "Songs of New Life" are more recent compositions, usually in Western style or popular Indian styles including "light" Carnatic songs—music with classical structures but accompanied on Western electronic keyboards with a built-in rhythm section.[210]

Thomas M. Thangaraj (b. 1942), a minister in the Church of South India and *Emeritus* Professor at Emory University's Candler School of Theology, has composed simpler songs in the Carnatic tradition in the repetitive *bhajan* structure where a leader sings a phrase and it is repeated by the congregation.[211] Hymns by Thangaraj in the *bhajan* form include "God of Creation," "Ocean of Love," "Rejoice, Hallelu," and "I was glad."[212] These songs may be accompanied on open fifths with an organ or on traditional

Indian instruments, the *sruti* box that plays sustained fifths, and the *harmonium*, an Indian keyboard instrument, both of which create sound by hand-pumped bellows.

An Indian folk hymn from the north is "Jeya Ho" ["We Bow Before You, O Great and Holy"] (STB 39) was first included in *Jaya Ho, Songs of Joy from India* 1955–1956.[213] This Hindi-language hymn may reflect the influence of the Dalit people in India (formerly known as the "Untouchable" caste). "Jeya Ho," translated as "victory be to you," takes the theme of victory that is offered by God. The call-and-response structure of this folk style is more accessible to Western congregations.

Southeast Asia

The Southeast Asia region consists of Brunei, Kampuchea (*Cambodia*), Indonesia, Philippines, Laos, Malaysia, Myanmar (*Burma*), Singapore, Thailand, and Vietnam.[214] The musical landscape of the region is a fusion of several ancient musical cultures including Chinese, Indian, and Arabic.[215] Aside from the pentatonic (five-tone) scale this area exhibits distinctive musical features such as those listed below.

- The use of gong-chime ensembles. Examples include *gamelan* and *dondang* ensembles of Indonesia, *kulintang* in Southern Philippines, Thailand's *pi phat* and other gong-circle ensembles in Kampuchea (*pin peat*) and Myanmar (*pat waing*). Remarkably, despite the strong Western influence in most churches, some of these ensembles are beginning to find their ways into the worship life of local congregations.[216]
- A by-product of the gong-chime ensemble is the performance practice of polyphonic stratification whereby "each voice is derived from the main melody, rather than independent of it, and all these voices are heard at the same time."[217] According to Malm, the shimmering sonic effect is achieved by means of "a system that marks music as temporal units according to the entrance of specific instruments in a specific order at specific times."[218]

- Bamboo is a common type of wood in this region and typically used to make musical instruments. Thus, it is normal to find bamboo instruments such as flutes, Jaw's harps, mouth organs (Thai: *khaen*), tuned stamping tubes, buzzers, etc. in this region. In fact, in the Philippines one may find an organ with its pipes made out of bamboo.[219]
- Generally speaking, the vocal production in this region is generally more "open" and not as nasal as the Eastern Asian region.
- Though ornamentation, gliding tones in the melodic line and improvisation remain important feature in the music of this region, they are not as dominant when compared to the practice of the Indian subcontinent.
- Unison singing, as in other parts of Asia, dominates though there is also a practice of responsorial (leader/chorus) singing in this region.
- This region also features specific scale systems like the equidistant intervallic tuning of Thai music, and the *pelog and slendro* tunings of Javanese gamelan. Sadly, due to dominating influence of the Western diatonic scale system, many such distinctive tunings, like the Thai scale system, are gradually abandoned.[220]

In addition, music in Southeast region also bears similar traits to the Northeast such as simplicity, melancholy, reflective, mystery and charm. In "Mary's Salidummay" (STB 102), the former principal of St. Andrew's Seminary in Manila, Henry W. Kiley (b. 1936), paraphrased and inserted the non-lexical but popular indigenous northern Philippine phrase of "Ay, Ay, Salidummay" into the liturgical text of the *Magnificat*. In this same work, he composed a melody out of a Kalinga (northern Philippine) motif. The result is a work that truly enables Filipino Christians to express their worship with much charm, dignity and sensitivity to their culture.

Example 7:11

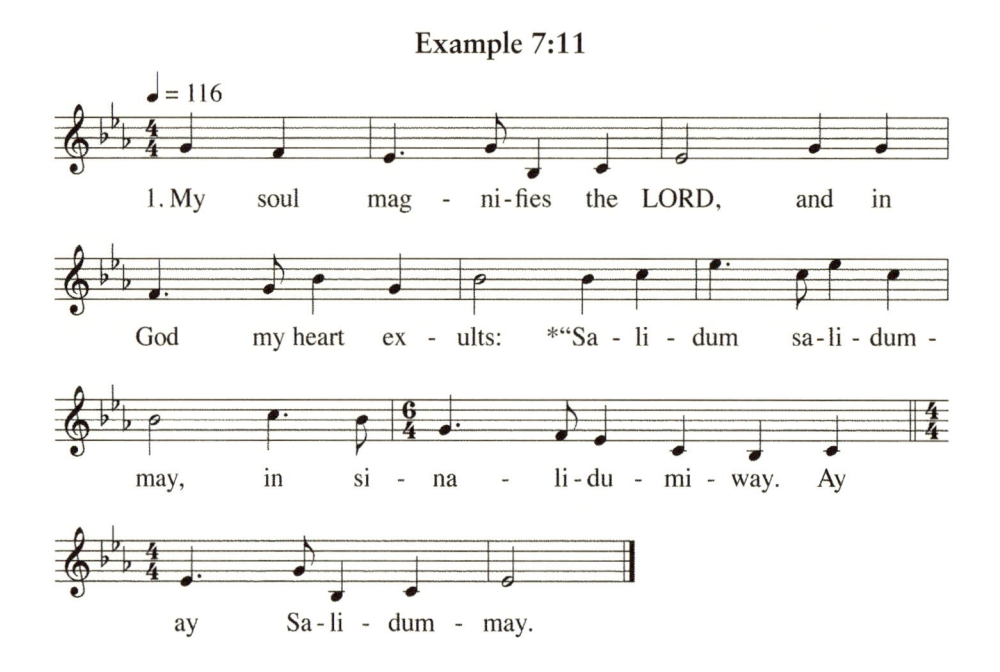

♩ = 116

1. My soul mag-ni-fies the LORD, and in God my heart ex-ults: *"Sa-li-dum sa-li-dum-may, in si-na-li-du-mi-way. Ay ay Sa-li-dum-may.

*The meaning of salidummay has long been forgotten, but Christians have adapted the word to express the mood of joy.

© 1990 Christian Conference of Asia, GIA Publications, Inc., agent.

Yet, as with the rest of Asia, there is no denying of Western influence in church music. Admittedly, in a country like the Philippines that had been dominated by the Spanish for four centuries, Western (Spanish) musical idioms have firmly taken roots and Western music performance practice can hardly be regarded as a foreign influence to its population. Such influence can clearly be seen in the Eucharistic hymn, "Kay Laking Hiwaga" ["What a Great Mystery", para. by James Minchin, b. 1942] [STB 82]. In this work, Dr. Francisco F. Feliciano (b. 1941), President of the Samba-likhaan (The Asian School of Music, Worship and the Arts) set his text to a lilting folk song from Bicol.[221] This hymn bears the traditional Filipino signature of a triple meter and the use of the guitar, a popular folk instrument in the country that tangibly reflects an entrenched Western influence within the culture.

An interesting feature of the musical idiom in Southeast Asia is the strong emphasis on communal participation and the connection between music, theatre and ritual. Without a doubt, various gong-chime ensembles in Southeast Asia also manifest this function. In "Lirih terdengar lagu kasih yang merdu" ["Soft the Master's Love Song," para. by James Minchin] [STB 203], Rudolf Pantou, a graduate from the Asian Institute for Liturgy and

Music and a member of YAMUGER, composed a hymn that uses the guitar to create the aural impression of the *gamelan*.[222] In so doing, he roots this soul stirring text within a specific cultural environment in a musical language that is easily understood. What might not be so obvious to outsiders is that folk entertainment that engages local Indonesian communities frequently features the use of gamelan, in particular the islands of Java and Bali. Thus, in his composition, Pantou seems to hint that the comfort being sought can be found in the God as personified by Christ. Such an intuitive approach clearly enables this hymn to resonate deeply with Javanese Indonesians.

Example 7:12

1. Soft the Master's love song, and beautiful to hear: "Come to me, you poor, all who stumble in distress; relief from toil I offer, come to me for rest."

*Put a matchstick between the guitar strings near the bridge to produce a gong-like sound.
© 1990 Christian Conference of Asia, GIA Publications, Inc., agent.

Equally effective, is the hymn "Nyanyikanlah nyanyian baru" ["Sing the Lord a New Song", para. by Rolando Tinio, b. 1937] [STB 100] composed by a Batak, the late Mdm. Tilly Lubis (1925–2002), also affiliated with YAMUGER. Resonating strongly with a creation motif, Lubis' decision to match the text with a traditional Batak melody gives further impetus for that work to be better accepted as a hymn by and for the Batak community.[223]

Thailand is the only nation in Southeast Asia that has never been a colony of any Western power. Unfortunately, what the nation has been able to avoid politically did not happen in the arena of church music as Western churches made inroads into that culture. Yet, in that situation, several visionaries have gradually changed the face of Christianity in Thailand. Through the work of the Thai Covenant Church, traditional musical ensembles like the *ranak ek, pong lam,* and *khaen* have found a place in Thai Christian worship. Pioneered by Jim and Joan Gustafson and their Thai co-workers, Pastors TongPan Phommedda and Banpote Wechkama in 1977, this work presently continues through the Thai Foundation for Music and Fine Arts ably led by Inchai (b. 1950) and Ruth (b. 1951) Srisuwan.[224] An example of this effort can be seen in the hymn "Phra-kham phi sawn hai rao ruu jak" ["From the Bible We Learn God's Will", para. by James Minchin] (STB 217) by Ruth and Inchai Srisuwan. Typically accompanied by the *khaen* (mouth organ) and *ching* (concussion bells), this hymn is frequently sung in house churches where the emphasis is on living out the Christian life in a local agrarian community. Illiterate church members are taught Christian doctrines through such songs and this is one such example.

Multi-racial immigrant countries like Malaysia and Singapore have a distinctive problem in terms of identifying what are truly local songs and how these might be adapted for Christian worship. Singaporean Samuel Liew's (b. 1942) initial setting of a Christian text, "Now Let Us Tell of Your Victory" (STB 22), to a folk tune did not quite work.[225] This problem of finding one's local voice is further compounded by the fact that local cultural expressions are closely linked to faith traditions such as Buddhism (and/or Taoism), Hinduism, and Islam. As a result, Christianity in these countries is often differentiated by its Western influence, particularly in its worship and church music expressions. An excellent example of this musical style is

Samuel Liew's "Call Me By My Name" (STB 265). Composed in 1964, this hymn found its way into *New Songs of Asian Cities*, the first editorial effort of I-to Loh and subsequently into *Sound the Bamboo*.[226] Liew, a former Methodist Malaysian pastor composed this song for a youth group he was leading in Kampar, Perak, West Malaysia.

Example 7:13

♩ = 80
Bm Em A7 Bm
1. A - lone I am yet not a -
F♯ Bm E A
lone; there're peo - ple all a - round.
D G Em A
I bear a name, yet I have none.
A7 Bm Em D A7
I'm lost, can I be found?
Refrain
D Em D
Just call me by my name, just call me
D7 A Bm F♯m
by my name, just call me by my
G A D A7 D
name, O my Lord, just call me by my name.

© 1990 Christian Conference of Asia, GIA Publications, Inc., agent.

Nevertheless, efforts are still made to try and root Christian worship in local idiom. The hymn of D. A. Chelliah, a Malaysian Lutheran, "Karthaadhi Karthar Iveree" ["This is the God Beyond all Gods," para. by James Minchin] (STB 139) is one such example as it retained the genius of South Indian musical idiom which invokes a sonic environment that is palpably soothing to the emigrated Indian population in Malaysia.

In the last decade, several including this writer have experimented in fusing musical idioms. For some like I-to Loh, the fusion has been primarily intra-Asian whereas for others such as the writer who is a Singaporean, the desire has been to develop a local voice which manifests both Asian and Western influences.[227]

Theological Foci of Asian Congregational Songs

While it is admirable that progress has been made in harnessing idiomatic features of the local culture in the process of music making, much of the textual content in Asian hymns has remained unchanged. Consistently, hymn writers have been primarily concerned with the praise of God and the anticipated salvific rewards in eternity. Few Asian hymns can be found to specifically speak on current "earthly" conditions such as deplorable socio-economic conditions, racism, sexism, globalization, and so forth, though such is the context of Asia in many instances. Nevertheless, there are exceptions. One remarkable example is the Indonesian hymn by S. Tarigan. Entitled "Sayur kubis jatuh harga" ["Oh, The Cabbage Price is Falling"] (STB 313), this hymn urges faith in God in the midst of devastating economic conditions. This is a poignant hymn and all too prophetic, in the midst of the current avian flu crisis that is enveloping this part of the world. Such a biological disaster has deprived countless families of the only means of sustaining their household economically as livestock is culled by authorities to minimize health risk with minimal compensation for such drastic act of prevention.

> Oh, the cabbage price is falling,
> the tomato plants are wilting,
> the close trees all have stopped blooming,
> and all my sales have come to nothing.
> Yet I worship and I praise God,
> and I sing and shout rejoicing,
> my salvation's from the Lord alone.

Geonyong Lee's hymn "O-so-so" ["Come Now, O Prince of Peace"] (STB 24) that urges for unity is deeply moving in the midst of political tension that is threatening to boil over in the Korean peninsula. I-to Loh's setting of Chun-ming Kao's (b. 1929) "Chhi-phe ho he sio" ["Watch the Bush of Thorns,"] para. by James Minchin) (STB 252) as well as the collaborative effort of Shengben Lin and Weifan Wang in "Dong tian yi wang, yu shui yi zhi" ["Winter has Passed, the Rain is O'er"] (STB 71) are examples of hymns written under persecution. Both hymns express faithfulness and steadfast commitment in the face of intense suffering.[228] Indeed, despite the very strong maxim of the separation of church and state in most parts of Asia and the fact that Christianity remains a minority faith tradition with very limited advocacy power in any given Asian society, such hymns testify to the love of God and the willingness of Christians to be the light and salt of the world as commanded by Christ in making a difference in the lives of others.

In an attempt to introduce prophetic texts with Asian musical idioms, I-to Loh has set several hymns by the New Zealand hymnwriter, Shirley Erena Murray (b. 1931). An example is Murray's *Hunger Carol* ("Child of Joy and Peace") (STB 144) with Loh's composition in an Indonesian *gamelan* style. The tune has been given the name SMOKEY MOUNTAIN, referring to a trash heap in Manila, Philippines, where people live and search for food through the refuse.

Finally, in these days of armed conflict and rumors of war, the Filipino hymn "Matulog pa, bunsong mahal" by Rolando Tinio (1937–1997) ["Sleep Through the Night, Beloved Child"] [STB 277] is a song that sings of hope in God to bring a father safely home to the family in the midst of violence. Indeed such a hymn transcends geographical location even as it is common knowledge that armed conflicts tear families apart even as current situations in the Middle East attest to this. Even now, armed conflicts all over the world continue to have a devastating impact on combatants, civilians and their loved ones.

Looking Ahead

In the last decade, there has been a gradual but definite move towards nurturing an Asian voice in church music. The Asian Institute for Liturgy and Music in Manila continues to play a significant effort in this effort, but other church-related institutions have joined this cause of empowering local churches. These include Tainan Theological College and Seminary in Taiwan where Loh served as its President (1994–2002) and Methodist School of Music together with Trinity Theological College in Singapore. These institutions have established graduate programs that strive to provide the Asian church with competent leaders in the field of church music and worship, equipping them with the necessary skills to develop a distinctive Asian emphasis in their worship and music ministry.[229] Such systematic training may greatly contribute to a dramatic transformation of church music practice in Asia for the twenty-first century.

Admittedly, many Asian churches continue to be enamored with "Praise and Worship" repertoire for their congregations, seeing this style as a panacea to Christian spirituality and church growth. In my view, this is a necessary step for some Asian churches to find their own voice in Christian worship, in particular highly urban societies like Singapore where western influence clearly dominates the cultural landscape.[230] However, just as larger churches in the west are gradually moving towards creating their own songs that better articulate their local context and concerns; in the not so distant future, I believe the churches in Asia will ultimately do the same.[231] Given this scenario, what is presently an exception in the Asian church i.e. singing songs that are locally composed reflecting local concerns, will inevitably become the norm.

PART V
A European Addendum
Music from Ecumenical Christian Communities
C. Michael Hawn

As the title of this chapter—"The Rise of Ecumenical Global Song"—indicates, ecumenical communities have sprung up during the twentieth century, and in some cases have partially shaped their spiritual identities by developing songs for daily prayer. Although it may be possible to consider the contributions of these communities under another stream of song, I have chosen to discuss them under the broad umbrella of ecumenical global song because their impact is worldwide and their missions are ecumenical. The influence the Taizé and Iona Communities, in particular, has been felt extensively in North American and European hymnals.[232]

Ecumenical Music from the Taizé Community

The Taizé Community has become a place of pilgrimage for young people from around the world. In 1940, Roger Louis Schutz-Marsauche (1915–2005), son of a Swiss Reformed pastor, arrived in the tiny hamlet of Taizé in southeastern France. In response to the conditions of occupied France during World War II, he cast his lot with the poor and disadvantaged. His dream was to live in community with others who would practice the essential dimensions of the Gospel in a manner that would offer a response of Christian reconciliation and hope in the face of the horrors of the war. Brother Roger, as he became known, found a place for such a community in the village of Taizé, just north of Cluny, a site of one of the great medieval monastic traditions of the church 1000 years earlier.

Today, the work of this ecumenical Community continues with approximately 100 brothers who, not unlike their predecessors in Cluny, have taken monastic vows, including poverty and chastity. These brothers, however, come from all over the globe and represent a wide spectrum of denominational beliefs. The Community includes Reformed, Anglican, and Catholic Christians. The overarching theme of Taizé is reconciliation through prayer. The brothers provide hospitality for thousands of pilgrims from around the globe each year and have served in some of the poorest and most helpless situations in the world, such as Calcutta, Haiti, and New York City.[233]

One cannot discuss Taizé music without understanding its context, that of common prayer. Brother Jean-Marie, who has been with the Community since 1981 and one of the brothers who prepares and leads daily prayer, indicates the importance of "common prayer" for the monastic community rather than daily office, i.e., "what we ought to do." Continuing, he observes that, "To say prayer is 'common' is to say that it brings us together."[234] The most significant aspects of this common prayer are singing and silence. "It is not that spoken prayer is unimportant. But the spoken work can be a little bit cerebral. There's a fullness to sung prayer, an element of wholeness."[235]

Taizé prayer is based upon the historic monastic service of daily prayer. Singing, silence, scripture (available in several languages) and prayer permeate morning, noon and evening prayers. The service draws from more contemplative roots where silence and reflection are central to worship and mantra-like music allows the participants to center their thought on the adoration of God. To many worshipers in the United States, prayer in the Taizé Community with fewer words and extended periods of silence may be at once disorienting and refreshing.

In the earlier days of the Community, the brothers used a variety of musical sources, including from their own faith traditions: Reformed and Lutheran. Their interest broadened to include compositions by others and to seek more contemporary musical forms.[236] French Jesuit scholar Joseph Gelineau (1920–2008) visited the Community in 1948 and developed with them the earlier versions of what would later become his psalm settings.[237] During 1950s there were relatively few visitors, making it easier to adopt this more sophisticated musical style.

By the 1960s and 1970s the brothers faced the challenge of larger visiting groups of young people. Brother Jean-Marie noted that the larger groups brought liturgical changes:

> Changes in the liturgy were now necessary. If the young people were to pray with us and not just watch or listen to us pray, we would have to adapt and simplify some things. And things were changing. For many people, the very language of faith was becoming harder to grasp. Times were changing. People were no longer coming to church to receive a teaching or to do their devotions or to fulfill religious and social obligations, as they had done for centuries. If they were coming, it was for different and more personal reasons: to find rest and refreshment, to live their lives with more meaning, or just to maintain a connection with God or else with the church they had grown up with. It was also becoming harder for people

to listen and retain what they heard. Modern life was noisier and more stressful.[238]

The structure of the liturgy remained the same, but the readings were shortened, more languages were employed, and the songs simplified. A period of experimentation followed with translations of songs sung in different languages at the same time and the use of a variety of instruments including gongs and other percussion—practices that proved not to be liturgically viable or tended toward the exotic.

The solution came from the singing of a simple canon. Robert Batastini (b. 1942) notes that Brother Robert (1922–1993) who joined the community in 1946, originated the idea for what has become know as the music of the Taizé Community.

> Brother Robert chose a six-measure canon by Praetorious, which could be sung in up to six parts and had only two Latin words and one Hebrew word: *Jubilate Deo, Alleluia*. The simplicity of form, textually and musically, lent itself to repetition and development—unison, two-voice, three-voice, and so on, and the eventual overlaying of instruments. The result was music that was accessible and textually uncomplicated, thus uniting the entire gathered assembly in a singe communal song while at the same time freeing the individual to lift his or her heart in prayer.[239]

Other canons came from a medieval collection of songs from Montserrat in Catalonia, *Libre Vermeil*. "Canons were of course easy to learn. The repetitive form seemed conducive to a more meditative style of prayer and yet had a certain joy and spontaneity to it that was appealing to people of different generations. They found a kind of bridge, and a few words were enough to allow people to pray."[240]

In 1974, Brother Robert shared his ideas, along with brief texts, mainly selected from scripture, with Jacques Berthier (1923–1994), a composer and friend of Taizé who became instrumental in providing music for the three common prayers. Berthier was organist of Saint-Ignace Church in Paris. "The form inspired the compositional genius of Berthier, who, working in close collaboration with Brother Robert, began a prolific outpouring of short songs and change for use in prayer at Taizé."[241] Berthier maintained a close relationship with the Community, helping them devise songs that could be easily sung by the young people coming from around the world. This accessible music includes a variety of forms[242]—chorales, *ostinati* (short, repetitive refrains), acclamations, responses and canons—in which worshipers with radically diverse liturgical and linguistic backgrounds are immediately able to participate. Taizé songs are sung during the prayers in several languages including Latin. Latin is common because it is a historical language of the church and places everyone on a common footing, unifying the singers in the mystery of common prayer. Judith Marie Kubicki comments on the accessibility of Taizé chants: "The simplicity and repetition of the musical format has the potential to draw in even the most hesitant of singers…. The multiplicity of melodic and harmonic elements, as well as the variety of languages employed, communicates the idea that diversity is not only tolerated but welcomed."[243]

Since the turn of the twenty-first century three of the brothers have been responsible for the new compositions. As visitors come from more and more countries, the brothers write in new languages such as Swedish, Portuguese, Lithuanian, and Croatian. More music comes from Christian Orthodox tradition because of the growing number of Orthodox young people coming to Taizé.[244]

Following Berthier's death in 1994, Fr. Gelineau contributed additional liturgical settings to the Community, but most new songs come from a variety of sources. Brother Jean-Marie comments on more recent compositions: "All the new songs composed are by members of the Community. We have also adopted some music from the Russian, Greek, and Rumanian Orthodox traditions not written for us but used already and familiar to many of the young people from these churches."[245]

Reflecting on Brother Roger's experience during the occupation of France and the importance of sung prayer during the difficult war years, Brother Jean-Marie notes,

> [S]inging isn't an accessory to what we do together in churches. It's not the ornamentation, which beautifies the other more important things. Singing is part of the foundation; it's part of what supports us. You know that. It's giving voice to our confidence in God and allowing it to fill us more deeply. Our chests and also our souls expand as we sing.[246]

The ecumenical spirit of the Taizé Community captured the imagination of the world church in the years following the Second Vatican Council (1962–1965). After Brother Roger's tragic death at the hand of a distraught pilgrim in August 2005, Brother Alois (b. 1954) succeeded him as prior. The spirit of hospitality continues with thousands of pilgrims making their way to the relatively isolated Community each year. The prayer—sung and spoken—remains a source of renewal and hope. This spirit is what prompted Pope John XXIII to comment after visiting Taizé, "Ah, Taizé—that little springtime!"[247]

Following the Wild Goose: Congregational Song from the Iona Community[248]

Music of the Iona Community has become a primary source for the ecumenical church since the late 1980s. While the major voice for the musical and liturgical reforms of the Community is John L. Bell (b. 1949), the heritage of the modern Iona Community extends back to the sixth century C.E.

The Iona of St. Columba (521–597 C.E.)

St. Columba, a monk from a wealthy house in Ireland, came to the island of Iona on the western coast of Scotland in 563 C.E. in order to establish a monastery. Much of the information on the life of Columba has been subject to embellishment by early accounts that are more hagiographic than historical. In the interest of separating fact from fiction and establishing their roots with Columba, the Iona Community commissioned Ian Bradley, senior lecturer in practical theology at St. Andrew's University and a minister in the Church of Scotland, to write a biography of Columba upon the 1400th anniversary of his death.[249]

Bradley suggests that three primary features make up Columba's character: he was "part pilgrim, part penitent and part politician." It is perhaps in these three areas of Columba's life that we can see both the foundation of his monastic life and continuity with the work of the contemporary Iona Community. The life of the *peregrini* or pilgrim has often been part of a monastic vocation. Columba's pilgrimage began with his decision to migrate from Ireland to Scotland under circumstances that are not entirely clear. As an ecclesiastical administrator and a missionary, he traveled widely for his day.

Bradley and many others leave no doubt that Columba was a penitent. His existence was ascetic by any standard. In addition to observing the seven daily hours of the offices during which all 150 psalms were chanted each week, early sources indicated that Columba would rise before sunrise, go down to the shore, and chant "the three fifties" or all 150 psalms before sunrise. Echoes of Celtic spirituality may be found in the music and the rule of the current Iona Community. Although not ascetic by the standards of Irish monastic life, the rule of the modern Iona Community encourages a kind of mutual accountability that distinguishes commitments of its members from many in modern society.[250]

Columba presided as abbot over a monastic *familia* (group of monasteries), offering hospitality to pilgrims and planting churches within a context of an alien culture. He lived a disciplined life balanced by periods of intense solitude and active political engagement. Esther de Waal notes that the "Celtic peoples are peoples who know suffering, deprivation, exile, oppression. And yet, they have learned through all of this to find the light in the darkness."[251] The balance between solitude and political engagement, and identification with those who suffer and experience oppression may be the richest spiritual trust of the Celtic context to the vision and work of the Iona Community today. John Bell and Graham Maule confirm the significance of the legacy Columba left on the small island of Iona:

> The Iona Community has always attempted to marry the work of peacemaking and political engagement with the practice of prayer. This has developed out of an understanding of the Incarnation, which is rooted deep in Celtic spirituality. Celtic

> Christians believe that when the Word became flesh in Jesus, a new significance was given to the material order and to human affairs. Creation and the work of humans then became arenas in and through which God could be praised.[252]

As a tribute to the saint, the Wild Goose Worship Group wrote a hymn, sung to the traditional Irish tune, ST. COLUMBA. Stanzas one, three and five follow:

> From Erin's shores Columba came
> To preach and teach and heal,
> And found a church which showed the world
> How God on earth was real.
>
> In hosting strangers, healing pain,
> In tireless work for peace,
> They served the servant Christ their Lord
> And found their faith increase.
>
> God grant that what Columba sowed
> May harvest yet more seed,
> As we engage both flesh and faith
> To marry word and deed.[253]

THE IONA OF GEORGE MACLEOD (1895-1991)

The legacy of Columba was paramount to George MacLeod, the founder of the modern Iona Community, who commented on the distortions of the Saint's ministry and its relevance today:

> The island of St. Columba.... How falsely men misread his work if they visualize his mission to the mainland as purely a 'religious' movement. True to his patron Martin of Tours, his whole evangel was compact of every aspect of man's living. Agriculture, fishing, education, craftsmanship—these were the

domains he insisted must be brought in thrall to the sovereign will of the All Highest. And, in our day and generation is not this essentially the challenge we must face?[254]

Much to the amazement of parishioners and clergy, MacLeod left a thriving parish ministry in industrial Clydeside, Govan—the dock area of Glasgow, to found the modern Iona Community in 1938. In spite of economic depression and high unemployment, worship at the Govan Old Parish Church was filled with people. He was admired for a pioneer ministry in a difficult area of Glasgow. MacLeod had serious doubts, however, about the ability of the established Church of Scotland to meet the needs of working class people and young persons. He wanted to experiment with a new way of theological preparation that would bring together industrial workers and ministers in community.

At the crux of his concern, was the way that ministers were educated separately from and ignorant of the working people that would undoubtedly populate their parishes in the future. So, he set off to a small island, distant and nearly inaccessible from the populated areas of Scotland, with twelve young ministers and artisans, equally divided, to rebuild the ruins of Iona Abbey. They built communal huts that would allow the small band to begin this experiment of community, from which they could eventually restore the ruins of the old Cistercian Abbey built on the site of Columba's original settlement.[255]

As the plan evolved, the two groups learned from each other. The summer months were spent on the island in study, work and worship. The winter months were spent in an industrial urban setting ministering in pairs in housing projects and experimenting in different ways of living in Christian community. It was not the intent of the founder to set up permanent residence on the remote island of Iona, but to use it as a place for training and an impetus for mission as it had been in the days of Columba.[256]

We know much of MacLeod's vision for those early years through the official newsletter from Iona entitled the *Coracle*—named for the small boat like the one used by Columba to travel from Ireland to Scotland—which was first published in October 1938. It helped to define the mission of the community for a broader audience. The rebirth of the Iona Community was a collective experiment or laboratory in community. Volunteers, living in a common hut, sleeping, eating, working and worshipping together, were forming this community within the Church of Scotland.

John Bell, commenting on MacLeod's vision states: "MacLeod's initial hope was that the rebuilt abbey might become an ecumenical seminary, but as the building-work progressed, he realised that a more worthy cause would be to make it a centre for reconciliation of people and also of strands of Christian witness, such as prayer and politics which for many people were mutually exclusive."[257]

MacLeod stated forthrightly that the Iona experiment was based on community, worship and laity. The times of retreat to the island were to be balanced by ministry in the "housing schemes" of Govan.[258] He believed that the Church of Scotland had lost its original vision: "The glory of the Church of Scotland used to be summed up in the phrase 'Kirk and Mart.'"[259] Programs that once had been under the purview of the church (caring for the poor, providing education, physical fitness, and even social life of the people) had now been superseded by the state. It was MacLeod's hope to form a new community that would encourage the Church of Scotland to find a renewed identity.

The importance of change was an early theme of MacLeod's ministry and continues to be a primary motif in the work of the Wild Goose Worship Group. The world is changing. Society is changing. Therefore, the church and its worship must change. It was from MacLeod that John Bell draws on the theme of a church that today is recalcitrant to change. Bell traces this attitude, in part, to sentiments expressed in Victorian hymns like Henry Francis Lyte's, "Abide with Me," the third line of stanza two which reads, "change and decay in all around I see."[260] Bell considers the nature of change in his reflection, "Changeless and Changing," based upon Hosea 2:14-23 and John 15:1-17:

> God is love and that love is constant and changeless. But when I say that God is changeless, I realize that I say not only a very comforting thing but a very dangerous thing. Because it

only takes a little thought or a little thoughtlessness to deduce that we should be changeless too. If from Scripture we learn that we are made in God's image, and we learn that God is changeless, we presume that we should be changeless too. But it doesn't work that way. The proof that we have been grasped by the changeless love of God is that we never remain the same, but are transformed, converted, turned upside down, inside out.[261]

The major themes of the hymns of the Iona Community reflect the poetic embodiment of this spirit.

By 1967 the restoration of the Abbey was completed and the Very Rev. Lord MacLeod of Fuinary relinquished leadership of the Iona Community. In 1985, the original huts used to house the community, built in the late 1930s, had outlived their usefulness as summer housing for young people. The MacLeod Center, just up the road from the Abbey, replaced the old huts. This facility is devoted to reconciliation, designed for families and is fully handicap accessible, and still honors the community's commitment to young people.

Full members of the Iona Community live by a five-fold rule.[262] While the majority of Iona's nearly 250 members are in Britain, the present Iona Community is a global ecumenical "movement of . . . over 1,500 Associate Members and about 1,400 Friends" from many denominational traditions in the United States, Africa, India, Australia and New Zealand.[263]

John Bell and Graham Maule and the Formation of the Wild Goose[264] Worship Group

John Bell grew up in Kilmarnock, a rural town south of Glasgow. He received degrees in Arts and Theology from the University in Glasgow. After a sabbatical year in student politics and two years working with an English-speaking congregation in Amsterdam, he was ordained by the Church of Scotland in 1978 and appointed Youth Coordinator for the Presbytery of Glasgow. In 1980 he was admitted to membership of the Iona Community, having applied to be a member not primarily because it was a place of liturgical innovation, but because it was "a place where the potentials of the socially marginalized as well as the socially successful would be attested."[265]

Out of this commitment he developed a core of volunteers that planned end-of-the-month youth workshops, bringing together young people for fellowship, reflection and worship. At the conclusion of the evening, all would prepare worship together. These monthly workshops called Last of the Month ran from 1982-1986 and attracted 250-500 young people. The workshops and worship were designed around biblical themes relevant to the lives of the young people, e.g., the Ten Commandments, Beatitudes, etc. Those attending were often on the fringe of the church and their knowledge of the biblical tradition was negligible.[266]

John Bell comments on Graham Maule's (b. 1958) role in these early days: "One of the initial volunteers who soon became a job-sharing colleague was Graham Maule, an architecture graduate who, in his own words decided that he could not 'make bread from stones.' He decided to forgo a lucrative career to live in one of the most socially deprived neighborhoods of Glasgow."[267]

In between Last of the Month workshops, John and Graham worked with volunteers to be a presence in poor and working class neighborhoods, not as social workers, but as friends and neighbors in the community. The volunteers, mostly in their twenties, were students or persons who wanted to take time out from work to discover more about themselves or change the direction of their lives. At its height there were about thirty people, living a simple lifestyle, often surviving on unemployment benefits, providing a caring presence for children and young people at risk in poorer neighborhoods.

In 1983, Bell and Maule brought together eight of the volunteers to reflect on the worship needs of the young people. By this time they were in the employ of the Iona Community, which enabled them to have easier contact with teenagers of different denominational backgrounds and with those totally outside the Church. Those they met with for six evenings of reflection eventually became the nucleus of what was known as The Wild Goose Worship Group. Bell, Graham and a succession of other people ormed a salaried unit within the Iona Community called The Wild Goose Resource Group in 1988.

The Worship Group consisted of volunteers who were a mixture of students, professional and working class people. Normally numbering between sixteen and twenty members, they met weekly to try out new songs, which Bell and Maule had written, to learn songs from the developing world, to experiment with new forms of corporate worship, and to pray. Much of the worship material that was initially published by the Iona Community found its genesis in this group who, though most could not read music, could all sing in harmony. In weekend workshops the Worship Group led conferences in which the paid Resource Group participated. What had been experiments in a crowded living room became liturgical materials used throughout Britain and abroad.

In 1984, the Iona Community began to publish in earnest. First books included a collection of MacLeod's prayers, *The Whole Earth Shall Cry Glory*, recordings of songs from the Iona Abbey, the preparation of *The Iona Community Worship Book*,[268] and the first musical collection of the group, *Heaven Shall Not Wait: Songs of Creation, the Incarnation, and the Life of Jesus*. In 1986, the first recording was released, *A Touching Place*.

In October 1986, Wild Goose Publications was formed as the entity responsible for producing and publishing materials for the Iona Community. The Wild Goose Resource Group (WGRG) became the entity responsible for producing and publishing materials for the Iona Community. The WGRG developed and promoted new forms of worship. Publishing interests evolved organically out of the need to revitalize worship.[269] As Kenneth Hull points out, many songs were "written in response to particular circumstances… [such as] the death of a child, or the unfairness and oppression of a life of poverty, or the feeling of impotence and despair in the face of natural disaster, or in thanksgiving for the blessing and example of everyday saints who live and work among us."[270]

The inclusion of world songs developed naturally out of the desire to be in solidarity with the poor and the oppressed around the globe. Early materials were drawn from the Swedish collection of South African songs entitles *Freedom Is Coming* (1984) edited by Anders Nyberg, other collections of songs from the 1983 World Council of Churches Assembly in Vancouver, and a few songs from Malawi and neighboring countries arranged by Tom

Colvin, a long-standing member of the Community. Formal publications of world song began with *Many and Great: Songs of the World Church*, Vol. 1 (1990 in UK edition; 1992 in the United States). *Sent by the Lord: Songs of the World Church*, Vol. 2, soon followed this in 1991 abroad and 1992 in the United States. Many recordings, song collections, anthems and books have followed since that time.[271]

The work of the Wild Goose Worship and Resource Groups was not limited to publications, however. Bell speaks of the public events planned by the Wild Goose Groups: "In 1990, they initiated a series of monthly events in Glasgow, initially called Last Night Out. Since 2003, the direct descendant has been called Holy City. Each Holy City event is an intergenerational occassion with a pattern of themed workshops during the first half of the evening followed by worship, which maximizes participation in song, prayer and symbolic action.

> These regular gatherings and the annual engagements the Resource Group has on Iona has encouraged a diversification in musical styles. Short, easily remembered chants, not dissimilar to those of Taizé, were once regarded as anathema to Scottish protestants, but where these have been used to accompany prayer, intersperse scripture reading or enable movement, their worth has been attested. Hence the publication of short songs first in the *Come All You People* and *There is One Among Us* collections, and in 2008 with a more adventurous and global collection called *We Walk His Way*.[272]

In 1996, the Worship Group established the Big Sing, described by Graham Maule as "glorified singing-only workshops or events."[273] These non-liturgical experiences are aimed at providing people with the experience of group singing. In Scotland and Britain people have moved away from singing as a communal expression. Group singing is limited to the church, which is a forum that reaches relatively few persons, and football (soccer) matches. The Big Sing helps people explore their voices as part of a community experience in a non-threatening environment. Bell notes: "These gatherings can involve a small company of the enthusiastic and suspicious in a church hall, or—as at the annual Greenbelt Festival in England—can incorporate up to 1000 people sitting in the grandstand of a racing track. A cappella unison songs, as well as simple songs or chants in four-part harmony are included, with different parts being taught by different members of the leadership team."[274]

Though the impact of the music and liturgy from the Wild Goose Group is worldwide, the roots of the Wild Goose experiences may still be found in singing and worship events in Glasgow as it has for several decades. Maule notes that these events "create a context for road-testing our material and having it critiqued by a peer group. We believe that unless it works here in a rooted, local context it's not going to work (paradoxically?) in a wider, even international diaspora."[275]

Themes of Iona Liturgy and Music

Four themes characterize the music and worship of the Iona Community: (1) Group creative process developed by the Wild Goose Worship Group; (2) Folk music influences; (3) songs of the world church; and (4) the biblical foundation and theology of the songs within liturgy.

Group Creative Process of the Wild Goose Worship Group

"The songs from Iona are not composed in solitude on the beach of the tiny island off the western coast of Scotland with the waves lapping at the shore," John Bell has often said. Many were composed in the context of urban Glasgow in a flat behind a nineteenth-century church, next to one of the most polluted arterial roads in Scotland. The music of the WGWG is "the product of ongoing argument, experiment, study, discussion, questioning and listening to the conversation of ordinary people. They are also the product of being stunned by the unquestionable relevance of the Word of God, which eyes, blinded by bias, presumption, or cynicism, had long avoided."[276]

For fifteen years the WGWG developed songs as a part of a group creative process:
- someone has an insight or an idea that excites others and informs or challenges faith;

- John picks over it and drafts a rough copy of a song;
- Graham scrutinizes, corrects, and amends it;
- somehow a tune emerges from a folk tradition or mid-air;
- the tune is either left alone, given accompaniment, or harmonized;
- the Worship Group sing it through and comment on it;
- the song, now in its third version, is sung at public worship; and
- a final revision is made.[277]

Rather than a solitary act of composition, musical creation was a community activity. In the introduction to one song collection, Bell notes that few "of these songs are contemporary with the publication of the book. The vast majority have been sung, scrutinized and amended several times in the past five or six years and have proven their worth in places far from a printing press."[278] Although Bell's name appears as the author/composer of most of songs published in the early volumes of the Iona Community, his role could often be described as somewhere between the facilitator of a group creative process and a scribe, who artistically shaped the inspirations, conceptions and convictions of others into a final printed form.

Folk Music Influences

Scottish, Irish, and English folk songs are the sources of tunes for many of the texts written by the WGWG. As conveyors of story-songs, these ballads kept alive many of the myths of their communities of origin and were the mode for transmitting basic cultural legends from generation to generation as well as to other groups. Popular dance groups and instrumental ensembles, adding to the resurgence of Celtic tradition both within the British Isles and beyond those shores, have picked up their modal sounds not only by singers but also. Bell and Maule recognized this when they noted:

> We live in a country which has a glorious heritage of folk music, of fiddle and pipe tunes, of vocal melodies all in danger of disappearing into oblivion. But where are the spiritual songs which [that] have clothed themselves in this musical richness? Why is it that Africans, Asians, and Central Americans have

allowed the Gospel to take root in their folk music, but we in Britain have, by and large, avoided such an association as if Christ had never joyed to see children piping and dancing in the street?[279]

In the three larger volumes of song published by the Iona Community, *Heaven Shall Not Wait* (1987), *Enemy of Apathy* (1988), and *Love from Below* (1989), there were 150 hymns with stanzas, plus thirty-three shorter chants and responses. Forty-six, or nearly one-third of the songs with stanzas have their roots in the folk-song legacy of the British Isles: twenty-three Scottish, nine Irish, eleven English, and three Gaelic. Many of these songs draw upon the oral reservoir of Celtic culture that continues to be transmitted by musical groups and through electronic means today.

Songs of the World Church

The WGWG has contributed to the Euro-North American church a wealth of global sung prayers through the publication of the collections, *Many and Great* (1990) and *Sent by the Lord* (1991). Many of the songs are transcriptions from their countries of origin. Others have been arranged by Bell. A brief note about the origins and/or use of each song follows the score. Original languages (or transliterations in the case of Asian languages) are often included along with English language singing translations. It did not escape John Bell that these two books would appear in time for the 500th anniversary of the commemoration of the "discovery" of America by Christopher Columbus. Bell noted that "For many people in Central and South America, this is not a time for joy, but a time for deep regret as that occasion calls to mind the succession of waves of colonial, religious, and financial imperialism which has beleaguered many of the countries of the region right to the present day."[280]

At the time of this writing no additional volumes devoted entirely to world songs are planned. However, more recent publications include world songs as a matter of course along with folk songs from North America, the United Kingdom and Europe and materials written by Bell.[281] Bell and Maule felt that it was time to include world songs within the body of Western song as a symbol of unity rather than as special publications, the practice of segregating global song possibly signally that this body of literature is optional for Westerners.

Biblical and Theological Foundations of Songs from the Iona Community

Communicating the truth contained in scripture is central to the aims of the Iona Community and the work of the WGWG. As a renewal movement within the Church of Scotland, the Community places scripture at the center of liturgical life and the creative process of the WGWG. There are many ways that this is evident.

Celtic tradition is often noted for its Trinitarian way of being. This is illustrated beautifully in an old Irish poem attributed to Columba, the *incipit* of which is provided here:

> The path I walk, Christ walks it.
> May the land in which I am be without sorrow.
> May the Trinity protect me wherever I stay,
> Father, Son, and Holy Spirit.[282]

The three larger collections mentioned earlier, *Heaven Shall Not Wait* (1987), *Enemy of Apathy* (1988), and *Love from Below* (1989), find their over-arching shape in the structure of the Trinity. Volume one contains "Songs of Creation, the Incarnation, and the Life of Jesus." Volume two included "Songs of the Passion and Resurrection of Jesus, and the Coming of the Holy Spirit." These two volumes focus on a "retelling of the events of the gospels," while volume three includes "songs which deal more with the life of Christ's disciples" and "the celebration of our experience of faith."[283]

The WGWG brings the biblical narrative into its songs in a variety of ways. One common approach is through the style of a ballad that draws the singer into the story.

> A pregnant girl none will ignore:
> Her husband knocks a guest-house door.
> > Who is the girl?
> > Why knock the door?
> Thus starts a tale of which there's more.[284]

Sometimes the use of the first person perspective, such as in "The Beggar," draws the singer into the song, though not without a certain amount of irony and, perhaps, discomfort:

> I sit outside the rich world's gate,
> I rake the rich world's dross
> And marvel that my poverty
> Is what you call my cross.
>
> I am the beggar called your Lord,
> The squatter called your King;
> I am the Savior of the world,
> A torn and tattered thing.
>
> Chorus: O who has ears to hear my Cry?
> > And who has eyes to see?
> > And who will lift my heavy load?
> > And who will set me free?[285]

The Celtic sense of the presence of Christ in all of life's activities and encounters is a theme that runs throughout many songs. "We Met You, God" has seven stanzas, one for each day of the week. It is shaped by the creation narrative of Genesis 1, but each stanza ends with a different but distinctly Christological quote: "I am the way," "I am the truth," "I am the life," "I've chosen you," "Come, follow me," "You are my friend," etc.[286] "Today I Awake" draws directly from Celtic Trinitarian prayer, the four successive stanzas beginning:

> Today I awake
> And God is before me. . . .
> Today I arise
> And Christ is beside me. . . .
> Today I affirm
> The Spirit within me. . . .
> Today I enjoy
> The Trinity round me. . . .[287]

When encountering the life of Christ, the WGWG is not content to allow us the comfort of viewing this as only a historical event. Some songs place us in the middle of the drama as a character, such as *Easter Evening*, based upon one of a post-resurrection encounter with Christ, sung to the beautiful Scottish tune SILKIE.

> As we walked home at close of day,
> A stranger joined us on the way.
> He heard us speak of one who'd gone
> And when we stopped, he carried on.
>
> "Why wonder further without light?
> Please stay with us this troubled night.
> We've shared the truth of how we feel
> And now would like to share a meal."[288]

Psalm settings call for flexibility of musical style and perspective depending on the emotional context of the psalm. Some are contemporary paraphrases such as "Happy is the One," based upon Psalm 1:

> Happy is the one
> who does not take bad advice for a guide,
> nor walks the path on which sinners have trod,
> nor sits where the cynics mock.[289]

Another is a paraphrase of Psalm 130, employing the classic Psalter tune SOUTHWELL commonly associated with the text from the Greek by Synesius of Cyrene, "Lord Jesus, think on me." This direct language is much more traditional than many texts by the WGWG, even reminiscent of the English-language Psalters of earlier centuries:

> Out of the direst depths
> I make my deepest plea.
> O graciously bow down your ear
> and listen, Lord, for me.
>
> If you kept note of sins,
> before you who could stand?
> But since forgiveness is your right,
> our reverence your command.[290]

Perhaps it is the Incarnation—drawn from biblical accounts and steeped in Celtic spirituality—that is most central to the work of the WGWG. Responding to the tendency to romanticize the birth of Christ, Bell notes in a characteristically direct commentary,

> To say that there is nothing wrong with traditional Christmas carols is to be less than discerning. Some—perhaps the majority—are good. But, there are some that tell patent lies about the Nativity or about Jesus himself.
>
> There is no biblical evidence to support the theory that "snow had fallen, snow on snow," but there is substantial evidence to suggest that Jesus did not "honor and obey" throughout all his wondrous childhood. What about him running away from his family when returning from Jerusalem? There is also the temptation to depict the characters in the Nativity story as less than full-blooded. Mary tends to be portrayed as anemic, docile, and constantly doting, not the kind of woman who could cope with a pile of dirty nappies.

Joseph is sometimes depicted as spineless, and the shepherds and wise men, perhaps too closely modeled on their Sunday-school Nativity play stereotypes, lack either humor or surprise.[291]

The allusions above to Christina Rossetti's (1830–1894) metaphor for the kind of world encountered by the Incarnate God expressed in the terms of a cold winter,[292] and Cecil Frances Alexander's (1818–1895) viewpoint on Jesus' childhood demonstrate ninteeth century notions of the Incarnation, a perspective that Bell considers to be "the verbal equivalent of Victorian stained glass."[293] Bell minces no words concerning the damage he feels that Victorian-era hymnody has done to the Christian faith: "The Victorians dumped on us a legacy of forced piety, sentimentalism, and deceptive images of God in their hymns. Their tunes, with mushy harmonies or pedantic melodies, were little better."[294] One might be tempted to dismiss Bell's comments as a personal soapbox or diatribe based upon individual taste. I believe, however, that the hymnody of the Victorian era represents for Bell and Maule a time in British society when classism elevated a few at the expense of many, and the arrogance of the waning British Empire affected the Anglican Church at its core. This sentiment manifests itself in a hymnody that lacks realism not only about the radical nature of the Incarnation, but also about the poor and oppressed whose estate in life had been ordered by God according to Cecil Frances Alexander in her hymn "All Things Bright and Beautiful."[295]

It is for this reason that the theology of the Incarnation and the narrative of the life of Christ are so central to the hymns of the WGWG. Compare the nativity scene set by Rossetti and Alexander to "Justice in the Womb" by the Wild Goose Worship Group:

> Not the foremost of her gender,
> Not the finest of her race;
> Favored now in reputation,
> Flound'ring then in deep disgrace.

Refrain: Though for her no rights or room,
  There is promise in the woman:
  There is justice in the womb.

Cowed and occupied her country,
Dented was her people's pride:
Such a girl, in such a nation,
Could have been a soldier's bride.

Forced to make a tiresome journey,
Flanked by her redundant groom;
All the brightness in her body
Longs to end the godless gloom.

All the power of heaven contracted,
Gathers in this mother's pain:
God, confounding expectations,
Sows her seed against the grain.[296]

One discovers in this text and others a rare combination of poetic realism and awe-filled mystery. The result is disturbing, discomforting and disquieting. For the WGWG will not allow you either to relegate the Incarnation to a historical observance or romantic recollection. Based upon Bell's experience with the empty sanctuaries and largely ineffective traditional religious structures of his homeland, he understands that the cynics who would rarely or never enter these places—especially some young people, working class folk, students, and poor—are looking for authenticity. The songs and liturgy of the Wild Goose Worship Group are not designed to prompt a sentimental moment of togetherness or a sensational surge of emotion. The point is not to feel good but to feel again—feel a sense of the holy and an experience of community that potentially awakens in the most recalcitrant skeptic an awareness of the Incarnation and how this mystery, in the richest sense of Celtic spirituality, pervades all of our existence.

Summary of Wild Goose Contributions

In addition to smaller collections developed by the WGRG, John Bell has served as editor for two hymnals. *Common Ground: A Song Book for All Churches* (1998) has been described by Bell as "arguably the first of its kind in Europe if not the Northern Hemisphere ... [with songs] selected on an equal basis by Roman Catholics, Methodists, Episcopalians, Congregationalists, and Presbyterians."[297] More recently, Bell returned to his roots, editing the *Church Hymnary,* fourth edition (2005), the official hymnal for the Church of Scotland containing 825 items, many from North American sources that have never appeared in a European hymnal. Given the vast corpus and influence of Wild Goose publications and John Bell's own peripatetic travel schedule (sometimes eight months a year), Kenneth Hull properly asserts that, "Taken as a whole, the Wild Goose material probably represents the most original and significant contribution to the repertoire of congregational song of the 1990's."[298] What specifically are some of the contributions of the Wild Goose movement? The WGRG has left us with more than collections of music, potential anthems, and a few liturgical innovations. I suggest that we are left with an approach for liturgical renewal that is needed among main-line churches on both sides of the Atlantic. I offer the following as a summary of this renewal movement.

- Restore singing to the people, even if it is counter-cultural.[299]
- use as little accompaniment as possible and allow singing to build and sustain the worshipping community.
- Explore the folk-song resources of your region and acquaint yourself with them. These contain the essence of your culture.
- Explore the songs of the world church. These are the prayers of others and, by singing them, we sing in solidarity with all of God's people.
- Shape the flow of the liturgy in the manner of your heritage. One does not have to reinvent the shape of the liturgy, just breathe new life into old bones.
- Be knowledgeable about your spiritual heritage, including hymns. For if we are not familiar with the great hymns which have shaped Christian life and faith through centuries, we have little by which to judge modern writing.[300]

- Look at biblical content in light of contemporary need. Don't settle for pat answers and traditional observations. Give the assembly an opportunity to tell you what they think the scripture is saying.
- The security and comfort of liturgy must be balanced with an awareness of those who experience insecurity, discomfort and injustice in its many manifestations—political oppression, racial discrimination, economic deprivation, gender exclusion, class struggles, etc.
- Preparing liturgy needs to be a community experience, not a solitary act by the minister or musician at the computer.
- Enliven the liturgy with metaphor—symbols, rituals, movement, poetry, drama, song, narrative—minimizing the one-way medium of the sermon and spoken word.

Finally, be open to the Spirit of the Wild Goose in liturgy which may alight at anytime in unexpected and disturbing ways.

Conclusion

Those who have persevered to this point in stream seven have encountered literally a world of congregational song, but only a snapshot of what the worldwide church is singing. In many cases readers have seen names that are totally new to them in the field of hymnology and ideas that defy set assumptions about hymns and congregational song. Although predicting the future is futile, it is possible that a revision of this book in fifty years would require that this swelling stream be considered as several separate rivers. The other possibility is that Western musical traditions may have swallowed this stream to the point that it becomes an ancillary tributary. If the latter happens, the loss of congregational musics would be analogous to losing languages. The loss of the music of the world church would deny all of the Christian church ways of expressing our prayers and praise before a Creator that is the God of the cosmos. The challenge for the North American church posed by Erik Routley at the beginning of this stream remains relevant. The church must "attend to the need for a truly ecumenical hymnody which will have little to do ... with the processes of missionary work, but will provide a vehicle for the praises of a growing world-church."

Notes —

1. See specifically, William Carey: *An Enquiry into the Obligations of Christians to Use Means for the Conversion of the Heathens in which the Religious State of the Different Nations of the World, the Success of Former Undertakings, and the Practicability of Further Undertakings are Considered* (Leicester, England: 1792), for a perspective on eighteenth-century missionary views in England. Available at www.wmcarey.edu/carey/enquiry/anenquiry.pdf. Accessed on March 23, 2013.

2. One can make a case for the plainsong of the Roman Catholic Church, the metrical psalms of the Geneva Psalter, and the chorales of the German Reformation, for example, as global song from Europe as well, though none traveled as broadly and quickly as did the hymns carried by eighteenth- and nineteenth-century Protestant missionaries. See Carlton R. Young, "Old and New Global Song and Mission," *Music and Mission: Toward a Theology and Practice of Global Song*, ed. S T Kimbrough, Jr. (New York: General Board of Global Ministries, GBGMusik, 2006), 9-13.

3. W. R. Stevenson, "Missions, Foreign," *Dictionary of Hymnology*, ed. John Julian (London, John Murray, 1892), 739–759.

4. Erik Routley, *Ecumenical Hymnody* (London: Independent Press Ltd., 1959), 5.

5. Routley, *Ecumenical Hymnody*.

6. Routley, *Ecumenical Hymnody*, 16. *Cantate Domino: An Ecumenical Hymnbook*, 4th ed., ed. Erik Routley (London: Bärenreiter, 1980). The melody-only edition (1974) was not edited by Routley. Although listed as the 4th edition, four previous hymnals under the name *Cantate Domino* were published in 1924, 1930, 1938, and 1951.

7. Routley, *Ecumenical Hymnody*, 17.

8. Philip V. Bohlman, *World Music: A Very Short Introduction* (New York: Oxford University Press, 2002), 6.

9. By Western historical practice, I am referring to hymns in stanzas, especially from Europe and later the United States, from the Reformation to the mid-twentieth century.

10. For an introductory discussion, see Carlton R. Young, "Ethnic and Minority Hymns in United States Mainline Protestant Hymnals 1940-1955: Some Qualifying Considerations," *The Hymn* 49:3 (July 1998), 17-27.

11. See Philip Jenkins, *The Next Christendom: The Coming of Global Christianity* (New York: Oxford University Press, 2002), 79-105, for a detailed discussion of the growth of Christianity in the Southern Hemisphere and its influence on the shape of Christianity in the Northern Hemisphere.

12. Timothy D. Taylor laments this in *Beyond Exoticism: Western Music and the World* (Durham: Duke University Press, 2007) noting that "world music has been reduced to a single 'style' that is used in [advertisements] to signify 'globalization,' marking the most recent triumph over the capitalist market over this music." (13)

13. For additional perspective, see Timothy Taylor's discussion of the problems with "globalization" in *Beyond Exoticism*, 113-139.

14. Taylor, *Beyond Exoticism*, 2.

15. Taylor, *Beyond Exoticism*, 2-3.

16. Taylor, *Beyond Exoticism*, 3.

17. South African Freedom Song that expressed resistance to apartheid in the last half of the twentieth-century is a case in point. Another example includes selected songs composed

in the midst of political oppression in Latin America, e.g., some hymns by Federico Pagura, discussed later in this chapter.

18 For a briefer summary, see Mark P. Bangert, "Liturgical Music, Culturally Tuned," *Liturgy and Music: Lifetime Learning*, eds. Robin A. Leaver, Joyce Ann Zimmerman (Collegeville, MN; The Liturgical Press, 1998), 360-383.

19 See Mark P. Bangert, "Dynamics of Liturgy and World Musics: A Methodology for Evaluation," *Worship and Culture in Dialogue*, ed. S. Anita Stauffer (Geneva: The World Lutheran Federation, 1994), 183-203.

20 See John Blacking, *How Musical Is Man?* (Seattle: University of Washington Press, 1973), 6-7.

21 For a more complete discussion of the criteria for choosing global song for worship, see C. Michael Hawn, "Praying Globally—Pitfalls and Possibilities of Cross-cultural Liturgical Appropriation," *Christian Worship Worldwide*, ed. Charles E. Farhadian (Grand Rapids: Wm. B. Eerdmans Press, 2007), 205-229.

22 Additional international venues, especially in Asia, are the gatherings sponsored by the YMCA and YWCA. For example, the Asian Alliance of YMCSs engaged I-to Loh as editor of the song collections *Songs of Our People* (1987) for the 12th YMCA Leader's Conference in Tozanso, Japan, and *Songs of Our People II* (1991) for the 13th Leader's Conference in Bangkok. Thailand. *Worship with Singing/Cultes avec Chants/Adoración y Canto* was produced for those attending the World YWCA Council in Kenya (2007) reflecting carefully and thematically prepared liturgies with a mixture of global song staples and fresh materials.

23 See Anscar Chupungco, *Liturgical Inculturation: Sacramental, Religiosity, and Catechesis* (Collegeville, MN: The Liturgical Press, 1992), 29, for a definition of liturgical inculturation. Alyward Shorter also provides a complementary definition in *Toward a Theology of Inculturation* (Maryknoll, NY: Orbis Books, 1988), 11.

24 Technically, Scandinavia consists of Norway, Sweden, and Denmark. Finland, Iceland, and the Faeroe Islands are often included in the region.

25 The *Ten-year Report of The Milwaukee Symposia for Church Composers* (1992), an ecumenical document with no standing in the Roman Catholic Church, elaborated on the proposals of Vatican II in the section entitled, 'Cross-Cultural Music Making.' Through this document liturgical inculturation also caught the attention of many Protestants.

26 Historical exceptions do exist. See Anthony Ruff, *Sacred Music and Liturgical Reform: Treasures and Transformations* (Chicago: Hillenbrand Books, 2007), 102-104, for hymns used in the Mass in Germany.

27 Trans. Peter Schütte, in Marc Ashley Foster, "*Missa Luba*: A New Edition and Conductor's Analysis," A Dissertation Submitted to the Faculty of the Graduate School at The University of North Carolina at Greensboro in Partial Fulfillment of the Requirements for the Degree Doctor of Music Arts, 2005, 8.

28 Foster, *Missa Luba*, 11.

29 Guido Haazen, arr., *Missa Luba* (New York: Lawson-Gould Music Publishers, 1969). For a recording see *Missa Luba: An African Mass* directed by Boniface Mganga (New York: Philips, 1990), No. 426 836-2.

30 For a discussion of the role of the leader in oral tradition performance practice, see C. Michael Hawn, chapter 8: "The Church Musician as Enlivener," *Gather into One: Praying and Singing Globally* (Grand Rapids, MI: Wm. B. Eerdmans, 2003), 241-270.

31. Stephen Mbunga's doctoral dissertation, *Church Law and Bantu Music: Ecclesiastical Documents and Law in Sacred Music as Applied to Bantu Music* (Schieneck-Beckenried, Switzerland: Novelle Revue de Science Missionaire, Supplement 13, 1963), was written on the cusp of Vatican II and proved to be quite prophetic in encouraging the development of African styles of church music.

32. For more information of the development of the African Mass, see Christopher Klein, *Messekompositionen in Afrika* (Germany: Edition Re, 1990).

33. David Dargie, *African Sunday Marimba Mass: Song Book*, 2nd Ed., privately published by David Dargie in 2003. Additional information from David Dargie, personal correspondence received 25 June, 2004.

34. These are discussed in José María Vigil and Angel Torrellas, eds. *Misas Centro Americana* (Managua: CAV-CEBES, 1988, with cassette). It contains the music of three Central American Masses: *Misa Popular Nicaragüense* (c. 1968), *Misa Campesina Nicaragüense* (c. 1975), and *Misa Popular Salvadoreña* (c. 1978-1980).

35. For more information on Routley's contribution to global song, see C. Michael Hawn, "Cantate Domino: Erik Routley and Global Song," *The Hymn* 53:4 (October 2002), 12-13.

36. Tércio Bretanha Junker from São Paulo, Brazil and C. Michael Hawn from the United States served as the primary music directors with assistance from Jorge Lockward (Dominican Republic/USA) for the Porto Alegre Assembly. Planning the common ecumenical prayers proved to be a difficult task at times with the exception of choosing the music. As was noted by several members of the WCC Worship Committee, "The music is what really holds our ecumenical prayers together." For a discussion of the role of music in the worship at the IX Assembly, see Jan Janssen, "God's Grace in a Tent," *The Ecumenical Review* 58:3-4 (July/October 2006), 292.

37. Though there were some attempts to develop more *animateurs* through regional conferences, the WCC was not able to sustain these. One example was a workshop that took place in San José, Costa Rica from March 5-13, 1988. The results of this gathering may be found in *Todas Las Voces: Taller de Música y Liturgia en América Latina*, ed. Pablo D. Sosa (San José: Ediciones Sebila, c. 1988).

38. See *In God's Hands: Common Prayer for the World*, eds. Hugh McCullum and Terry MacArthur (Geneva: World Council of Churches, 2006).

39. Another ecumenical collection entitled *Unisono: A Multilingual Book of Ecumenical Hymns* (Graz: Verlag Zeitpunkt Schnider, 1997), edited by Markus Jenny, Andreas Marti, and Franz Karl Prassl, was prepared by Internationalen Arbeitsgemeinschaft für Hymnologie (IAH). Though appearing similar to *Thuma Mina* at first glance, virtually all of its hymns are drawn from Euro-North American sources.

40. For more information on John Bell, see C. Michael Hawn, chapter 6: "The Wild Goose Sings: John Bell and the Music of the Iona Community," *Gather into One: Praying and Singing Globally*, 189-223.

41. Discussion with Geoff Weaver, London, England, June March 28, 2008. A more recent collection complied by Geoff Weaver is *In Every Corner Sing: Song's of God's World* (Salisbury, Wiltshire, England: RSCM, 2008).

42. The most recent publication is *Lambeth Praise*, ed. Geoff Weaver (St. Mary's Plain, Norwich, England: Canterbury Press, 2008).

43. Telephone interview with David Peacock, August 19, 2008.

44 The LWF has also contributed a framework for examining the relationship between worship and culture. See the "Nairobi Statement on Worship and Culture: Contemporary Challenges and Opportunities," *Christian Worship: Unity in Cultural Diversity*, ed. S. Anita Stauffer (Geneva: World Lutheran Federation, 1996), 25-28.

45 See the Bread for the Journey website for more information: www.bfjmusic.com. Accessed March 22, 2013.

46 See S T Kimbrough, Jr., "Practical Considerations for Promoting Global Song," *The Hymn* 51:4 (October 2000), 22-29, and *Music and Mission: Toward a Theology and practice of Global Song* (New York: General board of Global Ministries, GBGMusik, 2006), ed. S T Kimbrough, Jr.

47 Some of the preceding material first appeared in C. Michael Hawn, "Christian Global Hymnody: An Overview," *Music And Mission*, Ed. S T Kimbrough, Jr., 23-40.

48 A festschrift with DVD honoring Mary Oyer was recently published: *Nurturing Spirit Through Song: The Life of Mary K. Oyer*, eds. Rebecca Slough and Shirley Sprunger King (Telford, PA: Cascadia Publishing House, 2007).

49 Correspondence from Robin Harris, June 13, 2008. See www.worldofworship.org, for more information. Though formed by Evangelicals, Paul Neeley states that "ICE is a network open to anyone who can affirm a basic creed such as the Nicene Creed." Correspondence from Paul Neeley, March 22, 2013.

50 See http://ethnodoxology.org. Accessed on March 22, 2013. Paul Neeley notes that *Ethnodoxology* is the continuation of an earlier journal that began ten years earlier. Correspondence from Paul Neeley, June 19, 2008.

51 *The Garland Encyclopedia of World Music*, ed., Bruno Nettl and Ruth M. Stone (New York: Garland Publishing., 1998-2002.

52 *The New Grove Dictionary of Music and Musicians*, 2nd ed., ed. Stanley Sadie and John Tyrell (2001).

53 The *Canterbury Dictionary of Hymnology* is an online global hymnology resource that is available October, 2013. See http://hymnology.org.uk/dictionary/Welcome though the site requires a subscription and a password.

54 John Baptist Ntahokaja, *The African Ecclesial Review*, Masaka, 3:1 (1961), 75, as quoted in Stephen B. G. Mbunga, *Church Law and Bantu Music: Ecclesiastical Documents and Law in Sacred Music as Applied to Bantu Music* (Schieneck-Beckenried, Switzerland: Novelle Revue de Science Missionaire, Supplement 13, 1963), 30.

55 See James M Riccitelli, "Developing Non-Western Hymnody," *Practical Anthropology* (November-December, 1962), 241-256, 270. This majority of this issue is devoted to articles by missionaries on the problems and possibilities of composing and adapting hymnody for indigenous peoples.

56 Arthur M. Jones cites African settings of the ordinary of the Mass dating from at least 1939 in *African Hymnody in Christian Worship: A Contribution to the History of Its Development* (Gwelo, Rhodesia: Mambo Press, 1976), 47-53 . Interestingly, however, he neglects to mention the most widely circulated of these, *Missa Luba*. The accuracy of Jones' work in selected writings has come under some criticism for the "selection and analysis of his evidence." See Lucy Durán and Gregory Barz, "Jones, Arthur Morris," *The New Grove Dictionary of Music and Musicians*, 13, 2nd Ed., eds. Stanley Sadie and John Tyrrell (New York: Oxford University Press, 2001), 188.

57 Influences of Corbitt's work as a music missionary may be found in J. Nathan Corbitt,

The Sound of the Harvest: Music's Mission in Church and Culture (Grand Rapids: Baker Books, 1998).

58 A recent overview of music and missions in Africa may be found in *Music in the Life of the African Church*, ed. Roberta King (Waco, Texas: Baylor University Press, 2008).

59 J. H. Kwabena Nketia, "The Scholarly Study of African Music: A Historical Review," *Africa. The Garland Encyclopedia of World Music*, Volume 1, ed. Ruth M. Stone (New York: Garland Publishing, Inc., 1998), 51.

60 Nketia, "The Scholarly Study of African Music," 53.

61 Nketia, "The Scholarly Study of African Music."

62 Lucy Durán, "Tracey, Hugh (Travers)," *Grove Music Online* ed. L. Macy, http://www.grovemusic.com. Accessed June 15, 2007.

63 See http://www.ru.ac.za/ilam for information on the International Library of African Music including publications and recordings. After a hiatus following the publication of Volume 7 in 1992, the Journal has resumed publication with Volume 8 (2007) as the *African Music: Journal of the International Library of African Music* under the editorship and director of ILAM, Diane Thram. An extensive series of CDs of African music is available through the ILAM Web site.

64 Throughout this section I rely heavily on the analysis of African music provided by the renowned Ghanaian ethnomusicologist J.H. Kwabena Nketia. A recent line of thinking, however, disputes the traditional approaches to African musical analysis that draw upon comparisons to Western musical practices. Fellow Ghanaian Kofi Agawu presents an alternative proposal for how to think about African music in his book *Representing African Music: Postcolonial Notes, Queries, Positions* (New York: Routledge, 2003).

65 John E. Kaemmer, "Southern Africa: An Introduction," *Africa: The Garland Encyclopedia of World Music*, 701.

66 Blantyre Covenant, Article 17, "The Worshipping Church in Africa," *Black Sacred Music: A Journal of Theomusicology*, ed. John Michael Spencer, 7:2 (Fall 1993), 38.

67 John E. Kaemmer, "Southern Africa: An Introduction," *Africa: The Garland Encyclopedia of World Music*, 701

68 J.H. Kwabena Nketia, "Music in African Cultures: A Review of the Meaning and Significance of Traditional African Music," mimeographed (Legon, Accra, Ghana: Institute of African Studies, University of Ghana, 1966), 20; quoted in John Miller Chernoff, *African Rhythm and African Sensibility: Aesthetics and Social Action in African Musical Idioms* (Chicago: University of Chicago Press, 1979), 36.

69 Mbunga, *Church Law and Bantu Music*, 29.

70 For a more complete introduction to cyclic song, see C. Michael Hawn, Chapter 7: "Form and Ritual: Sequential and Cyclic Musical Structures and Their Use in Liturgy," *Gather into One: Praying and Singing Globally*, 224-240.

71 From a manuscript by Judith A. Bangsund, "Hymns as Theological Expression: A Case Study in the Evangelical Lutheran Church in Tanzania," (March 2001) later published in *Africa Theological Journal* 24:1 (March 2001), 77-95.

72 See J.H. Kwabena Nketia, *The Music of Africa* (New York: W. W. Norton, 1974), 177-188, for a discussion of "Speech and Melody."

73 African Initiated Congregations (AICs), sometimes known as African Indigenous or Independent Congregations, are Christian churches that originated independently of colonial missions and are generally more Pentecostal in spirit.

74 Christopher Brooks, "Foreign-Indigenous Interchange: The Yoruba," *Africa. The Garland Encyclopedia of World Music*, 403-404.

75 See Nketia, *The Music of Africa*, 139-167, for information on "Organization of Vocal Music" and "Vocal Melody and Polyphony."

76 See Nketia, *The Music of Africa*, 206–217, for information on the "Interrelations of Music and Dance."

77 Kofi Agawu makes this observation in *African Rhythm: A Northern Ewe Perspective* (Cambridge UP, 1995), 6, but it applies to most African cultures.

78 Agawu, *African Rhythm*, 7.

79 See Nketia, *The Music of Africa*, 168-174, for information on the "Rhythmic Structures of Vocal Music."

80 See Nketia, *The Music of Africa*, 67-107, for information on "Musical Instruments" in Africa.

81 See Nketia, *The Music of Africa*, 125-138, for information on "Rhythm in Instrumental Music."

82 See Nketia, *The Music of Africa*, 21-34, for information on "Music in Community Life."

83 Thomas Turino, "The Music of Sub-Saharan Africa," *Excursions in World Music*, ed. Bruno Nettl, et al., (Englewood Cliffs, NJ: Prentice Hall, 1992), 181-182.

84 I also experienced similar diversity of singing styles when I participated in Xhosa Methodist worship in November 1998 in East London, South Africa.

85 James R. Krabill outlines six stages in Chapter Four, "Encounters" What Happens to Music When People Meet," in *Music in the Life of the African Church*, ed. Roberta King (Waco, Texas: Baylor University Press, 2008). His stages are importation, adaptation, alteration, imitation, indigenization, and internationalization. Though Krabill's stages are similar to the seven genres outlined above, my approach, unlike Krabill's, does not suggest progressive stages through which church music must pass, but seven ways that colonial and African cultures interact in the composition of hymns. Individual composers may focus only on one or two of these genres without moving on to others. Likewise, a composer may enter at any point in the spectrum of practices outlined above.

86 Page numbers within the text in the following section refer to the entry by W. R. Stevenson, "Missions, Foreign," in *Dictionary of Hymnology*, ed. John Julian (1892, rev. 1907), 739-759.

87 Carlton R. Young, *Companion to The United Methodist Hymnal* (Nashville: Abingdon Press, 1993), 808.

88 Arthur M. Jones, *African Hymnody in Christian Worship*, 46.

89 Emily Brink and Bert Polman, Eds., *Psalter Hymnal Handbook* (Grand Rapids, Michigan: CRC Publications, 1998), 382.

90 See *The United Methodist Hymnal* (1989), 661.

91 See *E Korin S'Oluwa (Sing unto the Lord): Fifty Indigenous Christian Hymns from Nigeria*, Arranged and Composed by Godwin Sadoh (Colfax, NC: Wayne Leupold Editions, Inc., 2005).

92 Much of Jones's research centered on the controversial topic of the similarities between xylophones in Indonesia and Africa and the theory, though not according to some scholars substantiated by historical evidence, that the African xylophone came from Indonesia.

93 See Lucy Durán and Gregory F. Barz, "Jones, Arthur Morris," *Grove Music Online* ed. L. Macy, http://www.grovemusic.com. Accessed 15 June, 2007.

94 Howard Olson, *Lead Us, Lord* (Minneapolis: Augsburg Press, 1977), 4.

95 Howard Olson, *Set Free* (Minneapolis: Augsburg Fortress Press, 1993), 2.

96 Howard Olson, telephone interview with author, February 20, 2004.

97 Emily Brink and Bert Polman, Eds., *Psalter Hymnal Handbook* (Grand Rapids, Michigan: CRC Publications, 1998), 506.

98 Tom Colvin, *Come, Let Us Walk this Road Together: 43 Songs from Africa* (Carol Stream, IL: Hope Publishing Company, 1997), "Preface" (no page number provided).

99 Colvin, *Come, Let Us Walk this Road Together.*

100 Colvin, *Come, Let Us Walk this Road Together.*

101 Interview with Robert Kauffman, Seattle, Washington, February 10, 2004.

102 From "Reflections on the Arts Workshop" Nyakatsapa, Northern Rhodesia (April 24-29, 1961), unpublished notes.

103 Olof Axelsson, "The Development of African Church Music in Zimbabwe," *Papers Presented at the Symposium on Ethnomusicology* (Grahamstown, South Africa: Rhodes University, September 24-26, 1981), 5.

104 Atah Annan Mensah, "Compositional Practices in African Music," *Africa: The Garland Encyclopedia of World Music*, 217.

105 Recordings include "Drums in the Church" (1964).

106 See John E. Kaemmer, *Music in Human Life: Anthropological Perspectives on Music* (Austin: University of Texas Press, 1993).

107 Interview with John Kaemmer, Seattle, Washington, February 10, 2004.

108 See "Southern Africa: An Introduction" (700-721) and "Music of the Shona of Zimbabwe" (744-758).

109 Weman (1897-1992) wrote of his travels to southern Africa in 1954 and 1956–1957 in *African Music and the Church in Africa* (Uppsala, Sweden: Studia Missionalia Uppsaliensis, Svenska Institutet för Missionsforskning, 1960). For Weman, African music reflected the inner life of the African—"an essential part of [the African's] inmost being; it has the power to liberate, and it is in the music and dance that the African can best be himself." (20).

110 Olof Axelsson, *African Music and European Christian Mission*, Masters Thesis (Uppsala University, 1971). Stig-Magnus Thorsén provides additional information on Weman and Axelsson in "Swedish Missionaries' Image of Music in Africa," Unpublished paper presented at the Swedish—South Africa Research Network, Seminar in Pretoria, September 18-19, 2003.

111 In a conversation with Axelsson's daughter, Maria Minnaar, July 13, 2007, she recalled that her father made up to 100 sets of marimbas. While he did not play the marimba, he was skilled in playing the mbira. Minnaar, an expert marimba player and teacher, is publishing collections of marimba music and conducting research on the origins and history of the Zimbabwean marimba.

112 Thorsén, "Swedish Missionaries' Image of Music in Africa," 10.

113 Thorsén, "Swedish Missionaries' Image of Music in Africa," 11.

114 Thorsén, "Swedish Missionaries' Image of Music in Africa," 11.

115 Conversation with Maria Minnaar, July 13, 2007.

116 Minnaar, July 13, 2007.

117 Kaemmer found out later that many of the songs for the Holy Week drama may not have been totally original, but included consciously or sub-consciously folk songs, a common practice in oral composition and transmission. Thus the text/music for the drama may have been at least to some degree made use of the technique of contrafactum.

118 See Mary Hopkin, "African Marimba Music Hits Hermiston," *Tri-City Herald*, May 1, 2000.

119 I heard Maraire lead a marimba ensemble with his "Alleluia" in Harare in December 1998 just two years before his death. The occasion was the opening liturgy of the World Council of Churches Assembly with Patrick Matsikenyiri leading the assembly in singing. I assumed that it was common to have marimba ensembles in churches, but was informed later by Maria Minnaar that this was quite unusual as the marimbas were mostly used in schools and rarely in churches. With the percussive five-piece marimba accompaniment, however, this was indeed a celebrative Easter selection with many cross-rhythms (two-against-three).

120 *Ngoma: dze United Methodist Church Ye Zimbabwe* (Harare: Conference Board of Publications and Communications, [1964] 1995). L.G. Zhungu, Chairman of the hymnal project, acknowledges Matsikenyiri's contributions to the hymnal in the Forward, especially for "noting mistakes in some songs and missed lines and verses in some songs." (3).

121 For more on Matsikenyiri, see C. Michael Hawn, Chapter 5: "The Spirit of Ngoma: Patrick Matsikenyiri and Indigenous Song in Zimbabwe," *Gather into One: Praying and Singing Globally*, 148-188.

122 See *Sing! Imba! Hlabela! Zimbabwe: Short Songs and New Compositions from Zimbabwean Churches*, Comp. Patrick Matsikenyiri and Maggie Hamilton (Birmingham, UK: Christian Aid Office, 1998) and Patrick Matsikenyiri, *Njalo (Always): A Collection of 16 Hymns in the African Tradition*, ed. Dan Damon (Nashville: Abingdon Press, 2006).

123 See *Global Praise 2*, ed. By S T Kimbrough, Jr. and Carlton Young (New York: General Board of Global Ministries/GBGMusik, 2000), 83.

124 David Dargie. "Xhosa Church Music," *Music and the Experience of God*, eds. David Power, Mary Collins, and Mellonee Burnim. (Edinburgh: T. & T. Clark Ltd., 1989), 65.

125 Dargie's recordings are to be housed at the International Library of African Music in Grahamstown, South Africa along with Hugh Tracey's collection.

126 David Dargie, *Workshops for Composing Local Church Music: Methods for Conducting Music Workshops in Local Congregations*, No. 40. (Delmenville, South Africa: Lumko Missiological Institute, 1983), 5.

127 For more information on the work of David Dargie, see C. Michael Hawn, Chapter 4: "Singing Freedom: and South African Liberation Song," *Gather into One: Praying and Singing Globally*, 104-147.

128 For more information on Ntsikana and Bokwe, see John Knox Bokwe,. *Ntsikana: The Story of an African Convert*, 2nd Ed. (Lovedale, South Africa: Lovedale Mission Press, 1914); David Dargie, "The Music of Ntsikana," *South African Journal of Musicology* 2 (1982), 7-28; Janet Hodgson, "Ntsikana's 'Great Hymn', A Xhosa Expression of Christianity in the Early Nineteenth 19th-Century Eastern Cape," *Communications* 4.

University of Cape Town (1980), 21-31; J. A. Millard, "John Knox Bokwe," *Malihambe - Let the Word Spread* (Pretoria, South Africa: Unisa Press, 1999).

129   The Xhosa language Methodist hymnal, *Incwadi Yenkonzo Nezingoma* (Cape Town, South Africa: Methodist Book Depot and Publishing House, 1954) contains eleven of Soga's hymns, demonstrating his continued popularity through the mid-twentieth century. The Presbyterian *Incwadi Yamaculo Amaxhosa* (Lovedale: Lovedale Press, 1929, rev. 1974) includes twenty-six of Soga's hymns.

130   More complete biographical information on the South African hymn writers mentioned in this section is available in the *Canterbury Dictionary of Hymnology*, ed. J. Richard Watson, to be published online in October 2013.

131   For a more extensive discussion of the background of the South African Freedom Song in the context of the history of South African hymnody, see C. Michael Hawn, "The Truth Shall Set You Free: Song, Struggle, and Solidarity in South Africa," *Resonant Witness: Conversations Between Music and Theology*, eds. Jeremy S. Begbie and Steven R. Guthrie (Grand Rapids: Wm. B. Eerdmans, 2011), 408-433.

132   David Dargie, Interview, Dallas, Texas, March 21, 2000.

133   John M. Janzen, *Ngoma: Discourses on Healing in Central and Southern Africa* (Berkeley: University of California Press, 1992), 111-118.

134   A summary from Hawn, *Gather into One*, 144-145.

135   *Freedom Is Coming: Sons of Protest and Praise from South Africa*. Ed. Anders Nyberg (Uppsala, Sweden: Utryck; Ft. Lauderdale, FL: Walton Music Corporation, 1984). A more recent collection is *Freedom Is in Your Hand*, Ed. Anders Nyberg (Ft. Lauderdale: Walton Music, 2003). Also see *Sing Freedom! Songs of South African Life*, ed. Margaret Hamilton (London: Novello/Christian Aid, 1993).

136   For example, Australian Lutheran composer Robin Mann (b. 1949) was at the Budapest assembly and brought back South African Freedom Songs to his country and incorporated them into his *All Together* song series (Adelaide: Openbook Publishers, 1980, 1983, 1991, 1996, 2001, 2007).

137   At the conclusion of this section is a list of sources for the music cited. See Appendix B for specific references to hymn and sources.

138   Daniel Ramírez, "Hymnody as Ideology in Latino Protestantism," in *Singing the Lord's Song in a Strange Land: Hymnody in the History of North American Protestantism*, eds. Edith L. Blumhofer and Mark A. Noll (Tuscaloosa: The University of Alabama Press, 2004), 200.

139   Ramírez, "Hymnody as Ideology in Latino Protestantism," 201.

140   Ramírez, "Hymnody as Ideology in Latino Protestantism," 203.

141   For example, a simple bound soft-cover Catholic book from El Salvador, *El Pueblo Canta* [The People Sing], is actually a compilation of twelve earlier *cantos cancioneros* (song collections) into one volume in 1992. Each song has text only with guitar chords in the Latin American style. Simple drawings add interest to the volume. Each of the original twelve collections maintains its own numbering and there is no index. Recordings for some of the songs have been informally made. In Latin American, the total number of volumes printed usually accommodates just enough for local use with little thought given to a broader distribution. Needless to say, such collections are difficult for mainline denominations to acquire and, without musical notation or recordings, have little chance of being incorporated into hymnals.

142 See *Regocijate y Canta* [Rejoice and Sing] (Kearney, NE: Morris Publishing, 1995), an informal collection initiated by an individual Methodist congregation, Primera Iglesia Metodista Unidad de Corona (New York). While some composers are indicated—both Latino and Anglo—the composers of most songs are listed as *desconocido* (unknown).

143 Spanish words by Guillermo Cuéllar ©1988, GIA Publications, Inc. Used by permission. English translation by C. Michael Hawn.

144 Spanish words by Guillermo Cuéllar ©1988, GIA Publications, Inc. Used by permission. English translation by C. Michael Hawn. A very helpful introduction to the early post-Vatican II Masses from Central America is José María Vigil and Angel Torrellas, *Misas Centro Americanas: Transcripción y Comentario Teológia* (Managua: CAV-CEBES, 1988).

145 Pablo Sosa, "Spanish American Hymnody: A Global Perspective," *The Hymnology Annual: An International Forum on the Hymn and Worship*, Vol. 3, ed., Vernon Wicker (Berrien Springs, MI: Vande Vere Publishing Ltd, 1993), 68.

146 Roberto Escamilla, "Fiesta Worship," *The Interpreter* 20 (June 1976), 2.

147 Raquel Gutiérrez-Achón, "An Introduction to Hispanic Hymnody," in *¡Alabadle! Hispanic Christian Worship*, ed. Justo L. González (Nashville: Abingdon Press, 1996), 105.

148 Gutiérrez-Achón, "An Introduction to Hispanic Hymnody," 109.

149 Jorge Lockward, "Songs from Hispanic Sources," *Sing! a New Creation: Leader's Edition* (Grand Rapids: MI: CRC Publications, 2002), 436.

150 *The Garland Encyclopedia of World Music*, Vol. 2: *South American, Mexico, Central America, and the Caribbean*, eds. Dale A. Olsen and Daniel E. Sheehy (New York: Garland Publishing, Inc., 1998), indicates a vast number of dance forms in the index under "dance and movement" (1043-1046). This index by country and form is a valuable resource.

151 *The Garland Encyclopedia of World Music*, Vol. 2. See the index for valuable references to "African descendants," "African slaves," and specific entries for various African-influenced cultures, e.g., Afro-Bolivian, Afro-Brazilian, Afro-Caribbean, etc. (1032).

152 See Pedrito U. Maynard-Reid, *Diverse Worship: African-American, Caribbean and Hispanic Perspectives* (Downers Grove, IL: InterVarsity Press, 2000). In addition to broad historical and liturgical orientations to the various cultures, Maynard-Reid addresses general issues of Caribbean (138-149) and Hispanic (187-193) church music styles.

153 Raquel Mora Martínez, "A Survey of Hispanic Hymnody as Represented in *The New Century Hymnal*," *The New Century Hymnal Companion*, ed. Kristen L. Forman (Cleveland: The Pilgrim Press, 1998), speaks of the theme of the journey, (155).

154 Martínez, "A Survey of Hispanic Hymnody as Represented in *The New Century Hymnal*," 154.

155 The information on Pablo Sosa and his music comes from a larger article. See. C. Michael Hawn, chapter three: "The Fiesta of the Faithful: Pablo Sosa and the Contextualization of Latin American Hymnody," *Gather into One: Praying and Singing Globally*, 32-71.

156 Sosa, "Pagura. . . El Cantor," *Por Eso Es Que Tenemos Esperanza: Homenaje al Obispo Federico J. Pagura* (Quito: CLAI, 1995), 73-74. Trans. M. Aaron Hawn.

157 Sosa, "Pagura. . . El Cantor," 79. Trans. M. Aaron Hawn. The *baguala*, "Todo acabó en una tumba," is available in *Libro de Liturgia y Cántico* (346). This is a Good Friday text that uses a slower *vidala* or expanded *baguala* form. Perera wrote the melody first and then the text by Pagura followed.

158 The Central-American folk Masses discussed earlier in this chapter came over a decade later and were not part of the Argentine efforts to inculturate church music.

159 For more information see the section "Tango" in Ercilia Moreno Chá, "Argentina," *The Garland Encyclopedia of World Music*, Vol. 2, 263-265.

160 Sosa, "Pagura... El Cantor," 75. Trans. M. Aaron Hawn.

161 All three hymns can be found in *Libro de Liturgia y Cántico* as numbers 478, 579, 458 respectively.

162 Sosa discusses the "Porque" hymns in "Pagura... El Cantor," 81-85.

163 Sosa, "Pagura... El Cantor," 82. Trans. M. Aaron Hawn.

164 Carlton R. Young, *Companion to The United Methodist Hymnal* (Nashville: Abingdon Press, 1993), 311, 795.

165 Young, *Companion to The United Methodist Hymnal*, 311.

166 Gertrude Suppe (1911-2007) was an important collector and cataloguer of Spanish-language hymnals during the 1980s and 1990s. Her singing translations into English may be found in several hymnals including *The United Methodist Hymnal* (1989).

167 Young, *Companion to The United Methodist Hymnal*, 563-564.

168 Young, *Companion to The United Methodist Hymnal*, 438-439.

169 Young, *Companion to The United Methodist Hymnal*, 820-821.

170 Though not appearing broadly at this time, João Wilson Faustini (b. 1931) has a single-author collection of his hymns entitled *When Breaks the Dawn: Hymns from Brazil* (Colfax, North Carolina: Wayne Leupold Editions, Inc., 2006).

171 Many of the most widely used Caribbean hymns may be found in *Let Us Sing: Hymns, Songs and Choruses*, compiled by Godfrey Taylor, Claudette Campbell and Delores Flemming (Kingston, Jamaica: Carlong Publishers, 2003).

172 S T Kimbrough, Jr., ed. *Companion to Songbooks Global Praise 1 and Global Praise 2* (New York: GBGMusik, 2005), 97.

173 Many of Jordan's songs as well as those by other Caribbean composers may be found in the *A. E. C. (Antilles Episcopal Conference) Caribbean Hymnal* (Trinidad: AEC, 1998).

174 *A. E. C. Caribbean Hymnal*, 62.

175 *A. E. C. Caribbean Hymnal*, 50.

176 *A. E. C. Caribbean Hymnal*, 87.

177 Paul F. Bradshaw, *The Search for the Origins of Christian Worship: Sources and Methods for the Study of Early Liturgy*, 2nd ed. (New York, NY: Oxford University Press, 2002), 16.

178 Bradshaw, *The Search for the Origins of Christian Worship*, 16.

179 Yet, if we include the Middles East and Asia Minor as a part of Asia, then it is even possible to see this region as the birthplace of two other world religions, namely, Christianity and Islam.

180 The first edition of *Hymns of Universal Praise* (Shanghai: Christian Literate Society, 1936) was a joint effort by Sheng Kung Huei (a union of the Anglican and Episcopal Churches in China, the Church of Christ in China, including Presbyterians and twenty-four other denominations), the East China Baptist Convention (Southern Baptists), The Methodist Church (north and south), and the North China Congregational Church. See Allen Artz Wiant, *A New Song for China: A Biography of Bliss Mitchell Wiant* (Victoria, British Columbia: Trafford Publishing, 2005), 203.

181 For more information, see Emily F. Brink, "Glimpses of Recent Chinese Hymnody Including a Review of the 2006 Edition of *Hymns of Universal Praise*," *The Hymn* 59:2 (Spring 2008), 8-24.

182 The Three-Self Church in China is the ecclesial body officially recognized by the Chinese government. Unrecognized congregations also play a significant role in the Christian community. No one hymnal is used by these congregations, sometimes called "house churches." Of particular importance in the unrecognized congregations are the *Canaan Hymns*, a body of more than 1400 hymns conceived by one woman from the Henan Province, Xiao-min Lü.

183 Numerous other Chinese hymnals are either denominationally or regionally based. Most are largely Western in approach with some attention to Asian authors and composers. For example, see *Hymns of United Worship*, ed. Mary Gan Yoke Thue (Hong Kong: Chinese Christian Literature Council, Ltd., 1997) produced for the World Federation of Chinese Methodist Churches. While largely Western in style, a section at the end of the hymnal (nos. 248-260) is reserved for Chinese composers. The Baptist hymnal, *Century Praise*, ed. Richard R. Lin (Hong Kong: Chinese Baptist Press Ltd., 2001) appears in a bilingual version, but contains relatively few original contributions by Chinese authors or composers.

184 I-to Loh, ed., *Sound the Bamboo* (Hong Kong: Christian Conference of Asia, 2000), Carlton R. Young, ed., *The United Methodist Hymnal* (Nashville, TN: United Methodist Publishing House, 1989). See Appendix B for a listing of all hymns and their sources.

185 Due to space constraint, this article does not specifically describe regional ethnic groups and their unique musical cultures as in the case of the indigenous people of Taiwan. For a detailed description and analysis of Taiwanese indigenous music cultures, see I-to Loh, "Tribal Music of Taiwan: With Special Reference to the Ami and Puyama Styles" (PhD Dissertation, University of California at Los Angeles, 1982). For an ethnomusicological approach towards the performance practice of Asian church music see I-to Loh, "A Glimpse at Multipart Practices in Traditional Asian Music," in *Asian Workshop on Liturgy and Music* (National Art Center, Makiling, Philippines: Asian Institute for Liturgy and Music, 1987), 263.

186 There are many types of five-note (pentatonic) scales. For a quick overview, refer to I-to Loh, "Asian Christian Music," in *A Dictionary of Asian Christianity*, ed. Scott W. Sunquist (Grand Rapids, MI: Wm. B. Eerdmans Publishing Co., 2001), 569-574. We can also find six- and seven-note scale systems in this region of Asia, the diatonic musical system of the West notwithstanding. Nevertheless, the pentatonic scale seems to be largely preferred.

187 For additional background information for this hymn and its creators, see I-to Loh, *Sound the Bamboo: Asian Hymns in Their Cultural Contexts (A Companion to Sound the Bamboo: C.C.A. Hymnal 2000)* (Chicago, IL: GIA Publications, Inc., 2011).

188 One such study is I-to Loh, "Tribal Music of Taiwan: With Special Reference to the Ami and Puyuma Styles" (Ph.D., UCLA, 1982).

189 See C. Michael Hawn, *Gather into One: Praying and Singing Globally* (Grand Rapids, MI: Wm. B. Eerdmans Publishing Co., 2003), 72-103; Don Pitman, "I-to Loh: Finding Asia's Cultural Voice in the Worship of God," in *And God Gave the Increase: 1 Corinthians 3:6-9: Stones of How the Presbyterian Church (U.S.A.) Has Helped in the Education of*

Christian Leaders around the World, ed. June Ramage Rogers (Louisville, KY: Office of Global Education and Leadership Development of the Worldwide Ministries Division, 1998) and, Swee Hong Lim, "Giving Voice to Asian Christians: An Appraisal of the Pioneering Work of I-to Loh in the Area of Congregational Song" (PhD Dissertation, Drew University, 2006).

190 Carlton R. Young, *Companion to the United Methodist Hymnal*, 398.

191 Young, *Companion*, 858.

192 Young, *Companion*, 569.

193 *Sound the Bamboo* uses a translation by Frank W. Price entitled "Golden Breaks the Dawn."

194 See Allen Wiant, *A New Song for China*, 202-207, for a more complete discussion of *Hymns of Universal Praise*.

195 Wiant, *A New Song for China*, vi.

196 The first edition of *The Pagoda* was published with the assistance of a friend at Boston University School of Theology, Lynn Rohrbaugh, and her company the Cooperative Recreation Service (Delaware, Ohio, 1946). This author had access to a later edition published following the departure of the Wiants from China as *The Pagoda: Thirteen Chinese Songs*, Third Ed. (1952).

197 Introduction to the Third Edition, *The Pagoda*. [n.p.].

198 "Preface," *The Pagoda*, Third Edition. [n.p.].

199 The Wiants' second son, Leighton, suggested that Mildred was an even better translator than Bliss, though often in the background in comparison to her husband. Information on Mildred Wiant was provided in a telephone interview with C. Michael Hawn on October 22, 2008.

200 Allen Wiant, *A New Song for China*, 213.

201 Wiant, *A New Song for China*, vii.

202 Information on Boris and Clare Anderson was supplied by I-to Loh in correspondence with the author, August 10, 2007, and appears in a more complete form in I-to Loh, *Sound the Bamboo: Asian Hymns in Their Cultural Contexts*, 392-393.

203 Ragas (modes) are life- and time-cycle specific and misuse of such ragas is to invite disaster and therefore strenuously avoided.

204 The Indian musical instrument, *Veena*, is a drone-playing zither. It is usually played together with the melody-playing *Sitar* (zither), the *Ching* (finger cymbal), and the *Tabla* (hand drum). However, other different instrumental combinations exist, including the use of the *Harmonium* (hand-pumped portable reed organ). Instrument like the *Sitar* also contain a passive drone system that shimmers in the background even as one plays the melody.

205 Loh, ed., *Sound the Bamboo*. xviii.

206 Bart Shaha is presently holding the appointment of General Secretary of the World Alliance of YMCAs.

207 See *Sound the Bamboo*, No. 59 for the embellished version of this Tamil Indian hymn. A Telugu Indian hymn "Sarennam, O Divine Light" (STB 47) is another example of a hymn that uses "Saranam" as an indication of deep reverence.

208 See www.punjabonline.com/servlet/entertain.entertain?Action=Intro. Accessed March 22, 2013.

209 M. D. Thomas, editor, *Christian Hymns, Lyrics and Songs of New Life* (Chennai, Tamil Nadu, India: The Christian Literature Society, 1949, twenty-third edition, 2007).

210 Based on Michael Hawn's experience in southern India during January and February 2008 at Madurai Theological Seminary, while the Seminary actively teaches classical Indian music, the majority of the Church of South India congregations sing Western Gospel songs and Indian repertoire in a "light" style.

211 For a discussion of the Carnatic music tradition of southern India, see T. Viswanathan and Matthew Harp Allen, *Music in South India* (New York: Oxford University Press, 2004).

212 "God of Creation" and "Ocean of Love" are available in *Global Praise I*, songs 8 and 50. "Rejoice, Hallelu" and "I was Glad" may be found in C. Michael Hawn, ed., *Halle, Halle: We Sing the World Round* (Garland, TX: Choristers Guild, 1999), songs two and nine.

213 Young, *Companion*, 436.

214 Vietnamese hymns are rare in North American hymnals. *The United Methodist Hymnal* contains one, "My Prayer Rises to Heaven" (No. 498) by Nguyen Dao-Kim. Oregon Catholic Press has published two collections devoted to Vietnamese hymns, *United in Faith and Song: Hymns and Songs in Vietnamese and English* (2001) and *Chon Ngài* (2006) with hymns only in Vietnamese. Rufino Zaragoza, OFM, serves as the Project coordinator for these hymnals.

215 This is a region where several musical cultures are pervasive, both indigenous and imposed. Lying between the trade route to China from Europe, several European powers in the likes of English, Dutch, Portuguese, and Spanish have colonized this region and left their marks from the sixteenth to early twentieth century. Earlier on, China and India have also flexed their influences on this region and some countries still bear this imprint, such as the island of Bali, and the Indo-China countries of Cambodia, Laos, Myanmar, and Vietnam. Traders from Arab countries have also left their influence, particularly the practice of Islam in countries like Brunei, Indonesia, Malaysia, Singapore, and parts of the Philippines and Thailand.

216 The writer learned of the *gondang* being used in Christian worship in 1996 at the 2nd Ecumenical Seminar on Liturgy and Music in Manila when it was demonstrated by the participants from Sumatra, Indonesia. The use of *gamelan* in Christian worship has been documented in several publications including Mark P. Bangert, "Dynamics of Liturgy and World Musics: A Methodology for Evaluation," in *Worship and Culture in Dialogue*, ed. S. Anita Stauffer (Geneva: World Lutheran Federation, 1994), 183, and I-to Loh, ed., *Kristus Sundaring Bali (Christ the Light to Bali): New Balinese Hymns* (Quezon City, Metro Manila: Asian Institute for Liturgy and Music, 1988).

217 David Morton, "Polyphonic Stratification in Traditional Thai Music," *Asia Pacific Quarterly* 1, no. 3 (1971), 78. For more information about polyphonic stratification, see Loh, ed., *Kristus Sundaring Bali (Christ the Light to Bali): New Balinese Hymns*, 263.

218 William P. Malm, *Music Cultures of the Pacific, the Near East, and Asia* (Englewood Cliffs, NJ: Prentice-Hall, 1967), 43.

219 See www.villarfoundation.org/page?id=37&menu=4. Accessed March 22, 2013.

220 For a brief explanation of this scale and the performance practice of indigenous Thai church music, see I-to Loh, *Rak Phra Jao, Rao Pen Thai (The Love of God Sets Us*

Free): A Collection of New Thai Hymns (Quezon City, Metro Manila: Asian Institute for Liturgy and Music, 1989).

221 See www.sambalikhaan.org. Accessed March 22, 2013.

222 Y.A.M.U.G.E.R. is the acronym for Yayasan Musik Gereja di Indonesia (Indonesian Institute for Sacred Music). It is a Christian organization that advocates for the contextualization of church music in Indonesia. Its ministries include the collection and publication of indigenous hymns and the training of church musicians. See www.yamuger.or.id/. Accessed March 22, 2103.

223 See www.country-studies.com/indonesia/peoples-of-sumatra.html and http://sitogol.tripod.com. Accessed March 22, 2013.

224 For a brief discussion about this undertaking in contextualized worship in Thailand, see Lim, "Giving Voice to Asian Christians," 219-221. See also, www.thaicov.org/resources/documents/. Accessed March 22, 2013, and I-to Loh, ed., *Rak Phra Jao, Rao Pen Thai (the Love of God Sets Us Free): A Collection of New Thai Hymns* (Quezon City, Metro Manila: Asian Institute for Liturgy and Music, 1989).

225 Samuel Liew set his lyrics to RASA SAYANG, a much-loved folksong in the region of Malaysia, Singapore and Indonesia.

226 I-to Loh, ed., *New Songs of Asian Cities* (Tokyo: East Asia Christian Conference-Urban and Industrial Mission Committee (EACC-UIM), 1972). For more information about this publication, its significance for the Asian church and Loh's involvement, see Lim, "Giving Voice to Asian Christians," 23-24.

227 Samples of the Lim Swee-Hong's compositions can be found in the *Global Praise* song collections, volumes one, two, and three, published by the General Board of Global Ministries, GBGMusik, New York. See also works published by Hope Publishing, www.hopepublishing.com/html/main.isx?sitesec=40.2.1.0&hymnID=386. Accessed March 22, 2013.

228 Additional information of these hymns can be found in I-to Loh, ed., *Sound the Bamboo: Asian Hymns in Their Cultural Contexts*.

229 Other institutions that are seeking to develop this focus in church music include Taiwan Seminary in Taipei, Taiwan, Methodist Theological Seminary in Sibu, Sarawak, East Malaysia, and Jakarta Theological Seminary in Indonesia. Though not having a graduate program in church music, all of the Bachelor of Divinity students at Tamilnadu Theological Seminary in Madurai, India receive instruction in Indian classical and folk-music traditions, and develop Asian-influenced liturgies for daily chapel worship.

230 For an in-depth discussion on this phenomenon, see Lim, "Giving Voice to Asian Christians," 222-230.

231 Many mega-churches as well as emerging churches in North America are encouraging their worship teams to create congregational songs that reflect their concerns. For example, see www.willowcreek.com/servicebuilder/music.asp, and www.solomonsporch.com. Accessed March 22, 2013. Australia's Assembly of God congregation Hillsong is very influential in parts of Asia.

232 The Chemin Neuf (New Way) Community, for example, describes itself as a "Roman Catholic community with an ecumenical vocation." Founded in 1973 in Lyon, France, some of the music from this community is finding its way into recent European collections. See www.chemin-neuf.org. Accessed March 22, 2013.

233 For more complete introductions to the Taizé Community, see J. L. Gonzalez Balado, Story of Taizé (New York: Continuum International Publishing Group. 2003) and Kathryn Spink, *A Universal Heart: The Life and Vision of Brother Roger of Taize*, 2nd Ed. (Chicago: GIA Publications, Inc., 2006).

234 Brother Jean-Marie, "Prayer at Taizé: Singing and Silence," *Christian Century* 118:10 (March 2001), 16.

235 Brother Jean-Marie, "Prayer at Taizé: Singing and Silence," 16.

236 Correspondence with Brother Jean-Marie, July 11, 2007.

237 A compact disc of the Taizé brothers singing psalms appropriate for seasons throughout the Christian Year, including twelve settings by Gelineau, in the ancient Roman Church at Taizé, is *Taizé dans L'Église Romane: à travers l'année liturgique* (Paris: Studio SM 1994, 1991), available from GIA Publications, CD-266.

238 Jean-Marie of Taizé, "Jubilate Deo Award: Building a Bridge of Reconciliation," *Pastoral Music* 31:1 (October-November 2006), 45.

239 Robert Batastini, "Songs from the Community of Taizé," *Sing! A New Creation: Leader's Edition* (Grand Rapids: CRC Publications, 2002), 418.

240 Jean-Marie of Taizé, "Jubilate Deo Award: Building a Bridge of Reconciliation," 46.

241 Jean-Marie of Taizé, "Jubilate Deo Award," 46.

242 Judith Marie Kubicki, *Liturgical Music as Ritual Symbol: A Case Study of Jacques Berthier's Taizé Music* (Leuven, The Netherlands, 1999), provides a structural analysis of Berthier's music. She suggests four genres (1) *ostinato* response and chorales, (2) litanies, (3) acclamations, and (4) canons) with detailed analysis (54-75).

243 Kubicki, *Liturgical Music as Ritual Symbol*, 178.

244 Jean-Marie of Taizé, "Jubilate Deo Award: Building a Bridge of Reconciliation," 46.

245 Correspondence with Frere Jean-Marie, July 11, 2007.

246 Jean-Marie of Taizé, "Jubilate Deo Award: Building a Bridge of Reconciliation," 43.

247 For more information on the Taizé Community, see www.taize.fr. For music from the Taizé Community in the North America, contact GIA Publications, Inc., www.giamusic.com.

248 This is a condensation and updating of more extensive essays that first appeared in C. Michael Hawn, *Gather into One: Praying and Singing Globally* (Grand Rapids: Wm. B. Eerdmans, 2003), 223, and "The Wild Goose Sings: Themes in the Worship and Music of the Iona Community," *Worship* 74:6 (November 2000), 504-521.

249 Ian Bradley, *Columba: Pilgrim and Penitent* (Glasgow: Wild Goose Publications, 1996), 23.

250 See David N. Power, "Affirmed from Under: Celtic Liturgy and Spirituality," *Studia Liturgica* 27:1 (1997), 1-32, for an excellent scholarly treatment of Celtic hymnody and Psalter prayers, as well as verse related to the Celtic affinity with nature, penance, martyrology, and devotion to saints and to Christ, with examples drawn primarily from the *Antiphonary of Bangor*.

251 Esther de Waal, "The Celtic Way of Prayer," *Cistercian Studies Quarterly* 32:3 (1997), 372.

252 John L. Bell and Graham Maule, *Love + Anger: Songs of Lively Faith and Social Justice* (Glasgow: Wild Goose Publications, 1997), 8.

253 John L. Bell and Graham Maule, *Love from Below: The Seasons of Life, the Call to Care, and the Celebrating Community* (Glasgow: Wild Goose Publications, 1989), 123.

254 *The Coracle: Rebuilding the Common Life; Foundation Documents of the Iona Community* (Glasgow: Wild Goose Publications, [1938] 1988), October 1938, 4.

255 Omitted here is a discussion of the founding of the old Benedictine Abbey in the thirteenth century, repairs to the abbey in the fifteenth century, and the decline of the abbey up to the time of MacLeod during the mid-twentieth-century.

256 For more information, see *What is the Iona Community?* (Glasgow: Wild Goose Publications, 1988).

257 Correspondence from John Bell, May 13, 2008.

258 *The Coracle* (May 1939), 18.

259 *The Coracle* (May 1939), 16.

260 See John Bell, "Reforming Worship: Change is Not a Dirty Word," *Reformed Worship* 40 (June 1996), 5. Ian Bradley, *Abide with Me: The World of Victorian Hymns* (London: SCM Press, 1997), graciously notes that "John Bell, the leading contemporary Scottish hymn writer, has pointed to the damage done to the cause of reform and moving on in the life of churches by the deadening effect of [this line] from 'Abide with me'. . ." (234). Later, he adds that "it is good for [Victorian hymnody enthusiasts] to be confronted with the withering judgment of a leading contemporary hymn-writer such as John Bell. . . ." (245).

261 John L. Bell, *Wrestle and Fight and Pray: Thoughts on Christianity and Conflict* (Edinburgh: Saint Andrew Press, 1993), 5-6.

262 See *What is the Iona Community?* 8-12, for a complete description and explanation of "The Rule and Concerns of the Iona Community."

263 See http://iona.org.uk for more information. Accessed on March 22, 2013.

264 On August 13, 2001, I heard Brian Woodstock, then warden of the Iona Community, relate a story about the origins of the wild goose as a symbol of the Holy Spirit. Ron Ferguson, an earlier leader of the Community, was asked by George MacLeod, about the Celtic origins of the wild goose symbolism. Ferguson told MacLeod that he had borrowed the idea from MacLeod some years earlier. Ferguson then asked MacLeod if the wild goose was indeed a symbol of the Holy Spirit. MacLeod responded, "It is now."

265 Correspondence from John Bell, May 13, 2008, and John Bell, "Flight of the Wild Goose," *Reformed Liturgy and Music* 34: 2 (2000), 15.

266 "We will not take what is not ours," for example, is a song based on the eighth commandment—You shall not steal—that grew out of this experience. See Bell and Maule, *Love from Below*. 75.

267 Correspondence from John Bell, May 13, 2008.

268 *The Iona Community Worship Book,* Rev. ed. (Glasgow: Wild Goose Publications, 1991).

269 After a time of negotiation with Robert Batastini, G.I.A. Publications, Inc. was chosen to publish and distribute the songs produced by the WGRG and the first publication *Heaven Shall Not Wait: Songs of Creation, the Incarnation, and the Life of Jesus,* Vol. 1, originally published in 1987, appeared in 1989 in the G.I.A. edition. This was followed by companion volumes *Enemy of Apathy: Songs of the Passion and Resurrection of Jesus, and the Coming of the Holy Spirit,* Vol. 2, (1988/1990), and *Love from Below: The Seasons of Life, the Call to Care, and the Celebrating Community*, Vol. 3 (1989/1991).

270 Kenneth R. Hull, "A Decade of Wild Goose Songs," *Reformed Liturgy and Music* 34:2 (2000), 20.

271 A complete listing of available materials from Iona may be found at www.ionabooks.com with an additional link to song resources and recordings. In the United States, see GIA Publications, Inc.: http://www.giamusic.com/product_search.cfm?loc=series&advanced=1&series=Iona and the Book Service of The Hymns Society in the United States and Canada, www.thehymnsociety.org/books, for publications by John Bell and the Iona Community. All sites accessed on March 22, 2013.

272 Correspondence with John Bell, May 13, 2008.

273 Correspondence with Graham Maule, August 31, 2007.

274 Correspondence with John Bell, May 13, 2008.

275 Correspondence with Graham Maule, August 31, 2007.

276 John L. Bell and Graham Maule, *Heaven Shall Not Wait: Songs of Creation, the Incarnation, and the Life of Jesus* (Chicago: GIA Publications, Inc., ([1987], 1989), 8.

277 Bell and Maule, *Heaven Shall Not Wait*, 8.

278 John L. Bell and Graham Maule, *The Courage to Say No: Twenty-three Songs for Lent and Easter* (Chicago: GIA Publications, 1996), 4.

279 *Heaven Shall Not Wait*, 7.

280 John L. Bell, ed., *Sent By the Lord: Songs of the World Church*, Vol. 2 (Chicago: GIA Publications, Inc., [1991], 1992), 7.

281 For example, see *Come All You People: Shorter Songs for Worship* (1994) in which the theme song comes from Zimbabwe, *The Courage to Say No: Twenty-three Songs for Lent and Easter* (1996), and *Love + Anger: Songs of Lively Faith and Social Justice* (1997) with songs from Rwanda, Pakistan, South Africa, India and South America along with Western folk materials and original melodies.

282 Oliver Davies and Fiona Bowie, *Celtic Christian Spirituality: An Anthology of Medieval and Modern Sources* (London: SPCK, 1995), 38.

283 *Love From Below*, 6.

284 Stanza 1, "The Carol of the Nativity," *Heaven Shall Not Wait*, 46.

285 Stanzas one and five, and the refrain, "The Beggar," *Love from Below*, 61.

286 "We Met You," *Heaven Shall Not Wait*, 12-13.

287 "Today I Awake," *Love From Below*, 13.

288 Stanzas one and two, "Easter Evening," *Enemy of Apathy*, 68-69.

289 Stanza one, "Happy is the one," John L. Bell, *Psalms of Patience, Protest and Praise* (Chicago, GIA Publications, Inc., 1993), 4.

290 Stanzas 1 and 2, *Psalms of Patience, Protest and Praise*, **48-49**.

291 John L. Bell, *Innkeepers and Light Sleepers: Seventeen New Songs for Christmas* (Chicago, GIA Publications, Inc., 1992), 7.

292 While there is merit to Bell's opposition to the literal biblical accuracy of Rossetti's use of snow at the actual time and place of the Nativity, I find Rossetti's ability to paint a metaphorical picture of the world's bleakness and longing to be effective. If fault is to be found, it is not with Rossetti but with the assumption that northern world images of cold and snow should be transplanted to the southern hemisphere, where a heat wave often occurs during Christmas. For an alternative southern hemisphere Christmas hymn, see New Zealander Shirley Erena Murray's hymn "Carol our Christmas, an Upside Down Christmas."

293 Bell, *Innkeepers and Light Sleepers*, 7.

294 Quoted in Bradley, *Abide with Me*, 245.

295 The entire infamous stanza reads,
"The rich man in his castle,
The poor man at his gate,
God made them, high or lowly,
And ordered their estate."
Lionel Adey, *Hymns and the Christian "Myth"* (Vancouver: University of British Columbia Press, 1986), referring to this stanza notes, "Idolatry comes in when a system that reflects the economic and power structure of a given time and place is treated as divinely ordained and immutable. For long periods before the scientific and industrial revolutions, the divine will and the social structure were easily confounded" (12). In all fairness, however, perhaps this stanza should be read in the light of one that Alexander wrote two years earlier in 1846 in a collection entitled, *Verses for Holy Seasons*:
"The poor man in his straw-roofed cottage,
The rich man in his lordly hall,
The old man's voice, the child's first whisper,
He listens, and He answers all."
296 "Justice in the Womb," *Innkeepers*, 20–21.
297 John Bell, "Flight of the Wild Goose," 18. *Common Ground* is imported from Scotland and available from GIA Publications, Inc.
298 Hull, "A Decade of Wild Goose Songs," 24.
299 Bell describes how to approach congregational singing in his books *The Singing Thing: A Case for Congregational Song* (Chicago: GIA Music, 2000) and *The Singing Thing Too* (Chicago: GIA Music, 2007).
300 Introduction, *Heaven Shall Not Wait*, 7.

—Final Stanza—

Final Stanza

Streams and Tributaries

C. Michael Hawn

What about the future of congregational song? In a slim, posthumously published volume, Erik Routley outlines the history of Western hymnody from the perspective of congregational song. Using a center-periphery model, Routley compares songs created nearer to the centers of ecclesial authority with songs coming from the fringe, noting that, "hymns . . . have flourished most vigorously on the far edges of the church: at what some might call its growing points and others its vulnerable or even heretical points."[1] As we have already seen, what were once the "edges" of the church's witness world-wide have now become the center of Christian growth.

In an interview with Kenneth Hull in 1990, John Bell continues along a similar line of thinking, placing the role of the Taizé and Iona Communities in the broader context of institutional churches using a center-periphery spectrum:

> I think that always in the church you've had people who work in the center, and those who work at the periphery. And, when historically and biblically the folk at the center haven't

managed to communicate the goods, sometimes it has been the people on the periphery like the prophets who have done that. Now, I think in present-day ecclesiastical terms a lot of the churches in Western Europe are now very self-obsessed: with property and buildings, with their tradition, and with the fact that people don't come. And, when you're very obsessed with your own existence, then I think you lose the edge on material that might speak to people today who are disenchanted with the church but who still would want to hang in with some kind of religious faith. And, because Taizé and Iona in their respective countries are on the kind of margins of the church and set back as it were from central church structures and church bureaucracy and church terminology and language, I think we are maybe given the possibility to respond in a way that has more imagination in it.[2]

If nothing else, I hope that the essays contained in this book have caused readers to question their assumptions concerning who is at the center and who is on the fringe of the creative process of congregational song. Indeed, congregational singing in the twenty-first century is not about who is at the center or the periphery. The migration of peoples and accessibility of various forms of media have facilitated a hymnological flat earth that is limited only by provincial attitudes, lack of imagination, and inadequate pedagogical understanding. Hymnals since the mid-1980s have by and large opened the ecumenical and global world of congregational song to us.

Furthermore, this book has attempted to demonstrate that congregational song in North America has increased in quantity and diversity during the last half of the twentieth century and the initial decade of the twenty-first century. Streams, however, are never static. In quiet, almost imperceptible ways streams change the landscape, crossing one another, forming new streams, deepening in some places while becoming shallower in others.

How might such a survey look in 2050? I propose that we will have more streams than now. Given the exploding population of Latinos throughout the United States, at least one stream devoted to Spanish-language congregational song will be necessary. The many currents found in African-American congregational song may divide and form separate streams. Hip Hop and Rap, for example, already shows signs of becoming a significant voice in the African-American church.[3] These forms may be claimed by other ethnic groups as well. Stream seven, Ecumenical Global Song, is already potentially overflowing its banks. As communities who represent these songs continue to immigrate to North America, they may require separate and broader consideration. New voices are emerging, including Stuart Townend's Celtic sounds, which are being embraced across many streams. The Emergent Church movement is producing a plethora of grassroots musicians, some of who will find broader acceptance. Increasingly, texts and music will cross streams. For example, a stream two classical text may be set to Stream Six music.[4] Regardless, this overview is but a point along the journey in the continuing expansion of congregational song.

What is perhaps most needed in the church is the recognition that congregational song, in the words of Albert van den Heuval, not only tells us "who we are" as the gathered body of Christ, but also describes who we may become. Spiritual formation through congregational singing has often been acknowledged, but less often fully explored. The church needs to recognize and nourish those who have the gifts to teach us to sing. This office, be it labeled cantor, worship leader, *animateur*, or, as I have suggested elsewhere, enlivener,[5] is one of the most important positions in the life and worship of the church. Those who assume this role must be musically trained, theologically astute, and liturgically sensitive. It is one skill to elicit song from a dedicated group of choral musicians or a semi-professional praise team. It is another gift to draw out of the congregation its song.

To some, this book may be an attempt to describe the field of congregational singing from a North American perspective at the cusp of the twenty-first century. Though this is accurate, the implications of this study may be greater. This book may also be a broad description of Christian spirituality in North America through the lens of congregational song.[6] In addition to providing a broad overview of Christian spirituality in North America the spectrum of seven streams may be a way to understand the underlying spirituality of a particular congregation. Indeed, understanding the heart song that is at the core of a congregation's sung faith is a primary way of establishing the theological and liturgical identity of an assembly. A congregation, however, is also a part of the church universal. A stream that is not expanding is by nature gradually shrinking. Healthy congregational singing is organic by nature—rooted in a life-giving, identity-shaping source while responding to the evolving environment that surrounds it. On the one hand, a song diet that lacks an understanding of the contributions of the saints may atrophy. On the other hand, a song diet that dwells in the past may be in danger of contributing to a liturgical museum. A healthy singing congregation sings with the saints, both past and present. It sings deeply from within its faith tradition and widely from the witness of the broader church. The path toward this fuller experience of singing varies from congregation to congregation. The song of the people at its best forms faith, shapes identity, and nourishes community. Congregational singing in North America, increasingly a counter-cultural movement, provides an important indicator of the spiritual identity and health of a congregation.

Finally, all our songs are, at best, penultimate in their significance. As long as the Spirit moves, the church will continue to sing and create new songs. When we allow ourselves to be inhabited by the people's song, we join with the saints who have born witness of faith through the centuries past, connect with the breadth of the church universal now, and hear the echoes of eternity coming back to us from the cosmos. Singing in worship provides a cosmic connection with the faithful of the past, those who struggle in the present, and the all who long for the fulfillment of our hopes. Singing connects the temporal existence of humanity with the eternal realm of the cosmos. Aurelius Clemens Prudentius, the fourth-century Spanish monk, recognized the cosmic joining of earth and heaven in his hymn on the nature of Christ:

O ye heights of heaven adore him;
Angel hosts, his praises sing;
Powers, dominions, bow before him,
And extol our God and King;

Let no tongue on earth be silent,
Every voice in concert ring,
Evermore and evermore.

(Trans. John Mason Neale, 1851)

Notes —

1 Kenneth Hull, "An Interview with John Bell," *The Hymn* 43:1 (January 1992), 5.
3 In addition to many YouTube sites and other examples available on the Internet, see, for example, a collection published by the Episcopal Church, USA: *The Hip Hop Prayer Book*, ed. Timothy Holder (Harrisburg, PA: Church Publishing, 2006).
4 For example, Lim Swee Hong provides a Praise and Worship-style setting for Charles Wesley's "Ye Servants of God" in *Global Praise 2*, eds. S T Kimbrough, Jr., and Carlton R. Young (New York: GBGMusik, 2004), 116.
5 See C. Michael Hawn, *Gather into One: Praying and Singing Globally* (Grand Rapids, MI: Wm. B. Eerdmans, 2003), chapter 7, for a discussion of the role of the enlivener.
6 I explore this theme more substantially in "Streams of Song: The Landscape of Christian Spirituality in North America," in *The Changing World Religion Map*, ed. Stanley D. Brunn (Dordrecht, the Netherlands: Springer, 2013).

Appendix A
Seven Streams of Song:

An Overview of Congregational Song Since Vatican II

An Overview of Seven Streams of Song: Congregational Song since Vatican II

©C. Michael Hawn, Perkins School of Theology, Southern Methodist University

1. Roman Catholic Liturgical Renewal Hymnody	2. Protestant Contemporary Classical Hymnody	3. African American Spirituals and Gospel Songs	4. Revival/Gospel Songs	5. Folk Song Influences	6. Pentecostal Songs Azusa Street Revival (1906)	7. Global and Ecumenical Song Forms
Themes: Sacraments Psalm settings Lectionary Community Offices Refrain forms	Themes: Justice/Environ Lectionary Scriptural paraphrases Worship and the Arts Inclusive Lang. Sacraments Christian Year	Themes: Personal experience Salvation Refuge in times of trouble Praise of God	Themes: Salvation Spreading the Gospel Christological focus Triumphal Faith	Themes: Scriptural storytelling Narratives Social concerns Guitar	Themes: Praise of God Adoration of Jesus Use of scriptural fragments Personal, first person	Themes: Freedom Justice Liturgical music Liturgical Inculturation Modern Missions Sung prayer
Precursors: Of the Father's Love O Come, O Come Emmanuel" Where Charity and Love Prevail	Precursors: God of Grace and God of Glory (Fosdick) Hope of the World (Harkness) Lift High the Cross (Kitchin-Newbolt) Where Cross the Crowded Ways (North)	Precursors: Lift every Voice and Sing (Johnson) Precious Lord We Shall Overcome Sweet, Sweet Spirit (Akers) Stand by Me (Tindley) Leave it There (Tindley) Yes, God is Real (Morris)	Precursors: 19th Century Gospel Songs Early 20th Century Contributions: Great is Thy Faithfulness (Chisholm) How Great Thou Art (Boberg-Hine) Victory in Jesus (Bertlett)	**Precursors:** O Love, How Deep Tomorrow Shall be My Dancing Day Let There Be Peace on Earth (Miller-Jackson) Blowing in the Wind (Dylan) To Everything Turn (Seeger)	Precursors: Spirit of the Living God (Iverson) His Name is Wonderful (Mieir) There's Something About that Name (Gaither) Publishers: Hosanna/ Integrity Maranatha CCLI	Precursors: Many and Great, O God (Renville) Here, O Lord, Your Servants Gather (Yamaguchi-Stowe) In Christ There is No East or West (Oxenham)

Appendix A

1. Examples:
- Alleluia, Give Thanks (Fishel)
- Blest Are They (Haas)
- Cantemos al Señor (Rosas)
- Celtic Alleluia
- Cuando el Pobre
- Gather Us In (Haugen)
- Here I Am, Lord (Schutte)
- Make Me a Channel (Sebastian)
- My Soul Gives Glory (Winter)
- On Eagle's Wings (Joncas)
- One Bread, One Body (J Foley)
- Santo, Santo, Santo (Cuéllar)
- Taste and See
- Te Ofrecemos Padre Nuestro (Misa Popular Nicaragüense)
- Tú has venido (Gabarain)
- Una Espiga
- You Satisfy the Hungry Heart (Westendorf)

2. Examples:
- Jubilate Group (UK)
- All Who Love and Serve Your City (Routley)
- Blessed be the God of Israel (Perry)
- Earth Prayer (Murray)
- God of Many Names (Wren)
- God of the Sparrow (Vajda)
- I Come with Joy (Wren)
- O Day of peace (Daw)
- Silence, Frenzied, Unclean Spirit (Troeger)
- Tell Out My Soul (Dudley-Smith)
- We Utter Our Cry (Kaan)
- What does the Lord Require (Bayly)
- When in Our Music (Pratt Green)
- Womb of Life (Duck)

3. Examples:
- Appearance of Spirituals in mainline hymnals
- Bless the Lord (Crouch)
- Come Sunday (Ellington)
- Give me a clean heart (Douroux)
- Let It Breaathe on Me (Lewis-Butts)
- My Tribute (Crouch)
- Praise Ye the Lord (Cleveland)
- Someone asked the Question (Franklin)
- The Lamb (M McKay)
- The Lord is in His Holy Temple (G Burleigh)
- Through It All (Crouch)
- Total Praise (Smallwood)

4. Examples:
- Because He Lives (Gaither)
- Freely, Freely (Owens)
- He Touched Me (Gaither)
- People Need the Lord (Nelson & McHugh)
- Share His Love (Reynolds)
- Shine, Jesus, Shine (Kendrick)

5. Examples:
- Bring Forth the Kingdom (Haugen)
- I Was There to hear Your Borning Cry (Ylvisaker)
- Lord of the Dance (Carter)
- Pass It On (Kaiser)
- She Comes Sailing (Light)
- The First One Ever (Egan)
- Two Fisherman (Toolan)
- We Are the Church (Avery & Marsh)
- What Does the Lord Require (Strathdee)
- When Jesus the Healer (P Smith)
- Use of Southern Folk Tunes and Shaped-note melodies
- British, Irish and Scottish tunes

6. Examples:
- Alleluia (Sinclair)
- As the Deer (Nystrom)
- Awesome God (Mullins)
- El Shaddai (Card-Thompson)
- Emmanuel, Emmanuel (McGee)
- Great is the Lord (Smith)
- How Majestic is Your Name (Smith)
- I Love You Lord (L Klein)
- Majesty, Worship His Majesty (Hayford)
- My Life is in You (Gardner)
- Seek Ye First (Lafferty)
- Shout to the Lord (Zshech)
- Spirit Song (Wimber)
- Thy Word is a Lamp (Grant)
- We Will Glorify (Paris)

7. Examples:
Taizé chants:
- Bless the Lord
- Ubi caritas

Africa:
- Jesu, Jesu (Colvin)
- Jesu Tawa Pano
- Thuma Mina Siyahamba (Nyberg: *Freedom is Coming*)

Asia:
- Saranam, (D. T. Niles)
- Come Now, O Prince of Peace (Lee)

South America:
- Tenemos Esperanza (Pagura)

Iona:
- Goodness Is Stronger Than Evil
- Will You Come and Follow me

Leaders:
- John Bell
- David Dargie
- I-to Loh
- P Matsikenyiri
- Pablo Sosa

357

Appendix B
Stream Seven—

Sources for Hymns Cited

African Songs Cited with sources

Key: ELW *Evangelical Lutheran Worship* (2006)
      FWS *The Faith We Sing* (2000)
      GP1 *Global Praise 1* (1996)
      GP2 *Global Praise 2* (2000)
      GP3 *Global Praise 3* (2004)
      SNG *Sing! A New Creation* (2001)
      PCH *Panorama of Christian Hymnody* (Rev. ed. 2005)
      UMH *The United Methodist Hymnal* (1989)

Sources	PCH	UMH	GP1	GP2	GP3	FWS	ELW	SNC
Freedom is Coming (South Africa)						2192		
God sends us His Spirit (Colvin)	929							
Gracious Spirit (Niwaglia)	927				104		401	166
Haleluya! Pelo tsa rona (South Africa)							535	263
Halleluya (Maraire)					22			
Jesu, tawa pano (Matsikenyiri)			36			2273	529	5
Jesus, we want to meet (Olude)		661						
Kyrie eleison (Reindorf)					35			50, 53
Masithi-Amen siakudimisa (Molefe)			4			2067	846	
Njoo kwetu, Roho mwema (Niwaglia)	927				104		401	166
**Nkosi Sikelel' iAfrika (Sontonga)								
*Nkosi, Nkosi (Xhosa)								
*Ntsikana's Song								
Siyahamba (South Africa)						2235	866	293
That Boy-Child of Mary (Colvin)	930						293	
Thuma mina (Xhosa) (Send Me, Lord)		497					549 809	280
Uyai mose (Gondo)						2274	819	
Uyai mweya wakachena (Matsikenyiri)				83				
Wa wa wa (Aladura)				64		2124		4
Yesu, Yesu (Jesu, Jesu) Fill Us with Your Love (Colvin)	928	432					708	

*These songs are included in C. Michael Hawn, *Halle, Halle: We Sing the World Round* (Garland, TX: Choristers Guild, 1999).
**Because of its nationalistic nature, this important song is not in North American hymnals. It may be found easily in a variety of arrangements and languages on the Internet.

Caribbean, Central and Latin American Songs Cited

Key: PCH *Panorama of Christian Hymnody* (2005)
        GP1 *Global Praise 1* (1996)
        GP2 *Global Praise 2* (2000)
        GP3 *Global Praise 3* (2004)
        Him *El Himnario (1998).
        Him **El Himario Presbiteriano* (1999).
        Him *Himnario Unido (1999)
        FyC *Flor y Canto* (2001).
        LLC *Libro de Liturgia y Cántico*, (1998).
        MVC *Mil Voces Para Celebrar* (1996).

*The contents of these hymnals are the same.

Appendix B

Sources	PCH	GP1	GP2	GP3	Him	FyC	LLC	MVC
Arriba los corazones (Jaén)			41		258	611	396	323
Bendito el Rey (Pagura)	975				67		334	134
Canção da caminhada (Monteiro)		15						
Cantai ao Senhor/Cantad al Señor (Brazil)				57	1		598	
Cantemos al Señor (Rosas)	966				5		600	20
Cristo Vive (Hoy celebramos) (Arias)					165		353	150
Cristo vive (Martínez)	973							
Darkness now enfolds us (Jordan)			56					
El cielo canta alegría (Sosa)			28		26	403	575	271
En el principio (Rosas)	967							
En medio de la vida (Arias)	976				355		512	375
Enter into Jerusalem (Lung)			3					
Fruto del amor divino (Prudentius/Pagura)					83		318	52
Halle, Halle, Hallelujah (Mulrain)	969	31						
How great your name (Jordan)				14				
Jesús es mi Rey soberano (Mendoza)	963				42		569	54
Le lo le lo lay lo (Santo) (Loperena)			24					
Mantos y Palmas (Ruíz)	964				132		33	136
Mil voces para celebrar (C Wesley/Pagura)					47		578	1
¡Miren, qué bueno! (Sosa)	972	41			218		468	278
Momento Novo/ Momento nuevo (Brazil)	980					687	490	290
Porque él venció (Pagura)							478	
Porque hay un mundo (Pagura)							579	
Pues si vivimos (Mexico)	965				282		462	378
Santo, Santo, Santo, mi corazon (Argentina)		49						

Sources	PCH	GP1	GP2	GP3	Him	FyC	LLC	MVC
Santo, santo, santo (Cuéllar)					10	637	273	33
¿Señor, qué es nuestro templo si tu no estas presente? (Pagura)					19			373
Solitario (Pagura)								
Somos pueblo que camina					252		393	
Te Ofrecemos Padre Nuestro					246			322
Tenemos Esperanza (Pagura)	974				397		458	129
The right hand of God (Prescod)		60						
The thirsty deer longs for the steam (Mulrain)		24						
There was a man named Jonah (Mulrain)			31					
Todo acabó en una tumba (Pagura)							346	
Tua Palavra é lâmpada (Monteiro)			33					
Tua Palavra na vida/Esa palbra en la vida (Monteiro)		65			315			
Um menino (Monteiro)	978							
Vamos todos al banquete (Cuéllar)			36				410	292
Vem, Jesus nossa esperança/ Ven Jesús, nuestra esperanza (Maraschin)	977				60			
Vem, Santo Espiritu/ Ven, oh Tú que haces nuevos (Monteiro)	979				178			

APPENDIX B

Asian Hymnody Song Sources Cited

Key: STB (*Sound the Bamboo*, 2000)
      UMH (*The United Methodist Hymnal*, 1989)
      GP1   *Global Praise 1* (1996)
      GP2   *Global Praise 2* (2000)
      GP3   *Global Praise 3* (2004)

Sources	STB	UMH	GP1	GP2	GP3
Call Me By My Name (Liew)	265				
Chhi-phe ho he sio (Watch the Bush of Thorns) (Kao)	252				
Chin Chu Siong-te cho thi^n toe (God Created Heaven and Earth) Taiwan/Boris and Clare Anderson	173	151			
Dong tian yi wang, yu shui yi zhi (Winter has Passed, the Rain is O'er)	71		20		
Esho hae Probhu (Come, Lord Jesus Christ) (Shaha)	8				129
God of Creation (Thangaraj)			8		
Here, O Lord, Your Servants Gather (Yamaguchi)	242	552			
Hunger Carol (Child of Joy and Peace)	144		17		
*I was glad					
Jeya Ho (Hindi)	39	478			
Karthaadhi Karthar Iveree (This is the God Beyond all Gods) (Celliah)	139				
Kay Laking Hiwaga (What a Great Mystery) (Feliciano)	82				49/50
Khudaayaa, raeham kar (Have Mercy on Us, Lord) (Liberius)	120				
Lirih terdengar lagu kasih yang merdu (Soft the Master's Love Song) (Pantou)	203				
Mary's Salidummay (Kiley)	102				

Sources	STB	UMH	GP1	GP2	GP3
Matulog pa, bunsong mahal (Sleep Through the Night, Beloved Child) (Tinio)	277				
Now Let Us Tell of Your Victory (Liew)	22				
Nyanyikanlah nyanyian baru (Sing the Lord a New Song) (Tinio)	100			13	
Ocean of Love (Thangaraj)			50		
Ohoradiya (Lee)	101				
O-so-so (Come Now, O Prince of Peace) (Lee)	241		16/16a		
Phra-kham phi sawn hai rao ruu jak (From the Bible We Learn God's Will) (Sriswan)	217				
Qing zao qi-lai kan (Rise to Greet the Sun) (Chao Tzu-ch'en/Hu Te-ai/Wiant)	155	678			
*Rejoice, Hallelu					
Saranam, Saranam (Refuge) (Niles)	59	523			
Sarennam, O Divine Light (Dyvasirvadum)	47				
Sayur kubis jatuh harga (Oh, The Cabbage Price is Falling) (Tarigan)	313				
The Rice of Life (Fowler)	190				
Yellaam Yesuvee (Christ is All to Me) (Gnanamani)	55				

*These songs are included in C. Michael Hawn, *Halle, Halle: We Sing the World Round* (Garland, TX: Choristers Guild, 1999).

Bibliography

Abbington, James. *Let Mt. Zion Rejoice! Music in the African American Church*. Valley Forge: Judson Press, 2001.

____, ed. *Readings in African American Church Music and Worship*. Chicago: GIA Publications, 2001.

Adams, Jere V., ed. *Handbook to the Baptist Hymnal*. Nashville: Convention Press, 1992.

Adey, Lionel. *Hymns and the Christian "Myth"*. Vancouver: University of British Columbia Press, 1986.

Agawu, Kofi. *African Rhythm: A Northern Ewe Perspective*. Cambridge University Press, 1995.

____. *Representing African Music: Postcolonial Notes, Queries, Positions*. New York: Routledge, 2003.

Akins, Debra. "Praise and Worship Tours on the Rise," *Billboard* 116:17 (April 24, 2004): 20.

Apel, Willi. *Harvard Dictionary of Music*, 2nd ed. Cambridge, MA: Belknap Press of Harvard Univ. Press, 1969.

Axelsson, Olof. *African Music and European Christian Mission*. Masters Thesis, Uppsala University, 1971.

____. "The Development of African Church Music in Zimbabwe," *Papers Presented at the Symposium on Ethnomusicology*. Grahamstown, South Africa: Rhodes University, September 24-26, 1981, 2-7.

Baker, Frank. *Representative Verse of Charles Wesley*. Nashville: Abingdon, 1962.

Balado, J. L. Gonzalez. *Story of Taizé*. New York: Continuum International Publishing Group, 2003.

Bangert, Mark Paul. "Dynamics of Liturgy and World Musics: A Methodology for Evaluation," In *Worship and Culture in Dialogue*, edited by. S. Anita Stauffer, 183-203. Geneva: Lutheran World Federation, 1994.

_____. "Liturgical Music, Culturally Tuned," *Liturgy and Music: Lifetime Learning*, edited by Robin A. Leaver and Joyce Ann Zimmerman, 360-383. Collegeville, MN; The Liturgical Press, 1998.

_____. "Welcoming the Ethnic into our Church Musical Diet." *Cross Accent: Journal of the Association of Lutheran Church Musicians* 5 (January 1995): 4-7.

Bangsund, Judith A. "Hymns as Theological Expression: A Case Study in the Evangelical Lutheran Church in Tanzania." *Africa Theological Journal* 24:1 (March 2001): 77-95.

Batastini, Robert. "Songs from the Community of Taizé." In *Sing! A New Creation: Leader's Edition*, edited by Emily Brink, 418-419. Grand Rapids: CRC Publications, 2002.

Beary, Shirley L. "The Stamps-Baxter Music and Printing Company: A Continuing American Tradition, 1926-1976." DMA diss., Southwestern Baptist Theological Seminary, 1977.

Bell, John L. "Flight of the Wild Goose," *Reformed Liturgy and Music* 34:2 (2000): 15-18.

_____. *Innkeepers and Light Sleepers: Seventeen New Songs for Christmas*. Chicago: GIA Publications, Inc., 1992.

_____. *Psalms of Patience, Protest and Praise*. Chicago: GIA Publications, Inc., 1993.

_____. "Reforming Worship: Change is Not a Dirty Word," *Reformed Worship* 40 (June 1996): 5-11.

_____, ed. *Sent By the Lord: Songs of the World Church*, Vol. 2. Chicago: GIA Publications, Inc., [1991], 1992.

_____. *The Singing Thing: A Case for Congregational Song*. Chicago: GIA Music, 2000.

_____. *The Singing Thing Too*. Chicago: GIA Music, 2007.

_____. *Wrestle and Fight and Pray: Thoughts on Christianity and Conflict*. Edinburgh: Saint Andrew Press, 1993.

Bell, John L. and Graham Maule. *Enemy of Apathy: Songs of the Passion and Resurrection of Jesus, and the Coming of the Holy Spirit*, Vol. 2. Chicago: GIA Publications, Inc., [1988] 1990.

_____. *Heaven Shall Not Wait: Songs of Creation, the Incarnation, and the Life of Jesus*, Vol. 1. Chicago: GIA Publications, Inc., [1987] 1989.

_____. *Love + Anger: Songs of Lively Faith and Social Justice*. Glasgow: Wild Goose Publications, 1997.

_____. *Love from Below: The Seasons of Life, the Call to Care, and the Celebrating Community*, Vol. 3. Chicago: GIA Publications, Inc., [1989] 1991.

_____. *The Courage to Say No: Twenty-three Songs for Lent and Easter*. Chicago: GIA Publications, 1996.

Best, Harold M. *Music Through The Eyes of Faith*. New York: Harper Collins, 1993.

Bishops Committee on the Liturgy. *Music in Catholic Worship*. Washington, DC: National Conference of Catholic Bishops, 1972, 1982.

Blacking, John. *How Musical Is Man?* Seattle: University of Washington Press, 1973.

Blount, Brian K. and Leonora Tubbs Tisdale, eds. *Making Room at the Table: an invitation to multicultural worship*. Louisville, KY: Westminster John Knox Press, 2001.

Boccardi, Donald. *The History of American Catholic Hymnals Since Vatican II*. Chicago: GIA Publications, Inc., 2001.

Bokwe, John Knox. *Ntsikana: The Story of an African Convert*, 2nd ed. Lovedale, South Africa: Lovedale Mission Press, 1914.

Bohlman, Philip V. *World Music: A Very Short Introduction*. New York: Oxford University Press, 2002.

Boyer, Horace C. "African American Gospel Music," *African Americans and The Bible: Sacred Texts and Social Textures,* edited by Vincent L. Wimbush, 464-488. New York: Continuum, 2000.

_____. "An Analysis of His Contributions: Thomas A Dorsey: 'Father of Gospel Music,'" *Black World* 23:9 (July, 1974): 21-22.

Bradshaw, Paul F. *The Search for the Origins of Christian Worship: Sources and Methods for the Study of Early Liturgy,* 2nd ed. New York, NY: Oxford University Press, 2002.

Bradley, Ian. *Abide with Me: The World of Victorian Hymns*. London: SCM Press, 1997. 2nd ed. London: Faber and Faber, 2011.

_____. *Columba: Pilgrim and Penitent*. Glasgow: Wild Goose Publications, 1996.

Brother Jean-Marie of Taizé, "Jubilate Deo Award: Building a Bridge of Reconciliation." *Pastoral Music* 31:1 (October-November 2006): 43-46.

_____. "Prayer at Taizé: Singing and Silence." *Christian Century* 118:10 (March 2001): 16-17.

Brink, Emily R. "Acts and Letters: Song Search Results." *Reformed Worship* 79(March, 2006): 26-27

_____. "Erik Routley as Hymn Writer and Composer." *The Hymn*. 53 (October 2002): 4-7.

_____. "Glimpses of Recent Chinese Hymnody: Including a Review of the 2006 Edition of *Hymns of Universal Praise*." *The Hymn* 59:2 (Spring 2008): 8-24.

Brink, Emily and Bert Polman, eds. *Psalter Hymnal Handbook*. Grand Rapids, Michigan: CRC Publications, 1998.

Brooks, Christopher. "Foreign-Indigenous Interchange: The Yoruba," *Africa. The Garland Encyclopedia of World Music*, Volume 1, edited by Ruth M. Stone, 400-414. New York: Garland Publishing, Inc., 1998.

Brunn, Stanley D., ed. *The Changing World Religion Map*. Dordrecht, the Netherlands: Springer, 2013.

Carmichael, Alexander. *Carmina Gadelica*. Edinburgh: Floris Books, [1900-1928], 1992.

Canedo, Ken. *Keep the Fire Burning: The Folk Mass Revolution*. Portland, OR: Pastoral Press, 2009.

Carey, William. *An Enquiry into the Obligations of Christians to Use Means for the Conversion of the Heathens in which the Religious State of the Different Nations of the World, the Success of Former Undertakings, and the Practicability of Further Undertakings are Considered*. Leicester, England: 1792. Accessed April 6, 2013. www.wmcarey.edu/carey/enquiry/anenquiry.pdf.

Chernoff, John Miller. *African Rhythm and African Sensibility: Aesthetics and Social Action in African Musical Idioms*. Chicago: University of Chicago Press, 1979.

Christensen, Phil and Shari MacDonald. *Our God Reigns: The Stories Behind Your Favorite Praise and Worship Songs*. Grand Rapids, MI: Kregel Publications, 2000.

Christensen, Richard L., ed. *How Shall We Sing the Lord's Song: An Assessment of The New Century Hymnal*. Craigville, MA: Confessing Christ, 1997.

Chupungco, Anscar. *Liturgical Inculturation: Sacramental, Religiosity, and Catechesis*. Collegeville, MN: The Liturgical Press, 1992.

Clyde, Arthur G. *The Language of the New Century Hymnal*. Cleveland: The Pilgrim Press, 1996.

Collins, Dori Erwin and Scott C. Weidler. *Sound Decisions: Evaluating Contemporary Music for Lutheran Worship*. Minneapolis: Augsburg Fortress Press, 1997.

Colombari, Bari and Michael Prendergast, eds. *The Song of the Assembly: Pastoral Music in Practice.* Portland, OR: Pastoral Press, 2007.

Colvin, Tom. *Come, Let Us Walk this Road Together: 43 Songs from Africa.* Carol Stream, IL: Hope Publishing Company, 1997.

Cone, James H. *Speaking the Truth: Ecumenism, Liberation, and Black Theology.* Grand Rapids, MI: William B. Eerdmans Publishing Co., 1986.

Cone, James H. *The Spiritual and the Blues.* Maryknoll, NY: Orbis Books, 1972.

Corbitt, J. Nathan. *The Sound of the Harvest: Music's Mission in Church and Culture.* Grand Rapids: Baker Books, 1998.

Costen, Melva Wilson. "Published Hymnals in the Afro-American Tradition." *The Hymn* 40:1 (January 1989): 7-13.

Crawford, Richard. *America's Musical Life: A History.* New York: W. W. Norton, 2001.

Crouch, Andy. "A Humbling Experience: Contemporary Worship's Simple Aesthetic," *re:generation quarterly* 3:1 (Winter 1997): 11-13.

Cross, Virginia Ann. "The Development of Sunday School Hymnody in the United States of America, 1816-1869." DMA diss., New Orleans Baptist Theological Seminary, 1985.

Cushman, Candi. "Salt or Sugar?" *World* (May 13, 2000): 23.

Dargie, David. *African Sunday Marimba Mass: Song Book*, 2nd ed. Privately published by David Dargie, 2003.

_____. "The Music of Ntsikana." *South African Journal of Musicology* 2 (1982): 7-28.

_____. *Workshops for Composing Local Church Music: Methods for Conducting Music Workshops in Local Congregations*, No. 40. Delmenville, South Africa: Lumko Missiological Institute, 1983.

_____. "Xhosa Church Music," *Music and the Experience of God,* edited by David Power, Mary Collins, and Mellonee Burnim, 62-69. Edinburgh: T. & T. Clark Ltd., 1989.

Davies, Oliver and Fiona Bowie. *Celtic Christian Spirituality: An Anthology of Medieval and Modern Sources.* London: SPCK, 1995.

Deiss, Lucian. *Spirit and Song of the New Liturgy.* Cincinnati: World Library, 1976.

de Waal, Esther. "The Celtic Way of Prayer," *Cistercian Studies Quarterly* 32:3 (1997): 367-377.

Dictionary of North American Hymnology: A Comprehensive Bibliography & Master Index of Hymns and Hymnals Published in the United

States and Canada 1640-1978. CD-ROM. Boston: The Hymn Society in the United States and Canada, 2003.

Dox, Thurston J. *American Oratorios and Cantatas: A Catalog of Works Written in the United States from Colonial Times to 1985*. Metuchen, NJ: Scarecrow Press, 1986.

DuBois, W. E. B. *The Souls of Black Folk*. New York: Dover Publications, Inc., 1903, 1994.

Durán, Lucy and Gregory Barz. "Jones, Arthur Morris," In *The New Grove Dictionary of Music and Musicians*, Vol. 13, 2nd ed, edited by Stanley Sadie and John Tyrrell, 188. New York: Oxford University Press, 2001.

Durán, Lucy. "Tracey, Hugh (Travers)," In *Grove Music Online*, edited by L. Macy. http://www.grovemusic.com. Accessed 15 June 2007.

Echols, Paul C. "Hymnody" In *The New Grove Dictionary of American Music*, edited by H. Wiley Hitchcock and Stanley Sadie, 4 vols. London: Macmillan, 1986.

Escamilla, Roberto. "Fiesta Worship," In *The Interpreter* 20 (June 1976): 2.

Eskew, Harry and Hugh T. McElrath. *Sing with Understanding: An Introduction to Christian Hymnology*, 2nd ed. Nashville: Church Street Press, 1995.

Fleming, Jo Lee. "James D. Vaughan, Music Publisher, Lawrenceburg, Tennessee, 1912-1964." SMD diss., Union Theological Seminary, 1972.

Foley, Edward, ed. *Ten-year Report of The Milwaukee Symposia for Church Composers*. Washington, D.C.: The Pastoral Press, 1992.

Foster, Marc Ashley. "*Missa Luba*: A New Edition and Conductor's Analysis." DMA diss., The University of North Carolina at Greensboro, 2005.

Frame, John M. *Contemporary Worship Music, a Biblical Defense*. Phillipsburg, NJ: Presbyterian & Reformed Publishing, 1997.

Francis, Mark R. *Liturgy in a Multicultural Community*. Collegeville: Liturgical Press, 1991.

Gaither, Bill and Ken Abraham. *It's More Than the Music: Life Lessons for Loving God, Loving Each Other*. N.pl.: Warner Faith, 2003.

Garratt, David and Dale Garratt. *Scripture in Song*, 2 vols. Auckland, NZ, Costa Mesa, Cal.: Scripture in Song, 1979-1981.

Gelineau. Joseph. *Voices and Instruments in Christian Worship*: *Principles, Laws, Applications*. Translated by Clifford Howell. London: Burns and Oates, 1964.

Goff, James R., Jr. *Close Harmony: A History of Southern Gospel*. Chapel Hill & London: University of North Carolina Press, 2002.

Gutiérrez-Achón, Raquel. "An Introduction to Hispanic Hymnody," In ¡Alabadle! *Hispanic Christian Worship*, edited by Justo L. González, 101-110. Nashville: Abingdon Press, 1996.

Haazen, Guido, arr. *Missa Luba*. New York: Lawson-Gould Music Publishers, 1969.

Hamilton, Margaret, ed. *Sing Freedom! Songs of South African Life*. London: Novello/Christian Aid, 1993.

Hamilton, Michael S. "The Triumph of the Praise Songs." *Christianity Today* 43:8 (July 12, 1999): 29-35.

Hammond, Paul Garnett. "Music in Urban Revivalism in the Northern United States, 1800-1835." DMA diss., Southern Baptist Theological Seminary, 1974.

Harmon, Kathleen. *The Ministry of Cantors*. Collegeville: Liturgical Press, 2004.

_____. *The Mystery We Celebrate, the Song We Sing: A Theology of Liturgical Music*. Collegeville: Liturgical Press, 2008.

_____. "*Sing to the Lord* and Psalmody in the Life of the Church." *Pastoral Liturgy* 41:5 (September/October 2010): 9-12.

Harrison, Douglas. *Then Sings my Soul: The Culture of Southern Gospel Music*. Champaign, IL: Univ. of IL Press, 2012.

Hawn, C. Michael. "Cantate Domino: Erik Routley and Global Song." *The Hymn* 53:4 (October 2002): 12-13.

_____. "Christian Global Hymnody: An Overview." In *Music and Mission*, edited by S T Kimbrough, Jr. New York: General Board of Global Ministries, GBGMusik, 2006.

_____. "Congregational Singing from Down Under: An Interview with Australian Robin Mann," and "Congregational Singing Down Under: The Hymns of Elizabeth Joyce Smith, Melbourne, Australia." *The Hymn* 56:4 (Fall 2005): 8-18.

_____. "Congregational Singing Down Under: An Introduction to Current Australian Hymnals." *The Hymn* 56:3 (Summer 2005): 16-21.

_____. "Congregational Singing from Down Under: Experiencing Hillsong's 'Shout to the Lord.'" *The Hymn* 57:2 (Spring 2006): 15-24.

_____. *Gather into One: Praying and Singing Globally*. Grand Rapids, MI: Wm. B. Eerdmans, 2003.

_____, ed. Halle, Halle: *We Sing the World Round. Songs for the World Church for Children, Youth, and Congregation*. Teacher's Edition. Garland, TX: Choristers Guild, 1999.

_____. *One Bread, One Body: Exploring Cultural Diversity in Worship.* Bethesda, MD: The Alban Institute, 2003.

_____. "Praying Globally—Pitfalls and Possibilities of Cross-cultural Liturgical Appropriation." In *Christian Worship Worldwide,* edited by Charles E. Farhadian, 205-229. Grand Rapids: Wm. B. Eerdmans Press, 2007.

_____. "Shaping Up: The Role of the Hymnal in Faith Formation." *Worship Leader* (January 2013). http://worshipleader.com/shapingup/. Accessed April 6, 2013.

_____. "Streams of Song: The Landscape of Christian Spirituality in North America." In *The Changing World Religion Map,* edited by Stanley D. Brunn. Dordrecht, the Netherlands: Springer, 2013.

_____. "The Consultation on Ecumenical Hymnody: An Evaluation of its influence in Selected English Language Hymnals Published in the United States and Canada since 1976." *The Hymn* 47:2 (April, 1996): 26-37.

_____. "'The Tie That Binds': A List of Ecumenical Hymns in English Language Hymnals Published in Canada and the United States Since 1976." *The Hymn* 48:3 (July 1997): 25-37.

_____. "The Truth Shall Set You Free: Song, Struggle, and Solidarity in South Africa." In *Resonant Witness: Conversations Between Music and Theology,* eds. Jeremy S. Begbie and Steven R. Guthrie, 408-433. Grand Rapids: Wm. B. Eerdmans, 2011.

_____. "The Wild Goose Sings: Themes in the Worship and Music of the Iona Community." *Worship* 74:6 (November 2000): 504-21.

Hargreaves, Sam. *Jesus Is My Girlfriend?* Dissertation, London Bible College, 2001.

Hodgson, Janet. "Ntsikana's 'Great Hymn', A Xhosa Expression of Christianity in the Early 19th Century Eastern Cape." *Communications* 4 University of Cape Town (1980): 21-31.

Holder, Timothy, ed. *The Hip Hop Prayer Book*. Harrisburg, PA: Church Publishing, 2006.

Hopkin, Mary. "African Marimba Music Hits Hermiston." *Tri-City Herald*, May 1, 2000.

Howard, Jay R. and John M. Streck. *Apostles of Rock: The Splintered World of Contemporary Christian Music.* Lexington, KY: The University Press of Kentucky, 1999.

Huijbers, Bernard. *The Performing Audience,* 2nd ed., with Redmond McGoldrick. Cincinnati: North American Liturgy Resources, 1976.

Hull, Kenneth R. "A Decade of Wild Goose Songs." *Reformed Liturgy and Music* 34:2 (2000): 20-34.

———. "An Interview with John Bell." *The Hymn* 43:1 (January 1992): 5-11.

Hustad, Donald P. *Dictionary-handbook to Hymns for the Living Church*. Carol Stream: IL; Hope Publishing Co., 1978.

———. *Jubilate II: Church Music in Worship and Renewal*. Carol Stream: Hope Publishing Company, 1993.

"Hymns and Tunes Recommended for Ecumenical Use." *The Hymn* 28:4 (October 1977): 192-209.

Incwadi Yenkonzo Nezingoma. Cape Town, South Africa: Methodist Book Depot and Publishing House, 1954.

Iona Abbey Music Book: Songs from the Iona Abbey Worship Book. Glasgow: Wild Goose Publications, 2003.

Jackson, George Pullen. *Another Sheaf of White Spirituals*. Gainesville: University of Florida Press, 1952.

———. *Down East Spirituals and Others*. New York: J. J. Augustin, 1943.

———. *Spiritual Folk-Songs of Early America*. New York: J. J. Augustin, 1937.

———. *White Spirituals in the Southern Uplands*. Chapel Hill: University of North Carolina Press, 1933.

Janssen, Jan. "God's Grace in a Tent." *The Ecumenical Review* 58:3-4 (July/October 2006): 291-296.

Janzen, John M. *Ngoma: Discourses on Healing in Central and Southern Africa*. Berkeley: University of California Press, 1992.

Jenkins, Philip. *The Next Christendom: The Coming of Global Christianity*. New York: Oxford University Press, 2002.

Jenny, Markus, Andreas Marti, and Franz Karl Prassl, eds. *Unisono: A Multilingual Book of Ecumenical Hymns*. Graz: Verlag Zeitpunkt Schnider, 1997.

Jones, Arthur M. *African Hymnody in Christian Worship: A Contribution to the History of Its Development*. Gwelo, Rhodesia: Mambo Press, 1976.

Kaatrud, Paul Gaarder. "Revivalism and the Popular Spiritual Song in Mid-nineteenth Century America: 1830-1870." PhD diss., University of Minnesota, 1977).

Krabill, James R. "'Encounters' What Happens to Music When People Meet." In *Music in the Life of the African Church*, edited by Roberta King, 57-79. Waco, Texas: Baylor University Press, 2008.

Kaemmer, John E. *Music in Human Life: Anthropological Perspectives on Music*. Austin: University of Texas Press, 1993.

_____. "Southern Africa: An Introduction," *Africa: The Garland Encyclopedia of World Music* Vol. 1, edited by Ruth M. Stone, 700-721. New York: Garland Publishing, Inc., 1998.

Kubicki, Judith Marie. *Liturgical Music as Ritual Symbol: A Case Study of Jacques Berthier's Taizé Music*. Leuven, The Netherlands, 1999.

Kimball, Dan. *The Emerging Church*. Grand Rapids, MI: Zondervan, 2003.

Kimbrough, S T, Jr., ed. *Companion to Songbooks Global Praise 1 and Global Praise 2*. New York: GMGMusik, 2005.

_____. "Practical Considerations for Promoting Global Song." *The Hymn* 51:4 (October 2000): 22-29.

_____, ed. *Toward a Theology and Practice of Global Song*. New York: General Board of Global Ministries, GBGMusik, 2006.

King, Roberta, ed. *Music in the Life of the African Church*. Waco, Texas: Baylor University Press, 2008.

Klein, Christopher. *Messekompositionen in Afrika*. Germany: Edition Re, 1990.

Klein, Joe. *Woody Guthrie: A Life*. New York: Knopf, 1980.

LaRue, John C. "Worship Style Synthesis." *Your Church* (Nov/Dec 2001): 72.

Leaver, Robin A. and James H. Litton, eds. *Duty and Delight: Erik Routley Remembered,* Executive Editor Carlton R. Young. Carol Stream, IL: Hope Publishing Company, 1985.

Leaver, Robin A. and Joyce Ann Zimmerman, eds. *Liturgy and Music: Lifetime Learning*. Collegeville, MN: Liturgical Press, 1998.

Light, Alan. "Say Amen, Somebody!" *Vibe Magazine* (October 1997): 91-94, 96.

Lim, Swee Hong. "Giving Voice to Asian Christians: An Appraisal of the Pioneering Work of I-to Loh in the Area of Congregational Song." PhD diss., Drew University, 2006.

Lincoln, C. Eric and Lawrence H. Mamiya. *The Black Church in the African American Experience*. Durham, NC: Duke University Press, 1990.

Lockward, Jorge. "Songs from Hispanic Sources." In *Sing! a New Creation: Leader's Edition*, edited by Emily Brink, 434-437. Grand Rapids: MI: CRC Publications, 2002.

Loftis, Deborah Carlton. "'For Everyone Born, A Place at the Table': Hospitality and Justice in the Hymns of Shirley Erena Murray." In *Hearts and Minds in Praise of God: Hymns and Essays in Church Music in Honor of Hugh T. McElrath*, edited by J. Michael Raley and Deborah Carlton Loftis, 237-250. Franklin, TN: Providence House Publications, 2006.

Loh, I-to. "A Glimpse at Multipart Practices in Traditional Asian Music." In *Asian Workshop on Liturgy and Music*. National Art Center, Makiling, Philippines: Asian Institute for Liturgy and Music, 1987.

_____. "Asian Christian Music." In *A Dictionary of Asian Christianity*, edited by Scott W. Sunquist, 569-574. Grand Rapids, MI: Wm. B. Eerdmans Publishing Co., 2001.

_____, ed. *Kristus Sundaring Bali* [*Christ the Light to Bali*]: *New Balinese Hymns*. Quezon City, Metro Manila: Asian Institute for Liturgy and Music, 1988.

_____, ed. *New Songs of Asian Cities*. Tokyo: East Asia Christian Conference-Urban and Industrial Mission Committee (EACC-UIM), 1972.

_____. *Rak Phra Jao, Rao Pen Thai* [*The Love of God Sets Us Free*]: *A Collection of New Thai Hymns*. Quezon City, Metro Manila: Asian Institute for Liturgy and Music, 1989.

_____. *Sound the Bamboo: Asian Hymns in Their Cultural Contexts* (a Companion to *Sound the Bamboo: C.C.A. Hymnal 2000*). Chicago, IL: GIA Publications, Inc., Forthcoming.

_____. "Tribal Music of Taiwan: With Special Reference to the Ami and Puyuma Styles." PhD diss., UCLA, 1982.

Lorenz, Ellen Jane. *Glory, Hallelujah! The Story of the Campmeeting Spiritual*. Nashville: Abingdon, 1978.

Luff, Alan. "The Twentieth-Century Hymn Explosion: Where the Fuse Was Lit." *The Hymn* 58:4 (Autumn 2007): 11-21.

MacLeod, George. *The Coracle: Rebuilding the Common Life; Foundation Documents of the Iona Community*. Glasgow: Wild Goose Publications, [1938] 1988.

Manalo, Ricky. "Sing to the Lord: Cultural Perspectives." In *Perspectives on Sing to the Lord; Essays in Honor of Robert W. Hovda, Series V*, 39-54. Silver Spring, MD: NPM Publications, 2010.

Mann, Robin, ed. *All Together* song series. Adelaide: Openbook Publishers, 1980, 1983, 1991, 1996, 2001.

Mbunga, Stephen. *Church Law and Bantu Music: Ecclesiastical Documents and Law in Sacred Music as Applied to Bantu Music*. Schieneck-Beckenried, Switzerland: Novelle Revue de Science Missionaire, Supplement 13, 1963.

Malm, William P. *Music Cultures of the Pacific, the Near East, and Asia*. Englewood Cliffs, NJ: Prentice-Hall, 1967.

Mankin, Jim. "L. O. Sanderson, Church of Christ Hymn Writer." *The Hymn* 46 (January 1995): 27-31.

Mansfield, Brian. "Praise Hymn with an Upbeat." *USA Today*, October 19, 2001.

Martínez, Raquel Mora. "A Survey of Hispanic Hymnody as Represented in *The New Century Hymnal*." In *The New Century Hymnal Companion*, edited by Kristen L. Forman, 154-162. Cleveland: Pilgrim Press, 1998.

Matsikenyiri, Patrick. *Njalo [Always]: A Collection of 16 Hymns in the African Tradition*. Edited by Dan Damon. Nashville: Abingdon Press, 2006.

Matsikenyiri, Patrick and Maggie Hamilton, eds. *Sing! Imba! Hlabela! Zimbabwe: Short Songs and New Compositions from Zimbabwean Churches*. Birmingham, UK: Christian Aid Office, 1998.

Maynard-Reid, Pedrito U. *Diverse Worship: African-American, Caribbean and Hispanic Perspectives*. Downers Grove, IL: InterVarsity Press, 2000.

McClain, William B. *Come Sunday: The Liturgy of Zion: A Companion to Songs of Zion*. Nashville: Abingdon Press, 1990.

McCullum, Hugh and Terry MacArthur, eds. *In God's Hands: Common Prayer for the World*. Geneva: World Council of Churches, 2006.

McLaren, Brian. *A Generous Orthodoxy*. Grand Rapids, MI: Zondervan, 2004.

Mensah, Atah Annan. "Compositional Practices in African Music." In *Africa: The Garland Encyclopedia of World Music*, Vol. 1, edited by Ruth M. Stone, 208-231. New York: Garland Publishing, Inc., 1998.

Millard, J. A. "John Knox Bokwe." In *Malihambe - Let the Word Spread*. Pretoria, South Africa: Unisa Press, 1999.

Miller, Donald E. *Reinventing American Protestantism: Christianity in the New Millennium*. Berkeley and Los Angeles, CA: University of California Press, 1997.

Moring, Mark. "I Could Sing of Your Love Forever." *Campus Life* 59:6 (January 2001): 20-22.

Morton, David. "Polyphonic Stratification in Traditional Thai Music." *Asia Pacific Quarterly* 1:3 (1971): 78.

Musicam sacram. Acta Apostolicae Sedis 65, 1967.

Music, David W. *Christian Hymnody in Twentieth-Century Britain and America: An Annotated Bibliography*. Westport, Connecticut: Greenwood Press, 2001.

"Nairobi Statement on Worship and Culture: Contemporary Challenges and Opportunities," *Christian Worship: Unity in Cultural Diversity,* edited by S. Anita Stauffer, 25-28. Geneva: Lutheran World Federation, 1996.

Nketia, J.H. Kwabena. *The Music of Africa*. New York: W. W. Norton, 1974.

_____. "The Scholarly Study of African Music: A Historical Review," *Africa: The Garland Encyclopedia of World Music*, Vol. 1, edited by Ruth M. Stone, 13-73. New York: Garland Publishing, Inc., 1998.

Nettl, Bruno and Ruth M. Stone, Eds. *The Garland Encyclopedia of World Music*. New York: Garland Publishing, 1998-2002.

Nyberg, Anders, ed. *Freedom Is Coming: Songs of Protest and Praise from South Africa*. Uppsala, Sweden: Utryck; Ft. Lauderdale, FL: Walton Music Corporation, 1984.

_____. *Freedom Is in Your Hand*. Ft. Lauderdale: Walton Music, 2003.

Olsen, Dale A. and Daniel E. Sheehy, eds. *The Garland Encyclopedia of World Music*, Vol. 2: *South America, Mexico, Central America, and the Caribbean*. New York: Garland Publishing, Inc., 1998.

Olson, Howard. *Lead Us, Lord*. Minneapolis: Augsburg Press, 1977.

_____. *Set Free*. Minneapolis: AugsburgFortress Press, 1993.

Peterson, John W. and Richard Engquist. *The Miracle Goes On*. Grand Rapids: Zondervan Publishing House, 1976.

Pinn, Anthony B. *The Black Church in the Post-Civil Rights Era*. Maryknoll, New York: Orbis Books, 2002.

Plantinga, Cornelius, Jr. "Theological Particularities of Recent Hymnody." *The Hymn* 52 (October 2001): 8-15.

Pecklers, Keith F. *The Unread Vision: The Liturgical Movement in the United States of America: 1926-1955*. Collegeville: Liturgical Press, 1998.

Pecklers, Keith F. and Bryan D. Spinks. "The Liturgical Movement." In *The New Westminster Dictionary of Liturgy and Worship*, edited by Paul Bradshaw, 283-289. Louisville/London: Westminster John Knox Press, 2002.

Pittman, Don. "I-to Loh: Finding Asia's Cultural Voice in the Worship of God." In *And God Gave the Increase: 1 Corinthians 3:6-9: Stories of How the Presbyterian Church (U.S.A.) Has Helped in the Education of Christian Leaders around the World*, edited by June Ramage Rogers. Louisville, KY: Office of Global Education and Leadership Development of the Worldwide Ministries Division, 1998.

Pollard, Deborah Smith. *When the Church Becomes Your Party: Contemporary Gospel Music*. Detroit: Wayne State University Press, 2008.

Power, David N. "Affirmed from Under: Celtic Liturgy and Spirituality." *Studia Liturgica* 27:1 (1997): 1-32.

Polman, Bert. "The Praise and Worship hit parade: a brief analysis of some of the most-sung choruses of 1990." *Reformed Worship* 20 (June 1991): 33-35.

Porter, Thomas Henry. "Homer Alvan Rodeheaver (1880-1955): Evangelistic Singer and Publisher." EdD diss., New Orleans Baptist Theological Seminary, 1981.

Price, Deborah Evans. "Praise and Worship Genre Blessed with Global Growth." *Billboard* (February 15, 2003): 1.

Price, Deborah Evans. "Praise & Worship: Thank Heavens for the Music!" *Billboard* (April 24, 2004). Accessed September 17, 2005 via LexisNexis.

Ramírez, Daniel. "Hymnody as Ideology in Latino Protestantism." In *Singing the Lord's Song in a Strange Land: Hymnody in the History of North American Protestantism*, edited by Edith L. Blumhofer and Mark A. Noll, 196-218. Tuscaloosa: The University of Alabama Press, 2004.

Redman, Robb. *The Great Worship Awakening: Singing a New Song in the Postmodern Church*. San Francisco: Jossey-Bass, 2002.

_____. "Welcoming to the Worship Awakening." *Theology Today* 58:3 (October 2001): 369-83.

Regocijate y Canta [*Rejoice and Sing*]. Kearney, NE: Morris Publishing, 1995.

Reynolds, William J. *Companion to Baptist Hymnal*. Nashville: Broadman, 1976.

Reynolds, William J. "The Contributions of B. B. McKinney to Southern Baptist Church Music." *Baptist History and Heritage* 21 (July 1986): 41-49.

Riccitelli, James M. "Developing Non-Western Hymnody." *Practical Anthropology* (November-December, 1962): 241-256, 270.

Romanowski, William D. "Where's the Gospel?" *Christianity Today* 41:14 (December 8, 1997): 44-45.

Rothenbusch, Esther Heidi. "The Role of *Gospel Hymns Nos. 1 to 6* (1875-1894) in American Revivalism." PhD diss., University of Michigan, 1991.

Routley, Erik. *A Panorama of Christian Hymnody*. Edited and expanded by Paul A. Richardson. Chicago: GIA, 2005.

_____. *Christian Hymns Observed*. Princeton: Prestige Publications, Inc., 1982.

_____. *Companion to Westminster Praise*. Chapel Hill, NC: Hinshaw Music, 1977.

_____. *Ecumenical Hymnody*. London: Independent Press Ltd., 1959.

_____. *Hymns Today and Tomorrow*. Nashville: Abingdon Press, 1964.

_____. *The English Carol*. New York: Oxford University Press, 1959.

Ruff, Anthony. *Sacred Music and Liturgical Reform: Treasures and Transformations*. Chicago/Mundelein: Liturgy Training Publications, 2007.

Ruth, Lester. "Lex Amandi, Lex Orandi: The Trinity in the Most Used Contemporary Christian Worship Songs," Manuscript, 2005.

Sacrosanctum Concilium. Acta Apostolicae Sedis 65, 1964.

Sadie, Stanley and John Tyrell, eds. *The New Grove Dictionary of Music and Musicians*, 2nd ed. New York: Oxford University Press, 2001.

Sadoh, Godwin. *E Korin S'Oluwa [Sing unto the Lord]: Fifty Indigenous Christian Hymns from Nigeria*. Colfax, NC: Wayne Leupold Editions, Inc., 2005.

Saliers, Don E. *Music and Theology*. Nashville: Abingdon Press, 2007.

_____. "The Integrity of Sung Prayer." *Worship* 55:4 (July 1981): 290-303.

Sanders, Cheryl J. *Saints in Exile: The Holiness-Pentecostal Experience in African American Religion and Culture*. New York: Oxford University Press, 1996.

Saward, Michael. *Jubilate Everybody: The Story of Jubilate Hymns*. London: Jubilate Hymns, 2003.

Schaefer, Robert. *Catholic Music through the Ages*. Chicago/Mundelein, IL: Liturgy Training Publications, 2008.

Scheer, Greg. *The Art of Worship: A Musician's Guide to Leading Modern Worship*. Grand Rapids: Baker Books, 2006.

Schilling, S. Paul. *The Faith We Sing*. Philadelphia: The Westminster Press, 1983.

Schoenbachler, Tim. *Folk Music in Transition: The Pastoral Challenge*. Phoenix: Pastoral Arts Associates, 1979.

Shorter, Alyward. *Toward a Theology of Inculturation*. Maryknoll, NY: Orbis Books, 1988.

Sing to the Lord: Music in Divine Worship. Washington, DC: United States Conference of Catholic Bishops, 2007.

Spencer, John Michael, Ed. Blantyre Covenant, Article 17, "The Worshipping Church in Africa." *Black Sacred Music: A Journal of Theomusicology* 7:2 (Fall 1993).

Slough, Rebecca and Shirley Sprunger King, eds. *Nurturing Spirit Through Song: The Life of Mary K. Oyer*. Telford, PA: Cascadia Publishing House, 2007.

Smith, Efrem and Phil Jackson. *The Hip-Hop Church: Connecting with the Movement Shaping Our Culture*. Downers Grove, IL: InterVarsity Press, 2005.

Spink, Kathryn. *A Universal Heart: The Life and Vision of Brother Roger of

Taize, 2nd ed. Chicago: GIA Publications, Inc., 2006.

Sosa, Pablo David. "Pagura... El Cantor," *Por Eso Es Que Tenemos Esperanza: Homenaje al Obispo Federico J. Pagura*. Quito: CLAI, 1995.

_____. "Spanish American Hymnody: A Global Perspective." *The Hymnology Annual: An International Forum on the Hymn and Worship*, Vol. 3, edited by Vernon Wicker. Berrien Springs, MI: Vande Vere Publishing Ltd, 1993.

_____., ed. *Todas Las Voces: Taller de Música y Liturgia en América Latina*. San José: Ediciones Sebila, c. 1988.

Southern, Eileen. "Hymnals of the Black Church." *Readings in African American Church Music and Worship*, edited by James Abbington, 137-151. Chicago: GIA Publications, 2001.

Spretnak, Charlene. *States of Grace: The Recovery of Meaning in the Postmodern Age*. San Francisco: HarperCollins, 1991.

Stansbury, George William, Jr. "The Music of the Billy Graham Crusades 1947-1970: An Analysis and Evaluation." DMA diss., Southern Baptist Theological Seminary, 1971.

Stevenson, W. R. "Missions, Foreign." *Dictionary of Hymnology*, edited by John Julian, 739-759. London, John Murray, 1892.

Sweet, Leonard. *Post-Modern Pilgrims*. Nashville, TN: Broadman & Holman Publishers, 2000.

_____. *SoulTsunami*. Grand Rapids: Zondervan, 1999.

Taylor, Timothy D. *Beyond Exoticism: Western Music and the World*. Durham: Duke University Press, 2007.

The Iona Community Worship Book, Rev. ed. Glasgow: Wild Goose Publications, 1991.

The Milwaukee Symposia for Church Composers: A Ten-Year Report. Washington, DC: The Pastoral Press and Chicago: Liturgy Training Publications, 1992.

The Snowbird Statement on Catholic Liturgical Music. Salt Lake City: The Madeleine Institute, 1995.

Thorsén, Stig-Magnus. "Swedish Missionaries' Image of Music in Africa." Unpublished paper presented at the Swedish—South Africa Research Network, Seminar in Pretoria, September 18-19, 2003.

Turino, Thomas. "The Music of Sub-Saharan Africa." *Excursions in World Music*, edited by Bruno Nettl, et al., 165-195. Englewood Cliffs, NJ: Prentice Hall, 1992.

Turner, Nancy M. "The *Chalice Hymnal:* Broken Bread—One Body." *The Hymn* 48:1 (January, 1997): 33-38.

Twit, Kevin. "My Grandmother Saved It, My Mother Threw It Away; and

Now I'm Buying It Back: Why Young People Are Returning to Old Hymn Texts." *Reformed Worship* 70 (December, 2003): 30-31.

van den Heuvel, Albert. *Risk: New Hymns for a New Day*. Geneva: World Council of Churches, 1966.

Vigil, José María and Angel Torrellas, eds. *Misas Centro Americana*. Managua: CAV-CEBES, 1988.

Viswanathan, T. and Matthew Harp Allen. *Music in South India: The Karnatic Concert Tradition and Beyond*. New York: Oxford University Press, 2004.

Walker, Wyatt Tee. *Somebody's Calling My Name: Black Sacred Music and Social Change*. Valley Forge, PA: Judson Press, 1979.

_____. *Spirits That Dwell in Deep Woods III*. New York: Martin Luther King Fellows Press, 1991.

_____. "The Soulful Journey of the Negro Spiritual: Freedom's Song." *Negro Digest* (July, 1963): 93-94.

_____. *The Soul of Black Worship: A Trilogy—Preaching, Praying, Singing*. New York: Martin Luther King, Jr. Fellows Press, 1984.

Watson, J. Richard, ed. *Canterbury Dictionary of Hymnology*. Canterbury and Wm. B. Eerdmans Presses, Forthcoming, 2008.

Wainwright, Geoffrey. *Doxology: The Praise of God in Worship, Doctrine, and Life.* New York: Oxford University Press, 1980.

Weman, Henry. *African Music and the Church in Africa*. Uppsala, Sweden: Studia Missionalia Uppsaliensis, Svenska Institutet för Missionforskning, 1960.

Westermeyer, Paul. *Let Justice Sing: Hymnody and Justice*. Collegeville: The Order of St. Benedict, Inc., 1998.

_____. *Let the People Sing: Hymn Tunes in Perspective*. Chicago: GIA, 2005.

What is the Iona Community? Glasgow: Wild Goose Publications, 1988.

White, James F. *Protestant Worship: Traditions in Transition*. Louisville: Westminster/John Knox, 1989.

Wiant, Allen Artz. *A New Song for China: A Biography of Bliss Mitchell Wiant*. Victoria, British Columbia: Trafford Publishing, 2005.

Wilhoit, Melvin Ross. "A Guide to the Principal Authors and Composers of Gospel Song of the Nineteenth Century." DMA diss., Southern Baptist Theological Seminary, 1982.

_____. "Sing Me a Sankey: Ira D. Sankey and Congregational Song." *The Hymn* 42 (January 1991): 16-17.

_____. "The Birth of a Classic: Sankey's 'The Ninety and Nine.'" *We'll Shout and Sing Hosanna: Essays on Church Music in Honor of*

William J. Reynolds, edited by David W. Music, 229-253. Fort Worth, TX: School of Church Music, Southwestern Baptist Theological Seminary, 1998.

_____. "Alexander the Great: Or, Just Plain *Charlie*." *The Hymn* 46 (April 1995): 20-28.

Witvliet, John D. "Expanding the Conversation: Knitting Together Worship and Congregational Life." *Reformed Worship* 79 (March 2006): 2-3.

_____. *The Biblical Psalms in Christian Worship: A Brief Ecumenical Introduction and Guide to Resources*. Grand Rapids: Wm. B. Eerdmans, 2007.

Ylvisaker, John. *What Song Shall We Sing?* Minneapolis: Augsburg Fortress, 2005.

York, Terry W. "Add One Hymn," *The Hymn: A Journal of Congregational Song,* 55:3 (July 2004): 29-33.

_____. *America's Worship War.* Peabody, MA: Hendrickson Publishers, Inc, 2003.

_____. "Charles Hutchinson Gabriel (1856-1932): Composer, Author, and Editor in the Gospel Tradition." D.M.A. diss., New Orleans Baptist Theological Seminary, 1985.

Young, Carlton R. *Companion to the United Methodist Hymnal*. Nashville: Abingdon, 1993.

_____. "Ethnic and Minority Hymns in United States Mainline Protestant Hymnals 1940-1995: Some Qualifying Considerations." *The Hymn* 49:3 (July 1998): 17-27.

_____. *Music of the Heart: John & Charles Wesley on Music and Musicians*. Carol Stream, IL: Hope, 1995.

Zhungu, L.G., chairman. *Ngoma: dze United Methodist Church Ye Zimbabwe*. Harare:Conference Board of Publications and Communications, [1964] 1995.

Contributors

James Abbington is Associate Professor of Church Music and Worship, Candler School of Theology, Emory University, Atlanta, Georgia. He holds degrees from Morehouse College, with graduate degrees from the University of Michigan (Ann Arbor), MMus, and a DMA. Dr. Abbington serves as executive editor of the African-American Church Music Series by GIA Publications, Inc. (Chicago). He served as co-director of music for the Hampton University Ministers' and Musicians' Conference. In 2010, Hampton's Choir Directors'-Organists' Guild honored Abbington by naming their Church Music Academy after him. He has also served as the national director of music for both the Progressive National Baptist Convention and the NAACP. Selected publications include *Readings in African- American Church Music and Worship* (2001), *Let Mt. Zion Rejoice! Music in the African American Church* (2001), *Let the Church Sing On! Reflections on Black Sacred Music, Chicago* (2009), and *Readings in African-American Church Music and Worship*, Vol. II (2013). Musical editions include *New Wine in Old Wineskins: A Contemporary Congregational Song Supplement: Volume 1* (2007) and *King of Kings: Organ Music of Black Composers, Past and Present: Volume 1* (2008), Volume 2 (2009).

John L. Bell, F. H. S., received his education at the University of Glasgow. Joining the Iona Community in 1980, he began his work with the Community in 1983 as a Youth Coordinator, and has become the primary troubadour for congregational song on behalf of the Community for three decades. He is known worldwide as a writer, composer, teacher, editor of hymnals and song collections, and song leader. With Graham Maule, he has co-authored over 250 texts, and has written an additional 150 himself. He has also composed more that 275 tunes and arranged many other folk tunes, especially from Scotland, Ireland, and England.

Emily R. Brink, F.H.S., is currently a Senior Research Fellow at the Calvin Institute of Christian Worship and Adjunct Professor of Church Music and Worship at Calvin Theological Seminary, Grand Rapids, Michigan. In 1983, Dr. Brink became the first music and liturgy editor for the Christian Reformed Church in North America until she retired from that position in 2006. She was founding editor of *Reformed Worship*, a quarterly journal she edited for twenty years (1985-2006), available online at www.reformedworship.org; served as editor of the *Psalter Hymnal* (1987); *Songs for LiFE,* a children's hymnal (1995); *Sing! A New Creation* (2001); and co-editor with George Black and Nancy Faus of *Holding in Trust: Hymns of the Hymn Society in the United States and Canada* (1992). She has also contributed articles and chapters to several journals and books. Dr. Brink served as president of the Hymn Society in the United States and Canada from 1990-1992 and was named a Fellow of the Hymn Society in 2004.

Sr. Kathleen Harmon, SNDdeN, is Music Director for programs of the Institute for Liturgical Ministry in Dayton, Ohio. She is one of the authors of the annual publication *Living Liturgy: Spirituality, Celebration, Catechesis for Sundays and Solemnities.* Her books include *The Ministry of Music: Singing the Paschal Mystery* (2004); *The Ministry of Cantors* (2004); and *The Mystery We Celebrate, The Song We Sing: A Theology of Liturgical Music* (2008). She has done extensive liturgy and liturgical music education and consultation throughout the United States and Canada. Dr. Harmon holds a graduate degree in church music from Westminster Choir College and a doctorate in liturgy from Drew University.

C. Michael Hawn, F.H.S., is the University Distinguished Professor of Church Music and Director of the Master of Sacred Music Program at Perkins School of Theology, Southern Methodist University, Dallas, Texas. He joined the faculty in 1992 after teaching for fifteen years in two Southern Baptist seminaries and serving congregations as minister of music in Kentucky, Georgia, North Carolina, and Texas. Dr. Hawn has received numerous fellowships for the study of global hymnody and worship, and has conducted research and taught in forty countries. His publications include over 400 articles and books, including the global song collection *Halle, Halle: We Sing the World Round* (1999), *Gather into One: Praying and Singing Globally* (2003), and *One Bread, One Body: Exploring Cultural Diversity in Worship* (2003). Since 2004 he has written a weekly column entitled "History of Hymns" for the *United Methodist Reporter*. Hawn contributed over twenty entries to the *Canterbury Dictionary of Hymnology* (2013), primarily in the area of sub-Saharan African hymnody. In 2006, Michael Hawn was the music director for the Ninth Assembly of the World Council of Churches in Porto Alegre, Brazil. He was elected Fellow of the Hymn Society in the United States and Canada in 2008.

Lim Swee Hong, is the Deer Park Assistant Professor of Sacred Music at Emmanuel College of Victoria University in the University of Toronto, and the Director of the Master of Sacred Music Program. Before joining Emmanuel in 2012, Dr. Lim served as an Assistant Professor of Church Music at Baylor University. Prior to his work at Baylor, he served as a Lecturer of Worship, Liturgy, and Music at Trinity Theological College, Singapore. He currently serves as the Co-Moderator of the Worship Committee for the Tenth General Assembly of the World Council of Churches for its meeting in Busan, South Korea (2013), and also served as a member of the Worship Planning Committee for the 2011 Ecumenical Peace Convocation sponsored by the World Council held in Jamaica. In 2006, he was elected chairperson of the Worship and Liturgy committee of the World Methodist Council for the quinquennium of 2006-2011. Lim holds a PhD in Liturgical Studies from Drew University, where his dissertation won the Helen LePage and William Hale Chamberlain Prize for Outstanding Dissertation. He also holds a Master of Sacred Music from Perkins School of Theology, Southern Methodist University. He completed his undergraduate work in Church Music at the Asian Institute for Liturgy and Music in the Philippines. He has published numerous articles on global hymnody and is a prolific composer of hymns.

Deborah C. Loftis became the Executive Director of the Hymn Society in the United States and Canada in 2009. Prior to this she was Professor of Church Music at the Baptist Theological Seminary at Richmond (1999-2008). Dr. Loftis holds degrees from Furman University (European History), The Southern Baptist Theological Seminary (musicology), and a PhD in musicology and ethnomusicology from the University of Kentucky. In addition she holds a Masters in Library and Information Science from the University of Alabama. Her PhD dissertation was titled "Big Singing Day in Benton, Kentucky: A Study of the History, Ethnic Identity and Musical Style of Southern Harmony Singers" (1987). She co-edited *Minds and Hearts in Praise of God: Hymns and Essays in Church Music in Honor of Hugh T. McElrath* (2006), served as the issue editor of the *Review & Expositor* (Spring, 2009) on Worship and Spiritual Formation, and has numerous articles on hymnody with a focus on the hymns of Georgia E. Harkness. Drawing upon her skills as a music librarian, Dr. Loftis provided cumulative indexes for *The Hymn*, the journal of the Hymn Society in the United States and Canada in 1982 and 1998 while supplying an annual index for the journal from 1980 through 2011.

David W. Music, F.H.S., is Professor of Church Music at Baylor University, Waco, Texas, where he has served since 2002. He previously taught at Southwestern Baptist Theological Seminary and California Baptist College, and served for six years as Editor of *The Hymn*, the journal of the Hymn Society in the United States and Canada. Dr. Music has written numerous books in the field of hymnology and prepared editions of music which include *Hymnology: A Collection of Source Readings* (1996), *Christian Hymnody in Twentieth-Century Britain and America: An Annotated Bibliography* (2001), *Oliver Holden (1765-1844): Selected Works* (1998), *A Selection of Shape-Note Folk Hymns from Southern United States Tune Books, 1816-61* (2005), and *"I Will Sing the Wondrous Story": A History of Baptist Hymnody in North America*, written in collaboration with Paul A. Richardson (2008).

He co-authored *Singing Baptists: Studies in Baptist Hymnody in America* (with Harry Eskew and Paul A. Richardson, 1994) and the fifth edition of William J. Reynolds's *A Survey of Christian Hymnody* (with Milburn Price, 2010). Dr. Music was elected a Fellow of the Hymn Society in the United States and Canada in 2010.

Greg Scheer is Minster of Worship at the Church of the Servant, Grand Rapids, Michigan, and Music Associate at the Calvin Institute of Christian Worship. Before this he served as minister of music in congregations in Pennsylvania, Florida, and Iowa. He received his MA in music theory and composition from the University of Pittsburgh. His writings include *The Art of Worship: A Musician's Guide to Leading Modern Worship* (2006) and contributions to *Reformed Worship*, *The Hymn*, *Call to Worship*, and *Worship Leader*. He edited *Global Songs for Worship* (2010), a collection of fifty-seven worship songs with lyrics in the original language as well as English translations. A composer of over 500 songs and arrangements, his music is available from Augsburg Fortress, Abingdon, GIA, WorshipToday, Faith Alive, and at www.gregscheer.com.

Pablo D. Sosa was born in Argentina and is known throughout the world as a composer, church musician, worship and song leader. He is a pastor in the Evangelical Methodist Church in Argentina. He received his education from the Facultad Evangélica de Teologia (now known as Instituto Universitario ISEDET, Buenos Aires), Westminster Choir College (Princeton, NJ), the Hochshule für Musik (Berlin), and the School of Sacred Music at Union Theological Seminary (New York). Among his most influential projects was his role as editor of *Cancionero Abierto*, a collection of primarily new Latin American songs begun in 1974 and concluded in 1994. He has also served as an animateur for several assemblies of the World Council of Churches including the Sixth Assembly in Vancouver (1983) that introduced global song to the world church.

Tables and Examples Index

List of Tables

Chapter Three

    Table I Anglo-American and British Hymns Commonly Sung in African-American Churches 79-80

    Table II African-American Hymnals and Hymnal Supplements Published Since Vatican II 82-84

    Table III African-American Hymns Most Commonly Sung in African-American Churches 85-86

Chapter Four

    Table I Representative Gospel Song Writers of the Period 1960-1980 124

    Table II Representative Gospel Song Writers of the Period 1980-2000 125

Chapter Six

    Table I An Overview of Songs Cited 192-193

Chapter Seven

    Table I Spanish- and Portuguese-Language Hymnals 279-280

Musical and Textual Examples Cited

Example 2:1 "New Songs of Celebration Render" (Erik Routley) 43

Example 2:2 "These Things Did Thomas Count as Real" (Thomas Troeger) 46

Example 2:3 "In an Age of Twisted Values" (Martin E. Leckebusch) . . . 48

Example 2:4 "Sing to God with Joy and Gladness" (John Bell) 53

Example 2:5 "In Christ Alone" (Stuart Townend and Keith Getty) . . . 54

Example 2:6 "God Weeps" (Shirley Erena Murray) 56

Example 2:7 ANNIVERSARY SONG (Jane Marshall) 61
Example 2:8 EAST ACKLAM (Francis Jackson) 62
Example 5:1 "What Does the Lord Require" (Jim Strathdee) 148
Example 5:2 "Joy Comes with the Dawn" (Gordon Light) . . . 151-152
Example 5:3 "Two Fishermen" (Suzanne Toolan) 157-158
Example 5:4 "O He Is Born" (Felicia Edgecombe) 160-161
Example 5:5 *Sorrowing Song* (Robin Mann) 162
Example 6:1 "Seek Ye First" (Karen Lafferty) 181
Example 7:1 "Amen Siakudumisa" (Stephen Cuthbert Molefe) . . . 221
Example 7:2 "Wa, Wa, Wa Emimimo" (Aladura, West Africa) 234
Example 7:3 "Alleluia" (Abraham Dumisani Maraire) 252
Example 7:4 "Jesu tawa pano" (Patrick Matsikenyiri) 254-255
Example 7:5 "Vamos todos al banquete" (Guillermo Cuéllar) 264
Example 7:6 "Santo, santo, santo" (Guillermo Cuéllar) 265
Example 7:7 "Winter has Passed, the Rain is Over" (Weifan Wang) . . . 284
Example 7:8 "Yellaam Yesuvee" (Y. Gnanamani) 290
Example 7:9 "Khydaayaa, raeham kar" (R. F. Liberius) 291
Example 7:10 "Esho hae Probhu" (Bart Shaha) 292
Example 7:11 *Mary's Salidummay* (Filipino) 296
Example 7:12 "Soft the Master's Love Song" (Rudolf Pantou) 297
Example 7:13 "Call Me By My Name" (Samuel Liew) 299

Short Articles

Chapter Seven
   Missa Luba: A Case Study for Musical Inculturation 218-219
   Hugh Tracy: The Mentor of Missionaries 230-231
   Current Congregational Song Practice in Africa—
      Two Examples 237-239
   Composing An African Hymn—A Case Study 241-242
   A Case Study: "Siyahamba" 260-261
   Writing Hymns in South America: A Case Study 270-274
   The Role of Missionaries in the Development of
   Asian Hymns 286-289

List of Recorded Musical Examples

Introduction to the Recording:

While the scholarship in this book may enhance the reader's understanding of the streams of song that are part of the church's experience since Vatican II, music making is primarily an aural/oral experience. In the Introduction to the book, you will find a section on "General Trends Observed" (XXXVI). This recording should assist the reader in perceiving the variety of musical styles and sounds that make up the seven streams proposed in this book. Listen for Solo/Congregational Balance (XXXVI), Written and Oral Tradition (XXXVIII), Variety of Accompanying Instruments (XXXVIII), and Variety of Song Structures (XL). Although not a precise science, each stream may, in part, be identified by the musical styles and soundscapes that you will hear. Finally, how does each musical style express the embedded theology and possible liturgical use(s) of each song in its original context? Enjoy the rich diversity of the gifts of the Spirit that belongs to the church in the twenty-first century.

—C. Michael Hawn

Numbers after the country of origin refer to relevant pages in the book.

Stream One: Roman Catholic Renewal Song
Shepherd Me, O God	Marty Haugen	(USA), 9
Blest Are They	David Haas	(USA), 9

Stream Two: Classic Contemporary Protestant Hymnody
When In Our Music God Is Glorified	ENGLEBERG/Fred Pratt Green	(UK), 50
Christus Paradox	PICARDY/Sylvia Dunstan	(Canada), 59

Stream Three: African-American Congregational Song
The Storm is Passing Over me	Charles Tindley	(USA), 84
He's Done So Much for Me	Theodore R. Frye and Lillian Knowles	(USA), 92

Stream Four: Gospel and Revival Songs
Because He Lives	Bill and Gloria Gaither	(USA), 119
How Great Thou Art	Stuart Hine	(UK), 114

Stream Five: Folk Hymnody

Lord of the Dance	Sydney Carter	(UK), 143
The Summons	KELVINGROVE/John Bell	(Scotland), XV, 163

Stream Six: Praise & Worship Music

Shout to the Lord	Darlene Zschech	(Australia), 187
Lord, I Lift Your Name on High	Rick Founds	(Ireland), 54

Stream Seven: Global and Ecumenical Congregational Song

Masithi-Amen Siakudumisa	S. C. Molefe	(South Africa), 221
Ahomna	Ntsikana	(South Africa), 257
Wa wa Wa Enimimo	Aladura	(Nigeria), 234
Jesu, Tawa pano	Patrick Matsikenyiri	(Zimbabwe), 254-255
Give Thanks to the Lord	I-to Loh	(Taiwan), 282
Un Menino	Simei Monteiro	(Brazil), 276-27
Goodness is Stronger than Evil	John Bell	(Scotland), 307ff.
Ubi Caritas	Taizé Community	(France), 303-307
El cielo canta alegría	Pablo Sosa	(Argentina), XVII, 268

The following items are taken from the recording Halle, Halle: We Sing the World Round. CGC41 Copyright © 1999 Choristers Guild.

Amen Siakudumisa by S.C. Molefe; transc. David Dargie. (Words and music: Lumko Institute, transcription: David Dargie. Administered by Choristers Guild)

Ahomna by Thozama Dyani, transc. David Dargie. (Words and music: Thozama Dyani and David Dargie. Administered by Choristers Guild.)

Wa wa wa Emimimo, transc. I-to Loh. (Translation and music transcription: World Council of Churches, Geneva, Switzerland.)

Jesu tawa pano by Patrick Matsikenyiri, descant by Jorge Lockward. (Words and music: General Board of Global Ministries.)

O Give Thanks to the Lord (Transcription and english adaptation copyrighted by I-to Loh.)

Um Menino by Simei Monteiro, translation: Michael Hawn. (Text and music: Simei Monteiro, Administered by Choristers Guild.)

Index of Hymns and Songs

Hymns and Songs (*Italics* are used when the title differs from first line)
*indicates that a portion of the hymn is cited.
Author of the text is indicated where known.
Uppercase titles, not first lines

10,000 Reasons (Bless the Lord) (Myrin/Redman) 193
A Child (Monteiro) 277
A mighty fortress is our God (Luther) 13
A Praying Spirit (Clark) 85
A pregnant girl none will ignore (Bell/Maule) *320
A virgin unspotted (trad. English) 134
Abba, Father (Landry) 9
Abide with me (Lyte) 311
Adoro te devote (Latin Chant) 11
Ain't it a shame (Stamps-Baxter) 109
Alegría (Pagura) 273
Alleluia (Maraire) *252

All creatures of our God and King (Francis of Assisi) 197
All glory to Jesus (Peterson) 115
All hail the power of Jesus' name (Perronet) 183
All the earth (Deiss) 14
All things bright and beautiful (Alexander) 323
All to Thee (Baker) 124
All who hunger, gather gladly (Dunstan) 44
All who love and serve your city (Routley) 50
Amazing grace (Newton) 79, 137, 138

Amazing Love (Kendrick) 185
Amen siakudumisa (Molefe) 219, *221, 237, 259, 262
Ancient of Days (Harvill/Sadler) 192
Aquí estoy, Señor (Schutte) 17
Arriba los corazones (Jaén) 278, 363
As we walked home at close of day (Bell/Maule) *321
As the deer (Nystrom) 183, 192, 357
At the Cross (Watts/Hudson) 79
Awake! Awake, and greet the new morn (Haugen) *150, 156
Awesome God (Mullins) 11

Baby, baby (Grant) 186
Ballad of the green berets (Sadler) 142
Baptized in water (Saward) 52
Be not afraid (Dufford) 8, 17
Be Strong in the Lord (Fettke/Johnson) 124
Be thou my vision (Irish) 11
Because He Lives (Gaither) 118, 119
Bendito el Rey (Pagura) 271
Bless His Holy Name (Crouch) 85
Blessed assurance (Crosby) 79
Blessed be the King (Pagura) 271
Blessed Be the Name (Clark) 79, 164
Blessed be your name (Redman) 193, *196
Blessed Quietness (Ferguson) 79
Blest be the God of Israel (Perry) 60
Blowing In the Wind (Dylan) 142
Break now the Bread of Life (Lathbury) 47
Breathe (Barnett) 150, 193
Brighten the Corner Where You Are (Gabriel/Ogden) 109

Call me by my name (Liew) *299
Child of joy and peace (Murray) 301, 365
Canção da caminhada (Monteiro) 277, 363
Carol our Christmas, an upside down Christmas (Murray) 344 n292
Cantad al Señor (anon.) 277, 363
Cantai ao Senhor (anon.) 277, 363
Cantemos al Señor (Rosas) 276, 357, 363
Can't Nobody Do Me Like Jesus (Crouch) 85
Captivate Me (Haigh) *164

Index of Hymns and Songs

Carol of the Nativity, The (Bell/Maule) *284
Celebrate Jesus (Oliver) 184, 192
Certainly, Lord (spiritual) *136
Chhi-phe ho he sio (Kao) 301, 365
Chin Chu Siong-te cho thiⁿ toe (anon.) 289, 365
Christ is all to me (Gnanamani) 289, *290, 366
Christ is risen, Christ is living (Kaan) 274
Christ is the world's light (Pratt Green) 67 n23
Christ Lives (Arias) 274
Clap your hands (Repp) 7
Climb every mountain (Rodgers/Hammerstein) 127 n26
Cloaks and palms (Avila) 275
Come, Lord Jesus Christ (Shaha) 291, *292
Come, creating Spirit (Monteiro/Murray) 277
Come now, come, O Holy Spirit (Matsikenyiri) *253
Come now is the time to worship (Doerksen) 193
Come now, O Prince of Peace (Lee/Pope) 285, 301, 357, 366
Come, praise God all hearts together (Jaén) 278
Come, thou fount of every blessing (Robinson) . . . . *xxv, 137*
Come, thou long-expected Jesus (C. Wesley) 276
Come to be our hope, Lord Jesus (Maraschin) 276
Count Your Blessings (Oatman, Jr.) 79, 108
Cristo Vive (Arias) 274, 363
Cristo vive (Martínez) 274, 363
Crown him with many crowns (Bridges) 64

Darkness now enfolds us (Jordan) 278, 363
Du är helig (Harling) 255
Deep and wide 110
Deeper, deeper (Jones) 85
Die Stem van Suid-Afrika (Langenhoven) 259
Do Lord (African-American spiritual) 110
Dong tian yi wang, yu shui yi zhi (Wang) 301, 365
Down at the cross (Hoffman) 79
Draw me close (Carpenter) 190, 193
Draw the circle wide (Light) 149, 166
Draw us in the Spirit's tether (Dearmer) 61

Easter Evening (Bell/Maule) *321
Esho hae Probhu (Shaha) 291, *292, 365

397

El cielo canta alegría (Sosa)	269, 363
En el principio (Rosas)	276, 363
En medio de la vida (Arias)	274, 363
Enemy of Apathy (Bell/Maule)	163
Enter into Jerusalem (Lung)	276, 363
Este momento (Sosa)	270
Farther Along (Stevens)	79
Father, help your people (Kaan)	50
Father welcomes all his children (Mann)	161
For all the saints who've shown your love (Bell)	53
För livets skull (Harling)	225
For sake of life (Harling)	225
For the bread which you have broken (Benson)	60
For the fruit of this creation (Pratt Green)	61, *62
For Those Tears I Died (Stevens)	124
Forever (Tomlin)	193
Forever Reign (Morgan/Ingram)	193
Freedom is coming (South Africa)	261
Freely, Freely (Owens)	124, 357
From all that dwell below the skies (Watts)	*209
From Erin's shores Columba came (Bell/Maule)	*309
From the Bible we learn God's will (Srisuwan/Minchin)	298, 366
Fruto del amor divino (Pagura)	270, 363
Gather Us In (Haugen)	*153
Gentle Mary laid her child (Cook)	134
Get all excited (Gaither)	117
Getting Used to the Family of God (Gaither)	117
Give to the winds thy fears (J. Wesley/Jars of Clay)	197
Give me a clean heart (Douroux)	85
Give Us Clean Hands (Hall)	193, *195
Gloria, gloria, gloria (Sosa)	269-270
Glorify Thy Name (Adkins)	180, 192
Glory be to the Father (trad./Avery/Marsh)	145
Glory to His Name (Oatman, Jr.)	79
God be merciful to me (Redhead/Jars of Clay)	64
God bless Africa (Sontonga)	258
God created heaven and earth (Anderson)	289, 365

Index of Hymns and Songs

God gave to man the woman (Edgecombe) *159
God has smiled on me (Jones, Jr.) 85
God is love (Rivers) 13
God of creation (Thangaraj) 293
God of This City (Tomlin) 193
God of Wonders (Tomlin) 193
God rest you merry gentlemen (traditional English) 134
God sends us the Spirit (Colvin) 264, 361
God, the sculptor of the mountains (Thornburg) 68 n36
God weeps (Murray) *56
God will lift up your head (Jars of Clay) 197
God Will Take Care of You (Martin) 79
Golden breaks the dawn (Chao/Price) 339 n193
Good Christian men (friends) rejoice (Neale) 133
Good King Wenceslas (trad. English) 134
Gracious Spirit, heed our pleading (Niwaglia/Olson) 245, 361
Grains of wheat (Gabaráin) 154
Grant to us, O Lord (Deiss) 14
Great Hymn (Ntsikana) 258
Great is the Lord (Smith) 183
Greater is he that is in me (Wolfe) 120, 124
Guide me, O thou great Jehovah (Williams) 64, 79

Hail Mary, gentle woman (Landry) 9
Haleluya! Pelo tsa rona (South Africa) 261, 361
Halle, Halle, Hallelujah (Mulrain) 278
Hallelujah! We sing your praises (South Africa) 261-262
Happiness Is the Lord (Stanphill) 116
Happy is the one (Bell) *321
Have mercy on us, Lord (Liberius) 290, *291, 365
Have you got good religion? (Spiritual) *136
Healer of our every ill (Haugen) 153
Hear Our Praises (Morgan) 188
Heaven Came Down (Peterson) 127 n27
Heaven is singing for joy (Sosa) 269
He Is Coming Soon (Landgrave) 125
He is exalted (Paris) 11, 184, 192
He Knows My Name (Walker) 188
He Touched Me (Gaither) 118, 178, 357
He'll Understand and Say "Well Done" (Campbell) 85

He's Alive (Francisco)	179-180
He's my foundation	97
Here I Am, Lord (Schutte)	8, 123
Here I Am to Worship (Hughes)	193
Here in this place (Haugen)	*153
Here, O Lord, your servants gather (Yamaguchi/Stowe)	285, 356
Here we are (Repp)	7
Higher Ground (Oatman, Jr.)	79
Holy and anointed one (Barnett)	186, 192
Holy Is the Lord (Tomlin/Giglio)	193
Holy, holy, holy (Cuéllar)	264, *265, 357
Holy, holy, holy (Heber)	79, 240
Holy, holy, holy, my heart adores you (anon.)	270, 357, 363
How firm a foundation (anon)	79
How great your name (Jordan)	278, 363
How Great Thou Art (Boberg/Hine)	114, 356
How Great You Are (Posthuma)	193
How lovely, Lord, how lovely (Duba)	60
How majestic is your name (Smith)	183, 192, 357
Hoy celebramos (Arias)	274, 363
Hunger Carol (Murray)	301, 365
I am the bread of life (Toolan)	15, 155, *156
I am the light of the world (Strathdee)	147
I am thine, O Lord (Crosby)	79
I believe (Shirl/Graham/Drake/Stillman)	127 n26
I come with joy to meet my Lord (Wren)	50
I come with joy, a child of God (Wren)	50
I Could Never Outlove the Lord (Gaither)	118
I Could Sing of Your Love Forever (Smith)	186, 188, 193
I danced in the morning (Carter)	144
I don't feel no ways tired (Burrell)	85
I Exalt Thee (Sanchez, Jr.)	180, 192
I Have Come from the Darkness (Chaplin)	124
I Know Who Holds Tomorrow (Stamphill)	116
I Know Whom I Have Believed (Whittle)	122
I must tell Jesus (Hoffman)	79
I need thee every hour (Hawks)	64, 79
I need words (Crowder)	195

Index of Hymns and Songs

I remember	97
I saw three ships (trad. English)	134
I see the Lord (Falson)	187
I sit outside the rich world's gate (Bell/Maule)	*320
I want Jesus to walk with me (Spiritual)	*74
I want to walk as a child of the light (Thomerson)	14, 124
I was glad (Thangaraj)	393
I was there to hear your borning cry (Ylvisaker)	147
I will call upon the Lord (O'Shields)	183, 192
I worship you almighty God (Corbett)	184
I'd rather have Jesus (Shea)	114
I'll Fly Away (Brumley)	80
If I had a hammer (Seeger/Hays)	7
If it had not been for the Lord (Douroux)	85
If That Isn't Love (Rambo)	124
If walking is our vocation (Monteiro)	277
I'm going to live the life I sing about in my song (Dorsey)	99
In an age of twisted values (Leckebusch)	*48
In Christ alone (Townend/Getty)	*54, 193, 198
In dulci jubilo (macaronic carol)	133
In the beginning (Rosas)	276
In the Garden (Miles)	80, 190
In the middle of life (Arias)	274
In the secret (Park)	190, 193
Innocent sounds (Wesley)	135
Is Your All on the Altar? (Hoffman)	80
Isn't the Love of Jesus Something Wonderful (Peterson)	115
It only takes a spark (Kaiser)	145
It Is Well with My Soul (Spafford)	80
It Took a Miracle (Peterson)	115, 116
It was on a Friday morning (Carter)	*144
Jaya Ho (Hindi)	294
Jeannie with the Light Brown Hair (Foster)	108
Jerusalem, my happy home (anon,)	137
Jesu a fe pade (Olude)	242
Jesu, Jesu fill us with your love (Colvin)	246, 357, 361
Jesu, tawa pano (Matsikenyiri)	*254-255, 262, 357, 361
Jesus calls us here to meet him (Bell/Maule)	163
Jesus draw me close (Founds)	192

Jesús es mi Rey soberano (Mendoza) 275, 363
Jesus is all the world to me (Thompson) 80
Jesus Is Lord of All (Gaither) 118
Jesus Is Lord of All (McClard) 120, 124
Jesus Is the Song (Danner) 124
Jesus, keep me near the cross (Crosby) 80
Jesus, you're the center of my joy (Smallwood) 85
Jesus, the very thought of thee (attr. Bernard of Clairvaux) 204 n37
Jesus, we are here (Matsikenyiri) *254-255, 262, 357, 361
Jesus, we love to meet (Parsons) 242
Jesus, we want to meet (Adebesin/Olude) 242
Jeya Ho (anon.) 294, 365
Joy comes with the dawn (Light) 150
Just a cup of water (Edgecombe) 159
Just a Little Talk with Jesus (Derricks) 85
Justice in the Womb (WGWG, Iona) *323-324

Karthaadhi Karthar Iveree (Chelliah) 300
Kay laking hiwaga (Feliciano) 296, 365
Keep in mind (Deiss) 14
Keep Me Every Day (Eiland) 80
Knowing You (Kendrick) 193
Khudaayaa, raeham kar (Liberius) *291, 365
Kyrie eleison (with tropes by Haigh) *163-164
Kyrie eleison (Reindorf) 262, 361

Lågorna är många (Frostenson) . . . . xxiv n1
Lamb of Glory (Nelson) 125
Le lo le lo lay lo (Loperena) 264, 265, 363
Lead me, guide me (Akers) 85
Lead Me to Calvary (Hussey) 80
Leave It There (Tindley) 85, 356
Let all the world in every corner sing (Herbert) 61
Let us all go to the banquet (Cuéllar) *264
Let us talents and tongues employ (Kaan) xxxix
Let's just praise the Lord (Gaither) 117, 118
Lift every voice and sing (Johnson) 99, 356
Lift Him Up (Oatman, Jr.) 80
Like a Lamb Who Needs the Shepherd (Carmichael) 124
Like the murmur of the dove's song (Daw) 60

Index of Hymns and Songs

Little country church (Love Song) 201 n1
Lirih terdengar lagu kasih yang merdu (Pantou) *296-297, 365
Look, how good it is! (Sosa) 259
Lord, help me to hold out (Cleveland) 85
Lord, Here Am I (Crosby) 125
Lord, I lift your name on high (Founds) 183, 192
Lord Jesus, think on me (Synesius of Cyrene) 322
Lord of the Dance (Carter) 143, 144
Lord, what is our temple if you are not present? (Pagura) 271
Lord, you have come to the lakeshore (Gabaráin) 11, 154
Love divine, all loves excelling (Wesley) 63
Love the Lord (Brewster) 193
Love was when (Wyrtzen) 124

Majesty (Hayford) 182, 192, 357
Mansion over the hilltop (Stamphill) 116
Mantos y palmas (Avila) 275, 263
Many are the light beams (Frostenson) . . . . xxiv n1
Mary's salidummay (Kiley) *295-296, 365
Masithi—Amen (Molefe) 219, *221, 237, 259, 262, 361
Matulog pa, bunsong mahal (Tinio) 301, 366
Meekness and majesty (Kendrick) 185
Mighty to Save (Fielding/Morgan) 193
Mil voces para celebrar (C. Wesley/Pagura) 271
¡Miren, qué bueno! (Sosa) 269, 363
Momento novo (collaborative work) 277, 363
Must Jesus bear the cross alone (Allen) 80
My darling Clementine (folk song) 257
My faith looks up to thee (Palmer) 80
My hope is built on nothing less (Mote) 80
My Jesus, I love you (Featherstone) 204 n37
My life is in you (Gardner) 184, 357
My Lord Is Near Me All the Time (Gaultney) 124
My prayer rises to heaven (Dao-Kim) 340 n214
My Redeemer Lives (Morgan) 188
My Tribute (Crouch) 85, 357

Near To the Heart of God (McAfee) 108
Near to thy heart (Peterson) 115
Nearer my God to thee (Adams) 80

403

Never been scared	97
New moment (collaborative work)	277, 263
New songs of celebration render (Routley)	*42-43
Njoo kwetu, Roho mwema (Niwaglia)	245, 262, 361
Nkosi, nkosi (Xhosa, *Kyrie eleison*)	262, 361
Nkosi Sikelel' iAfrika (Sontonga)	258, 259, 361
No One Like You (Crowder/Parker)	195
No, Not One (Oatman, Jr.)	80
No temas más (Dufford)	8
Not the foremost of her gender (WGWG, Iona)	*323-324
Now behold the Lamb (Franklin)	96
Now let us tell of your victory (Liew)	298
Nyanyikanlah nyanyian baru (Lubis)	298
O come, O come, Emmanuel (Latin Chant)	11, 356
O for a thousand tongues to sing (Wesley)	*137
O God of earth and altar (Chesterson)	*xxiii
O happy day (Doddridge)	95, 96
O he is born (Edgecombe)	*159-160
O How I Love Jesus (Whitfield)	80
O Jesus, my King and my Sovereign (Mendoza)	275
Our cities cry to you, O Lord (Clarkson)	48
Out of the direst depths (Bell)	*322
O sing unto the Lord (Rosas)	276, 357
O What a Wonder It Is (Whitney)	125
Ocean of love (Thangaraj)	340, 366
Of the Father's love begotten (Prudentius/Neale)	134, 270
Oh, freedom! Oh, freedom! (Spiritual)	*74
Oh, how he loves you and me (Kaiser)	145
Oh love, how deep, how broad, how high (á Kempis)	133
Oh, the cabbage price is falling (Tarigan)	*300, 366
Ohoradiya (Psalm 150) (Lee)	285, 366
Oh, to be kept by Jesus (Frazier)	85
On Eagle's Wings (Joncas)	9, 357
On the Jericho road (Stamps-Baxter)	110
One bread, one body (Foley)	8, 357
One more step (Carter)	143
Open the eyes of my heart (Baloche)	189, 193
Open to You (Haigh)	*165
O-so-so (Lee)	285, 301, 366

Index of Hymns and Songs

Our cities cry to you, O Lord (Clarkson) 48
Our God (Redman/Myrin/Tomlin/Reeves) 193
Our Love Is Loud (Crowder) 195

Pan de vida (Hurd) 17
Pass It On (Kaiser) 145, 182, 357
Pass me not, O gentle Savior (Crosby) 80
Peace is flowing like a river (Landry) 9
People Need the Lord (Nelson/McHugh) 123
Pescador de Hombres (Gabaráin) 11, 154
Phra-kham phi sawn hai rao ruu jak (Srisuwan) 298, 366
Porque él venció (Pagura) 273, 363
Porque él entró en el mundo (Pagura) 273
Porque hay un mundo (Pagura) 273, 363
Praise Be to Jesus (Gaither) 118
Praise God from whom all blessings flow (Ken/Avery/Marsh) 145
Praise Him (Harper) 85
Praise him, praise him (Crosby) 80
Precious Lord, take my hand (Dorsey) 85
Priestly people (Deiss) 14
Pues si vivimos (anon.) 275, 363
Puff the Magic Dragon (Lipton/Yarrow) 202-203 n16

Qing zao qi-lai kan (Chao) 287, 366

Rain Down (Cortez) 127 n36
Redeemed, how I love to proclaim it (Crosby/Butler) 123
Refuge (tr. Niles) 292
Rejoice, Hallelu (Thangaraj) 293, 366
Revelation Song (Riddle) 193
Revive Us Again (Mackay) 123
Rise to greet the sun (Wiant) 287, 366
Room at the Cross for You (Stanphill) 116

Santo, santo, santo (Cuéllar) *264-265, 364
Santo, santo, santo, mi corazon te adora (anon.) 270, 363
Saranam, saranam (tr. Niles) 292, 357, 366
Sarennam, O divine light (Dyvasirvadum) 339 n207, 366
Savior, more than life to me (Crosby) 80
Say it loud (Kendrick) 185

Sayur kubis jatuh harga (Tarigan) 300, 366
Seek ye first (Lafferty) 146, 180, *181, 192, 357
Send us, Lord (South Africa) 262
¿Señor, qué es nuestro templo si tu no estas presente? (Pagura) 271, 364
Servant King (Kendrick) 185
Set my soul afire (Bartlett) 124
Share His Love (Reynolds) 120, 124
She comes sailing on the wind (Light) 149, 357
She Flies On (Light) 149, 357
She sits like a bird (Bell/Maule) 163
Sheaves of summer (Gabaráin) 154
Shepherd of love (Peterson) 116
Shine, Jesus, Shine (Kendrick) 54, 123, 185, 192, 357
Shout from the highest mountain (Repp) 7
Shout to the Lord (Zschech) 86, 188, 193
Shout to the North (Smith) 189
Show a Little Bit of Love and Kindness (Peterson) 115
Sign me up for the Christian jubilee (Yancy/Metcalfe) 85
Sing praise to the Father (Clarkson) 120
Sing the Lord a new song (Lubis/Tinio) 298
Sing to God with joy and gladness (Bell) 53
Sinner Saved by Grace (Gaither) 117
Siyahamba (South African freedom song) 14, *260-261, 357, 361
Sleep through the night, beloved Child (Tinio) 301, 366
Solitario (Pagura) 272, 364
So send I you (Clarkson) 119
Soft the Master's love song (Pantou/para. Minchin) *297, 365
Softly and tenderly Jesus is calling (Thompson) 80
Something beautiful (Gaither) 118
Something within (Campbell) 85
Somos el cuerpo de Cristo (Cortez) 11, 17
Somos pueblo que camina (*Misa Popular Nicaragüense*) 264, 364
Sons of God (Theim) 7
Soon and very soon (Crouch) 85
Sorrowing Song (Mann) *162
Standing on the promises (Carter) 80
Stomp (Clinton/Sall) 96
Surely goodness and mercy (Peterson) 127 n27
Sursum corda (Pagura) 273
Sweet Beulah Land (Parsons, Jr.) 124

Index of Hymns and Songs

Sweet, Sweet Spirit (Akers) 85
Taiwan the green (Ti'n/para. Anderson) *288
Take my life and let it be (Havergal) 123
Take my life, lead me, Lord (Rawls) 124
Tantum ergo 256
Te Deum . . . . xiii, 238, 239, 240
Te ofrecemos Padre nuestro (*Misa Popular Nicaragüense*) 264, 357
Tell out my soul (Dudley-Smith) 51, 357
Tenemos Esperanza (Pagura) *273, 357, 364
Thank you, Lord, for water, soil, and air (Wren) 50
That boy-child of Mary (Colvin) 246, 361
The angel Gabriel (trad. English) 134
The beggar (Bell/Maule) *320
The Blood That Stained the Old Rugged Cross (Stamps-Baxter) 109
The Call of South Africa (Afrikaans' national anthem) 259
The Family of God (Gaither) 117, 118, 119
The Glory Song (Gabriel) 108
The Heart of Worship (Redman) 189, 193
The Impossible Dream (Leigh) 127 n26
The King Is Coming (Gaither) 117
The Lord is my light (Bouknight) 86
The Ninety and Nine (Clephane) 107, 112
The Old Rugged Cross (Bennard) 109, 112
The power of God (Smith/Williams) 95
(The reason) why we sing (Franklin) 96
The rice of life (Fowler) 285, 366
The right hand of God (Prescod) 278, 364
The Spirit is a-movin' (Landry) 9
The Stand (Houston) 193
The Summons (Bell/Maule) 163
The thirsty deer longs for the steam (Mulrain) 278, 364
The true use of musik (Wesley) 134
The Wonder of It All (Shea) 114
The Wonderful Cross (Reeves/Tomlin/Watts) *197
There is a fountain filled with blood (Cowper) 80
There is a Redeemer (Green) 123, 184, 192
There Is None Like You (LeBlanc) 184
There was a man named Jonah (Mulrain) 287, 364
There's Something About That Name (Gaither) 117, 118, 356
These things did Thomas count as real (Troeger) *46

They'll know we are Christians by our love (Scholtes) 14, 270
This Day (Hawkins) 86
This is the day of new beginnings (Wren) 68 n36
This is the God beyond all gods (Chelliah/para. Minchin) 300
This is the moment (Sosa) 270
Thuma mina (South Africa) 262, 357, 361
Thy word (Grant/Smith) 184, 192
'Til the Storm Passes By (Lister) 116
'Tis so sweet to trust in Jesus (Stead) 80
Today I awake (Bell/Maule) *320-321
Todo acabó en una tumba (Pagura) 336 n157, 364
To God be the glory (Crosby) . . . . xl, 112, 114
Tomorrow shall be my dancing day (anon.) 144, 356
Total Praise (Smallwood) 86
Touch me, Lord Jesus (Campbell) 86
Trust and Obey (Sammis) 80, 112
Tú has venido a la orilla (Gabaráin) 154, 357
Tua Palavra é lâmpada (Monteiro) 277, 364
Tua Palavra na vida (Monteiro) 277, 364
Two fishermen (Toolan) *156-158

Ubi caritas (Hurd) 17
Ubi caritas (Latin Chant) 13
Um menino (Monteiro) 277, 364
Una espiga (Gabaráin) 154, 357
Un pan, une cuerpo (Foley) 17
Uyai mose (Gondo) 262, 361
Uyai mweya wakachena (Matsikenyiri) 253, 361

Vamos todos al banquete (Cuéllar) *264, 364
Vem, Jesus nossa esperança (Maraschin) 276, 364
Vem, Santo Espiritu (Monteiro) 277, 364
Veni Creator Spiritus (Latin hymn) 240
Victory in Jesus (Bartlett) 112, 356

Walking Up the King's Highway (Dorsey) 86
Watch the bush of thorns (Kao/Minchin) 301, 365
Wa, wa, wa Emimimo (aladura, Yoruba) *233-235
We are one in the Spirit (Scholtes) 14, 270
We are the body of Christ (Cortez) 11, 17

Index of Hymns and Songs

We are the church (Avery/Marsh) 146, 357
We are marching in the light of God (South Africa) . . . 14, *260-261, 357, 361

We are people on a journey (*Misa Popular Nicaragüense*) 264
We bow before you, O great and holy (anon.) 294
We bow down (Paris) 184, 192
We fall down (Tomlin) 189, 193
We Have Hope (Pagura) *273, 357, 364
We met you, God (Bell/Maule) *320
We offer you our Father (*Misa Popular Nicaragüense*) 264
We will glorify (Paris) 184, 357
We will not take what is not ours (Bell/Maule) 343 n266
We shall overcome (anon., adpt. C.A. Tindley) 7, 141, 356
We'll Understand It Better By and By (Tindley) 86
We're Marching to Zion (Watts/Lowry) 80
We've come this far by faith (Goodson) 86
Were you there when they crucified my Lord? (Spiritual) 136
What a fellowship (Hoffman) 80
What a friend we have in Jesus (Scriven) 80
What a great mystery (Feliciano/para. Minchin) 296, 365
What does the Lord require of you? (Strathdee) *147-148, 166, 357
What gift shall we bring (Marshall) *60-61
What wondrous love is this (trad. folk) *136, 138

When I survey the wondrous cross (Watts) 64
    Tomlin setting 197
When in our music God is glorified (Pratt Green) 357
When the Roll Is Called Up Yonder (Black) 111
When the trumpet of the Lord shall sound (Black) 111
When We All Get to Heaven (Hewitt) 80
When we are living (anon., tr. composite) 275
When we've been there ten thousand years (anon.) 137
Where are the Hebrew children? (Spiritual) 136
Where charity and love prevail (Westendorf) 13, 356
Where have all the flowers gone? (Seeger) 7, 142
Where is my wand'ring boy tonight (Lowry) 107
Where Shall I Be? (Jones) 86
Wherever He Leads I'll Go (McKinney) 112
Who Will Tell Them (Peterson) 116
Will you come and follow me (Bell/Maule) 166, 357

Winter has passed, the rain is o'er (Wang/Carroll) 283, 285, 365
Without Him (LeFevre) 124
Woke up this mornin' (spiritual) *74
Worthy of worship (York) 125

Yellaam Yesuvee (Gnanamani) *289-290, 366
Yesu, Yesu, [Jesu, Jesu] fill us with your love (Colvin) 264, 361
Yes, God Is Real (Morris) 3T3
Yield not to temptation (Palmer) 80
You Are Good (Houghton) 193
You are holy (Harling) 225
You Are My All in All (Jernigan) 192
You brought the sunshine (Clark) 95
You can't beat God's giving (Akers) 86
You have come down to the lakeshore (Gabaráin) 11, 154
Your Grace Is Enough (Maher) 193
Your word in our lives (Monteiro) 277, 364
Your word is a lamp (Monteiro) 277, 364

Index of Hymnals and Hymnal Supplements, Hymnaries, Psalters, and Hymn Collections Cited

9 Carols or Ballads (1964) 144

A Canção do Senhor na Terra Brasileira (1982) 276
A Collection of Spiritual Songs and Hymns, Selected from Various Authors (1801) 86
A Singing Heart (1987) 59, 127
A Year of Grace (1990) 45, 66
A. E. C. Caribbean Hymnal (1998) 337
A.M.E.C. Bicentennial Hymnal, The (1984) 82
A.M.E.Z. Bicentennial Hymnal, The (1996) 83
Africa Praise Songbook (1998) 225
African American Heritage Hymnal, The (2001) 83, 86, 88, 90
African Songs of Worship (1986) 222
Agape: Songs of Hope and Reconciliation (2003) 224
Aleluya: Let the Whole World Sing (1989) 225
All Together (1980, 1983, 1991, 1996, 2001) 67, 161, 171
Alleluia Aotearoa (1993) 67, 159, 167
Amaculo ase Lovedale (Lovedale Music) (1885) 258
Australian Hymn Book, The (1977) 54, 55, 67

Baptist Hymnal (1975) 145
Baptist Hymnal, The (1991) 124, 126, 127, 167
Beams of Heaven: Hymns of Charles Albert Tindley (2006) 83
Bongan' iNkosi (Praise the Lord) (c. 1978) 220
Borning Cry (2000, 2003) 147
Brazilian Songs of Worship (1989) 222, 276
Breaking Bread (1996, 2011, 2013) 17

Cáliz de Bendiciones: Himnario Discipulos de Cristo (1996) 279
Canaan Hymns (20th c.) 338
Cancionero Abierto (Open Songbook) (1974-1994) . . . 268, 269, 270, 371
Canções de Rua (Songs of the Street) (1992) 227
¡*Cantad al Señor!* (1991) 279
Cantate Domino (1924, 1930, 1938, 1951) 227, 327
Cantate Domino, 5th Ed. (1974) 210, 222, 242, 274
Cantico Nuevo (New Song) (1960) 269, 271, 274
Cantos de Alabanza y Adoración/Songs of Praise and Worship (1997) . . . 280
Caribbean Praise (2000) 226
Carmina Gaedelica (6 vols., 1900-1928/1992) 164
Carol Our Christmas (1996) 67, 344
Celebration Hymnal, The (1997) 124, 125
Celebremos (1979) 275, 280
Celebremos II (1983) 275, 280
Celebremos su Gloria (1992) 203, 280
Century Praise (2001) 338
Chalice Hymnal (1995) 43, 66, 147, 168, 170
Chalice Praise (2004) 147
Chon Ngài (2006) 340
Christian Harmony (1805) 135
Christian Hymns, Lyrics and Songs of New Life (1949) 293, 339
Christian Lyre, The (1831) 106
Christmas Carols New and Old (1871, 1878) 134
Church Hymnary, fourth edition (2005) 139, 167, 325
Church Hymnary, The (1973) 49
Come All You People: Shorter Songs for Worship (1994) 315, 344
Come, Let Us Walk This Road Together (1997) 245, 333
Common Ground: A Song Book for All Churches (1998) 325, 345
Coronation Hymns (1910) 169
Courage to Say No: Twenty-three Songs for Lent and Easter, The (1996) . . . 344

Den Svenska Psalmboken med Tillägg (2002) 261
Divine Hymns or Spiritual Songs (c. 1784) 135
Dunblane Praises (1964) 49, 50
Dunblane Praises 2 (1966) 49, 50

E. A. C. C. Hymnal (1963) 282, 289, 292
E Korin S'Oluwa (Sing unto the Lord) (2005) 332
El Himnario (1998) 279

Index of Hymnals and Hymnal Supplements, Hymnaries, Psalters, and Hymn Collections Cited

El Himario Presbiteriano (1999) 279, 362
El Pueblo Canta (The People Sing) (1992) 335
*Enemy of Apathy: Songs of the Passion and Resurrection of Jesus,
    and the Coming of the Holy Spirit* (1988) 318, 319, 343
English Hymnal, The (1906) 139
English Hymnal with Tunes, The (1933) 139, 169
Evangel, The (1909) 169
Liturgy Hymnal (1965) 7
Evangelical Lutheran Worship (2006) . . . . xlvii, 66, 360
Every Day in Your Spirit (1996) 68

Faith Forever Singing (2000) 67
Faith Makes the Song (2003) 68
Faith We Sing, The (2000) 168, 360
Fill Us with Your Love (1983) 245
Five New Hymns on the City (1954) 46
Flor y Canto (1989) 18, 280
Flor y Canto, segunda edición (2001) 280, 362
Flor y Canto, tercera edición (2011) 280
Foundery Collection (1742) 134
Fourteen New Rural Hymns (1955) 46
Free to Serve (1969) 245
Freedom is Coming (1984) 314, 335
Freedom Is in Your Hand (2003) 335

Gather (1988, 1994) 9-11, 15, 16, 20, 150
Gather Comprehensive (1994) 10, 11, 16, 20
Gather Comprehensive—Second Edition (2004) 10, 11, 16, 20
Gather—Second Edition (1994) 10, 11
Gather—Third Edition (2011) 10, 11
Genevan Psalter (1562) 42
Global Praise I (1996, rev. 1997) 225, 226, 280, 337
Global Praise II (2000) 225, 226, 280, 334
Global Praise III (2004) 225, 280
Global Songs 2 (1997) 225
Global Songs: Local Voices (1995) 225
Glory and Praise (1977, 1980, 1982) 8-9
Glory and Praise—Second Edition (1997) 9
Glory to God (2013) 48
Gospel Hymns Nos. 1-6 (1875-1891) 108, 125

413

Gospel Pearls (1921) 86, 90
Graduale Romanum (1974) 22
Graduale Simplex (1975) 22
Green Print for Song (1963) 143

Halle, Halle: We Sing the World Round (1999) 340, 361, 366, 369
Heaven Shall Not Wait: Songs of Creation, the Incarnation,
and the Life of Jesus (1986) 314, 318, 319, 343, 344, 345
Heavenly Highway Hymns (1956) 126
Hela världen sjunger (The Whole World Sings) (1997) 224
Himnario Bautista (1978) 279
Himnario Unido (1999) 280, 362
Himnos Selectos (1921) 275
Hinário para o Culto Cristao (1990) 279
His Fullness Songs (1906) 87
His Fullness Songs (1977) 82, 86, 87
Holding in Trust: Hymns of the Hymn Society in the
United States and Canada (1992) 66, 368
Hymnal 1940 (1943) 56
Hymnal 1982, The (1985) 203
Hymnal: A Worship Book (1992) 226
Hymnal for the Assembly (1947) 216
Hymnal for Young Christians (1967, 1970, 1973) 6-7
Hymnal of the Christian Methodist Episcopal Church, The (1987) 82
Hymnal of the Christian Methodist Episcopal Church
    Discipleship 2000 Edition, The (2000) 83
Hymns Ancient and Modern (1st ed., 1861) 240
Hymns and Sacred Poems (1749) 135
Hymns for the Family of God (1976) 119, 124, 127
Hymns for the Gospels (2001) 45, 66
Hymns for the Living Church (1974) 145
Hymns for Today's Church (1982) 47, 51-52, 66
Hymns Hot and Carols Cool (1963) 146, 170
Hymns of United Worship (1997) 338
Hymns of Universal Praise (1936, 1977, 2006) . . . 282, 286-287, 337, 338, 339
In Every Corner Sing (1992) 68
In Every Corner Sing: Song's of God's World (2008) 329
In Search of Hope and Grace (1991) 59
Incwadi Yamaculo Ase-rabe (1929) 258
Incwadi Yamaculo Amaxhosa (1929, 1974) 258
Incwadi Yenkonzo Nezingoma (1954) 335

Index of Hymnals and Hymnal Supplements, Hymnaries, Psalters, and Hymn Collections Cited

Innkeepers and Light Sleepers: Seventeen New Songs for Christmas (1992) . . 344, 345
Iona Abbey Music Book: Song from the Iona Abbey Worship Book (2003 . . 163, 171

Jaya Ho, Songs of Joy from India (1955-1956) 294
Jesus Only, No. 1 (1899) 87
Jesus Only, No. 1 revised and No. 2 (1901) 87
Journeysongs (1994, 2003) 16
Journeysongs—Third Edition (2012) 16

Kristus Sundaring Bali (Christ the Light to Bali): New Balinese Hymns (1988) . 340

Lambeth Praise (2008). 329
Laudamus (6 eds., 1952-1990) 216, 224
Lead Me, Guide Me (1987) 17-18, 82
Lead Me, Guide Me—Second Edition (2012) 17-18, 84, 87, 90, 100
Lead Us, Lord (1977) 244, 333
Leap My Soul (1976) 245
Let Us Sing: Hymns, Songs and Choruses (2002) 337
Libro de Liturgia y Cántico (1998) 279, 336, 337, 362
Lift Every Voice and Sing (1981) 82
Lift Every Voice and Sing II (1993) 83
Lift Up Your Hearts (2013) 48
Lord of the Dance 143
Love + Anger: Songs of Lively Faith and Social Justice (1997) 342, 344
Love from Below: The Seasons of Life, the Call to Care,
    and the Celebrating Community (1989) 318, 319, 342, 343, 344
Lutheran Book of Worship (1978) 41, 66
Lutheran Service Book (2006) 66
Lutheran Worship (1982) 66

Many and Great: Songs of the World Church (1990) 315, 318
Methodist Hymnal, The (1966) 242
Mil Voces Para Celebrar (1996) . . . . xxix, 280, 362
More Voices (2007). 59, 150
Mwimbieni Bwana (Sing to the Lord) (1988). 245

Ndwiyo Dzechechi Dzevu (Church Music of the Soil) (1963, 1965) 251
New Century Hymnal, The (1995) . . . . xlvii, 47, 66, 67, 168, 170
New Hymnal, The (1983). 282
New Hymns for the Lectionary (1986) 45, 66
New Metrical Psalter, A (1986) 66

New National Baptist Hymnal 21st Century Edition, The (2001) 83
New National Baptist Hymnal, The (1977) 82
New Oxford Book of Carols, The (1992). 169
New Progressive National Baptist Hymnal, The (1982) 82
New Songs of Asian Cities (1972) 299, 341
New Wine in Old Wineskins (2007, 2010) 83, 84, 367
Ngoma: dze United Methodist Church Ye Zimbabwe (1964, 1995) . . 253, 333
Njalo (Always): A Collection of 16 Hymns in the African Tradition (2006) . . 334

O Cântico da Vida (1991) 277
O Novo Canto da Terra (1987). 276
One Faith/Una Voz (2005) 19
Oramos Cantando/We Pray in Song (2005) 19, 280
Oxford Book of Carols, The (1928) 134, 140

Pagoda, The: Thirteen Chinese Hymns (1946, 1952) 287, 339
Pave the Way: Global Songs 3 (2004) 225
People's Mass Book (1961, 1964, 1970, 1976, 1984) 6, 13
Piae Cantiones (1562) 134
Praise Book, The (1983) 180
Praise! Our Songs and Hymns (1982) 115
Presbyterian Hymnal, The (1990) 66, 168, 203
Psalm Praise (1973) 51
Psalm for All Seasons (2012). 66
Psalms, The: 150 Metrical Psalms for Singing to Well-Known Hymn Tunes (2006) 66
Psalms of Patience, Protest, and Praise (1993 . . . . 53, 344
Psalter Hymnal (1987). 66, 203, 242, 368

Rak Phra Jao, Rao Pen Thai (The Love of God Sets Us Free):
    A Collection of New Thai Hymns (1989) 340, 341
Regocijate y Canta (Rejoice and Sing) (1995). 335
Rejoice in the Lord (1985) 57, 169
Repository of Sacred Music, Part Second (1813). 138
RitualSong (1996) 16, 150, 203
Russian Praise (1999) 225
Sacred Harmony (1780) 134
Sacred Harp, The (1844) 138
Sacred Melody (1761) 134
Sacred Songs and Solos (1873) 107, 240
Scripture in Song (1979, 1981) 159, 171

Index of Hymnals and Hymnal Supplements, Hymnaries, Psalters, and Hymn Collections Cited

Sechuana (1873). 240
Sèng-si (2009) 282
Sent by the Lord: Songs of the World Church (1991) 315, 318, 344
Servant Songs (1987) 159, 171
Set Free (1993) 244, 333
Seven New Social Welfare Hymns (1961) 46
Sing! A New Creation (2001) 67, 336, 342, 360, 368
Sing Alleluia: A Supplement to the Australian Hymn Book (1987) 67
*Sing! Imba! Hlabela! Zimbabwe: Short Songs and New Compositions
   from Zimbabwean Churches* (1998) 334
Sing for Peace (2004) 68
Sing Freedom! Songs of South African Life (1993) 335
Sing Glory: Hymns, Psalms, and Songs for a New Century (1999) 52
Songs for the Ransomed (1887) 169
*Songs for the World: Contemporary Settings of Charles Wesley
   Hymns from Five Continents* (2001) 226
Songs of Love and Praise: The Hymns of John Wesley (2003) 226
Songs of Our People (1987, 1991) 328
Songs of Praise (1925) 139
Songs of Sydney Carter: In the Present Tense (5 vols., 1969) 143
Songs of Zion (1981) 82, 83, 86, 87, 88, 99
Sound the Bamboo (1990, 2000)   282, 283, 289-291, 293, 299, 338, 339, 341, 365
Southern Harmony and Musical Companion (1835) 138
Spirit Anew: Singing Prayer & Praise (1999) 168
Spirit and Song (1999, 2005) 11
Spiritual Songs for Social Worship (1832) 106
Spirituals Triumphant Old and New (1927) 90
Supplement to the Book of Hymns (1982) 276
Supplement to the Kentucky Harmony (1820) 138

Tenemos Esperanza/Temos Esperança/We Have Hope (2003) 226, 280
Thánh Ca Dân Chúa (2009) 19
There Is One Among Us (2000) 315
This Far By Faith (1999) 83, 203
Thuma Mina: Internationales oekumenishches Liederbuch (1995) 223
To Sing God's Praise (1992) 45, 66
Together in Song: The Australian Hymn Book II (1999) 55, 139. 168
*Total Praise: Song and Other Worship Resources
   for Every Generation* (2011) 84, 89, 90
Touch the Earth Lightly (2008) 68

Tumshangilie Mungu (Let Us Praise God) (six editions, 1968-1987) . . 244, 245

Una Vos/One Faith (2005) 19
Unisono: A Multilingual Book of Ecumenical Hymns (1997) 329
United in Faith and Song: Hymns and Songs in Vietnamese and English (2001) 340
United Methodist Hymnal, The (1989) 168, 168, 170, 203, 276, 283, 292, 332, 337, 338, 339, 340, 360, 365

Virginia Harmony (1831) 138
Voices as One (1999) 12
Voices United (1996) 59, 147, 150, 168

We Celebrate Worship Resource (1994, 2007-2010) 14
We Pray in Song/Oramos Cantando (2005) 19
We Walk His Way (2008) 315
When Breaks the Dawn: Hymns from Brazil (2006) 337
Where the Promise Shines (1995) 59
With One Voice (ELCA, 1995) 168
With One Voice (New Zealand, 1982) 55, 168
With One Voice (UK, 1979) 55
World Praise (1993, 1995, 2000) 225

Worship & Rejoice (2001) 122, 124, 237, 139
Worship (1971) 15
Worship II (1975) 15
Worship—Fourth Edition (2011) 15
Worship—Third Edition (1986) 15, 168
Worship His Majesty (1987) 117
Worship with Singing/Cultes avec Chants/Adoración y Canto (2007) . . . 328
Worshiping Church, The (1990) 48, 124
Worshipping Ecumenically (1995) 224

Yes, Lord! (1982) 82, 86, 87
Youth Praise 1 (1966) 51
Youth Praise 2 (1969) 51
Youth Sings: A Praise Book of Hymns and Choruses (1951) 126

Zion Still Sings! For Every Generation (2007) 83, 86, 88

Index of Hymn Tunes

ANNIVERSARY SONG (Marshall) 60
AUGUSTINE (Routley) 60, 61
BEACH SPRING (anon.) 138
BECK (Beck) 127
BOURBON (anon.) 138
BRIDEGROOM (Cutts) 60
CENTRAL (Sosa) 274
CHURCH UNITED (Fedak) 67
CONSOLATION (MORNING SONG) (anon.) 138
DEO GRACIAS (anon.) 133
DETROIT (anon.) 138
DIVINUM MYSTERIUM 134
EARTH AND ALL STARS (Brokering) 60
EAST ACKLAM (Jackson) 61
ENGLEBERG (Stanford) 60
ES IST EIN' ROS ENTSPRUNGEN (anon.) 140
FINLANDIA (Sibelius) 183
FOREST GREEN (anon., arr. Vaughan Williams) 139
FOUNDATION (anon.) 138
GIFT OF LOVE (Hopson) 68
GREET THE NEW MORN 170
HAMBURG (Mason) 197
HARMONY GROVE (anon.) 138
HOLY MANNA (anon.) 138
JENNINGS-HOUSTON (Husberg) 68
KEDRON (anon.) 138
KELVIN GROVE (trad. Scottish) 163
KINGSFOLD (anon., arr. Vaughan Williams) 139

KING'S LYNN (anon., arr. Vaughan Williams) 139
KING'S WESTON (Vaughan Williams) 60
KINGDOM (Copes) 60
LINSTEAD (Potter) xxxix
MERLE'S TUNE (Hopson) 60
NETTLETON (anon.) 138
NEW BEGINNINGS (Young) 68
NEW BRITAIN (AMAZING GRACE) (anon.) 138
NOW (Schalk) 60
RASA SAYANG (Liew) 341
RESTORATION (anon.) 138
ROLL CALL (Black) 111
SALVE FESTE DIES (Vaughan Williams) 60
ST. COLUMBA (Irish traditional) 309
SILKIE (Scottish trad.) 321
SIMPLE GIFTS (Shaker melody) 144
SINE NOMINE (Vaughan Williams) 60
SMOKEY MOUNTAIN (Loh) 301
SOUTHWELL (Damon's *The Psalms of David*, 1579) 322
STUTTGART (Witt) 238
TEMPUS ADEST FLORIDIUM (anon.) 134
TOA-SIA (Taiwanese traditional) 289
TWENTY-FOURTH (DUNLAP'S CREEK) (anon.) 138
UNION SEMINARY (Friedell) 61
VINEYARD HAVEN (Dirkson) 60
WONDROUS LOVE (anon.) 138
WOODLANDS (Greatorex) 51

Name Index

NOTE: F.H.S. following a name denotes Fellow of the Hymn Society in the United States and Canada, a distinction bestowed upon those who have made significant contributions to hymn writing, hymnology or congregational singing.

á Kempis, Thomas 133
Abbington, James . . . . xxxii, 83, 84, 100, 367
Abraham, Ken 127
Adams, Sarah F. 80
Adebesin, Biodun 242
Adey, Lionel 345
Adkins, Donna 180, 192
Adler, Jerry 65
Agawu, Kofi 235, 331, 332
Akers, Doris 79, 84, 85, 86
Akins, Debra 205
Alexander, Cecil Frances 323, 345
Alexander, Charles M. 108, 109, 126
Alexander, Neil 88
Allen, Horace B. 66
Allen, Matthew Harp 340
Allen, Richard 86
Allende, Salvador 273
Alonso, Tony 10
Alois, Brother, of Taizé 307
Alstott, Owen 16, 280
Ambrosius xxxv
Anderson, Boris 288, 339, 365
Anderson, Clare 288, 339, 365

Angotti, John 12
Angrisano, Steve 11, 12
Apel, Willi 168
Arias, Mortimer 274, 363
Armstrong. Chris 202
Armstrong, Jeremy 205
Artis, Tracey 100
Augustine of Hippo 14, 35
Ault, Gary 34
Auza, Antonio 274
Avery, Richard Kinsey 145, 146, 170, 357
Avila, Rubén Ruíz 275
Axelsson, Olof 229, 230, 248, 249, 250, 261, 333

Bach, Johann Sebastian 235
Baez, Joan 141
Baker, Dave 34
Baker, Frank 169
Baker, Richard D. 120, 124
Bakke, Corean 225
Balado, J. L. Gonzalez 341
Baldwin, Chester 94
Balhoff, Mike 34
Baloche, Paul 189, 193
Banana, Canaan 253
Bangert, Mark P. . . . . xliii, 19, 224, 328, 340
Bangsund, Judith 232, 331
Barnett, John 186, 192
Barnett, Marie 190, 193
Barraclough, Henry 108
Bartlett, Gene 124
Barz, Gregory 330, 333
Batastini, Robert, F.H.S. . . . . . xii, 10, 66, 305, 342, 343
Baughen, Michael 51
Beary, Shirley L. 126
Beaumont, Geoffrey 49, 142
Beck, John Ness 125, 127
Beecher, Lyman 106
Begbie, Jeremy S. 335

Name Index

Bell, John L., F.H.S. 10, 15, 52, 53, 57, 163, 166, 171, 223, 307, 308, 311, 312, 313, 316, 317, 318, 325, 329, 342, 343, 344, 345, 349, 353, 357, 368
Bennard, George 109
Benoit, Dom Paul, OSB 13
Benson, Louis F. 60
Berthier, Jacques 305, 306, 342
Best, Harold M. 202
Betts, Richard 170
Bidgrain, Suzanne 217
Bikel, Theodore 141
Black, George 66, 368
Black, James M. 111
Blacking, John 20
Blake, Bishop Charles E. 92
Blankenship, Mark 125
Bliss, Philip P. 107
Blount, Brian K. 204
Blue, Robert .7
Blumhofer, Edith L. 335
Boatner, Edward 90
Boccardi, Donald, SM 34
Bock, Fred 117, 124
Bohlman, Philip V. 211, 327
Bokwe, John Knox 258, 260, 334
Bokwe, Selborne T. 258
Bolduc, Ed 12
Booth, Tom 11, 12
Booth, William 177, 199, 202
Boström, Tomas 225
Bouknight, Lillian 86
Boweni, Rev. 258
Bowie, Fiona 344
Bowman, Thea 17
Boyer, Horace C. 74, 83, 96, 99, 100, 101
Bradley, Ian 307, 308, 342, 343, 344
Bradshaw, Paul 33, 281, 337
Bramley, H. R. 134
Bray, Jillian 171
Brewster, Lincoln 193
Bridge, Barbara 16

Bridges, Robert	184
Bringle, Mary Louise	20, 54, 89
Brink, Emily, F.H.S.	xxxi, 66, 67, 68, 332, 333, 337, 368
Broaddus, Andrew	135
Broadus, Cordozar Calvin "Snoop"	95
Brokering, Herbert	60
Brooks, Christopher	233, 332
Brown, Grayson Warren	16, 17
Brown, James	95
Brown, Ruth	95
Brumley, Albert E.	80
Bunyan, John	258
Burchwell, Frederick	97
Burks, Leonard	90
Burleigh, Glenn	84, 89, 357
Burnim, Mellonee	334
Burrell, Curtis	85
Burrow, Marjorie-Gabriel	17
Butler, A.L.	124
Cabié, Robert	35
Caesar, Buddy	34
Cage, Byron	94
Camacho, Joe	11
Campbell, Claudette	337
Campbell, Lucie E.	79, 84, 85, 86
Campbell, Patricia Shehan	227
Campo-Flores, Arian	201
Canedo, Ken	8, 11, 16, 33, 34
Carey, William	327
Carlson, Trish	204
Carmichael, Alexander	171
Carmichael, Ralph	124, 145, 170
Carpenter, Delores	83
Carpenter, Kelly	190, 193
Carr, Kurt	89, 94
Carrell, James P.	138
Carroll, Ewing W., Jr	283
Carter, R. Kelso	80
Carter, Sydney Bertram	143, 162, 165, 166, 270

Name Index

Cartford, Gerhard 224
Castillo, José Luis 18
Cennick, John 135
Chá, Ercilia Moreno 337
Chao, Tzu-chen 287, 366, 367
Chaplin, Marian Wood 124
Chapman, J. Wilbur 108
Cheech and Chong 202
Chelliah, D.A. 300
Chen, Pen-li 283
Cheri, Richard 90
Chernoff, John Miller 331
Chesterton, Gilbert K. xxiii
Chiaroni, Glynnis 171
Child, Francis James 140
Chotsourian, Santiago xx1v
Christensen, Phil 202
Christiansen, Richard L. 67
Chupungco, Anscar 328
Clancy, Bryant 83
Clark, Elbernita "Twinkie" 85
Clark, Mattie Moss 87
Clark, William H. 79
Clarkson, Margaret, F.H.S. 48, 59, 119, 120, 127
Clayton, David L. 138
Clephane, Elizabeth 107, 125
Cleveland, James Jefferson 82, 99
Clyde, Arthur G. 66, 67
Coleman, Robert H. 169
Collins, Dori Erwin 203
Collins, Mary 334
Colombari, Bari 35
Columba, Saint 309, 342
Columbus, Christopher 318
Colvin, Tom 14, 225, 246, 247, 262, 315, 333, 357, 361
Cone, James H. 76, 77, 99
Conry, Tom 10
Cooke, Sam 95
Cooney, Rory 10
Copes, V. Earle 60

425

Corbett, Sondra	184
Corbitt, Nathan	229, 330
Core, John	59
Cortez, Jaime	10, 11, 17
Costen, Melva	100, 225
Cowper, William	80
Crawford, Richard	141, 169
Crosby, Fanny J.	xl, 79, 80, 111, 114, 119, 125
Cross, Virginia Ann	125
Crouch, Andraé	xl, 79, 84, 85, 87, 92, 96
Crowder, David	195, 197, 200
Cuddy, Kate	10
Cuéllar, Guillermo	220, 264, 336, 357, 364
Cushman, Candi	205
Cutts, Peter	60, 167
Cyprian of Carthage	xxiv
Dameans, The	7, 10, 34
Damon, Dan	xxxvii, 334
Danner, David	124, 127
Dargie, David	219, 256, 257, 259, 329, 334, 335, 357
Davies, Oliver	344
Davisson, Ananias	138
Daw, Carl P., Jr., F.H.S.	20, 45, 57, 60, 66, 357
Dawn, Marva	184
Day, David	98, 101
Daye, Terrance	94
de Unamuno, Miguel	xx
de Waal, Esther	308, 342
Dean, Brendan	204
Dean, Kenda Creasy	204
Dearmer, Percy	61, 139
Debarge	95
DeBruyn, Randall	16
Deiss, Lucien	9, 13, 35
Delgado, Conchita	279
Derricks, Cleavant	85
Dexter, Noel	278
Dirksen, Richard	60
Doerksen, Brian	193

Name Index

Donaldson, Andrew 223
Doran, Carol 45, 60, 66
Dorsey, Thomas A. 74, 75, 79, 84, 85, 86, 96, 99
Douroux, Margaret 79, 83, 84, 85, 357
Dowell, Jimmy 84
Dox, Thurston J. 126
Drake, Ervin 127
Duba, Arlo 60
DuBois, W. E. B. 71, 72, 99
Duck, Ruth 20, 59, 89, 150, 357
Ducote, Darryl 34
Dudley-Smith, Timothy, F.H.S. 50, 51, 52, 56, 357
Dufner, Delores 20, 89
Dufford, Bob 8
Duncan, Norah IV 11, 18, 188
Dunstan, Sylvia, F.H.S. 20, 44, 59
Durán, Lucy 330, 331, 333
Dylan, Bob 141, 142, 161, 169, 356

Eggleston, Jean 94
Echols, Paul C. 169
Edgecombe, Felicia 158, 159, 161
Eiland, F. L. 80
Engquist, Richard 126
Erdozain, Carmelo 18
Escamilla, Roberto 265, 275, 280, 336
Eskew, Harry, F.H.S. 138, 168, 169, 371
Eskridge, Larry 201
Eslinger, Elise Shoemaker 280
Espinosa, J.A. 18
Evers, J. Clifford 13
Excell, Edwin O. 137, 169

Falson, Chris 187
Farhadian, Charles E. 328
Farrell, Bernadette 10, 16, 17, 19
Farrell, Melvin 13
Farquharson, Walter 59, 150
Faus, Nancy 66, 368
Faustini, João Wilson 137

Fedak, Alfred V.	67
Ferguson, Manie P.	79
Ferguson, Ron	343
Fettke, Tom	124
Fielding, Ben	193
Find, Mrs..	248
Finney, Charles G.	106
Fisher, Bobby	12
Fitzpatrick, Dennis	7, 8
Flack, Roberta	95
Fleming, Jo Lee	126
Flemming, Dolores	337
Foley, John	8, 357
Forbis, Wesley L.	124
Forman, Kristen L.	170, 336
Fortunato, Frank	226
Foster, Marc Ashley	218, 328
Foster, Stephen C.	108
Founds, Rick	183, 192
Fowler, Andrew	285, 366
Frame, John M.	202
Frances, Esther	276
Francisco, Don	179
Franklin, Aretha	95, 100
Franklin, Kirk	89, 96
Fraser, Ian	49, 52
Frazier, David	84
Frazier, Thurston	85
Friedell, Harold	61
Frostenson, Anders	xxiv, 270
Fryson, Robert J.	89
Gabaráin, Cesáreo	xxxviii, 11, 16, 18, 154, 263, 357
Gabriel, Charles Hutchinson	126
Gaither, Gloria	85, 117, 118, 119, 120, 127, 182
Gaither, William J. (Bill)	85, 117, 118, 119, 120, 127, 178, 182, 205, 356, 357
Gan, Mary Yoke Thue	338
Gannon, Michael	13
Garbouzova, Ludmilla	225
Gardner, Daniel	184, 357

Name	Pages
Gardner, Mary	86
Gaultney, Barbara Fowler	124
Garner, Norris O.	89, 94
Garrett, Dale	159, 178
Garrett, Dave	159, 178
Gaye, Marvin	95
Gelineau, Joseph	15, 35, 304, 306, 342
George, William E.	83
Gerhardt, Paul	197
Getty, Keith	54, 198
Giglio, Louie	193
Gilbert and Sullivan	108
Glen, Genevieve	16, 20
Glover, Rob	10
Gnanamani, Y.	289, 366
Goddard, Josiah	135
Godoy, Carlos	220
Goff, James R., Jr.	126
Gondo, Alexander	262, 361
González, Justo L.	336
Goodson, Albert A.	84, 86
Gordon, G. J. R.	134
Gordon, Robert Winslow	140
Graham, Billy	114, 126, 127, 178
Graham, Irvin	127
Grant, Amy	100, 183, 184, 186, 192
Green, Fred Pratt, F.H.S.	14, 15, 20, 50, 61, 67
Green, Keith	184
Green, Melody	123, 184, 192
Gregoru, Wilton D.	90
Griffin, Tony	94
Gustafson, Jim	298
Gustafson, Joan	298
Gutierrez-Achón, Raquel	265, 266, 279, 280, 336
Guthrie, Steven R.	335
Guthrie, Woody	140, 141, 169
Haas, David	xl, 9, 10, 11, 15, 17, 33, 357
Haazen, Guido	218, 219, 328
Habjan, Germaine	7

Hagan, Harry	16, 20
Haigh, Anita	163, 164, 165, 171
Haigh, Nick	163, 164, 165, 171
Hall, Charlie	193, 195
Hamilton, Maggie (Margaret)	224, 334, 335
Hamilton, Michael S.	94, 100
Hammer, M. C.	95
Hammond, Fred	94
Hammond, Paul Garnett	125
Hampton, Calvin	15
Handel, George Friderich	134, 287
Handt, Hartmut	235
Hannah, Digby	161
Harbor, Rawn	17, 90
Hargreaves, Sam	204
Harkness E. Georgia	370
Harkness, Robert	108
Harling, Per	xxxviii, 222, 224
Harmon, Kathleen	xxxi, 35, 368
Harper, Donnie	85
Harris, Kim R.	18
Harris, Robin	226, 330
Harrison, Douglas	127
Hart, Sarah	12
Harvill, Jamie	192
Hastings, Thomas	106
Haugen, Marty	xxxvii, xl, 9, 10, 15, 17, 18, 58, 150, 153, 166, 170, 357
Hawkins, Edwin	86, 95, 96
Hawkins, Walter	89
Hawks, Annie S.	79
Hawn, C. Michael	xvi, xxiii, xxxiii, xlvi, xlvii, 66, 67, 171, 204, 205, 328, 329, 330, 331, 334, 335, 336, 338, 339, 340, 342, 353, 361, 366, 369
Hawn, M. Aaron	336, 337
Hayford, Jack	182, 192, 357
Haywood, Garfield T.	84
Heber, Reginald	29
Helmore, Thomas	133, 169
Henry V, King	133
Herbert, George	61
Hewitt, Eliza E.	80

430

Hill, Rowland 202
Hillert, Richard 244
Hintza, Otto 279
Hirmer, Oswald 220, 256
Hitchcock, H. Wiley 169
Hodgson, Janet 334
Hoernle, Winifred 230
Hoffelt, Robert O. 82
Hoffman, Elisha A. 79, 80
Holder, Timothy 353
Holland, M. Roger II 18, 90
Holst, Gustav 230
Hommerding, Alan J. 20
Hopkin, Mary 334
Hopson, Hal H. 60, 68
Houghton, Israel 89, 94, 184, 193
Houghton, Meleasa 89
Houston, Joel 193
Houston, Whitney 95
Hovda, Robert W. 36
Hovland, Egil 244
Howard, Jay R. 203
Howell, Clifford 35
Hu, Te-ai 287, 366
Huber, Jane Parker 11
Hudson, Ralph 169
Huff, Ronn 117
Hughes, Howard 15
Hughes, Tim 193
Huijbers, Bernard 10
Hull, Kenneth 314, 325, 343, 345, 349, 353
Hunter, Laymon T. 83
Hurd, Bob 16, 17, 19
Hurd, David 15
Hurd, Stephen 89, 94
Husberg, Amanda 68
Hussey, Jennie E. 80
Hustad, Donald P., F.H.S. 124, 126, 146, 170
Hutchins, Norman 94, 126
Hytrek, Theophane 36

431

Ingalls, Jeremiah	135
Ingram, Jason	193
Inwood, Paul	16, 17
Jackson, Francis	61, 62
Jackson, George Pullen	169
Jackson, Irene V.	82
Jackson, Jill	356
Jackson, Phil	97, 101
Jaén, Néstor S.J.	278
Janco, Steven	14
Janssen, Jan	329
Janzen, John M.	135
Jean-Marie, Brother, of Taizé	303, 304, 306, 342
Jenkins, Philip	327
Jenny, Markus	329
Jensen, Guy	171
Jernigan, Dennis	192
John Paul II, Pope	229
John XXIII, Pope	307
Johnson, Bernice	141
Johnson, Harrison	90
Johnson, James	356
Johnson, Linda Lee	124
Johnson, Norman	115
Joncas, Jan Michael	xxxvii, 9, 10, 11, 15, 17, 357
Jones, Arthur M.	241, 243, 330, 332, 333
Jones, Charles Price	79, 82, 83, 84, 85, 86, 87, 92
Jones, Isaiah, Jr.	85
Jones, Ivor	225
Jones, Kimberly Denise ("Lil' Kim")	95
Jordan, Louis	95
Jordan, Paschal O.S.B.	278, 337, 363
Joshua's Troop	94
Julian, John	210, 227, 240, 241, 258, 327, 332
Junker, Tércio Bretanha	329
Jussila, Päivi	224
"K" in Rippon's *Selection of Hymns* (1787)	79
Kaan, Fred, F.H.S.	xxxix, 14, 15, 20, 46, 50, 56, 67, 150, 259, 274, 357

Kaatrud, Paul Gaarder	107, 125
Kaemmer, John	229, 230, 231, 249, 250, 251, 331, 333, 334
Kaiser, Kurt F.	145, 170, 182, 357
Kao, Chun-ming.	301, 365
Kauffman, Robert	229, 230, 247, 248, 249, 250, 251, 333
Kee, John P.	94
Kendrick, Graham	54, 123, 185, 187, 192, 193, 198, 357
Kennedy, John	7
Kennedy, Robert.	7
Kenoly, Ron	184, 204
Key, Stephen	84, 89
Keyte, Hugh	169
Kiefer, Ralph	35
Kieffer, Aldine S.	109
Kiley, Henry W.	295, 365
Kimball, Dan.	194, 205
Kimbrough, S T, Jr.	83, 225, 226, 280, 327, 330, 334, 337, 353
King, B. B.	95
King, D.F.	82
King, E. J.	138
King, Martin Luther, Jr.	7, 73, 89, 99, 142
King, Roberta	226, 229, 331, 332
King, Shirley Sprunger	330
Kipping, Deon	89
Klein, Christopher	329
Klein, Joe	169
Klein, L.	357
Klusmeier, Ron	150
Knight, Gladys	95
Koizumi, Isao	286
Krabill, James R.	332
Krisman, Ronald	11, 280
Kubicki, Judith Marie	306, 342
Ladies of the Grail	15
Lafferty, Karen	146, 170, 179, 180, 192, 202, 357
Lakey, Othal Hawthorne	82
Landgrave, J. Phillip	125, 170
Landry, Carey	9, 17
LaRue, John C.	204

Lawrence, Donald	94
Lawson, Robert C.	84
Leach, Richard	57
Leaver, Robin A.	35, 328
Leavitt, Joshua	106
LeBlanc, Lenny	184
Leckebusch, Martin E.	48, 66
Lee, Geonyong	285, 301
Leech, Bryan Jeffrey	58
LeFevre, Mylon R.	124
Leigh, Mitch	127
Liberius, R. F.	290, 365
Liew, Samuel	298, 299, 341, 365, 366
Light, Alan	95, 100
Light, Deanna	14
Light, Gordon	149, 166, 170
Lim, Swee Hong	xxxiii, 225, 228, 339, 341, 353, 369
Lin, Richard R.	338
Lin, Shengben	301
Lincoln, C. Eric	72, 75, 98, 99, 101
Lister, Mosie	116
Lobinger, Fritz	256
Lockward, Jorge	225, 226, 266, 280, 329, 336
Lockwood, George	276
Loftis, Deborah	xxxii, 68, 370
Loh, I-to	222, 225, 226, 254, 282, 283, 285, 289, 290, 291, 293, 299, 300, 301, 301, 328, 338, 339, 340, 341, 357
Loh, Sian-chhun	282
Lomax, Alan	140, 141
Lomax, John A.	140
Loperena, William	264, 265
Lorenz, Ellen Jane	125, 169
Louis, Kenneth W.	18, 19
Lovelace, Austin C., F.H.S.	242, 244
Lovett, Kyle	97
Lowry, Robert	107
Lubis, Tilly	298
Luff, Alan	67
Lung, Richard Ho	12, 278, 363
Luther, Martin	177, 202

434

Name Index

Lyte, Henry Francis	311
MacArthur, Terry	222, 223, 329
Macdonald, Ian	149, 170
MacDonald, Shari	202
Mackie, R. C.	217
MacLeod, George	309, 310, 311, 312, 314, 343
Macmillan, Prime Minister Harold	247
Macy, L.	331
Maher, Matt	12, 193
Malm, William P.	294, 340
Mamiya, Lawrence	72, 75, 98, 99, 101
Manalo, Ricky	11, 17, 36
Mandela, Nelson	259, 262
Mankin, Jim	126
Manibusan, Jesse	12, 17
Manion, Tim	8
Mann, Robin	55, 67, 161, 162, 165, 171, 335
Mannion, M. Francis	36
Mansfield Brian	203
Maraire, Abraham Dumisani	249, 250, 251, 252, 253, 262, 334, 361
Maraschin, Jaci Correia	276, 277, 364
Marchionda, James	14
Marsh, Donald Stuart	145, 146, 170, 357
Marshall, Jane	xxxvii, 60
Marti, Andreas	329
Martin, Civilla D.	79
Martin, Roberta	84
Martínez, Bishop Joel	xxix
Martínez, Nicolás	274
Martínez, Raquel Mora	154, 170, 268, 280, 336
Mason, Charles Harrison	92
Mason, Lowell	106
Matsikenyiri, Patrick	222, 225, 249, 250, 252, 253, 254, 262, 334, 357, 361
Mattingly, Joe	12
Maule, Graham	163, 171, 308, 312, 313, 314, 315, 316, 317, 318, 323, 342, 343, 344
Maynard-Reid, Pedrito U.	336
Mbunga, Stephen B. G.	219, 231, 328, 330, 331
McAllister, Judy (Judith)	92, 94

McClain, William B.	76, 82, 87, 88, 99
McClard, LeRoy	129, 124, 380
McCoy, Myron F.	83
McCullum, Hugh	329
McDonald, Scott	170
McElrath, Hugh T., F.H.S.	68, 138, 168, 169, 370
McGranahan, James	107
McGuffey, Danny	204
McHugh, Phill	123, 125, 357
McKay, V. Michael	84, 357
McKinney, Baylus Benjamin	110, 112, 126
McLaren, Brian	194, 204, 205
McMahon, J. Michael	35
McPherson, Aimee Semple	176
Mejia, Alejandro	16
Mendoza, Vicente	275, 363
Mensah, Atah Annan	333
Mercer, Jesse	135
Metcalfe, Jerome	85
Miffleton, Jack	14
Miles, C. Austin	80
Millard, J. A.	334
Miller, Donald E.	201
Miller, Sy	356
Minchin, James	296, 298, 300, 301
Minnaar, Maria	250, 333, 334
Mitchell, Ian	7
Moffat, Dr.	240
Molefe, Stephen Cuthbert (1917-1987)	219, 237, 259, 262, 361
Monteiro, Simei (b. 1943)	222, 225, 276, 277, 363, 364
Moody, Dwight L.	74, 178
Moore, Bob	10
Morgan, Reuben	188, 193
Moring, Mark	205
Morolong	240
Morris, Kenneth	79, 84, 86
Mortensen, John	204
Morton, David	340
Mote, Edward	80

Mtambenengewe, Baba 247
Mulrain, George 225, 226, 278, 263, 364
Mullins, Rich 11, 357
Munizzi, Marth 89
Murphy, Gale Jones 90
Murray, A. Gregory 1
Murray, J. Glenn 17
Murray, Shirley Erena, F.H.S.. . . . . 55, 56, 68, 89, 150, 277, 301, 334, 357
Music, David, F.H.S. . . . . xxxii, xlvi, 126, 370
Mxadana, George 222
Myrin, Jonas 193

Nachtwey, Roger 7
Nasuti, Harry P.. . . . . 24, 35
Neale, John Mason 133, 134, 353
Neeley, Paul 226, 227, 330,
Nelson, Greg 123, 125
Nelson G., Eduardo 279
Nettl, Bruno 330, 332
Nettleton, Asahel 106
Newton, John 79, 135, 137
Newton, Leigh 161
Nguyen, Dao-Kim 340
Nketia, J. H. Kwabena. 230, 231, 331, 332
Nicks, Charles H. Jr. 84, 89
Niles, Daniel Thambyrajah (1908-1970) 281, 289, 292, 357, 366
Niwaglia, Wilson 245, 361
Nix, W. M. 86
Nix [-Allen], Verogla 82, 87, 99
Noll, Mark A. 335
Norful, Smokie 94
Norman, Larry 179, 200
Nowell, Irene. 35
Ntahokaja, John Baptist 228, 330
Ntsikana (Gaba), the prophet 217, 257, 258, 259, 334, 361
Ntsikana, William Kobe 258
Nyberg, Anders (b. 1955). 259, 261, 314, 335, 357
Nystrom, Martin 183, 192, 357

Oatman, Johnson, Jr. 79, 80
O'Brien, Francis Patrick 10
O'Connell, Matthew J. 35
O'Connor, Roc 8
Ogden, Ina 109
Oldenburg, Bob 170
Oliver, Gary 184, 192
Olsen, Dale A. 356
Olsen, Ted 203
Olson, Howard S. 229, 230, 243, 244, 245, 262, 333
Olude, A. T. Olajida 241, 242, 361
Owens, Carol 124, 357
Owens, Oliver J. 84
Oosterhuis, Huub 10
O'Shields, Michael 183, 192
Oyer, Mary, F.H.S. 226, 330

Pace, Joseph II 89
Page, Paul 14
Pagura, Federico José . . 270, 271, 271, 273, 274, 328, 336, 337, 357, 363, 364
Palmer, Horatio R. 80
Palmer, Ray 80
Paluch, J. S. 14
Paris, Twila 11, 184, 192
Park, Andy 190, 193
Parrott, Andrew 169
Parsons, Elizabeth 242
Parsons, Squire E., Jr. 124
Patterson, Bishop G.E. 93
Patterson, Joy 59
Paul VI, Pope 154
Pavlechko, Thomas xxxvii
Payne, Tony 225
Peacock, David (b. 1949) 224, 225, 329
Pearson, Carlton 93
Pecklers, Keith F. 33
Peloquin, C. Alexander 15
Perera, Homero 271, 272, 273, 274, 336
Perry, Michael 60
Peter, Paul, and Mary 141, 161

Peterson, John W. 114, 115, 116, 119, 127
Phillips, Philip 107
Phommedda, TongPan 298
Pinn, Anthony 95, 100
Pinochet, Augusto 273
Pitman, Don 338
Pius X, Pope 33
Pius XII, Pope 33
Plantinga, Cornelius, Jr. 202
Polan, Abbot Gregory 34
Pollard, Deborah Smith 93, 96, 100
Polman, Bert 203, 332, 333
Pope, Marion 285
Porter, Thomas Henry 126
Posthuma, Phil 193
Potter, Doreen xxxix
Power, David N. 334, 342
Prassl, Franz Karl 329
Prendergast, Michael 35
Prescod, Patrick 278, 364
Presley, Luther G. 126
Price, Deborah Evans 204, 205
Price, Frank W. 339
Price, Milburn 371
Proulx, Richard 11, 15, 18
Prudentius, Aurelius Clemens 271, 352, 363
Puig, Carlos 279
Purdue, Peter 35

Quick, Norman N. 82
Quinlan, Paul 7
Quinn, Frank C. 26, 35

Raley, J. Michael 68
Rambo, Dottie 124
Ramírez, Ariel 220, 267, 272
Ramírez, Daniel 263, 335
Randolph, James Weldon 84
Rawls, R. Maines 124
Reagon, Cordell 141

439

Redman, Beth 193, 205
Redman, Matt 185, 189, 193, 195, 196, 205
Redman, Robb 94, 100
Reeves, Jesse 193, 205
Reid, Stephen Breck 35
R.E.M.. 188
Repp, Ray 7, 142, 169
Reza, Mary Frances. 16, 18
Reynolds, William J., F.H.S. 120, 124, 126, 170, 371
Riccitelli, James M. 330
Richard, Cliff 178
Richardson, Paul A., F.H.S. . . . . xxxiv, 167, 170, 371
Riddle, Jennie Lee 193
Ridge, M. D. 16, 17
Riley, Teddy 95
Rivers, Clarence J. 13
Robert, Brother, of Taizé 305, 306
Roberts, Leon C. 17, 18
Robinson, Eddie 89
Robinson, Robert . . . . xxv, 137
Rodeheaver, Homer 108, 109, 110, 126
Rodgers and Hammerstein 127
Rogers, June Ramage 338
Rohrbaugh, Lynn 339
Rojas, Juan 280
Romanowski, William D. 203
Romero, Archbishop Oscar 220
Rosas, Carlos 18, 276, 357, 363
Rossetti, Christina 323, 344
Rothenbusch, Esther Heidi 125
Routley, Erik . . . . . xxvii, xxxiv, xxxvii, xlvi, 42, 43, 50, 55, 56, 60, 61, 66, 67,
    144, 167, 168, 170, 210, 222, 242, 274, 326, 327, 329, 349
Rowthorn, Jeffrey 58, 58
Rubalcava, Pedro 17
Ruebush, Ephraim 109
Ruff, Anthony 24, 33, 35, 36, 328
Ruiz, Alejandro 275
Ruiz, Rubén 275, 363
Russell, Rosemary 171
Ruth, Lester 177, 202

Sadie, Stanley	169, 330
Sadler, Sgt. Barry	142
Sadoh, Godwin	242, 332
St. Francis of Assisi	197
St. Louis Jesuits	8, 9, 10, 17
Saliers, Don	xlii, xliii, xliv, xlvii
Sammis, John H.	80
Sanchez, Pete, Jr.	180, 192
Sanders, Cheryl J.	91, 100
Sands, Ernest	17
Sanderson, Lloyd. O	110, 126
Sankey, Ira D.	74, 107, 109, 112, 115, 125, 126, 178, 240
Saward, Michael	52, 66, 67
Schaefer, Edward	26, 35
Schalk, Carl, F.H.S.	60
Scheer, Greg	xxxiii, 205, 371
Schilling, S. Paul	xli, xlvii
Schoenbachler, Tim	34
Scholtes, Peter	14, 270
Schubert, Franz	11
Schutte, Dan	8, 14, 19, 123, 357
Schütte, Peter	328
Schutz-Marsauche, Roger Louis	303, 306, 307, 342
Scriven, Joseph M.	80
Scorsese, Martin	169
Seeger, Pete	141, 142, 356
Shaha, Bart	291, 339, 365
Sharp, Cecil	140
Shaw, Martin	139
Shea, George Beverly	114
Sheehy, Daniel E.	336
Sheik, Duncan	188
Shepherd, Thomas	80
Shirl, Jimmy	127
Shorney, George, F.H.S.	56, 68
Shorter, Alyward	328
Slough, Rebecca	330
Smallwood, Richard	85, 86, 357
Smith, Chuck	179
Smith, Efrem	97, 101

Smith, Elizabeth J. 67
Smith, James Todd (a.k.a. L.L. Cool J.) 95
Smith, Joshua 135
Smith, Martin 185, 186, 188, 189, 192, 193
Smith, Michael W. 183, 192, 196
Smith, Tim E. 12
Simon, Paul 161
Soga, Tiyo 258, 335
Sontonga, Enoch Mankayi 258, 259, 361
Soper, Scott 16
Sosa, Juan J. 18
Sosa, Pablo David . . . xxvii, xxxviii, xlvi, 222, 265, 267, 268, 274, 329, 336, 357, 371
Sousa, John Philip 108
Southern, Eileen 86, 87
Spafford, Horatio G. 80
Spencer, John Michael 331
Spink, Kathryn 342
Spinks, Bryan 33
Spretnak, Charlene . . . . xvii, xxiv
Srisuwan, Inchai 298
Srisuwan, Ruth 298
Stainer, John 134
Stanphill, Ira F. 116, 127
Stanford, Charles Villiers 60
Stansbury, George W., Jr 126, 127
Stauffer, S. Anita 328, 330, 340
Stebbins, George C. 107
Stead, Louisa M. R. 80
Stevens, Marsha 124
Stevens, W. B. 79
Stevenson, Iris 87
Stevenson. W. R. 210, 240, 327, 332
Stillman, Al 127
Stone, Ruth M. 330, 331
Stonehill, Randy 179
Stowe, Everett M. 285, 356
Strathdee, Jean 147
Strathdee, Jim 147, 148, 166, 357
Strauss, Johann, Jr. 108
Streck, John M. 203, 204

Name Index

Stuempfle, Herman, Jr., F.H.S. 20, 58, 89
Suarez, Pedro. 279
Sullivan, Arthur S. 108
Sunday, Billy 108
Sunquist, Scott W. 338
Suppe, Gertrude C. 275, 337
Sutton, Joan Larie 279
Sweet, Leonard 194, 205
Synesius of Cyrene 322

Tam, Angela 282
Tarigan, S. 300, 366
Tate, Paul A. 12, 14
Taylor, Godfrey 337
Taylor, Timothy D. 213, 214, 237
Temple, Sebastian 14
Thangaraj, Thomas M. 293, 366
The Clark Sisters 92, 95
The Edwin Hawkins Singers 95
The Proclaimers 188
The Winans 92, 95
Thiem, James 7
Thomas, M.D. 209
Thomerson, Kathleen 14, 124
Thompson, Will L. 80
Thornburg, John . . . . xii, 59, 68
Thornton, Marilyn E. 83
Thorsén, Stig-Magnus 250, 333
Thue, Mary Gan Yoke 338
Thurman, Howard 147
Tice, Adam 89
Tindley, Charles A. 79, 83, 84, 85, 86, 356
Tinio, Rolando 298, 301, 366
Tisdale, Leonora Tubbs 204
Tomaszek, Tom 11, 12
Tomlin, Chris 12, 189, 193, 195, 197, 205
Toolan, Suzanne 15, 155, 156, 165, 170, 357
Torrellas, Angel 329, 336
Torrey, Reuben A. 108
Towner, Daniel B. 108

443

Townend, Stuart	54, 193, 198, 351
Townsend, Willa A.	86, 90
Tracey, Andrew	231, 249, 256
Tracey, Hugh	230, 247, 249, 258, 331, 334
Trautwein, Dieter	xix, 223
Troccoli, Kathy	12
Troeger, Thomas	15, 45, 46, 57, 66, 357
True, Lori	10
Truitt, Gordon E.	35
Turino, Thomas	237, 332
Turner, Nancy M.	66
Turner, Tina	95
Twit, Kevin	64, 197
Tyamzashe, Benjamin John Peter	219, 259
Tyrrell, John	330, 56
Vajda, Jaroslav, F.H.S.	58, 60, 357
Van den Heuvel, Albert	xxv, xxvi, xxvii, xlvi
Vaughan Williams, Ralph	60, 131, 139, 230
Vaughan, James D.	109, 126
Vermulst, Jan	13, 14
Verwoerd, Hendrik	247
Vigil, José María	329, 336
Viswanathan, T.	340
Vogt, Janet	11
Wade, Bonnie C.	227
Wainwright, Geoffrey	xlvi
Walker, Christopher	16, 17
Walker, Hezekiah	94
Walker, Tommy	188, 204
Walker, William	138
Walker, Wyatt Tee	71, 73, 75, 78, 99, 100
Wallace, Bob	149
Wang, Weifan	283, 301
Ward, Karen M.	83
Warner, Steve	10, 12, 14
Washington, Dinah	95
Watkins, Craig	97
Watson, J. Richard	227, 335

Name Index

Watts, Isaac 79, 80, 105, 197, 209
Weaver, Geoff 223, 225, 329
Weakland, Archbishop Rembert. 36
Webber, Christopher L. 66
Wechkama, Banpote 298
Weidler, Scott C. 203
Wemen, Henry 261
Wesley, Charles . xv, 50, 63, 67, 134, 135, 137, 169, 202, 226, 271, 276, 353, 363
Wesley, John . . . . xv, 134, 135, 197, 226
Westendorf, Omer 13, 357
Westermeyer, Paul, F.H.S. 47, 59, 67, 139, 169
Whalum, Wendell P., Sr. 98, 101
White, Benjamin Franklin 138
White, James F. 40, 65
Whitfield, Frederick. 80
Whitney, Rae 58, 125
Wiant, Allen Artz 337, 339
Wiant, Bliss Mitchel 282, 286, 287, 288, 337, 339, 366
Wiant, Leighton 339
Wiant, Mildred 286, 287, 288, 339
Wicker, Vernon . . . . xlvi, 336
Wilhoit, Melvin Ross 125, 126
Williams, Nolan B. 83
Williams, William 79
Wilmore, Gayraud 72
Wilson, Eli Jr. 83
Wilson, Jackie 95
Wilson, John W., F.H.S. 52, 66
Wimber, Carol 203, 204
Wimber, John 185, 189, 200, 203, 204, 357
Wimbush, Vincent L. 100
Wise, Joe 14
Witvliet, John D. 40, 65, 66
Wolfe, Lanny 120, 124
Wonder, Stevie 95
Woodstock, Brian 343
Work, Frederick J. 86
Work, John W. Jr. 86
Wren, Brian, F.H.S. 20, 50, 56, 57, 68, 89, 150
Wyeth, John 138

Wyrtzen, Don 124
Xiao-min, Lü. 338

Yackley, David 12
Yamaguchi, Tokuo 285, 356, 365
Yancy, Kevin 85
Ylvisaker, John 132, 146, 147, 166, 170, 357
York, Terry W. 125, 126, 201, 203, 205
Young, Carlton R., F.H.S. . . . . . xii, 68, 83, 146, 169, 170, 225, 226, 280
   286, 327, 332, 337, 338, 339, 353

Zaragoza, Rufino, OFM 340
Zhungu, L.G. 334
Zimmerman, Joyce Ann 35, 328
Zschech, Darlene 186, 187, 188, 193, 197, 204

Subject Index

African-American recordings, Influence of 93, 94
African-American secular artists, Influence of 75, 76, 95, 96
African diaspora 267
African hymnody, ... 228-262
    catalyst 257
    composition process of Dargie 257
    Colvin 245-247
    Kauffman 247-248
    Olson 243-245
    missionary contributions to 232-233, 243-250
    theology of 262
    varieties of 239-241
African Initiated Congregations (AIC) 331 n73
African Music Journal 231
African music, characteristics of traditional 231-237
African Music Society 231
African National Congress (ANC) 259
African Sunday Marimba Mass: Song Book 329 n33
Afrocentrism 78
Agincourt Song, The 133
Alabama bus protest (1955-1956) 73
Aladura ("owners of prayer") 233-234, 261
All African Church Music Journal 248
alterity (otherness) 214
Amadodana 260
American evangelicalism 175
American Society of Composers, Authors and Publishers (ASCAP) . . . 145
animateurs 222, 223, 253, 265, 278, 329 n37, 351, 371

apartheid 247, 256, 258, 259, 260, 261, 262, 327
Apostolic Church 91
Archive of American Folk Song 140, 141
Arts Workshops (Zimbabwe) 247-249, 252
Asian hymnody 281-302
    Carnatic music 293
    Hindustani music 289
    East Asia (China, Korea, Japan, Taiwan and Hong Kong) . . . 283-289
    South Asia (Bangladesh, Nepal, Pakistan, India and Sri Lanka) . 289-294
    Southeast Asia (Brunei, Kampuchea (*Cambodia*), Indonesia, Philippines, Laos, Malaysia, Myanmar (*Burma*), Singapore, Thailand, and Vietnam) . 294-300
    theological foci of 300-301
Asian School of Music, Worship and the Arts 296
Asian Workshop for Liturgy and Music 291
Azusa Street Revival (1906) 178, 356

baguala 271
bamboo instruments 295
bhajan (India) 293
Big Sing (Iona Community) 315s
Billy Graham crusades 114, 178
bi-lingual texts 286
Black Nationalism 81
Black Power 76
Black Theology 77-78, 81
Blantyre Covenant 331 n66
Book of Common Prayer 196
"boomers" 121, 182, 194
Born a King 115
Bread for the Journey 225
Brooklyn Tabernacle Choir 184
Brothers Four 141
Brownsville revival 184
Bulawayo marimba 249, 250, 251
business and CCM 6

CCM crossover 195
"call and response" 136, 166, 167, 219, 232, 237, 242, 251, 294
Calvary Chapel (California) 146, 179, 182
campmeeting songs 105, 106, 135-138, 164

Campus Life magazine 196
Canaan Hymns 338 n182
Cantata Folklorico para Pascua de Resurrección 271, 272
Canterbury Dictionary of Hymnology 227, 369
candombe 272
cantos cancioneros 335 n141
Carlton Pearson Recordings 93
Caribbean Mass (Lung) 12
Carmina Gaedelica 164
Carnatic (Karnatic) Music 293
carnavalito 269, 273
carol (*carole*) tradition 133-135
catalyst (for composition) 50, 57, 257
"Celebration Medley, The" 92
Celtic music/spirituality/tradition . 163-165, 198, 308, 317-320, 322, 324, 351
centonization 125 n2
chamarrita 269
chacarera 271
Chemin Neuf Community 341 n232
changgo 285
Charismatic movement/music/worship . . . xl, xli, 40, 48, 53, 94, 112, 122,
    178, 182, 200
Church of God in Christ, The (COGIC) 82, 92
Church of the Apostles (Seattle) 198
Christian "boy bands" 176
Christian Copyright Licensing International (CCLI) . 180, 183, 193 203, n24, 356
Civil Rights Movement . . . . . xvii, xxxii, 6, 73, 76,81, 95, 141, 142, 259
Common Cup Company, The 149-152
Community Mass (Proulx) 18
Consejo Latinoamericano de Iglesias (CLAI) 273
Consultation on Common Texts (CCT) 44
Consultation on Ecumenical Hymnody (CEH) . . . . xxvii-xxviii
Constitution on the Sacred Liturgy 4-5, 178, 217-218
contemporary Christian music (CCM) 8, 12, 121-123, 146,
    162, 179, 182-183, 186-187, 192, 195-196
Contemporary Christian Music (journal) 180
contemporary Christian worship 145, 176, 194
contrafactum 106, 234, 334 n117
Coracle (journal) 110, 342 n254
coritos 263, 266

Corpus Christi Mass (Proulx) 11
Council of British Missionary Societies 210
"country" gospel. 109
cueca 270, 274
cyclic musical structures . . . . . xl, xli, xlii, 167, 220, 232, 236, 261

Dameons 7, 10
Delirious 118
demographics, worldwide Christian 213
Dictionary of Hymnology (Julian) 210, 227, 240, 241, 258
Dictionary of North American Hymnology. 66 n5
dondang ensembles 294
Dunblane gatherings 49-53

ecumenical and missionary hymnody 210, 221, 229, 250, 326
Edwin Hawkins Singers, The 95, 96
"Emergencies" of 1960 and 1986 259
emerging worship 191, 196, 198, 200
English and Scottish Popular Ballads, The 140
English Folk-Song: Some Conclusions 140
English folk melodies 139-140
estribillos 220
EthnoDoxology (journal) 227
Ewe (Ghana) 235, 237
Evangelicals 176-178, 186, 187, 189, 199, 226
"Experiencing Music, Expressing Culture" 227

"Father of Gospel Music" 74
F.E.L. Publications 7
fiesta spirit 265, 268
five phases of worship (Wimber) 189
Fjedur 261
folk hymns/melodies. 132-133, 138
    social concerns 7
    theological perspectives 165-166
Folk Mass 7-9, 14, 25, 49, 142, 224, 225, 272

folk music 140
    with Iona Community 317-318
folk musicals 145, 178

Subject Index

Folk Songs of the Southern Appalachians 140
"four-hymn" Mass 26
Freedom Ride (1961) 73
Freedom Singers 141
Freedom Songs 14, 74, 238, 259-262
frontier camp-meeting 105, 106, 135-138, 164
frontier revivals 135, 177
"full, conscious, and active participation" 3, 4, 6, 28

gamelan 294, 295, 297, 301
"gapped" scale 106, 132
Garland Encyclopedia of World Music, The 227, 249
Gather hymnbooks 11, 15, 16, 20, 150
GCoMM Conferences 227
Gen Xers 194
GIA Publications . . . . xii, 10, 15, 16, 17, 19, 51, 57, 89, 90, 150, 155, 270
global music . . . . xxxiii, 10, 52, 161, 209-345
Global Praise Project 225-226
gong-chime ensembles 294, 296
gong-circle ensembles 294
Good News 142, 178
gospel chorus 110, 123
"gospel marches" 108
Gospel Music Hall of Fame 145
"gospel patter songs" 108
gospel song 86-96, 106-112
"gospel waltzes" 108
global hymnody 212-215
    transmission of 215
globalization 213, 300
"Grail-Gelineau" psalms 15, 304, 306
Gregorian Chant . . . . xliv, 5, 7, 13, 15, 20, 22, 25, 26, 28, 29
guitar . . . . xxxii, xxxviii, xxxix, xl, 7, 9, 10, 19, 51, 52,
    91, 132, 141, 142, 150, 166, 180, 181, 182, 187, 188, 189, 195, 200, 233,
    236, 238, 266, 296, 297

Habitat for Humanity 194
Hampton University Ministers' and Musicians' Conference . . . xxxii, 79, 367
harmonium (India) 294
"harp and bowl" worship 198

heterophonic accompaniment . . . . xxxvii, 283
hexatonic melody 110, 132
Hillsong 184, 187-188
Hip Hop (Holy hip hop) 91, 95-97, 351
Holiness-Pentecostal Worship. 87, 91, 177
Holy City events (Iona). 315
Hosanna! Music. 184
Hymn Society in the United States and Canada, The . . v, xi, xxxi, 47, 56, 57,
    277, 369, 370, 371
"hymn[ic] explosion" . . . . xxvi, xxvii, xxxi, 46, 59, 63, 263

improvisation. . . . . xxxvii, 75, 80, 148, 166, 236, 295
International Council of Ethnodoxologists (ICE) 226
International Library of African Music (ILAM) 230-231
inculturation, liturgical 29, 216, 218, 229, 262, 272
industry, Praise & Worship 8, 95, 175, 179, 182,183,
    185, 186, 190, 191, 196, 199, 200
Integrity Music 184-185, 187, 191
International House of Prayer (IHOP) 198
intimacy and CCM 177, 185, 189, 190, 200, 201

Iona Community. 10, 52-53, 57, 163, 223, 307-326
    Church of Scotland and 223, 245, 307, 310, 311, 312, 319, 325
    Cistercian Abbey at 310
    Celtic influence on 308, 317-320, 322, 324
    Coracle 310
    Columba legacy. 307-309, 310, 319
    five-fold rule of 312
    John Bell's work for 312-317
    MacLeod legacy 309-312, 314
    Wild Goose Worship Group 309, 311, 312-318
    Wild Goose Publications 312-316
    Wild Goose Resource Group (WGRG). 223, 314, 325
iPods in worship 63, 200

Jars of Clay 64, 197
jazz influence 6, 49, 110, 186, 238-239
"Jesus is my girlfriend" songs 190
"Jesus music" 121, 179, 180, 181

"Jesus movement" 146, 178, 198
"Jesus People" 178, 182
Jubilate Group, The 50, 51-52, 53
King James Version 146, 183
Kingston Trio 141
kulintang (Filipino) 294
kriti (India) 293

Ladies of the Grail 15
La Nueva Misa Mesoamericana 220
Last of the Month workshops (Iona) 313
Latin American hymns 262-280
    baguala 271
    candombe 272
    cantos cancioneros 335 n141
    carnavalito 269, 273
    chamarrita 269
    chacarera 271
    cueca 270-274
    dance 268, 269, 270, 272, 274
    fiesta spirit 265-266, 268
    gran fiesta 268
    liberation 264, 265, 268, 274, 278
    milonga 272
    musical characteristics 266-268
    Sanctus (Santo) settings 264, 265, 270
    tango 271-274
    theological characteristics 266-268
    zamba 271
Latin language 5, 9, 11, 13, 15, 16, 17, 18, 19, 22, 26,
    27, 28, 29, 44, 142, 219, 229, 240, 256, 271, 305, 306
Latino Pentecostal hymns 263
    coritos 263, 266
    theology of 263
Last Night Out events (Iona) 315
leadsheet format 187
Lectionary for Mass 22, 23
Light Music Group, 20th Century 142, 178
Liturgical Movement 3, 33 n3, 40-41
Lord of the Dance and other songs and poems 143

Love Transcending 115
Lumko Missiological Institute 256, 257

macaronic carol 134
Magnificat 295
makwaya (style) 260
Man of LaMancha 127 n26
Maranatha! Music 146, 179, 180-181, 185
March for Jesus (Kendrick) 185, 187
Mass
    African 218-219,
      bilingual (multilingual) texts 5, 6, 11, 12, 29
    Central and South American 262, 268
      cultural diversity and inculturation of . . . 15, 30, 218, 229, 262, 272
    Filipino settings 5
    "four-hymn" Mass 26
    Folk Mass . . . 6, 7, 8, 9, 14, 18, 19, 25, 49, 142, 224, 225, 272
      global music 10, 219, 224
    jazz settings 16
      Latin language 5, 11, 13, 15, 16, 19, 219
      missalettes 14
    multilingual texts 5, 6, 11, 12, 29
    Ordinary of the Mass 5, 218, 219, 220, 264
    Pacific Rim settings 5
    Roman rite 29
      Tridentine Mass (Pius V) 22
    vernacular in the mass . 5, 7, 8, 9, 10, 13, 21, 22, 26, 30, 142, 220, 272
    Vietnamese settings 5, 12, 19
Mass for Christian Unity (Vermulst) 13, 14
Mass for the Life of the World (Camacho/Haas) 11
Mass for Young Americans (Repp) 7, 142
Mass of a Joyful Heart (Angrisano/Tomazek) 12
Mass of Celebration (Bolduc) 12
Mass of Creation (Haugen) 10, 18
Mass of Glory (Canedo) 16
Mass of Life (Booth) 12
Mass of Rejoicing (Angotti) 12
Mass of St. Timothy (Maher) 12
Mass of the Bells (Peloquin) 15
Mazuva Ekupedzisa (*The Last Days*) 251

Subject Index

Methodist Holiness movement 177
mbira 236, 247, 248, 249, 251
Millennials 194
milonga 272
Milwaukee Symposia for Church Composers, The (1992) 28
Misa Campesina 220
Misa Criolla 220, 267, 272
Misa del Mundo (Manibusan) 12
Misa Popular Nicaragüense 220, 264
Misa Popular Salvadoreña 220, 264
Misa Santa Barbara (Fisher) 12
Missa 1 (Tyamzashe) 259
Missa Baba Yetu (Mbunga) 219
Missa Emmanuel (Proulx) 11
Missa Luba (Haazen) 218-219, 229
Missa Ubi Caritas (Hurd) 16
Moody Bible Institute 108
Motown 94
Música para Todos (Music for All) 269
Musicam Sacram 34 n18, 35 n24

Nairobi Statement on Worship and Culture 330 n44
"Nancy Dawson" 134
Natural High 145
Navidad Neuestra 267, 272
New Christy Minstrels 141
New Plainsong Mass (Hurd) 15
Newport Folk Festival (1963) 141
ngoma 233, 260
No Greater Love 155
North American Liturgy Resources (NALR) 9, 10
Northumbria Community 163, 165
Now We Can Start 14
ontological question, "What is a hymn" . . . . . . xli, 4, 211, 212, 231
oral tradition . . . . . xxxv, xxxvi-xxxvii, 73, 212, 219, 229, 232, 236,
    237, 239, 242, 244, 254, 257, 258, 269
organ (pipe, electronic, mouth, reed) . . . xxv, xxxviii, xxxix, 5, 39, 52, 60,
    91, 109, 166, 182, 190, 233, 239, 271, 275, 293, 295, 298
organum 235
Oregon Catholic Press (OCP) 9, 11, 12, 16, 17, 18, 19

Oxford Movement 133, 144
parody 125 n2, 218
Psallite Mass (Joncas) 11
paschal mystery 4, 25, 31, 32
Passion gatherings 194-195
pentatonic scale 132, 181, 283, 287, 294, 338 n186
Pentecostal Church (singing) . . . . xxxiii, 40, 55, 87, 91, 177, 178, 188, 198, 200, 263, 275
Pentecostal hymnody, Latino 263
Pentecostal revival 178
Peter, Paul, and Mary 141, 161
Pirates of Penzance, The 108
Poor People's Campaign (1968) 73
popular culture . . . . . xlv, 51, 64, 93, 96, 175, 176, 178, 189, 199, 200
popular music 63, 176-177, 179, 180, 189, 191
PostModerism 194, 198, 201
Praise and Worship . . . . . xxxiii, 12, 73, 89, 91-94, 175-205
    crossover music 11, 122, 195-196
    hymn revival in 197-198
        industry/marketing 176, 183, 185, 187, 191, 196
        intimacy in 177, 185, 189, 190, 200, 201
        musical analysis 181
        Pentecostal influence 177, 178, 188, 198, 200
        precursors to 177-178
        relationship to pop culture . . . 175, 176-180, 189, 191, 199, 200
        role of guitar 180-182, 187-189, 195, 200
        scripture song in 179-184, 188, 192, 199
        textual analysis 180, 183, 184, 186, 189, 190
prayer, liturgical vs. devotional 31
Promise Keepers 187
psalm tones, new 15
Purpose 142
ragas (India) 289, 293
R.E.M. 188
Reformed University Fellowship (RUF) 197
responsorial psalm singing 4, 22, 23, 24, 42
Revised Common Lectionary, The (1992) 44, 45, 64
revival hymnody 8, 105-108, 111-116, 120-125
rock and roll 94, 179
Roman Missal (1970/1975) 10, 22, 50

Subject Index

rhythm, African 218, 224, 231-232, 235, 237, 239, 242, 243, 246
"7-11 songs" 203 n18
Sacrosanctum Concilium 4, 217, 218
St. Louis Jesuits 8, 9, 10, 17
Salvation Army 236
Samba-likhaan 296
Sanctified Worship 91
Scripture song 179-184, 188, 192, 199
Second Great Awakening 105, 106, 135
Second Vatican Council (Vatican II) . . . . xl, xxvi, xxvii, xxxi, xxxiii, xxxiv, xliv, 3, 4, 6, 13, 18, 21, 23, 24, 26, 27, 28, 29, 32, 42, 44, 73, 81, 82, 86, 121, 142, 210, 211, 216, 217, 218, 219, 228, 229, 256, 262, 263, 268, 271, 272, 275, 307
sekere 235
Selma to Montgomery March (1965) 73
shape-note hymnody 109, 113, 138, 139
Sharpeville Massacre 247

Shona (Zimbabwe) 236, 237, 248, 251, 254, 262
Singspiration Music 115
Sit-In Movement (1960) 73
Snowbird Statement on Catholic Liturgical Music, The (1995) 27
sol-fa system 233, 241, 246, 258
"Sound of Africa" series 230
SoundScan statistics (CCLI) 186
SongDiscovery (CCLI) 187
Songs 4 Worship 191
Songs of Sydney Carter: In the Present Tense (5 vols.) 143
SonicFlood 191, 194
Sound of Music, The 127 n26
South Africa 10, 14, 210, 217, 219, 222, 230, 235, 237, 238, 247-248, 256-262, 314
    Amadodana 260
    apartheid 247, 256, 258-262
    Fjedur 261
    freedom songs 14, 259-262
    makwaya 238, 258, 260
    national anthem ("Nkosi Sikelel' iAfrika") 258-259
    hymn writers 257-262
    toyi-toyi 260

South African Freedom Songs	14, 259-262
South African National Anthem	258-259
Southern gospel hymnody	109-110
Spirituals (African-American)	xxxii, xxxviii, xxxix, xliv, 16, 17, 18, 73, 81, 87, 88, 92, 135-136
Spirituals (white)	135-136
sruti box (India)	xxxix, 294
Stamps-Baxter Music Company	109, 117
storytelling in hymns	165
tabla drums (India)	290
Tainan Theological College and Seminary	288, 302
Taizé Community	xv, xxxiii, xxxvi, xli, 10, 15, 57, 148, 155, 161, 196, 214, 303-307, 315
common prayer at	303, 306
history of	303-307
music of	303-307
musical forms	303-307
ostinati	306
talas (India)	293
tango	271-274
Tanzanian hymns	219, 232, 243-245
Tell It Like It Is	142, 145, 178
Thai Foundation for Music and Fine Arts	298
Thai traditional musical ensembles	298
"The Almanacs"	141
The Proclaimers	188
The Weavers	141
Third Day	195, 196, 199
Three-Self Church	282, 338 n182
tonal languages (Africa)	233-235, 242, 257
toyi-toyi (dance)	260
Träd in i dansen: Mässa i Viston (*Come, Join the Dance: A Mass in Song*) (1993)	224
translators of Chinese hymns	286-289
Tridentine Mass (Pius V)	22
Twentieth-century Folk Mass (Beaumont, 1960)	49, 142
Vatican II (See "Second Vatican Council")	
Victorian hymns	xliv, 61, 115, 311, 323, 343 n260
Vietnam protests	6, 73, 141, 142
Vineyard Fellowship	185-186, 189, 190

Subject Index

We Celebrate Worship Resource 14
West Angeles Church of God in Christ 92
Wild Goose 307
Wild Goose Worship Group (WGWG) 309, 311, 312-316, 23-326
    Big Sing events 315
    folk music influence 317-318
    Formation of 312-316
    group creative process in 316-317
    Holy City events 315
    Last Night Out events 315
    Last of the Month workshops 313
    songs from the world church 318-319
    theological foundations 319-326
Wild Goose Publications 312-316
Wild Goose Resource Group (WGRG) 223, 314, 325
"Winds of Change" speech 247
World Council of Churches (WCC) . . . . .xxv, 210, 217, 222-223, 228, 253, 268, 274, 276, 277, 287, 314
    VI General Assembly (Vancouver) 222, 223, 253, 314
    VII General Assembly (Canberra) 222, 223
    VIII General Assembly (Harare) 222, 223, 253, 334 n119
    IX General Assembly (Porto Alegre) 222, 227, 329 n36, 369
    X General Assembly (Busan) 223, 369
World Library of Sacred Music (WLSM) 13, 14
World Library Publications (WLP) 14
World Lutheran Federation (WLF) 216, 224, 261
World Student Christian Federation 216, 217, 222
Worship hymnals 15
Worship Leader 187, 197
WoW Worship 191, 205 n41
Willow Creek Community Church 194
"worship explosion" 187
"worship wars" 147

Xhosa (South Africa) . 217, 219, 220, 235, 236, 237, 256, 257, 258, 259, 262

Y.A.M.U.G.E.R. 297, 298, 341 n222
Yoruba hymns 233, 234, 242, 262
Youth for Christ 110
YMCA/YWCA (Asia) 291, 328 n22, 339 n206

459

Zaïrian Rite 229
zamba 271